Mercier Press is the oldest independent Irish
publishing house and has published books in the
fields of history, literature, folklore, music, art,
humour, drama, politics, current affairs, law
and religion. It was founded in 1944 by John
and Mary Feehan.

In the building up of a country
few needs are as great as that of a publishing
house which would make the people proud of
their past, and proud of themselves as a people
capable of inspiring and supporting a world of
books which was their very own. Mercier Press
has tried to be that publishing house. On the
occasion of our fiftieth anniversary we thank
the many writers and readers who have
supported us and contributed to our success.

We face our second half-century
with confidence.

THE COURSE
OF
IRISH HISTORY

EDITED BY

T.W. MOODY

FELLOW EMERITUS

TRINITY COLLEGE, DUBLIN

FORMERLY PROFESSOR OF MODERN HISTORY

AND

F.X. MARTIN

EMERITUS PROFESSOR OF MEDIEVAL HISTORY

UNIVERSITY COLLEGE, DUBLIN

1994 REVISED AND ENLARGED EDITION

EDITED BY F.X. MARTIN

Published in association with
Radio Telefís Éireann
by

MERCIER PRESS

MERCIER PRESS
PO Box 5, 5 French Church Street, Cork
16 Hume Street, Dublin 2

© Radio Telefís Éireann, 1967, 1984, 1994

ISBN 1 85635 108 4

A CIP for this book is available from the British Library.

First published 1967
Fifteenth impression 1980

Revised and enlarged edition 1984
Seventh impression 1993

Revised and enlarged edition 1994

10 9 8 7 6 5 4 3 2 1

Lay-out by Cor Klaasen

Printed in Ireland by Colour Books Ltd.

DEDICATION

To the memory of Theo Moody (1907-84)
in appreciation of his work as an historian
and of his services to
broadcasting.
His work on this new edition was completed
just before his death
on 11th February 1984.

CONTENTS

PREFACE TO THE 1967 EDITION

From 24 January to 13 June 1966 a series of twenty-one programmes was transmitted by the television service of Radio Telefís Éireann under the title 'The course of Irish history'. The text of these programmes, revised and slightly adapted, is here published with a selection of the televised illustrations.

The aim of the series was to present a survey of Irish history that would be both popular and authoritative, concise but comprehensive, highly selective while at the same time balanced and fair-minded, critical but constructive and sympathetic. To this end, twenty-one scholars, all of them specialists in their respective fields, have cooperated in a scheme which, while prescribing a general framework, has left each free to treat his part of the subject in his own way. Whatever unity this book possesses is not imposed, but arises from the nature of the subject itself: the contributors have no thesis to prove, no official line to follow.

Since each chapter originated as a script of less than half an hour's duration, each contributor has been faced with difficulties of selection, and there are certain to be readers who will disagree with the choice of subject matter. Moreover, as editors we should have liked to include a number of chapters on general topics, and in particular a larger element of social and economic history. But this proved impracticable. As an effort of scholarship the whole undertaking had to be executed under severe limitations of time, and this was part of the challenge we accepted. For we are convinced of an urgent need for general works on Irish history such as this, which offers the reading public a rapid, new, and up-to-date conspectus of the subject, based on the best scholarship available.

The book, we hope, will serve as a guide to, as well as a source of, historical knowledge. Citation of evidence and bibliographical apparatus would have been inappropriate, but at the end of the volume we have supplied references to all substantial quotations in the text and have provided a list of books for further reading, which cover the whole field of Irish history including topics not treated in the present survey. To facilitate readers in following the course of events and to supplement the information in the narrative, we have also added a chronology of Irish history.

The list of books for further reading (apart from sections I, II, XIII, XIV) is based on lists supplied by the contributors, but the editors accept full responsibility for the final selection of the items, the form of each entry and the general arrangement. Similarly the final selection, identification and descriptions of the illustrations have been the editors' responsibility.

The illustrations, which are a feature of the book, are not intended primarily as embellishment – though many of them, we think, are a pleasure to the eye – but rather as documents, exemplifying or supplementing points in the text. They mainly consist, therefore, of re-productions of contemporary pictures, drawings and photographs, and of photographs of field monuments and other objects of historical interest. In addition, they include a number of maps specially constructed to provide a geographical frame of reference for the narrative. In all cases we have sought to give precise identifications for each illustration, including source and, where appropriate, dating. In this task, as generally in the preparation of the illustrations, we have received invaluable help from Máire and Liam de Paor, which we acknowledge with gratitude. We also wish to make grateful acknowledgments to all the many institutions from which we have derived material, as specified in the list of illustrations that follows. We offer special thanks to the Commissioners of Public Works in Ireland, Bórd Fáilte Éireann, the National Library of Ireland, the National Museum of Ireland, and the Library of Trinity College, Dublin; also the Ordnance Survey of Ireland, on whose maps those drawn for this book are based.

Dublin, 18 November 1966   T. W. Moody
                                                              F. X. Martin

PREFACE TO THE REVISED EDITION

After seventeen years this book, we are persuaded, continues to serve a useful purpose; and having, for the first time since its publication in 1967, been given the opportunity to prepare a new edition, we have revised and updated it, subject to certain qualifications.

It would not have been feasible to rewrite the book, if for no other reason than that five of the original twenty-one contributors have died; and in any case if it were rewritten today by the same authors it would doubtless be a different book from the one that the original twenty-one produced with such phenomenal speed and harmony in 1965-6. For it reflects the state of historical scholarship of that time; and since then important advances have been made. Nevertheless, believing that in its essentials the book still holds its value, we agreed with Radio Telefís Éireann, to a plan that leaves the text largely unchanged but takes account, mainly in the bibliography but also at a number of critical points in the text, of new research.

We undertook (1) to correct misprints and literal errors, (2) to correct errors of fact, (3) to remedy any crucial omissions in the text, having regard to the scale and scope of the book, (4) to update the bibliography, (5) to revise and update the chronology, (6) to add chapter 22, continuing the story from 1966 to 1982, and (7) to revise and extend the index. All living contributors were invited to supply material under any or all of (1)-(5), and nearly all of them did so. Very little change was necessary under (1), but we have taken the opportunity to correct small inconsistancies in punctuation, spelling, and other usage. Under (2) sentences have been re-written and paragraphs replaced, especially in chapters 2 and 6. Under (3) we have contrived to insert new matter in several chapters without seriously disrupting the original text. Under (6) a new chapter, 'Ireland 1966-82', has been contributed by Professor J. H. Whyte, to whom we are indebted for his ready cooperation. Under (4),(5) and (7) extensive additions and alterations have been made.

There has been a phenomenal crop of new publications on Irish history, especially articles in periodicals, during the past seventeen years, and we have endeavoured to include the most significant of these in each of the categories into which the original 'Books for further reading' was divided. The reader who wishes to pursue this new scholarship is thus provided with a comprehensive guide; and, as in the original edition, the extended bibliography covers topics and aspects not dealt with in the text. Two further changes deserve comment: section II ('General works in special fields') has been greatly amplified in size, scope, and definition, and a new section (XIII) has been introduced to bring together works on Ulster history. As thus largely recast we hope that our 'Bibliography of Irish history' will be found serviceable and suggestive, not only to the general reader but also to the specialist, as a conspectus of twentieth-century historiography, in English and Irish, about Ireland.

The chronology, which was all too scanty for the period to 1534, has been expanded for that period, has been generally revised and developed, and has been extended to early 1984. It now amounts to a substantial supplement to the text. The index has been revised and extended both to include the new chapter and to supply gaps in the original coverage.

As thus revised and extended it is our hope that the book will continue to serve its purpose of providing a rapid survey of the whole course of Irish history that is both popular and authoritative, concise but comprehensive, within its limits, highly selective but balanced and fairminded, cool and critical but constructive and sympathetic, and signposting the way to deeper levels of knowledge.

Dublin, 9 February 1984   T.W.M.

                                                                        F. X.M.

A further chapter 'Ireland, 1982-94' by Dr Richard English has been added to the text and the chronology and index have been updated accordingly.

F.X. MARTIN, OSA
September 1994

LIST OF ILLUSTRATIONS

48 Pembroke Castle, Pembrokeshire, late 12th century

49(a) Norman knights, from the Bayeux tapestry, late 11th century *(Vetusta monumenta,* vi, 1819)

49(b) Norman foot-soldiers, from the Bayeux tapestry, late 11th century *(Vetusta monumenta,* vi, 1819)

50 Motte and bailey, Tipperary Hills, county Tipperary, 12th century (photo. Commissioners of Public Works in Ireland)

51 Carrickfergus Castle, county Antrim, early 13th century (photo. Bord Fáilte Éireann)

52 Cistercian abbey, Dunbrody, county Wexford, 13th century (photo. Commissioners of Public Works in Ireland)

53 Map of Ireland, *c.*1150 *c.*1250, by Liam de Paor

54 Charter of Dublin, 1171/2 (Muniments Room, City Hall, Dublin)

55 The medieval court of exchequer, late 14th century, from the Red Book of the Exchequer (J. T. Gilbert (ed.), *Facsimiles of the national manuscripts of Ireland,* iii, 1879)

56 Trim Castle, county Meath, early 13th century (photo. Commissioners of Public Works in Ireland)

57 St Mary's Church, New Ross, county Wexford, 1220-35: east window (photo. Commissioners of Public Works in Ireland)

58 Meeting between Art MacMurrough and the earl of Gloucester, June 1399, from British Museum, Harleian MS 1319 (J. T. Gilbert, *Facsimiles of the national manuscripts of Ireland,* iii, 1879)

59 Clara Castle, county Kilkenny, late 15th century (photo. Commissioners of Public Works in Ireland)

60 Franciscan abbey, Rosserk, county Mayo, mid-15th century (photo. Commissioners of Public Works in Ireland)

61 Carved figures from the cloister of the Cistercian abbey of Jerpoint, county Kilkenny, 15th century (photo. Commissioners of Public Works in Ireland)

62 King Henry VII, 1485-1509, by an unknown Flemish artist (National Portrait Gallery, London)

63 Map of Ireland, *c.* 1500, showing the Pale and the great lordships, after the map in E. Curtis, *A history of medieval Ireland,* 1938

64 King Henry VIII, 1509-47, after Holbein (National Portrait Gallery, London)

65 Irish groat of Henry VIII (National Museum of Ireland)

66 Irish warriors and peasants, by Albrecht Dürer, 1521 (National Gallery of Ireland)

67 Hugh O'Neill, from H. Adami, *La spada d'Orione* (Rome, 1680)

68 Armagh in ruins, *c.* 1600, from a map by R. Bartlett (G.A. Hayes-McCoy, *Ulster and other Irish maps, c. 1600,* 1964)

69 The battle of Kinsale, 1601, from [Thomas Stafford], *Pacata Hibernia,* 1633

70 Donegal Castle, *c.* 1615 (photo. Bord Fáilte Éireann)

71 Magherafelt and Salterstown, county Londonderry, from Sir Thomas Phillips's survey (D. A. Chart (ed.), *Londonderry and the London companies, 1600-29,* 1928)

72 King Charles I, 1625-49, by Daniel Mytens, 1631 (National Portrait Gallery, London)

73 Thomas Wentworth, 1st earl of Strafford, after Van Dyck (National Portrait Gallery, London)

74 Sir Phelim O'Neill: facsimile of contemporary print (British Museum, Department of Prints and Drawings)

75 Plan of Drogheda in 1657, by Robert Newcomen (John D'Alton, *History of Drogheda,* 1844)

76 Maps by J.G. Simms showing the proportion of land owned by catholics in Ireland according to counties, in 1641, 1688 and 1703

77 James Butler, 1st duke of Ormond, by Sir Peter Lely (National Gallery of Ireland)

78 Richard Talbot, duke of Tyrconnell (National Portrait Gallery, London)

79 Patrick Sarsfield, earl of Lucan (Franciscan House of Studies, Killiney, county Dublin.

80 James II landing at Kinsale, 12 March 1689: contemporary Dutch print (National Gallery of Ireland)

81 The battle of the Boyne, 1 July 1690, by Theodore Maas (National Library of Ireland)

82 An Irish cabin, from Arthur Young's *Tour in Ireland* (1780)

83 A wooden cross of the penal era (National Museum of Ireland)

84 Catholic chapel, James's Gate, Dublin, built in 1738-49 *(Catholic emancipation centenary record,* ed. M.V. Ronan, 1929)

85 Catholic chapel, Arles, county Leix, early 18th century (Francis Grose, *Antiquities of Ireland,* ii, 1795, facing p. 34)

86 Scene after open-air mass at a scathlan, Bunlin Bridge, county Donegal, 1867. *Sights and scenes in Ireland* [1896]

87 Charles O'Conor of Belanagare (National Library of Ireland)

88 James Caulfield, first earl of Charlemont, by William Cuming (National Gallery of Ireland)

89 Volunteer parade in College Green, 4 November 1779, by Francis Wheatley (National Gallery of Ireland)

90 Theobald Wolfe Tone, *c.* 1792 (National Library of Ireland)

91 The Parliament House and Trinity College, Dublin, *c.* 1793, by James Malton (National Library of Ireland)

92 The Custom House, Dublin, *c.* 1793, by James Malton (National Library of Ireland)

93 Belfast from Cromac Wood, *c.* 1780 (Ulster Museum)

94 The battle of Vinegar Hill, Enniscorthy, 21 June 1798: contemporary print (National Library of Ireland)

O'Growney memorial volume, 1904); (c) Eoin MacNeill (Cashman Collection, Radio Telefís Éireann)

120 National Volunteers in training, 1913 (Cashman Collection, Radio Telefís Éireann)

121 Citizen Army on parade, 1914 (photo. Keogh Bros., Dublin)

122 Funeral of O'Donovan Rossa, Glasnevin, 1 August 1915 (Cashman Collection, Radio Telefís Éireann)

123 Éamon de Valéra addressing anti-conscription meeting at Ballaghadereen, 1918 (Cashman Collection, Radio Telefís Éireann)

124 Dáil Éireann, 1919 (Radio Times Hulton Picture Library, M 91074)

125 Thomas James Clarke, by Seán O'Sullivan, R. H. A. (National Gallery of Ireland)

126 Seán Mac Diarmada, by Seán O'Sullivan, R. H. A. (National Gallery of Ireland)

127 Patrick Henry Pearse by Seán O'Sullivan, R. H. A. (National Gallery of Ireland)

128 James Connolly, by Seán O'Sullivan, R. H. A. (National Gallery of Ireland)

129 Thomas MacDonagh, by Seán O'Sullivan, R. H. A. (National Gallery of Ireland)

130 Éamonn Ceannt by Seán O'Sullivan, R. H. A. (National Gallery of Ireland)

131 Joseph Mary Plunkett, by Seán O'Sullivan, R.H.A. (National Gallery of Ireland)

132 1916 memorial: statue of Cuchulainn by Oliver Sheppard in the General Post Office, Dublin (photo. Bord Fáilte Éireann)

133 Sir Edward Carson addressing anti-home rule meeting *c.*1912 (Public Record Office, Belfast)

134 Sir James Craig, later Viscount Craigavon, prime minister of Northern Ireland, 1921-40 (Public Record Office, Belfast)

135 Joseph Devlin, Ulster nationalist leader (Public Record Office, Belfast)

136 John Miller Andrews, prime minister of Northern Ireland, 1940-43 (photo., dated 27 November 1940, J. R. Bainbridge, Belfast)

137 Sir Basil Brooke, later Viscount Brookeborough, prime minister of Northern Ireland, 1943-63 (photo. Leslie Stuart, Belfast)

138 Shipbuilding at Belfast, October 1956 (Central Office of Information, London)

139 Terence O'Neill, prime minister of Northern Ireland, visits Seán Lemass, taoiseach, 9 February 1965

140 Arthur Griffith (Cashman Collection, Radio Telefís Éireann)

141 Michael Collins, at the funeral of Arthur Griffith, 12 August 1922 (photo. Walsh, Dublin)

142 William Thomas Cosgrave, president of the executive council of the Irish Free State 1922-32, on a visit to New York in 1928 (Radio Times Hulton Picture Library, P 37331)

143 Éamon de Valéra, president of the executive council of the Irish Free State, 1932-7; taoiseach 1937-48, 1951-4, 1957-9; uachtarán 1959-73 (photo. taken on 3 December 1941, *Irish Press*)

144 John Alyosius Costello, taoiseach 1948-51, 1954-7 (photo. taken on 19 February 1948, *Irish Press*)

145 Irish soldier serving in the United Nations forces, by John F. Kelly, R.H.A.

146 Harold Wilson, prime minister of Great Britain, and Seán Lemass, taoiseach, signing the Anglo-Irish free-trade agreement at 10 Downing Street, 14 December 1965 (photo. Thompson Newspapers, London)

147 Map of Ireland, political

148 Ian Paisley (photo. Radio Telefís Éireann, 1973)

149 James Chichester-Clarke (photo. Pacemaker Ltd 1969)

150 Brian Faulkner (photo. Radio Telefís Éireann, 1969)

151 William Whitelaw (photo. Pacemaker Ltd. 1973)

152 Oliver Napier, Liam Cosgrave, Edward Heath, Brian Faulkner and Gerry Fitt at the Sunningdale Conference (photo. *Irish Times*)

153 James Prior (photo. Pacemaker Ltd 1982)

154 Jack Lynch (photo. Radio Telefís Éireann, 1972)

155 Liam Cosgrave (photo. Radio Telefís Éireann, 1973)

156 Charles Haughey (photo. Radio Telefís Éireann, 1973)

157 Garret FitzGerald (photo. Radio Telefís Éireann, 1978)

158 Haughey-Thatcher meeting, 8 December 1980 (photo. Colman Doyle)

159 John Hume (photo. *Cork Examiner*)

160 Gerry Adams (photo. Sinn Féin)

161 Albert Reynolds (photo. *Cork Examiner*)

162 John Major (photo. *Cork Examiner*)

163 President Mary Robinson (photo. Radio Telefís Éireann)

1

A GEOGRAPHER'S VIEW OF
IRISH HISTORY
by J. H. Andrews

Throughout the twentieth century Ireland has been among the weaker countries of the western world. It is small in area and population and has been slow in achieving success as a producer of non-agricultural wealth. Geographically it stands on the edge of things, a wall flower at the gathering of west-European nations, and despite its popularity with the tourist it has failed to attract any large body of permanent immigrants. Not all these characteristics are deeply rooted in the past. Ireland has been a small and sea-bound country, admittedly, for at least 8,000 years, ever since the upward movement of sea level that finally separated it from the Continent, and it has never been a great military power. Nevertheless, there have been times when its fertile soils, its copper, and its gold have attracted some of Europe's most vigorous colonising peoples and, later, when its scholars and missionaries have moulded the intellectual life of other lands. Before trying to understand these changes of fortune, we must look at the different regions of our country and study their relations both with each other and with the world outside.

In many parts of Ireland, nature has remained inhospitable for long periods, in some cases down to the present day. Around the edges, especially, much of its surface is raised or crumpled into highland masses and steep-sided glens, their upper slopes seared by winter gales, the goodness washed from their soils by drenching rain, their coarse grass and heather of little value except as rough grazing. In these areas the stony roots of the Irish landscape reach the surface – in the basalt cliffs of Antrim, for example; the spiky quartzite mountains of Donegal, Mayo, and Galway; the bare and fissured limestone pavements of north Clare; the sandstone masses of Kerry; and the schist and granite of the Wicklow glens. These hills, though they are seldom out of sight, make up only one eighth of Ireland's total area; but this is not to say that all the rest is fertile lowland. In much of the north, particularly, the lowland shown on the ordinary school-atlas map is really a maze of tightly packed small hills known as drumlins, low but quite steep, and patched together with fragments of bog or lake. For much of their history the drumlin belts have made a surprisingly effective obstacle to movement. Southwards they give way to smoother country, but this in turn is interrupted by thousands of acres of bare and lonely peat bog, some of it in the very centre of the island, another difficult kind of country in both the military and the agricultural sense.

This still leaves a large part of Ireland – half at least – as fully productive, but much of the good land is inextricably mixed with the bad, and until a few centuries ago the pattern was further complicated by the numerous patches of forest that fringed the bogs and clothed the lower slopes of many of the hills. Bog, mountain, and forest, though unfitted for tillage, provided useful summer grazing land for nearby farmers and a refuge where life could be sustained even when invading armies had burned the corn from the lowland fields. These strips of relatively unattractive country have many times helped to channel the course of Irish history, but their influence has never been quite decisive. Ideas and attitudes have flowed freely around and between them. One such attitude, perhaps the oldest Irish national characteristic, is our love of celebrating death, which was implanted as long ago as 3000 B.C. by the builders of the megalithic tombs. These imposing stone structures are found in every corner of the island and the same is true of many of our other pre-Christian and early Christian antiquities, several of which are distinctively Irish and found in hardly any other country. This cultural identity has prompted Irishmen to seek political union and political independence as well, but here they have been less successful in overcoming geographical difficulties. The traditional centre of the island, the hill of Uisneach, was not, as might have been expected, a national capital, but part of a political frontier zone, the meeting place of independent kingdoms. And although these kingdoms have long since passed into history

1 Mountains, bogs and drumlins, by J. H. Andrews

MOUNTAINS

BOGS

DRUMLIN AREAS

SCALE OF MILES

0   50

or legend, there is nothing legendary about the international boundary that still divides the country fifty miles further north. Nobody would claim that such political divisions, old and new, have been 'caused' by geography in any simple sense. Nothing about Irish geography is simple. But emerging from this intricate pattern we can distinguish at least two broad regional themes that no historian can ignore. One of them is the tendency for the north to stand aloof from the rest of the country; the other, which we shall look at first, is the gap between the east of Ireland and the west.

As one travels westwards from the Shannon, unfriendly and inaccessible regions crowd more closely together. In the east, the land is generally kinder, and if we draw one line from Lough Owel to Dundalk and another to meet the coast just south of Dublin (Fig.2) we have marked off the heart of this eastern zone, a part of Ireland which receives less rain, and contains less bog and mountain than any other compact area of similar size, and which forms a junction for routes that thread their way between the bogs and mountains to give access to smaller but equally

19

2 The 'eastern triangle', by J. H. Andrews

fertile districts like the lowlands of the Suir, Nore, and Barrow. Almost every period of our history has left conspicuous traces in this eastern triangle. Here is Newgrange, the most impressive of our prehistoric monuments, and Tara, the focus of an ancient road system and the most famous of the early centres from which Irishmen have sought political unification. Here was found the richest of our illuminated manuscripts, the Book of Kells, while the highest of our high crosses stands at Monasterboice and the earliest of our great Cistercian monasteries at Mellifont. In this triangle, at Dublin, the Norsemen placed the largest and most powerful of their Irish city states, so vital a centre that Strongbow the Norman hurried north to possess it within a month of his first landing at Waterford harbour. At Dublin, too, the English kings established their deputies, and at the other end of the triangle, at Dundalk, the Scottish invader Edward Bruce challenged them by having himself crowned king of Ireland. Here, in the Pale, the fifteenth-century English government resolved to keep one last precarious foothold; and here, at Maynooth, stood the fortress of their strongest and most ungovernable vassal, the great earl of Kildare. Here the primate of the Irish church placed his residence, at Termonfeckin, at a time when the archiepiscopal seat of Armagh was too much threatened by war and disorder to be considered safe. Here, finally, beside the Boyne, was fought the last

20

great battle of Irish history. The eastern triangle is the geographical nucleus from which men have seen their best chance of commanding the whole country. And yet the same district is also one of the most vulnerable parts of Ireland, the longest break in its defensive mountain ring, with the estuaries of the Liffey and the Boyne to beckon the invader onwards. The sea that washes its shore is too narrow to make an effective geographical barrier, and there have been many times when a united Irish Sea must have seemed as likely a prospect, politically, as a united Ireland. From this triangle, then, we are inevitably drawn eastwards to consider Ireland's relations with the outside world.

Our most distinguished geographer, Professor Estyn Evans, has placed the coastlands of the Irish sea among what he calls the 'Atlantic ends of Europe', a geographical province that stretches all the way from Norway to Brittany and Spain but which excludes eastern and central England. He has pointed out, for instance, that Ireland's first taste of civilisation and its first knowledge of metals came from prehistoric sea-farers making their way from island to island and peninsula to peninsula across these western seas. Historians tell of many other important journeys among the Atlantic ends of Europe. But as they take the story forward, one trend is inescapable: when we compare our modern emigrants with the saints and scholars of the past, Ireland's role in western Europe appears increasingly passive, involuntary, and dominated by England. Consider a few examples. The Romans brought their armies no further west than Pembrokeshire. Ireland viewed their empire with detachment, appropriated some of their best ideas, and then drew on this Roman legacy to maintain its own spiritual ascendancy of the Irish Sea long after the last of the legions had been disbanded. The Norsemen were more aggressive, and although their territorial conquests were confined to small areas near the coast, they struck two blows at the native civilisation of the interior, firstly by attacking the monasteries which were the custodians of this civilisation and secondly by securing each of the chief harbours with a fortified town. Towns were a new and alien settlement form, and one that Gaelic Ireland has never succeeded in fully assimilating. But the next invaders, the Normans, appreciated their value at once, and by

21

3 The mountains of Connemara (photo Bord Fáilte Éireann)

stringing others along the well-articulated river systems of the south and
east they drew this part of Ireland into feudal dependence on the English
kings. Their Tudor successors completed the sequence by going one stage
further: starting from a narrow foothold in the Pale they reconquered the
area of Norman influence and went on to conquer the north and west as
well.

Behind this sequence we can see a general European trend. Under the
Tudors, England had emerged as one of a number of large, compact,
land-based nation states, each well integrated within itself, but each in
conflict with one or more of the others. Several of them owed much of
their power to the quickening economic life of Europe's northern lowlands, and central England was one of the lowland areas most affected by
this trend: from being a prehistoric barrier region, it had become the obvious link between London and the Irish Sea – a shorter route, of course,
and now an easier one, than any of the sea routes from Ireland to the

22

4 Drumlins in south Donegal (photo. J. C. Brindley, University College, Dublin)

Continent. Even if Ireland had been united, England would still have been larger, richer, and more in touch with continental technology and military science. But Ireland was not united. It had remained an exception to the west-European rule. No Irish leader had recaptured the nucleus of the eastern triangle, or even sought to dominate any of the inland towns – such as Athlone, Kilkenny, or Athy – which have from time to time been suggested as alternative capitals of a united Ireland. By the standards of the middle sixteenth century, almost the whole island was a political vacuum, like the newly discovered countries of America. The conflict between the English and other European powers made it necessary to fill this vacuum, and it eventually became clear to the statesmen and strategists of Spain and France that the idea of the Atlantic ends of Europe could not be translated into political terms. While English troops poured into Dublin from Chester and Liverpool, continental forces had to seek a timid foothold on the extremities of Munster, and after they had been defeated Ireland's southern traffic dwindled down to a trickle of spies, smugglers, and fishermen. Today it is in the older details of our countryside and its folklore that the idea of Atlantic Europe must be sought, in the design of the Irish peasant house and much of its furniture, and in the stories, songs, attitudes, and some of the farming practices of its inhabitants. The student who seeks to understand the history of more recent times will find an interesting contrast to Professor Evans's view in the ideas of the English geographer, Halford Mackinder. In a map published in 1902 in his book *Britain and the British seas,*

Mackinder described the Irish Sea as 'the inland sea of Britain': not very tactfully put, perhaps, but we must admit that what has mattered most in the last few centuries of our history is the easy passage from Britain to Ireland's eastern coastlands. Because of it, our present-day laws and institutions have their origins in England.

There were limits to the process of anglicisation, however, and in so far as Ireland today enjoys political independence, the English conquest may be regarded as a failure. It certainly did not fail for want of thought or planning. The Elizabethans, for example, made a great effort to master the geography of the country, as we can see by studying the maps collected by their capable chief minister, Lord Burghley. His earliest specimens were crude and distorted, with little but artist's licence in the west and north-west. But he was constantly seeking out better ones, correcting and augmenting them with his own hand, and finding expert surveyors to supply new detail. As the map of Ireland was painfully filled in, key river-crossings and mountain passes were fully appreciated by English strategists for the first time. But in many areas, the far west for instance, there was little of importance apart from physical geography for the map-makers to add, and indeed the blankness of much of the Irish landscape was one of the most difficult problems facing the conquerors. They soon discovered that military victories were not enough: Ireland could not be secured without being brought to what the Elizabethans called 'civility', and to an Englishman civility meant towns, villages, and enclosed fields, the sort of orderly landscape that was still missing from Tudor Ireland except for a few favoured districts in the east. It was easy enough to plan such improvements on paper, not so easy to establish them on the ground. One method was by parcelling out tracts of land to English proprietors with English tenants, in the somewhat naive hope that Irishmen would be so impressed by these newcomers that they would hasten to imitate their way of life. Deciding where to put these colonies was an interesting geographical exercise. But it remained, for the most part, no more than an exercise. The new ruling class could carve out estates, build forts and barracks, cut down the woods, and drive new roads across the bogs; and in the seventeenth and eighteenth centuries they were doing all

5 Bogland in county Offaly (photo. Bord na Móna)

these things. But what they could not do, except in some parts of Ulster, was to persuade any large number of their countrymen to come and till the soil of Ireland.

It was a familiar problem in colonial territories. Where immigrant meets native in a landed society, economic war may go on smouldering long after the military conquest is over. The native is content with a lower standard of living than the settler. So unless the settler can earn more, acre for acre, from his farm, the native can outbid him by offering the landlord a higher rent. This is one reason why so many of the British immigrants stayed in the towns. It also explains why Scotsmen made better colonists than Englishmen: their expectations were more modest. The outcome of this economic competition depends to some extent on local geography, for it is on the better land that the progressive newcomer is likely to have an advantage over his less efficient native rival. Outside Ulster, the planters of the seventeenth century were nowhere numerous enough to displace the previous inhabitants completely and their biggest successes, such as they were, occurred in areas of fertile land and good communications. In the rural areas of the west they made hardly any impression. Yet the west was the very part of Ireland that had been most in need of civility when the Tudor conquest had begun.

So for all their efforts the English had not managed to wipe out the distinction between the richer east and the poorer west. This distinction appeared again with harsh clarity in a great series of official maps, memoirs, and statistical reports compiled in the decades that followed the union, and especially in the early years of Queen Victoria, many of them prepared under the direction or influence of Captain Thomas Larcom of the ordnance survey, whom we may perhaps regard as the ablest practical geographer ever to have worked in Ireland. The landscape revealed by the ordnance surveyors was much better furnished and more closely occupied than the one depicted on Lord Burghley's maps. Nevertheless, Ireland could still be divided into two broad regions, and with the important exception of Ulster these were pretty much the same two regions that could have been distinguished three hundred years earlier. In the east and south, the resident gentry were more numerous and more progressive; society was more diversified, both economically and in religious terms; farms were larger and farming more commercialised; towns were larger and more closely spaced; people were better housed and better educated. In all these matters the west lagged behind and in general the further west one travelled the poorer were the land and the people, until one reached the westernmost peninsulas of Europe, the 'parishes next to America'. The remarkable thing, though, was how little difference America had made to Ireland. In other west European countries, economic geography had been revolutionised by the discovery and development of the new world. But these changed space-relationships brought no great benefits to Ireland under British rule, certainly not to western Ireland. America had provided the potato in the sixteenth century; and now, in the nineteenth, it provided somewhere to emigrate to after the ruinous upsurge of population that the potato had helped to bring about. Through these changes, the west remained the most secluded and in some ways the most Irish part of Ireland.

East and west were not clearly distinct. Along most of their boundary they either overlapped, interpenetrated, or merged into one another. But in parts of Munster at least, where fertile bog-free lowland laps against the upland blocks of the south, the contrast between English and Gaelic influences was more abrupt and historically more consequential. One of our leading geographers, Professor T. Jones Hughes, has pointed out that it was not in the east or the west but in this critical frontier region

6 Hill and lowland in county Tipperary (photo. Bord Fáilte Éireann)

that modern Irish nationalism found some of its earliest expressions, ranging for example from a high incidence of agrarian unrest to the beginnings of the cooperative movement.

Here then is a possible view of Ireland in the decades before the treaty of 1921: the west, and especially the far west, remote on every side and for the most part crushingly poor; the east, and especially the old English Pale, attractive and accessible by land and sea; with the two finally integrated, one hopes, in the Ireland of today and tomorrow. It is an interesting view; but like many pictures drawn in Dublin it leaves out the north. Ulster has always had its own geographical personality, formed, as we might imagine, by taking qualities from each of the other regions, accentuating them, and combining them into something dramatic and highly coloured. Like the west – only more so – Ulster for long remained somewhat inaccessible by land, kept apart from the south by mountains, drumlins, forests, and water, which together formed the nearest Irish equivalent to the uplands that divided England from Scotland, just as the prehistoric earthworks known as the Black Pig's dyke are the nearest Irish equivalent of Hadrian's wall. What lay beyond this barrier, however, was not a handful of impoverished peninsulas, but something more like a whole Ireland in miniature, with its own version of the eastern triangle in the valleys of the Lagan and the Bann. For the English government, Ulster was the most intractable part of Ireland, and in trying to breach its frontiers they suffered several particularly humiliating defeats, defeats which stung them, when the wars were over, to devise the most

27

7 The Glen of Aherlow, county Tipperary: sixteenth-century forest, twentieth-century farmland (photo. Bord Fáilte Éireann)

thoroughgoing of all their plantation schemes.

Remoteness from Dublin was what gave Ulster a certain resemblance to the west. But like Dublin – only, again, more so – Ulster lay open to outside influence. A narrow gap, at its narrowest a mere thirteen miles, separated it from Scotland and along the shores of this gap English, Irish, and Scots had for many centuries confronted each other in a confused and shifting pattern of wars and alliances. A new era was inaugurated, however, when England and Scotland were united under James I in 1603. As king of Ireland, James had two advantages denied to his predecessor Elizabeth: his kingdom of Scotland gave him command of the narrow North Channel; and from the manpower of that kingdom he could stiffen his Ulster colony with energetic lowlanders who were reinforced by a new wave of immigration in the last decades of the seventeenth century. By combining agriculture with their national industry of linen-making these Scottish immigrants became almost the only people in modern Ireland to combine a high rural population-density with a relatively high level of prosperity. Irishmen, who have a habit of confusing Britain with England, often forget that James I's two British crowns played an important part in the division of their own country.

Ever since the Tudor conquest, most of our new settlers have been protestants, and as religious conversion is a rare experience in Ireland, a twentieth-century denominational map (Fig. 8) is the best way of measuring the overall effect of the plantation policy. Outside the north, this policy was clearly a failure. In the north it enjoyed considerable success. But the north, in common with the rest of Ireland, had its upland refuges, like the Sperrin mountains and the northern glens of Antrim, where the older

28

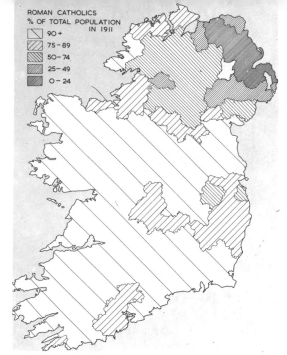

ROMAN CATHOLICS
% OF TOTAL POPULATION
IN 1911
90 +
75 – 89
50 – 74
25 – 49
0 – 24

8 Religious
distribution in
Ireland, 1911,
by J. H. Andrews

communities survived almost intact. This mixture of catholic districts and protestant districts was to be further complicated when Ulster, more than any of the other provinces of Ireland, experienced the industrial revolution of the nineteenth century, and when new factories attracted the descendants of pre-plantation Ulstermen to help to populate its growing towns. Some urban catholic majorities now appeared in certain rural hinterlands that remained predominantly protestant; and within the typical northern town each religious denomination kept to its own streets. Like Ireland as a whole, Ulster has remained divided within itself.

The geographical factors in Irish history cannot be adequately summarised in a short survey. They have helped to unite Ireland and to divide it, just as they have helped both to unite and to divide the British Isles. Their significance has changed and is still changing, generally for the better. Rivers have been harnessed; hillsides have been afforested with productive timber; bogs have been exploited for fuel and electric power, and will in future give way to cultivated land; and new industries are at last beginning to exploit the advantages of Ireland's central position among the land masses of the world. Geographical barriers are disappearing, and in time the consequences of these barriers will themselves begin to fade away – not only within Ireland but between Ireland and other countries.

2
PREHISTORIC IRELAND
by G. F. Mitchell

Everybody has some interest in the past, not only his own past, but also that of the society to which he belongs. The past has made us what we are, and we must all at some time have asked: where and what do I come from? what does it *mean* to be Irish? Historians can tell us about a good deal of Ireland's and our forefathers' past. They work by studying what men wrote years or centuries ago, and from these documents they try to reconstruct the story of a society. But men did not always write. In Ireland, writing began about fifteen hundred years ago. What happened before then, before history, we call prehistory, and for many people there is a fascination in the mute testimony of the peoples who lived thousands of years ago: a massive stone fort on the Atlantic cliffs, a great earthen mound on a hilltop, a circle of standing stones in some farmer's field.

The archaeologist investigates the forts and other monuments: he asks questions about them; he searches for smaller and less obvious works of early man. He goes to work like a detective piecing together clues to reconstruct a story: he removes from the earth scraps of pottery, implements of bone or flint or a polished axe-head. He is not primarily interested in the objects – often dull enough – which he finds, and he is not seeking for treasure in his excavations. He is trying to find out in the only way possible what people were like in prehistoric times.

The story the prehistorian has to tell must be related to its geographical setting. When we look at a map (Fig. 9) of western Europe at the end of the ice age we see that Spain and Portugal, and England and Ireland, stick out from the west of Europe into the Atlantic. While England and Ireland are now detached from the mainland, they nonetheless remain part of Europe. These areas which jut out from Europe, together with

Scandinavia, are highland areas. Lowlands extend from western France along both sides of the English channel, and stretch far to the east through the Low Countries and north Germany.

In the last ice age, which lasted from over 100,000 until about 15,000 years ago, conditions were too cold over much of Europe for trees to grow. Ice covered the highlands of the north and the mountains of central Europe. On the lowlands we had rich and fertile grassy plains, with great herds of deer and horses in western France, but farther north the grass was sparser and poorer, and the big game were fewer. At this time there must have been, in western France and parts of Spain a large population who lived by hunting this big game. They lived in caves, and at Lascaux and other places painted on cave walls wonderful pictures of the animals they hunted. This palaeolithic (or old stone age) art was the earliest art in the world. From it and from the tools of stone and bone we get a vivid picture of the way of life of these early men. These hunters moved on following the game into England, for the English Channel did not then exist. In England they have not left any pictures, but their flint implements have been found, and their living conditions must have been much the same as in France. They do not seem to have reached Ireland, because for a hundred years archaeologists have searched in vain for this type of tool. I do not believe they will ever be found here, because there were not then enough animals in Ireland to provide food for these hunting people.

Here in Ireland at the end of the ice age it must have been much as Lapland is today, with boggy grassland on flat ground and little vegetation on the hill slopes. As the climate got warmer, bushes began to grow again, just as in warmer parts of Lapland. It was at this time, about 10,000 B.C., that the giant deer became common in Ireland. These animals would have provided food for hunters, but, although there were hunting peoples in Holland and Denmark at the time, we have found no traces of them in Ireland. The country seems to have been still unpopulated, and the giant deer were more common here than elsewhere – probably because there were no men to hunt them.

Before we come to the first inhabitants of Ireland we must look at the

9 Western Europe at the end
of the ice age, *c.* 15000 B.C.,
by G. F. Mitchell

way Europe was changing. During the ice age a great deal of the world's water was frozen solid on higher ground; there was much less water in the sea, and the sea level was low. As a result land connected Ireland with England and England with the Continent. When the ice melted, sea level rose again, and by 6000 B.C. Ireland had been cut off from Britain, but the floor of the future North Sea still stood above sea level; forests and swamps stretched from Yorkshire to Denmark (Fig. 10). As the ice-sheets retreated northwards, the warmer climate allowed trees to grow again, and Europe, except for its lakes and rivers, became entirely covered by dense woodland. The deer and the horses that had roamed the grassy plains were driven out by the expanding forests: the hunters now had no big game, and had to live on birds and fish. Their movements too were restricted because of the growth of forests, and the people migrated along the rivers and by sea and lake shores, wherever they could find food.

These were the first people to come to Ireland. They had crossed from Scandinavia to Britain, and at about 6000 B.C., or perhaps a little earlier, they moved still farther west, probably across narrow straits of water towards the highlands of Antrim and Wicklow as these could be clearly seen from the British shore. We find them first near Coleraine in Derry and Tullamore in Offaly. As time went on they seem to have preferred the north-eastern half of the country to the south-western. Lakes are more common in the north-east, and food would have been more abundant there.

We can tell little about our first ancestors – these middle stone age or mesolithic people. We know that at the Coleraine site they lived in round huts with a central hearth, but we do not know how they disposed of their dead. All we have are the rubbish-dumps or kitchen middens they left behind them near the swamps and waters where their food supplies lived. The first arrivals used microliths, tiny blades of flint which were probably set as barbs in a wooden shaft. But these implements, very handy in arrows for shooting birds, do not seem to have been used by the later mesolithic people. Their tools are less exciting – a limited range of flint implements, used for skinning and cleaning birds and fish, hardly any bone, and a few stones for rubbing and hammering.

Barbed harpoons of bone are known outside Ireland, and were almost certainly used here also, not only for chasing seals and porpoises in the sea, but also for hunting deer, which could be ambushed when crossing rivers or venturing into woodland clearings. Deer like young shoots, and there is now evidence that mesolithic man made deliberate clearings, where the deer could be easily killed when they came to graze.

Man the hunter was utterly dependent on the bounty of nature. To feed himself and his family he had to hunt incessantly throughout the year, often by night as well as day. Only a tiny group of people could win sustenance from a very large area of forest and marsh, where they were in competition with other beasts of prey. But even before the first aborigines entered Ireland to try to scrape a living by hunting along the banks of its rivers and lakes, elsewhere in the world the great revolution was taking place, which was to win for mankind the empire of the earth – the first farmers were at work in the Middle East.

This neolithic or new stone age revolution was perhaps the most significant step forward in the history of man. From now on instead of being at the mercy of nature, man could control his environment. He learned from observing wild plants and grasses that by scattering the seeds he could cultivate grain. Wild beasts who came to graze in the special clearings were gradually tamed, perhaps by capturing a young animal, a calf, or a kid, and rearing it to maturity. These domestic herds provided not

SITES IN IRELAND AND
ASSOCIATED SITES IN
SCOTLAND ARE SHOWN

10 Ireland and Western Britain in mesolithic times, by G. F. Mitchell

only meat and hides, but also milk and hair. Food was stored in baskets
and leather bags, and this led eventually to the discovery of pottery.
Someone probably had the idea of daubing a basket with clay to make it
waterproof. When it was baked by the sun it became hard and firm, and
then it was found possible to make containers wholly of clay. This was the
first manufacture, and the earliest pots are round-bottomed and bag-
shaped, resembling the baskets and bags from which they derive. At the

same time people learned to polish their rough stone tools, and to make a more effective hoe or axe. As land was cultivated and exhausted more land was needed, and the clearing of forests began. The felling axe was invented (Fig. 11). Later Egyptian paintings show us the whole process – the trees being cut down with stone axes, the ground broken with stone hoes, and the crop being raised and harvested.

Expanding population in the Middle East forced these farming people to spread out in the never-ending search for new land. They pushed west along the Mediterranean to Spain and France, moved up through France to the Channel coast and on into Ireland, Great Britain and the Low Countries (Fig. 12). This expansion took quite a long time, but by various dating methods we can say that the neolithic colonisers reached north-west Europe by about 3000 B.C.

At Lough Gur in County Limerick we can observe the way of life of the first people to till the soil of Ireland. They were practical and observant, and knew that the soil would be richest where elm trees grew most freely, and so they settled on light limestone soils such as we have in south Limerick – an area that is still fertile and suitable for cattle-raising. At Lough Gur the late Professor Seán Ó Ríordáin excavated many of their houses. What the archaeologist finds are stains in the soil where wooden posts have rotted away, or remains of stone foundations. The houses must have had walls of turves on a wooden frame, and been thatched with rushes from the lake shore. Some of the houses were round – others were rectangular. By piecing together some of the many pottery fragments found, Ó Ríordáin showed that these people made round-bottomed pots with decorated rims for storing their food, and heavier flat-bottomed cooking-pots. They used stone axes of various sizes for cutting trees and hoeing the ground, and antler picks were also used in agriculture. Many small bone implements, borers, needles, awls, had domestic uses, and whorls of bone and stone were used in spinning wool for clothing. The women ground the grain by pushing a heavy rubbing implement across a block of stone.

As well as the crops they grew, these people ate great quantities of meat – from the refuse bones we know that they kept cows and also pigs

11 Polished stone axe with wooden handle, *c.* 3000 B.C. (National Museum of Ireland)

and sheep.

Arrows or spears with flint tips were probably used for hunting small game birds, and flint blades and scrapers took the place of our modern knives. Not all the objects left behind by these early farmers are utilitarian, for many beads of bone and stone and bracelets of lignite show they adorned themselves, and were interested in their appearance just as we are today.

We can still read the record of this first farming in the muds on the bottom of the lake. The plants which grew by its shores scattered their pollen in the air and much of this fell in the lake. If we take samples of the lake mud and count the pollen grains in it, in the lower levels we see much elm pollen coming from the virgin woodlands before the colonisers arrived. The farmers killed off the trees and the amount of elm pollen fell. In its place we find at a higher level in the mud the pollen of the cultivated fields – grasses, cereals, and weeds. These first farmers had no idea of using manure, and after a time the productivity of the fields was drastically reduced. The farmers moved on to new lands, and then the tree pollen reaching the mud increased again as the trees invaded the

36

12 The expansion of neolithic
farming, *c.* 3000 B.C., by
G. F. Mitchell

abandoned fields.

The people who lived at Lough Gur were self-sufficient in most things, but a certain amount of trading went on. Some of the axes found were of local stone, but others were imported from further afield where particularly suitable rocks were available. Tievebulliagh in County Antrim and Rathlin Island were two such places, and here stone axes were mass-produced in the first Irish factories. From the factories axes of a characteristic speckled stone were traded not only to the surrounding counties but also to Dublin, to Lough Gur, and to the south of England, in what was Ireland's first export-drive, 5,000 years ago.

Lough Gur was naturally not the only settlement of neolithic people, but it is the only place where many dwellings have so far been found. Others lived and worked at the axe factories, and there must have been a considerable settlement at Lyle's Hill, County Antrim. Here hundreds of fragments of neolithic pottery have been found, and no doubt many other sites still await discovery.

Not only do we know how these early farmers lived, we can tell something of their religious beliefs from the massive monuments they raised for their dead. Some of these are in the form of long galleries of huge stones in which the burials were placed, with a forecourt or central open court where ceremonies could take place. These court cairns, as they are called, are found mainly in the northern half of the country. At Ballyglass, in Mayo, the cairn had been built on top of the ruins of a wooden house.

37

The general term for such burial places is megalithic tombs (from the Greek *megos* large and *lithos* stone), and it is easy to see why they are so called, even when we look at the simplest tombs which survive. Dolmens – stone tripods with a capstone – are common throughout the country. All that now remains are the huge stones which formed the burial chamber, but originally they may have been covered by a cairn of stones or mound of earth. The most spectacular of the neolithic graves are the great megalithic cairns which we find in groups on the hills to the west of Lough Arrow, County Sligo; on the Lough Crew Hills in County Meath, in the valley of the Boyne, and on the Dublin-Wicklow mountains. Inside the cairns are elaborate burial chambers approached by a passage, and the type is known as a passage grave.

Such great cairns were constructed by a tribal group, and an immense amount of social organisation was required in their building. Many people were buried in the one passage grave – their bodies were burnt, and then the cremated bones were placed in the burial chambers, sometimes with pottery, beads of stone and bone, and tools for use in the next life. Great quantities of burnt bone have been found in some excavated tombs, showing that they were used over quite a period of time. We do not know exactly what beliefs the builders held, but some of them may have worshipped the sun since some tombs are placed with their entrances towards the rising sun. But their religion was a compelling one, and similar types of burial structures are known over large areas of Europe.

Another clue to their religious belief is the elaborate decoration of the stones in some of these tombs, such as at Newgrange, County Meath, where the finest passage grave in the country is to be seen. The spirals, lozenges, and zig-zag patterns which ornament the stones must have had a religious significance, and some are thought to be highly stylised versions of the human face and figure. These may represent the death-goddess worshipped for so long in the Mediterranean world.

While some of these tombs were still in use, other groups of people had reached Ireland's shores. A further great technological advance had taken place in the Middle East where men had learnt to recognise ores and make metal objects. Early prospectors were probably first attracted

13 Gold lunula from
Trillick, county Tyrone,
c. 1800 B.C. (National
Museum of Ireland)

by the bright colour of gold, but then they became aware of other metals such as copper. By fairly complicated processes they had learnt to reduce the ores to molten metal, and then cast objects in moulds. Metal objects could be made in any size, and another advantage was that broken or unfashionable articles could be melted down and remade.

Prospectors and metalworkers reached Ireland about 2000 B.C. and began their search for metallic ores – a search that continues to the present day. In nearly every case where a copper deposit has been worked in more recent historic times the miners have come across evidence of prehistoric mining. In any case there can be no doubt that these new colonisers were successful in their search, for many objects of bronze were soon being made. First of all simple flat axes, and then others decorated with zig-zag or spiral ornament. These are found in great quantity here, but were also exported to Britain and as far afield as Scandinavia. There is gold in the gravels of the Wicklow rivers, and distinctive gold ornaments were made in Ireland in this period which we call the early bronze age. One type of necklet was named a *lunula* (Fig. 13) because its outline resembled the crescent moon, and the lunulae also were exported to Britain and the Continent.

The early metal workers introduced a new type of pottery vessel into Ireland – very well made and beautifully decorated. The vessels probably were drinking cups, and are known by the term beaker. Pottery of this

39

type has been found in Ireland in megalithic tombs. But in this early part of the bronze age (from about 2000 to 1200 B.C.), a new style of burial was coming into fashion. Some groups were burying their dead, no longer cremated but each in a single grave, with a new style of decorated pot placed beside the body. Archaeologists assume that food for the dead man was placed in these vessels, so they are called food vessels. Sometimes bodies were still cremated, and the burnt bones were placed within a food vessel or a larger pottery vessel called an urn.

On the Hill of Tara a small mound – the Mound of the Hostages – was partly excavated by Seán Ó Ríordáin, and after his death by Professor Ruaidhri de Valéra. Here the megalithic people had built a tomb and covered it first with a cairn of small stones and then with a layer of clay. In this clay covering, the later arrivals placed many cremated burials in urns and with food vessels. One body, of a youth, had not been burned, and was evidently of some importance, since the boy had been buried with a necklace of beads of bronze, amber, and faience still in position around his neck. Faience is an artificial gemstone, a type of glass bright blue in colour which was manufactured in Egypt and the Near East about 1500 B.C. Amber, a form of fossil resin, comes from the shore of the Baltic, and was then very fashionable – as it is today – in necklaces and other jewellery. These luxury goods – faience and amber – were being imported probably in exchange for the gold and bronze objects Ireland was exporting at the time.

Though their tombs were not as elaborate as those of the earlier people, bronze age men built great circles of stone in which they held religious ceremonies. In a great circle at Grange, County Limerick – the largest in Ireland – fragments of broken beaker and food vessels were found near the bases of the stones – souvenirs perhaps of some ritual feast. Another circle at Lough Gur has an inner and an outer ring of stones, and although we cannot tell what rites took place in them these were the temples of the bronze age people.

About 800 B.C. new ideas from various parts of Europe penetrated into Ireland. Many new types of tool appeared, and more delicate work in wood and metal became possible. The style of warfare changed; close

14 The expansion of the Celts,
c. 400 B.C, by G. F. Mitchell

in-fighting with short heavy swords developed, and shields of bronze, leather or wood were used in defence. Farming was revolutionised by the introduction of simple ox-drawn ploughs; these could not turn the soil over in long furrows like the modern plough, but they could break up its surface, and so do away with a lot of hard spade-work.

The result appears to have been a great increase in wealth, and chieftains were able to accumulate stocks of gold. Neck-ornaments or gorgets were cut out of the sheet gold, and decorated with raised patterns. Bar gold was worked into penannular bracelets with expanded ends. Some gold ornaments were exported to England and beyond, and doubtless paid for luxury imports.

These bronze age people probably lived in simple settlements – single huts or groups of huts of wattle and daub surrounded by stockades in which the cattle could be kept safe. Or their homes may have been in clearings in the woodlands – log cabins surrounded by a wooden palisade like the homes of the American pioneers of one hundred years ago.

Another and more distinctive type of dwelling seems to have been coming into general use about this time. This is the crannog or lake-dwelling, an artificial island laboriously constructed in the waters of a lake. The idea goes right back to neolithic times, and the type of dwelling was to continue in use until medieval times. Whatever their type of

41

dwelling, wealthy people lived in style, and cooked meat for special feasts in large bronze cauldrons hung over the fire.

While Ireland was continuing to use bronze, another metal, iron, was coming into use in Europe. Iron ores are more common and therefore cheaper than those of copper, and iron for many purposes is superior to bronze. But the production of iron from its ores is more complicated, and technological difficulties slowed up its coming into common use. By about 600 B.C. however, iron-using tribes led by wealthy chiefs were establishing themselves in central Europe. These people spoke a Celtic language, an ancestor or early relative of the Irish that is spoken today. They were a group of different peoples who were linked by a common language and by various characteristics in their appearance, dress and way of life, and were known to the Greeks as *Keltoi,* or Celts. Aided perhaps by their superior weapons, they spread west to Spain, east to Asia Minor and north to England and Ireland. There seem to have been two movements into Ireland – one to the western half, by people coming directly from the Continent, and a second to north-east Ireland by a group coming from northern Britain (Fig. 14). It is clear in any case that the Celts were established here by about 150 B.C.

With the arrival of the Celts, Ireland entered on a new phase of her history. Apart from their ruined monuments, and their blood which probably still flows in our veins, little survives of the stone age hunters, the early farmers, the bronze age metal workers and herdsmen who had lived and died in Ireland for many hundreds of years. Their beliefs, their institutions, their traditions have passed away. But the Celtic immigrants were to dominate Ireland for more than a thousand years and even today, some remnants of their ways survive in the Irish-speaking households of the western seaboard. Theirs is the next part of the history of Ireland.

3

EARLY IRISH SOCIETY
(1st-9th Century)
by F. J. Byrne

Already before the Christian era Ireland was a Celtic country. The earliest waves of Celtic invaders may have arrived at the end of the Irish bronze age – in the sixth century B.C. The Celts had long dominated central and western Europe, and for a brief period of glory they terrorised Italy and Greece. They sacked Rome in 390 B.C., raided Delphi a century later, and founded the kingdom of Galatia far away in Asia Minor. In statues made by Greek artists who were impressed by their size and ferocity, we can almost recognise the very features of the chariot warriors of ancient Irish saga. The Celtic culture of the late iron age – from the fifth century on – is known as La Tène after a site in Switzerland. La Tène culture probably reached Ireland in the second century B.C. La Tène finds in Ireland include golden collars or torques – the typical ornament of the Celtic warrior; also war trumpets and beautifully ornamented sword scabbards.

Such finds are concentrated in Ulster and Connacht – the very area where Irish saga tradition places the scene of the epic 'Táin bó Cuailnge' and other legends of the heroic age. The stories of Cú Chulainn and Conchobar mac Nessa do reflect an historical situation. The Ulster capital of Emain Macha (Navan fort, near Armagh), is recorded as a city (*Isamnion*) on the map of Ireland drawn by Ptolemy of Alexandria in the second century A.D. The way of life of the heroes in the *Táin* is exactly that of the Celts in Gaul, as described by the Greek philosopher Poseidonios in the first century B.C. It is also very similar to that of the Homeric warriors in the *Iliad*. Still further east the Sanskrit epic poem, the *Mahābhārata,* depicts the same society of chariot-driving warriors in Northern India some centuries earlier.

All these legends reflect historical phenomena, although they do not record strict history. The term 'Celtic' is primarily linguistic, and Celtic, like Greek and Sanskrit, is a branch of the Indo-European family of languages. So are Germanic, Latin, Slavonic, and Persian. As the Indo-Europeans spread over Europe and parts of Asia in prehistoric times, they brought with them not only a language but common religious beliefs and a common semi-barbaric structure of society.

The Irish language derives from a dialect called Q-Celtic. The Celts of Gaul and Britain spoke P-Celtic, the ancestor of Welsh and Breton. Their word for 'horse' was *epos,* whereas the Q-Celts said *equos,* which in Irish developed to *ech,* Modern Irish *each.* There is some evidence to suggest that the Q-Celts came from Spain. The latest Celtic invaders – those who introduced the La Tène culture – may well have been P-Celts from Britain. Cú Chulainn's boyhood name of Sétantae is identical with that of a British tribe, the *Setantii,* who lived on the Lancashire coast. The *Menapii* of Belgium appear on Ptolemy's map of Ireland in Wexford – later they are found in Ulster under the Q-Celtic form of their name as the *Fir Manach.*

The earlier, non-Indo-European, population, of course, survived under the Celtic overlordship. One group in particular, known to the P-Celts as *Pritani* (Welsh *Prydyn*) and to the Irish as *Cruithni,* survived into historical times as the Picts or 'painted people' of Scotland. The Cruithni were numerous in Ulster too, and the Loíges of Leinster and possibly the Ciarraige of Connacht and north Kerry belonged to the same people. But when Irish history properly begins, in the fifth century A.D., all these peoples had become completely Celticised, sharing a common culture and a common Gaelic language. This language was introduced into Scotland by the Dál Riata of Antrim, who founded a powerful kingdom in Argyll. The movement of British Celts to Ireland was reversed in the fourth century when the Irish began raiding Roman Britain. The Romans called them *Scotti* and the Britons *Gwyddyl.* The Irish borrowed this Welsh name for themselves as *Goídil* – Modern Irish *Gaoidhil.*

These events marked the end of the heroic age. The great Ulster kingdom of Emain Macha was destroyed by the Connachta, probably as late

15 Gold collar from Broighter, county Londonderry, end of 1st century B.C.
(National Museum of Ireland)

as 450 A.D. – not 331 as you will find in most history books. In fact, when
Armagh was founded in 444 as the chief church in Ireland, Emain Macha
may still have been the most important political centre. Niall of the Nine
Hostages, a prince of the Connachta, seems to have won fame and power
by successful raids on Britain. From his brothers, Brión and Fiachra,
descended the great ruling families of Connacht. Niall's own descendants
took the dynastic name of Uí Néill. Three of his sons founded kingdoms
in north-west Ulster. Others ruled in the midlands, in Mide and Brega,
and waged successful war against the Laigin of Leinster. Around Emain
Macha itself the subject peoples seem to have thrown off the yoke of the
Ulaid and put themselves under the protection of the Uí Néill. They
formed a confederation of nine petty kindoms – a sort of satellite state
called the Airgialla, 'the hostage-givers' – from whom Niall got his
epithet of *Noígiallach*. The Ulaid themselves were driven east of the
Bann.

When documentary evidence becomes fuller in the seventh and eighth
centuries we see that Ireland has settled down to become an agricultural
country, divided into mainly small kingdoms. There were at least 150
such *tuatha,* although the population of Ireland may have been less than
half a million. The great war-lords who had dominated the land with their

45

chariots and hill-forts had gone. Heroic ages do not last long, but they are remembered forever. At this very time the Old Irish sagas were being composed by men who united native and Latin learning. Just as suburban Americans cherish the memory of the wild west, so Irish kings cast themselves in the rôle of Conall Cernach or Cú Chulainn. But the Irish nobleman was primarily a farmer. The battles which figure so prominently in the Annals rarely lasted longer than a summer's afternoon.

In this rural society there were no towns or villages. The only feature on the Irish landscape approximating to a town was the larger monastery. About the year 800 Óengus, the Céile Dé, in his poetical calendar of saints describes the scene:

The strong fortress of Tara has perished with the death of her princes; with its quires of sages great Armagh lives on.

The rath of Cruacha has vanished together with Ailill the victorious; fair above the kingdoms is the majesty in the city of Clonmacnoise.

The proud fortress of Allen has perished with her boastful host; great is victorious Brigit, beautiful her crowded city.

The fortress of Emain has faded away; only its stones survive; crowded Glendalough is the Rome of the Western world.[1]

The over-kings of the Uí Néill continued to call themselves 'kings of Tara', but they themselves lived more modestly in ring-forts or lake-dwellings such as the crannog at Lagore in County Meath, the home of the Uí Néill kings of south Brega.

The people lived in individual farms – the better homesteads were raths surrounded by an earthen rampart and stockade: the 'fairy forts' of the modern countryside. The king's house, according to the brehon laws, should have a double rampart – the outer ring being built by the forced labour of the king's lower-grade vassals – his *céili giallnai*. The king's most important functions were to lead his people in war and to preside over the *óenach*. This was an assembly held on regular occasions when the population of the *tuath* could meet to transact public and private business. There were also games and horse-racing – a survival from pagan funeral games, for the site of the *óenach* was normally an ancient tribal cemetery.

In the twelfth century the scribe of the Book of Leinster drew an imaginary sketch of the great banqueting hall of Tara as it was conceived to have been in the days of the legendary Cormac mac Airt (Fig. 17). It shows in detail the official seating protocol, and lists the portion of meat to be served to each guest according to his rank. This picture is not completely unreal: the Laws describe the seating arrangements in the less magnificent hall of a petty king in the eighth century. The door faces east, and beside it are the king's bodyguard of four mercenary soldiers.

The personal surety for the king's base vassals west of these. . . Envoys are placed to the west of him; guest-companies after them; then poets; then harpers.[2]

The Irish poets were not harpers. Even the *bard,* who was much inferior to the *filí,* was a member of the learned aristocracy and not a mere harper. The harper ranked as a freeman by virtue of his art, but other musicians, pipers, horn-players, and jugglers, were unfree. They were relegated to the corner near the door, beside the mercenaries.

In the other half of the house, on the north, a warrior and a champion guarding the door, each with his spear in front of him to prevent a disturbance of the banqueting hall. The king's noble clients west of these – they are the company who are in attendance on the king. The hostages are seated after them. A brehon after them. The king's wife west of him and then the king.[3]

Hostages whose lives were forfeit were placed in chains in the corner farthest away from the door, under the king's watchful eye: they may have derived some consolation from being in the best position to hear the harper!

The giving of hostages or pledges, as well as the employment of elaborate forms of guarantee and suretyship, played a very large part in Irish life, both public and private. The king was not a judge, nor could he enact laws except in certain emergencies. The brehons were men learned in the difficult traditional law, which enshrined a very archaic Indo-European social system.

Early Irish law finds its closest parallel in traditional Hindu law. The brehons maintained that it represented the law of nature, so that Christianity might add to but not subtract from it. They even defended

16 Hill of Tara, from the air (photo. Bord Fáilte Éireann)

polygamy on the grounds that it was practised by the Old Testament patriarchs! In the manuscripts of the law schools we find that the text of the law is written in large clear letters, quite distinct from the explanatory notes and commentaries of a later date which usually surround it. Although the manuscripts are as late as the fifteenth or sixteenth century, the text is in difficult Old Irish of the eighth or even the seventh century and has been preserved unaltered and sacrosanct.

The laws teach us much about Irish society in the eighth century – institutions such as fosterage of children, distraint of cattle to recover damages, ritual fasting as a method of asserting one's rights (this custom is found also in India). There are tracts on bee-keeping and on water-mills, and tracts on marriage and the position of women.

The two pivotal institutions in Irish life were the *fine* or joint-family, which was the social unit, and the *tuath* or petty kingdom – the political unit. To translate these terms as 'clan' and 'tribe' respectively, as is some-

48

times done, is not very helpful and can be positively misleading. There was no organic connection between these two units. The *fine* was the family group and included all relations in the male line of descent for five generations. It corresponds to the Hindu 'joint-family', and in it was vested the ultimate ownership of family land, *fintiu*. If anyone died without immediate heirs, his property was distributed among his more distant relations in well-defined proportions. The individual as such had few or no legal rights – these were contingent on his membership of the *fine*.

The brehon lawyers drew up a very elaborate scheme of the different degrees of relationship. The *geilfhine,* sometimes called *deirbfhine,* was the normal family group – basically the relationship between a man and his brothers; but it was extended over five generations to include his own children, his father's brothers, his grandfather's brothers, and even his great-grandfather and *his* brothers! Naturally, it was extremely unlikely that so many generations should be alive at the one time, but the lawyers had to provide for all possible contingencies. The next group, the *deirbfhine* or alternatively the *táebfhine,* brought in the first cousins for four generations; and the *iarfine* and *indfhine* the second and third cousins respectively.

The only term in general use outside of the law tracts is *deirbfhine,* though it is not always certain whether it refers to the first or second of the groups enumerated above. There was no system of primogeniture: land was shared equally between brothers; but the head of the senior line was the *cenn fine,* who represented the family in all its affairs. The *fine* were responsible for the misdeeds of its members and bore the duty of blood-vengeance if any member were slain. In practice they often accepted an *éraic* – a payment of blood-money from the slayer. If the latter had absconded, his *fine* were liable for the payment of the *éraic.* Women could not inherit land, but daughters might accquire a life interest in their father's land if they had no brothers.

In royal families each member of the king's *deirbfhine* was theoretically a *rígdamnae* – eligible to be elected king. If one branch of the family monopolised the kingship for four generations, the others were in danger of falling outside the magic circle of the *deirbfhine* and of losing their

17 Plan of banqueting hall, Tara, from Book of Leinster, 12th century (Trinity College, Dublin)

royal status forever. To avoid this fate they were often tempted to commit *fingal* – to slay their own kin. This was the worst crime in the Irish calendar, since there could be neither legal vengeance nor compensation for it. To prevent such occurrences a *tánaise ríg* or heir-apparent was usually elected during the king's lifetime. In practice, this would be the person who had most clients or vassals to support him. The ramifications of the *fine* make it easy to understand why Irish noble families were so careful to preserve their genealogies – a function which was committed to the learned *senchaid*.

Irish society was rigidly stratified. Besides the unfree classes – slaves, labourers, workmen, and the lower grades of entertainers – there were freemen and nobles. Rank depended on wealth as well as birth, and it was possible to rise or fall in status accordingly. Learning was also a qualification, for the *áes dána* or learned classes were equated in rank with the aristocracy, as were the Christian clergy. An *ollam* – a chief poet or brehon – was of equal status with a bishop or the king of a *tuath*. It was even possible for one of unfree status to acquire franchise by practising a skilled trade – smiths, physicians, and harpers were classified as freemen. Hence the word *sáer* for a craftsman. Irish law had a maxim that a man was better than his birth: *Is ferr fer a chiniud*.

All freemen were landowners. The lawyers catalogued elaborate sub-divisions of each class according to property qualifications. The *bóaire* or higher grade of freeman had to have land worth thrice seven *cumals* – that is to say an amount equalling the value of 63 milch-cows. The Irish had a simple agrarian economy and did not use coined money. The basic unit of value was a *sét* (Modern Irish *séad)*– a young heifer. A higher unit was the *cumal* – a female slave, reckoned as equal to six *séts*. We find similar units in Homeric Greece, and even the Latin word for money, *pecunia,* comes from *pecus*, 'cattle'. The *cumal* and *sét* are not always to be understood in their literal sense, for they were equated with sums reckoned in shekels and ounces of silver, and we find the *cumal* used as a measure of land, as in this description of the *bóaire's* property. His house is described in detail:

All the furniture of his house is in its proper place –
  a cauldron with its spit and handles,
  a vat in which a measure of ale may be brewed,
  a cauldron for everyday use,
  small vessels: iron pots and kneading trough and wooden mugs, so that he has
    no need to borrow them;
  a washing trough and a bath,
  tubs, candlesticks, knives for cutting rushes;
  rope, an adze, an auger, a pair of wooden shears, an axe;
  the work-tools for every season – every one unborrowed;
  a whetstone, a bill-hook, a hatchet, spears for slaughtering livestock;
  a fire always alive, a candle on the candlestick without fail;
  a full ploughing outfit with all its equipment. . .
There are two vessels in his house always:
  a vessel of milk and a vessel of ale.

51

He is a man of three snouts:
the snout of a rooting boar that cleaves dishonour in every season,
the snout of a flitch of bacon on the hook,
the snout of a plough under the ground;
so that he is capable of receiving a king or a bishop or a scholar or a brehon
from the road, prepared for the arrival of any guest-company.
He owns seven houses:
a kiln, a barn, a mill (a share in it so that it grinds for him),
a house of twenty-seven feet,
an outhouse of seventeen feet,
a pig-stye, a pen for calves, a sheep-pen.
He has twenty cows, two bulls, six oxen, twenty pigs, twenty sheep, four domestic
boars, two sows, a saddle-horse, an enamelled bridle, sixteen bushels of seed
in the ground.
He has a bronze cauldron in which there is room for a boar.
He possesses a green in which there are always sheep without having to change
pasture.
He and his wife have four suits of clothes.[4]

The Greeks and Romans always spoke of the Celts as wearing
trousers. But in Ireland only the lower classes seem to have worn them –
they were tight-fitting and could be short or long. They were usually worn
together with a short jacket. But the aristocracy, both men and women,
wore a voluminous cloak called a *brat* over a shirt or tunic – the *léine* –
which varied in length. The *brat* was often secured with a beautiful
brooch.

A man's status was expressed in very material terms by his *eneclann* or
'honour-price'. Damages due to him in a law-suit were assessed according to this price. Furthermore, he was not able to make a legal contract
for an amount worth more than this, nor was his evidence on oath valid in
cases involving a larger amount.

The detailed inventory of the contents of an aristocrat's house in the
same law-tract shows that it was basically the same as that of a prosperous
commoner. The furnishings are more luxurious, of course: articles of
yew-wood, bronze, silver and gold are mentioned. His hall had eight bed-
cubicles arranged along the walls and furnished with matresses, cushions,

18 Extract from brehon laws in Book of Ballymote, *c.* 1400 (Royal Irish Academy)

and hides. Although there was little privacy anywhere in the middle ages, it is clear from old Irish texts that separate huts or houses within the *liss* or stockaded enclosure served the functions of separate rooms in a modern house. It is obvious that the nobleman too was a farmer:

> He has implements for every sort of farm-work, with a plough and`its full legal equipment; he has two horses for harrowing. . .
> He is allowed to have pet animals:
> a deer-hound and horses, and a lap-dog for his wife.[5]

The element which really distinguished the aristocrat was *déis* – the possession of clients and vassals and the authority and influence which this entailed. Irish clientship was quite different from the feudal system of medieval Europe. The free or noble clients – the *sáer-chéili* – borrowed cattle from their lord with which to stock their own land. For this they paid a high rate of interest and accompanied the lord as part of his *dám* or retinue – the word *céile* in fact means 'companion'. The so-called *dáer-chéile* or *céile giallnai* on the other hand was not in fact 'unfree': he paid a lower rate of interest for his stock, but he also had to pay an annual food-rent and to perform certain menial services. He also had to provide free hospitality for the lord and his retinue during the *aimser chue* or 'coshering time' between New Year's Day and Shrovetide. Both forms of clientship were terminable on repayment of the original stock. A noble himself might be *céile* to another noble or to the king.

We are told of the *aire túise,* the highest grade of nobleman, that he was the *toísech* or chief of a large group of aristocratic kinsmen, a *cenél:*

> Twenty *séts* is his honour-price: he swears in compurgation, he is bond, surety, guarantor, debtor, or creditor and witness to that amount; he must be able to pay it whenever necessity arises, without having recourse to requisition or borrowing. . .
> So that he is of full assistance to the *tuath,* in representations, in oaths, in pledging, in giving hostages, in treaties across the border, on behalf of his kindred and in the house of a prince.
> He sustains legal agreements on behalf of his father and grandfather; he is able to enforce compensation by his own power; his oath overrides those of his inferiors in rank.[6]

19 Reconstruction of crannog, by W. F. Wakeman (W. G. Wood-Martin, *The lake dwellings of Ireland*, 1886)

It is easy to see that only through the patronage of such a person could the ordinary man hope to recover damages or debts due from a powerful neighbour. The nobles for their part were anxious to increase their political power by having as many clients as possible. Julius Caesar says that the Helvetians were unable to convict Orgetorix of treason because he appeared in court surrounded by his clients and debtors (*clientes obaeratosque*). The elaborate nexus of mutual responsibilities entailed both by membership of a closely-knit family group and by the relationship between client and patron in a small rural community ensured a reasonable measure of law and order in a society which had no police force, and where the state was not involved in most law-suits, such as those for manslaughter or assault.

Relations between different *tuatha* were conducted on similar personal lines by the kings. Most *tuatha* were tribute-paying, under the suzerainty of a greater king. Certain so-called *sáer-tuatha* did not have to pay tribute, because their own king belonged to the same dynasty as the over-king. But all sub-kings, whether tributary or not, acknowledged their inferior status by receiving gifts – termed *tuarastal* or 'wages' – from the over-king. The latter did not normally interfere in the government of the subject *tuatha*. Irish law recognised three grades of kings: the *rí tuaithe,* king of a single *tuath;* the *ruire* or over-king, also called *rí tuath,* king of several *tuatha;* and at the top the *rí ruirech* or *rí cóicid,* the king of a province.

If we look, for instance, at the kingdom of Ulaid as it was in the eighth century, we shall find that in County Down alone there were several

55

tuatha or petty kingdoms: Bairrche in the Mourne Mountains; Leth Cathail, now the baronies of Lecale; In Dubthrian, now the barony of Dufferin; Uí Echach Arda in the Ards peninsula; Uí Derco Chéin around Belfast; Dál mBuinne east of Lough Neagh – and some others as well. All of these formed the over-kingdom of Dál Fiatach, now represented by the diocese of Down. Other over-kingdoms were Dál nAraidi and Dál Riata in the north, which together form the present diocese of Connor; Uí Echach Cobo, the diocese of Dromore; and even Conaille Muirtheimne in the north of County Louth was an over-kingdom with two or three subject *tuatha*. Over all these stood the king of Ulster, *rí in Chóicid* – a position usually held by the king of Dál Fiatach, but sometimes by the king of Dál nAraidi or the king of Uí Echach Cobo.

Leinster presents a similar picture. The boundary between Laigin Tuathgabair and Laigin Desgabair is that between the dioceses of Kildare and Dublin-Glendalough on the one hand and Leighlin and Ferns on the other. The kingdom of Uí Failge comprised the baronies of Offaly in County Kildare together with that part of County Offaly which is in the diocese of Kildare. The kings of Uí Failge were related to the ruling Laigin dynasty and so were free from tribute. Not so the Loíges, whose chief territory lay in that part of County Leix which is in the diocese of Leighlin, though they had branches elsewhere in Leinster. It will be seen that the modern county boundaries have little relevance to early Irish history: part of County Offaly, for instance, was anciently in Munster, and still is in the diocese of Killaloe.

From the seventh century to the eleventh the overlordship of all Leinster was held by the northern Laigin, the kingship alternating fairly regularly between three branches of the dynasty – the Uí Dúnchada near Dublin (Dolphin's Barn is a corruption of Dunphy's Cairn, *Carn Ua nDúnchada*), the Uí Fáelán around Naas, and the Uí Muiredaig near Mullaghmast. But in the eleventh and twelfth centuries their southern cousins, the Uí Chennselaig, were to emerge supreme under the leadership of the Mac Murchada family. The Leinster baronies often preserve the boundaries of ancient *tuatha:* for example, Uí Dróna (Idrone), Fotharta (the baronies of Forth in Carlow and Wexford), Uí Bairrche

(Slievemargy in Leix and Bargy in Wexford).

Our dioceses very often coincide with early Irish over-kingdoms. An example is Ossory, which has preserved the name as well as the territory of Osraige – a kingdom which vacillated in its allegiance between Munster and Leinster. Kilmore is the enlarged kingdom of Bréifne as it was in the twelfth century; Clonfert is Uí Maine and Kilmacduagh Uí Fiachrach Aidne. Even such relatively small kingdoms as Corcomruad and Corco Loígde obtained their own dioceses of Kilfenora and Ross.

The law-tracts do not recognise a high king of Ireland even as late as the eighth century. One text in fact calls the king of Cashel the greatest of kings. Nevertheless, as we have seen, in the fifth century Niall and his sons had upset the ancient division of Ireland into five fifths by setting up new kingdoms in the north and in the midlands. The Uí Néill over-king styled himself king of Tara. We know that Tara was an important site even in prehistoric times, but we do not know precisely at what date the ancestors of Niall gained control of it. Both the Ulaid and the Laigin seem to have had ancient claims to the title, and possibly it had a religious rather than a political significance. The *Feis Temro* or 'Feast of Tara' originally symbolised the marriage of the priest-king to Medb, who was really a goddess and not a human queen. This feast was last celebrated by King Diarmait mac Cerbaill in the mid-sixth century. Diarmait was on good terms with Saint Ciarán of Clonmacnoise according to tradition, but the legend of the cursing of Tara in his reign by Saint Ruadán of Lorrha shows that the church disapproved of his attachment to certain aspects of the pagan past. Saint Adomnán of Iona, however, in his Life of Colum Cille, describes Diarmait in high-flown terms as having been ordained by God as ruler of all Ireland. Adomnán was writing at the end of the seventh century. His contemporary, Muirchú, in his Life of Patrick, talks of Lóeguire son of Niall reigning in Tara, 'the capital of the Irish' (*caput Scottorum*), and gives him the title of *imperator*. These claims were not universally accepted. But the Uí Néill certainly presented a new phenomenon on the political scene. In particular, they demanded from Leinster the payment of a large cattle tribute, the *bóruma*. As the king of Leinster was technically a *rí cóicid,* he should not have had to pay tribute

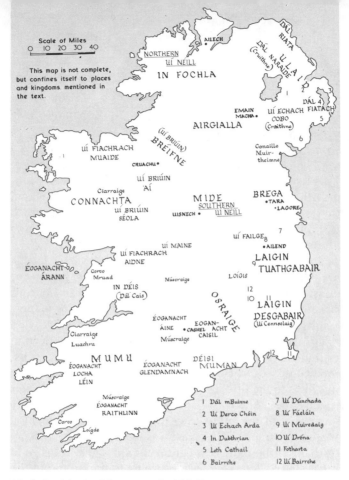

Scale of Miles
0 10 20 30 40

This map is not complete, but confines itself to places and kingdoms mentioned in the text.

AILECH

DÁL RIATA

NORTHERN
UÍ NEILL

IN FOCHLA

(Cruithne)
ULIA

ULAID

DÁL 4

EMAIN
MACHA
UÍ ECHACH FIATACH
COBO
(Cruithne)
5

AIRGIALLA

UÍ FIACHRACH
MUAIDE

(UÍ BRIÚIN)
BRÉIFNE

CRUACHU

Conaille
Muir-
theimne

6

UÍ BRIÚIN
ÁI

Ciarraige

CONNACHTA
UÍ BRIÚIN
SÉOLA

MIDE
SOUTHERN
UÍ NEILL

UISNECH

BREGA
TARA
LAGORE

7

UÍ FAILGE₈
AILEND

UÍ MAINE

UÍ FIACHRACH
AIDNE

ÉOGANACHT
ÁRANN

Corco
Mruad

IN DÉIS
(Dál Cais)

Múscraige

LAIGIN
TUATHGABAIR

LOÍGIS

12

OSRAIGE

10   11
LAIGIN
DESGABAIR
(Uí Cennselaig)

ÉOGANACHT
ÁINE

EOGAN-
ACHT
CAISIL

CASHEL

Ciarraige
Luachra

Múscraige

DÉISI
MUMAN

12   11

MUMU
ÉOGANACHT
LOCHA
LÉIN

ÉOGANACHT
GLENDAMNACH

Múscraige
ÉOGANACHT
RAITHLINN

Corco
Loígde

1 Dál mBuinne

2 Uí Derco Chéin

3 Uí Echach Arda

4 In Dubthrian

5 Leth Cathail

6 Bairrche

7 Uí Dúnchada

8 Uí Fáeláin

9 Uí Muiredaig

10 Uí Dróna

11 Fotharta

12 Uí Bairrche

20 Ireland in the 8th century, by F.J. Byrne

to anyone. The *bóruma* was never paid willingly, and many of the Uí Néill 'high kings' fell in battle in the attempt to levy it.

Meanwhile, Munster was ruled by the Eóganacht dynasty. This was divided into several groups with kingdoms planted strategically throughout Munster, dominating earlier peoples such as the Múscraige and the Corco Loígde. The king of any one of these groups was eligible to become king of Cashel. From the beginning Cashel seems to have been a Christian centre, and several of its kings were also bishops or abbots. County Clare had been conquered from Connacht early in the fifth

58

century, and the Eóganacht had colonised it with a subject people. These may have been related to the Déisi – at all events they were called In Déis, which simply means 'the vassals'. Later they were to emerge from obscurity under the name of Dál Cais.

At first the Eóganachta ignored the pretensions of the Uí Néill. But they became alarmed at their interference in Leinster. Cathal mac Finguine in the eighth century and Feidlimid mac Crimthainn in the ninth both challenged the Uí Néill supremacy. It was in the middle of the ninth century, however, during the crisis provoked by the viking invasions, that Máel Sechnaill I, of the southern Uí Néill, first made the high kingship a reality. In 851 he secured the submission of the king of Ulaid, and a few years later brought the king of Osraige to heel. Then he invaded Munster and obtained hostages from the whole province. But the existence of the high kingship depended very much on the ability of the claimant. Among those who vindicated their claim was Flann Sinna, who erected the Cross of the Scriptures at Clonmacnoise in memory of his treaty with the king of Connacht. He also slew the scholarly king and bishop of Cashel, Cormac mac Cuilennáin, at a battle in Leinster in 908. He was succeeded by Niall Glúndub, the ancestor of the O'Neills; Niall fell fighting the Dublin Norse near Islandbridge in 919 at the head of an army which was more representative of a national effort than that which fought under Brian at Clontarf a century later.

The absence of political unity makes the cultural unity of the country all the more remarkable. From the time of the earliest documents we find a sophisticated and uniform language in use throughout Ireland. The *áes dána* or 'men of art' constituted the most important element of early Irish society. They included the *filid* – a word very inadequately translated as 'poets' – as well as the brehons and the historians and genealogists. They alone enjoyed franchise outside their own *tuatha* and travelled freely throughout Ireland. They were all originally druids. Greek authors tell us of the importance of the druids and poets among the continental Celts, and Caesar says that the pupils of the Gaulish druids had to learn by heart an immense number of verses. His account tallies closely with what we know of the Irish bardic schools as late as the seventeenth century. With

59

the triumph of Christianity the druids as such disappeared. The poets gave up their more pagan and magical functions, but otherwise they and the other members of the learned caste continued to enjoy their full privileges.

They adapted the Latin alphabet to produce a native Irish literature, and in collaboration with the Christian monks tried to provide Ireland with a history as respectable and ancient as that of Babylon, Egypt, Greece, and Rome. The result was the *Lebor Gabála,* which related the successive invasions of Ireland by Parthalón, Nemed, the Fir Bolg, the Tuatha Dé Danann, and the Milesians. It is possible that these stories may preserve some genuine traditions: for instance, the Fir Bolg may be the Belgae: but in general the *Lebor Gabála* is an extremely artificial compilation. The Tuatha Dé Danann are in fact the Celtic gods worshipped by the pagan Irish. The church tolerated Celtic mythology if it was disguised as history.

The compromise arrived at between the church and the poets is reflected in the legend of the convention of Druim Cett in 575, where the poets were said to have been rescued from banishment by the intercession of Colum Cille. As a result, Ireland was in an almost unique position in the middle ages: here learning and literacy were not the preserve of the Christian clergy. As late as 1539, a formal treaty between Manus O'Donnell and O'Connor Sligo invokes the satire of the poets and excommunication by the clergy as penalties for its violation. And just as the Romans extirpated the druids from Gaul and Britain, so too in the sixteenth century, when Gaelic society was on the verge of extinction, the Elizabethan pamphleteers reserved their most bitter venom for the 'lewd rhymers' – the poets who were the true bearers of the ancient Celtic tradition.

THE BEGINNINGS OF CHRISTIANITY
(5th and 6th centuries)
by Tomás Cardinal Ó Fiaich

Since the historian depends mainly on written documents for his knowledge of the past, Irish history properly speaking must begin with St Patrick, the author of the earliest documents known to have been written in Ireland. Indeed it is extremely doubtful if our ancestors had any method of writing before his time except the Ogham alphabet, a cumbersome system of representing letters by groups of short lines varying in number and position. The system sufficed for short inscriptions on tombstones and the like, but if a modern novel were to be written in it, it would require a surface over a mile in length. St Patrick wrote a Latin which was rugged and abrupt, with little of the grace and dignity of the classical language, but for all his shortcomings as a scholar his writings provide us with our only contemporary narrative of the conversion of Ireland to Christianity.

Now there were certainly Christians in Ireland before St Patrick's arrival. Trade relations with Roman Britain and Gaul saw to that. Some scholars from Gaul may even have sought refuge in Ireland during the barbarian invasions of the empire. At any rate Irish Christians were sufficiently numerous by the year 431 to justify the appointment of a bishop for them by Rome in that year.

What does St Patrick tell us about himself in his writings? A little about his family background and captivity. He was a native, he says, of Roman Britain, the son of Calpurnius of the village of Bannavem Taberniae; at the age of sixteen he was captured by Irish raiders along with thousands of others and spent six years in captivity in Ireland tending sheep in the woods and on the mountain. During this period he turned to God and to matters of religion, which he had neglected in his youth, and finally succeeded in making his escape. Back in Britain he was welcomed by his relatives as a long-lost son and they implored him to remain with them. He might have done so were it not for a vision which he recounts in his *Confession* half a century later with remarkable vividness:

And there I saw in the night the vision of a man whose name was Victoricus, coming as it were from Ireland, with countless letters. And he gave me one of them and I read the opening words of the letter which were 'The voice of the Irish' and as I read the beginning of the letter I thought that at the same moment I heard their voice — they were those beside the Wood of Foclut which is near the Western Sea — and thus did they cry out as with one mouth: 'we ask thee, boy, come and walk among us once more'.[1]

St Patrick does not tell us where exactly he received his ecclesiastical training but in his old age he could write of his desire to go to Gaul to visit 'the saints of the Lord', and this suggests that it was in Gaul he studied. A seventh-century biography makes him a disciple of St Germanus of Auxerre, the site of whose monastery is still pointed out along the banks of the River Yonne. A stay on the island of Lérins, off the French Mediterranean coast, to which a primitive form of monasticism had spread from the middle-east, is also a possibility.

Without going beyond the saint's own words we can learn many details of his missionary work in Ireland. He 'baptized thousands', 'ordained clerics everywhere', 'gave presents to the kings', 'was put in irons', 'lived in daily expectation of murder, treachery, or captivity', 'journeyed everywhere in many dangers, even to the farthest regions beyond which there lived nobody', and rejoiced to see 'the flock of the Lord in Ireland growing splendidly with the greatest care and the sons and daughters of kings becoming monks and virgins of Christ'. It is probable that most of his missionary work took place north of a line running from Galway to Wexford. Most of the churches which later claimed St Patrick in person as their founder are situated in this half of the country. Of the twenty churchmen whose obits are entered in the annals in the generation after St Patrick's death, almost all are associated with the same area. And while paganism put up a stiff fight before being overthrown, Ireland was

21 Ogham stone, Coolnagort, Dungloe, county Kerry 5th–8th century (photo. Commissioners of Public Works in Ireland)

the only country in western Europe whose conversion produced no martyrs. Perhaps that was the reason why an Irish cleric, in the earliest sermon which has survived in the native tongue, elaborated his theory of the three kinds of martyrdom, white and green as well as red:

Is í an bán-martra do dhuine, an tan scaras, ar son Dé, re gach rud a charas (This is white martyrdom to a man, when he renounces everything he loves for God; this is green martyrdom to him, when by fasting and labour he does penance').[2]

The Irish monks had reason to know.

To fill in the details of his life left unrecorded by the saint himself — to give him an anchorage in time and place — has been the task of medieval biographers and modern scholars. Where was the elusive Bannavem Taberniae, his native village? Until the nineteenth century it was usually identified with Dumbarton on the Clyde. But an area so far north seemed inconsistent with Patrick's Roman citizenship and this induced modern scholars to seek his birthplace further south. The Severn valley, the island of Anglesey, and Ravenglass in Cumberland, have all received strong support in recent times, but the question is still unresolved. Or again where was the mysterious Wood of Foclut, whose people called Patrick back to Ireland? Faughill in North Mayo, Achill, Magherafelt in south Londonderry, Killultagh in south Antrim, Kilclief on Strangford Lough have all been advanced because of similarities in the Irish forms of the names. Or where did the saint spend his years of captivity? Slemish and Croagh Patrick have both their advocates. Most disputed of all the questions connected with the saint at present is the problem of giving definite dates to his Irish mission. We are certain that it began in the second or third quarter of the fifth century and lasted about thirty years. But did the saint arrive in Ireland in 432 and die in 461 or did he arrive in Ireland in 456 and die about 490? The earlier dating fits better into the continental background and the saint's associations with Auxerre. The later dating agrees better with the fact that some of the saint's disciples in Ireland survived until well into the sixth century. It is this problem of dating the saint's work in Ireland which has brought forward the theory of the two Patricks, a Roman missionary who came in the 430s, and a British missionary who arrived a generation later. But there we enter the region of textural criticism which had better be left to the scholars. The saint who proclaimed himself 'the most unlearned of men' must surely be enjoying the battles of the scholars in pursuit of him.

The system of church government which Patrick introduced into Ireland would naturally have been the episcopal one which he saw all around him in Britain and Gaul. The laws of a synod held before his death assume the existence of bishops with fixed sees, each exercising jurisdiction within his own diocese. But Patrick also introduced the

22 Beginning of
St Patrick's
Confession, in Book
of Armagh,
9th century
(Trinity College,
Dublin)

monastic life into Ireland and wrote with gratitude of the great numbers of his new converts who embraced it, something then unusual in most of western Europe. The trend towards monasticism which from the beginning had thus enjoyed an important but by no means predominant position within the Irish church became more pronounced after the saint's death. Within a century new monasteries had ousted many of the older Patrician foundations as the important centres of religion and learning; and ultimately Ireland became unique in western Christendom in having its most important churches ruled by a monastic hierarchy, many of whom were not bishops. Even Armagh, the church which was looked upon as in a special way Patrick's own, soon accommodated itself to the new system. Patrick's immediate successors there were bishops; before the end of the fifth century one of them, Cormac, is styled first abbot, and for the next two centuries the ruler of Armagh church was both bishop and abbot. The process was not completed till the eighth

23 Skellig Michael from the air (photo. Bord Fáilte Éireann)

century, by which time the abbot of Armagh was no longer a bishop, but had as a subordinate member of his community a bishop for the administration of those sacraments for which episcopal orders were necessary.

Whence came the impulse for this sixth century flowering of monasticism? The tendency of the Irish temperament towards an ascetic way of life surely contributed to it, as also the strong and attractive personalities of the great monastic founders. But some of the impulse also came from abroad, from Scotland and Wales. Ninian's foundation in Galloway, called *Candida Casa,* 'The White House', from the unusually bright appearance of the walls, was the training-ground of St Enda, whose later monastery on the largest of the Aran Islands was the school where many Irish abbots served their apprenticeship. But Aran's renown as a school of asceticism was soon eclipsed by the monastery of St Finnian of Clonard, who under the influence of the Welsh reformers, Cadoc and Gildas, placed a new emphasis on sacred study as part of the monastic life and thus attained the position which caused the martyrologies to name him 'the teacher of the saints of Ireland'. His twelve outstanding disciples at Clonard are linked together under the picturesque title of 'the twelve apostles of Ireland' and each became in turn an outstanding monastic founder in his own right — Colum Cille in Durrow, Derry, and Iona, Ciarán in Clonmacnoise, Brendan in Clonfert, Molaisse in Devenish, Cainneach in Aghaboe, Mobhi in Glasnevin. Others, too, who had not been pupils of Finnian, followed the example of his disciples and thus arose a second wave of foundations during the sixth century which owed nothing to Clonard – Bangor founded by Comgall, Moville by Finnian, Glendalough by Kevin, Tuam by Jarlath, Cork by Fionnbar. Religious establishments for women were less numerous but no less celebrated; some of them like St Brigid's foundation at Kildare and St Moninne's at Killeavy near Newry went back to the end of the fifth century, while others like St Ita's at Killeady, County Limerick, Caireach Deargan's at Cloonburren, County Roscommon, and St Safann's at Cluain Bronaigh in Meath followed later. Indeed St Brigid's foundation at Kildare was unique in sixth-century Ireland in being a double monastery for both men and women, each group following the same rule and using a common church, with the government of the whole community held jointly by the abbess and the bishop-abbot.

Monasteries established by the one founder tended to retain close ties with one another – such as Durrow, Derry, Iona, and the others founded by St Colum Cille and his disciples. These groupings of monastic churches, no matter where they were situated, would have been some-what on the lines of the present-day link-up of the various Franciscan or Dominican houses in Ireland in a single province under one provincial.

The difference was that nowadays these groupings of the regular clergy exist side by side with groupings of the secular clergy into dioceses arranged on a geographical basis; in early Ireland the monastic groupings replaced dioceses altogether. Another peculiar feature of the early Irish monasteries was the tendency in many of them to choose their abbots as far as possible from the family to which the founder belonged. Thus, of the first twelve abbots of Iona, all with two exceptions belonged to the Cenél Conaill from which Colum Cille himself was descended. This tendency undoubtedly helped to open the way for the later assumption of power in some of the large monasteries by local ruling families. Even from the beginning, however, Clonmacnoise was a notable exception.

A sixth-century Irish monastery must not be pictured like one of the great medieval monasteries on the Continent. It was much closer in appearance to the monastic settlements of the Nile valley or the island of Lérins than to later Monte Cassino or Clairvaux. Even the Latin word *monasterium,* when borrowed into Irish under the form *muintir,* was applied not to the buildings but to the community. For a modern equivalent one could think of the army camps to be found in various parts of the country during the 1940s, each a collection of wooden huts for sleeping in, grouped around a few larger buildings used by the whole community. A modern holiday-camp with rows of wooden chalets grouped around a few central halls would be closer to it in appearance than a modern Mount Melleray.

From Adomnán's Life of Colum Cille, written in Iona in the seventh century, when some of those who had entered the monastery under the founder were still alive, we can reconstruct the authentic picture in great detail. Instead of a communal residence the monks lived in individual cells constructed of wood or wattles, the abbot's cell slightly apart from the rest. In the west of Ireland, where wood was even then scarce, the cells were more likely constructed of stone and those are the only ones which have stood the test of time. Besides the cells of the monks the monastic enclosure included within it the *church,* usually built of oak, with a stone altar, sacred vessels, relics and handbells for summoning the congregation (on the rare occasion when the church was of stone, this

24 Page from the Cathach, late 6th century (Royal Irish Academy)

was of sufficient interest to be given a special name, the *damliag,* from which St Cianán's foundation at Duleek, County Meath, took its name); the *refectory* with its long table, and adjoining it the *kitchen* containing an open fire, cooking utensils, and a large cauldron of drinking water; the *library* and *scriptorium* with manuscripts suspended in satchels by leather straps from the walls and an ample supply of writing materials — waxed tablets, parchment, quills and stylos, ink-horns and the rest. A workshop and forge were situated nearby, while outside the rampart came the cultivated lands and pastures belonging to the monastery, furnished with farm buildings and in addition a mill and limekiln.

'Pray daily, fast daily, study daily, work daily', wrote Columbanus in his rule,[3] and the monastic life became a round of divine worship, mortification, study and manual labour. With the exception of those brethren who worked on the farm the monks assembled daily in the church for the various canonical hours. Sundays and saints' feastdays were solemnised by rest from labour and the celebration of the eucharist in addition to the divine office. Easter was the chief feast of the liturgical year, a time of joy after the austerities of Lent. Christmas was also a festival of joy, preceded by a period of preparation.

While the whole life of the monk and his retirement from the world was meant to be one great act of self-denial, additional mortification was imposed at fixed intervals. Every Wednesday and Friday throughout the year, except during the period from Easter to Pentecost, was observed as a fast day, when no food was taken till the late afternoon, unless when hospitality to a guest demanded relaxation of the rule. During Lent the fast was prolonged every day except Sunday till evening when a light meal was allowed. The ordinary diet consisted of bread, milk, eggs, and fish, but on Sundays and festivals and on the arrival of a guest meat was probably permitted. The monks wore a white tunic underneath and above it a cape and hood of coarse, undyed wool. When working or travelling they wore sandals. At night they slept in their habits. Their tonsure, unlike the Roman shaving of the crown of the head, took the peculiar Irish form of shaving the hair to the front of the head and allowing the hair at the back to grow long.

The principal subject of study was the sacred scriptures, much of which was committed to memory, especially the Psalms. Columbanus, a pupil of sixth-century Bangor, and Adomnán, a pupil of seventh-century Iona, show an extensive knowledge of Latin classical authors in their writings, especially of Virgil and Horace, and pagan authors must be included among the liberal writings studied in Irish monasteries as mentioned by the Venerable Bede. Lives of the fourth- and fifth-century continental saints such as Sulpicius Severus' Life of St Martin of Tours and Constantine's Life of St Germanus found their way into the Irish monasteries at an early date and were used for reading to the community. Recent research has pointed to close cultural connections between Ireland and Spain in the sixth and seventh centuries; and the writings of Isidore of Seville reached Ireland before being brought by Irish monks to Central Europe.

70

25 Early Irish monastery: reconstruction by Liam de Paor

Copying of manuscripts formed an important part of the monastic occupations. The monastic scholar *par excellence* was the scribe, and Colum Cille and Baíthín, the first two abbots of Iona, laid the foundations of a scribal art which with its later illuminative elements, formed one of the greatest glories of Irish monasticism. Of all the surviving manuscripts, however, only a handful go back to the period with which we are dealing, around the year 600. One is the Cathach, a fragmentary copy of the Psalms, traditionally looked upon as the copy made by Colum Cille in his own hand which led to the battle of Cúl Dreimhne and the saint's exile from Ireland. It is now preserved in the Library of the Royal Irish Academy, Dublin, and shows the Irish style of writing before it was

71

subjected to any seventh-century continental influences. Another is a copy of the four Gospels, arranged in the order Matthew, John, Luke, Mark, now in the Library of Trinity College, which may have been written at Bobbio while Columbanus was still alive. Two other manuscripts of the same period from Bobbio are now in the Ambrosian Library, Milan, and a fourth Bobbio manuscript which was looked upon as having belonged to Columbanus himself is now in Turin. Showing none of the brilliant illumination of Irish manuscripts of a century or two later, they are still precious relics from the very dawn of Irish Christianity.

The manual labour in which the early Irish monks engaged was primarily agricultural. Ploughing, sowing, harvesting, threshing are all mentioned as occupations of the sixth-century Iona monks. Others were engaged in making the various articles required for domestic use, and the need for sacred vessels of all kinds inspired an artistic approach to metalwork. Since fish formed such an important element in the diet, it is not surprising that the monks of Iona, as of all monasteries situated near the sea or the larger rivers, spent long hours in their boats. Like all true fishermen they liked to tell later of the 'big ones' which did not get away, and so Adomnán heard of the two huge salmon which Colum Cille's companions netted on the River Boyle in Roscommon more than a century before.

Some of the Irish monasteries seem to have had very large communities. Medieval sources refer to 3,000 monks of both Clonard and Bangor, but if this is not simply an exaggeration it must be taken to include all their daughter-houses as well. Upwards of a hundred would probably be the normal number during the sixth century in the larger monasteries — for instance Columbanus had two hundred monks divided among his three foundations in Gaul. By the early seventh century, when many English students flocked to Ireland, the numbers in some monasteries reached a few hundred. The great majority of the monks in each foundation were laymen and remained so, but a small number of the office holders were in sacred orders. At the head of the community stood the abbot, who often nominated his own successor. He was assisted by the vice-abbot or prior, who looked after the material resources of the

Iona
Derry
Armagh · Bangor
Aran · Kells
Clonmacnoise · Clonard
Lismore
Lindisfarne
Whitby
Glastonbury
Péronne · Liège · Cologne
Jumièges · · Fulda
·Laon ·Trier ·Wurzburg
·Regensburg
Auxerre· ·Reichenau ·Vienn
Luxeuil· ·Rheinau ·Salzburg
·St. Gall
Bobbio·
Lucca· ·Fiesole
Scale of miles
300

26 Centres of Irish Christian influence in Europe, 6th–8th century, by Liam de Paor

house, and by a group of the older brethren called the *seniores*. One of these was usually in bishop's orders and one or two were ordained to the priesthood to celebrate mass and administer the sacraments. Other posts in the monastery were those of scribe, cellarer, cook, guestmaster, miller, baker, smith, gardener, porter, and so on. Many monasteries had one or more anchorites who secluded themselves from the rest of the community and lived lives of silence and prayer.

It is well known that Irish monastic discipline was strict but a few instances from the rule of Columbanus will show just how severe it sometimes was. The smallest penalty, imposed for minor infringements of the

73

rule, was the recitation of three psalms. Corporal punishment, inflicted on the hand with a leather strap could vary from six to one hundred strokes. Periods of extra silence, fasting on bread and water, expulsion, and exile were other penalties. The most severe, imposed by Columbanus for murder, was ten years exile, of which some at least were to be spent on bread and water. Corporal punishment was nowhere prescribed in the Irish civil law and its introduction as a form of monastic chastisement is therefore all the more surprising. When the Irish monks went to the Continent, however, they found it, together with the more extreme fasts and vigils, opposed by their continental recruits and ultimately abandoned it.

The great era of Irish monastic expansion abroad falls later than our period but already during the sixth century the pioneers of it had left Ireland. In its initial stages it had nothing of the character of the modern foreign missionary movement; in fact it was not an organised movement at all. The motive uppermost in the minds of the *peregrini* was that of mortification and self-sacrifice — to renounce home and family like Abraham and seek a secluded spot where the ties of the world would not interfere with their pursuit of sanctity. Colum Cille's journey to Iona in 563 did not differ essentially, therefore, from Enda's journey to Aran a generation before. But once in Scotland he found unlimited scope for his missionary zeal in the conversion of the Picts. Thus he became the prototype to later generations of the patriotic exile, thinking longingly in a foreign land of the little places at home he knew so well:

> Ionmhain Durmhagh is Doire,
> Ionmhain Rath-Bhoth go nglaine
>> Ionmhain Druim Thuama is mín meas,
>> Ionmhain Sord is Ceanannas.

> Da mba liom Alba uile
> Óthá a broinne go a bile,
>> Do b'fhearr liomsa áit toighe
>> Agam ar lár caomh-Dhoire.[4]

Colum Cille's mission inspired his namesake Columbanus to go further afield a generation later and England, France, Belgium, Germany, Switzerland, Austria, and Italy would soon re-echo to the tramp of Irish monks. Luxeuil, the greatest of Columbanus's foundations in France, was destined to influence directly or indirectly nearly one hundred other houses before the year 700. His journey from Luxeuil to Italy like another Patrick or another Paul was surely one of the great missionary voyages of history — twice across France, up the Rhine to Switzerland, across Lake Constance to Bregenz in Austria, southward through the Alps and Northern Italy till he founded his last monastery at Bobbio in 613.

To stand by his tomb in Bobbio is therefore to realise what the advent of Christianity meant to the Irish people. He was still proud of that people: 'we Irish, living at the edge of the world, followers of Saints Peter and Paul — there has never been a heretic or a schismatic among us'. He still retained his individuality, that independence of spirit which had hurled anathemas at kings and queens and requested a pope not to allow 'the head of the church to be turned into its tail. . . for in Ireland it is not a man's position but his principles that count.'[5] He was still reluctant to give up his Irish method of calculating Easter or the episcopal exemption which the Irish monasteries enjoyed. To this native inheritance he added a mastery of Latin learning which few of his contemporaries could emulate, fashioning the new language into letters and sermons, poems and songs, even into a rowing chorus:

> The tempests howl, the storms dismay,
> But skill and strength can win the day,
>   Heave, lads, and let the echoes ring;
> For clouds and squalls will soon pass on
> And victory lie with work well done
>   Heave, lads, and let the echoes ring.[6]

The original Latin of this song is a far cry from the stumbling prose of St Patrick with which we began. It is a clear indication that the native and foreign elements in the Irish heritage are being welded into a new Christian culture and that Ireland which received much from Europe since the arrival of St Patrick has now also much to offer in return.

5

THE GOLDEN AGE OF EARLY CHRISTIAN IRELAND

(7th and 8th centuries)

by Kathleen Hughes

We have seen how Christianity came to Ireland, how church schools were set up and young clerics were given a Latin education. Irish scholars made rapid progress, for though Patrick in the fifth century was writing a very stumbling Latin, a century or more later Columbanus, Master of the Schools at Bangor in Ulster, could express himself fluently in Latin. Teachers in Irish ecclesiastical schools must have been hard at work during the fifth and sixth centuries. The boys learned Latin and studied the scriptures; and the ablest of them could enjoy reading classical authors and could write excellent Latin verse.

But there were other schools in Ireland as well, schools of poets and of lawyers which, for a considerable time, remained completely separate from the learning brought by the church. They had a long history and were honoured and respected by the people. The scholars educated in these secular schools formed a professional body, as closely-knit as the clergy in Ireland today, and they contributed a great deal to the life of the country. They knew the law which governed men's actions, they could recite the genealogies (which were similar to one's birth-certificate and title-deeds today), they entertained and instructed people with their stories and histories. They told their traditions before men went into battle, to inspire them with reminders of the heroic past, they praised the warriors' courage and prowess, they lamented those who were slain in war. These learned men of the pre-Christian period had to go through a long and severe training before they reached the top of their profession; but reading and writing were no part of it. Memory, not literacy, was the basis of their education, so that an Irish man of learning who could repeat, with complete accuracy, many complicated stories, whose sayings had grace, wit, and fluency, could yet write down none of his fine tales or clever remarks.

The education provided in the church schools on the one hand and the schools of poets and lawyers on the other was completely different, not only in subject matter but in its whole method and approach. One of the most exciting and important historical facts of the seventh century is that these two quite separate worlds, the Latin and the Irish, began to borrow ideas and techniques from each other. For instance, by this time some of the poets and lawyers had not only learned to read and write, which must have been fairly easy: they had also begun to apply their new knowledge to the Irish language and to their own traditional body of learning. The old method of learning by memory in the secular schools did not cease, but rather some poets and lawyers were coming into closer contact with clergy of Latin education, and were wanting to record their own learning in writing in the new manner. These two kinds of education, written Latin and oral Irish, *could* have remained completely distinct. When the Romans went to Celtic Britain, Latin schools were set up, but, as far as we know, British oral literature was not written down. Some people can remember Irish-speaking grandparents who learned to write English at school, but who could not write Irish, though Irish was the language of their daily lives and they spoke it with grace and elegance. Some seventh-century Irish scholars applied the foreign methods of Latin scholarship to their own, and were sufficiently proud of it. One of the early Irish law tracts has a story telling how this came about. The hero is a man called Cenn Fáelad who was wounded at a battle fought in 636 and who was taken to Toomregán for nursing, to a house at the meeting of three streets between the houses of three professors.

And there were three schools in the place; a school of Latin learning, a school of Irish law, and a school of Irish poetry. And everything that he would hear of the recitations of the three schools every day, he would have it by heart every night. And he fitted a pattern of poetry to these matters and wrote them on slates and tablets, and set them in a vellum book.[1]

27　Gallarus Oratory, county Kerry (photo. Commissioners of Public Works in Ireland)

We cannot be certain that things took place exactly like this, but something similar must have happened. So spoken learning came to be written down and permanently recorded.

The borrowing was not all in one direction. The bishops who had drawn up church laws in the fifth or sixth century had forbidden their converts to bring disputes before the secular law courts: Christians were not to appeal to the pagan brehons. But by the seventh and eighth centuries church authorities and secular lawyers must have been on easy terms. By this time the brehons had been converted and the clergy, by reason of their orders, had been given a position among the noble grades of society. When church leaders now drew up their ecclesiastical laws they were influenced by the secular lawyers, and tried to phrase their own legislation in the Irish manner. They had to find, or make up, Latin words to describe Irish legal practices unknown to classical Roman law. By the seventh and eighth centuries there must have been a considerable amount of friendly contact between ecclesiastical and secular lawyers.

Nor did the church cut herself off entirely from the Irish poets. Adomnán, writing his Life of Colum Cille at the end of the seventh century, tells us that when a poet visited the monastery of Iona he would usually be asked to entertain the monks by singing to them something of his own composition. Were the monks accustomed to hear in this way praises of former kings and heroes, perhaps the ancestors of their founder, and songs of battles? Monks and laymen were not cut off from each other. Monastic education was not reserved exclusively for those who were to enter religion, it was also given to the sons of church tenants and to some laymen who in adult life would farm and raise families. So there must have been people in Ireland, educated in the church, who could read and write Latin, but who knew and loved the old tales.

Many of these tales were of violence and bloodshed, not of peace and love. Listen to the boast of a pagan Ulster hero:

I swear by that by which my people swear, since I took spear in my hand I have never been without slaying a Connachtman every day and plundering by fire every night, and I have never slept without a Connachtman's head beneath my knee.[2]

Churchmen could not well approve such conduct. Indeed a seventh-century sermon urges self-sacrifice, not self-assertion. 'It is right', says the preacher,

that every one of us should suffer with his fellow in his hardship, and in his poverty and in his infirmity. We see from those wise words. . . that fellow-suffering is counted as a kind of cross.[3]

But even while some clerics, like this one, preached the true morality of Christ, others, writing the lives of the saints, were influenced by the generally accepted idea of what a hero should be like – brave, successful, hospitable, quick-witted. So although Patrick, on his own confession, was many times robbed, bound, and in danger of death, his seventh-century biography shows him in triumph, worsting his pagan opponents, killing the king's druid, cursing the king's host. Brigit is the perfect example of Irish hospitality: she can (by a miracle) milk her cows three times in one day to provide a meal for visitors; she can outwit a king (in the cause of charity), as well as any pagan hero could have done and with far more charm. The monastic scribes who wrote such saints' lives had

79

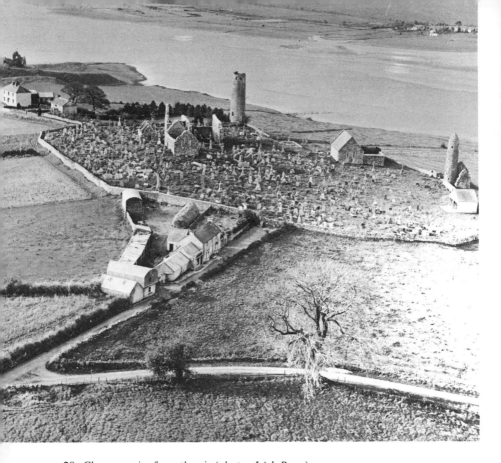

28 Clonmacnoise from the air (photo. *Irish Press*)

been brought up on the Irish hero tales.

The church did not suppress the learning of the secular poets and story-tellers, and ultimately much of it came to be recorded in writing and preserved in monastic libraries. Of course no man's learning, either Latin or Irish, will of itself get him into heaven. One scholar, writing a grammar book, put in a cautionary verse to this effect:

Grammar, learning, glosses plain,
Even philosophy is vain;
Arithmetic and letters all
In Heaven's hall God shall disdain.[4]

Yet Irish, as well as Latin, could be used in the service of God. So someone wrote a grammar in the Irish tongue, and clerics used Irish in their school-teaching. The division between Latin and Irish worlds became less sharp in the seventh century than it had been when Christianity was first introduced. Laymen and clerics came together. Latin and Irish learning met and mingled, Christian artists used the designs of the earlier Irish craftsmen. Perhaps we may even see Christian and secular symbols alongside one another on the slab at Drumhallagh in County Donegal. In the lower arms of the cross are two bishops with their croziers. Above, in duplicate, is a figure with his thumb in his mouth, like the Irish hero Finn who sucks his thumb to obtain knowledge.

The monasteries which housed the Latin schools, in their physical structure, followed Irish building techniques, although the Irish clergy must have been aware of continental styles. The whole settlement was enclosed behind a *rath* or cashel, like the monastery on Inishmurray, where the door and the stepped walling are very like those from secular forts. Inside were a number of cells where the monks lived. This plan may be contrasted with that of a continental Benedictine monastery in the early ninth century. Here the living quarters of the monks adjoined the church in a cloister, where the monks slept together in a common dormitory, and ate together in a common refectory. Irish monks did not adopt this style of building, based on the Roman villa and court-yard. The early cells and churches were of wood, or of stone without mortar, each stone overlapping the one beneath on the inside, until at the top the roof could be joined with one stone. Chapels like this can still be seen: at Gallarus (Fig. 27) the mason fitted his stones together with such skill that the building stands complete and weather-proof to this day. Near the church was a graveyard, often with the tomb of a holy man beside the church entrance, and crosses stood within and around the monastic enclosure as the sacred sign which guarded its approaches.

In the seventh and eighth centuries many of the monasteries which had been founded much earlier rose to positions of wealth and power. As one poet put it, writing about 800:

> Little places taken
> First by twos and threes,
> Are like Rome reborn
> Peopled sanctuaries.[5]

Such were the churches of Armagh, Clonmacnoise, Kildare, Glendalough, and others. Many of them had been founded near native forts, but the forts had declined while the power of the churches had risen. The same poet tells us of the lost glory of King Ailill's chief fort of Connacht and the present splendour of Clonmacnoise, and of Glendalough's importance.

Ailill the king is vanished
Vanished Croghan's fort:
Kings to Clonmacnoise now
Come to pay their court.

Navan town is shattered
Ruins everywhere:
Glendalough remains
Half a world is there.[6]

Such monasteries were usually easily accessible, on the main roads; they were cities, places of refuge, hostels, penitentiaries, schools and universities, as well as religious centres. Other monasteries, by contrast, were in remote and isolated places: Sceilg Mhichíl in the stormy Atlantic, or Kildreelig on Bolus Head, inside its stout rampart above the steep slope of the cliff edge. Men might retire to the desert to fast and pray. Some of our sources show us saints intent only upon God, with the lightest grasp upon material things, like St Brigit who

loved not the world:
she sat the perch of a bird on a cliff[7]

– the saint who has nothing and desires nothing but God. For Irish monastic life, in its enthusiasm and lack of uniformity, had its roots in the eastern desert where monasticism began. But there was no standard norm. While some monks retired to forests or islands 'to be sitting awhile, praying to God in some place' others attended church councils, drew up laws, went on visitation, collected revenues, ran the schools. Such men were in constant touch with the world.

Masters of monastic schools were eager to have Latin books from the Continent. They welcomed new works, and were looking for better texts of known authors. We know that books written in Spain were coming to Ireland in the seventh century, for some of the works of Isidore, bishop of Seville, seem to have reached Ireland within a few decades of his death.

30 Ardagh chalice, early 8th century (National Museum of Ireland)

Irishmen were also taking their own books to the Continent with them. St Columbanus founded monasteries at Luxeuil in Burgundy and Bobbio in North Italy. At both these monasteries, and at St Gall founded by the disciple of Columbanus, there were very soon important libraries.

Others beside Columbanus went to the Continent as 'pilgrims for Christ', in search of 'salvation and solitude'; they soon found themselves preaching the gospel, and setting up communities. One of the most famous was St Fursey, buried at Péronne in north-eastern Gaul, a monastery where the monks loved Patrick. Irishmen constantly stayed

31 Athlone crucifixion plaque, 8th century (National Museum of Ireland)

here, so it became known as 'Perona Scottorum' (Péronne of the Irish) These houses supported scribes who copied books, and they attracted men of learning. Scholars on pilgrimage took books out with them and brought books home in their luggage. For example, a service-book from Bangor, probably written at the very end of the seventh century, found its way to Bobbio, we do not know for certain how, but most probably carried there by some monk in his book-satchel. Among the treasures of St Gall are books written and illuminated by Irish artists in a specifically Irish style. From about the middle of the seventh century up to the Carolingian renaissance art and learning in Gaul were at a low ebb, and some of the Irish foundations with their active book production stand out the more brilliantly in contrast with the general gloom. No doubt some Irish pilgrims, having visited their continental brothers, went on as far as Jerusalem, for Adomnán abbot of Iona, who died in 704, on information supplied by a Gaul, wrote an account of the holy places, though as far as we know he was never able to get there. The ninth-century copy of this book has plans which would have been of use to the tourist as well as of interest to the scholar in the library at home.

The fusion of Irish and Latin cultures is nowhere more clearly seen than in seventh and eighth-century Irish art. In the pre-Christian period the patrons of Celtic art were the warrior aristocracy: it was for them that the smiths produced personal ornaments, weapons, and horse-trappings. By the eighth century the church had become a great patron. A church might be small and dark, but its altar must have gleamed with book-cover or reliquary or altar-vessels. Many of these ornaments are in gilt-bronze, decorated with gold filigree arranged in intricate patterns, inlaid with enamel and precious stones, so that the surface has an exquisite variety of texture, yet, at the same time the eye can easily grasp a coherent design. The seventh-century compiler of the Life of Brigit tells us that the church at Kildare contained two tombs, of St Brigit and bishop Conláeth, placed to the right and left of the altar. 'These tombs', he says, 'are richly decorated with gold and silver and many coloured precious stones; they have also pictorial representations in relief and in colours, and are surmounted by crowns of gold and silver.'[8] Once Irish smiths had made crowns for warriors; in the seventh century they were also turning their skill to glorify Christ and his saints.

The pagan Irish artist had sometimes carved statues, which, to our eyes, seem grotesque and brutal lumps of stone. Yet in abstract design he had been a master. The Christian artist repeated the old motifs of curves and spirals: the scribe liked to decorate his books with them, the smith put them on his metal work, the sculptor carved them on his crosses. But the Christian artist also needed to show Christ in human form, as a child in the virgin's arms, as a man tempted as we are, as the redeemer bearing the sins of the world yet triumphant over death. So new designs entered Irish art, sometimes influenced by types which came originally from the eastern end of the Mediterranean, sometimes by patterns from nearer home, copying the appearance of English jewellery.

Yet for all the foreign influence it received and adopted, Christian art

32 Funeral procession on base of north cross, Ahenny, county Tipperary,
8th century (photo. Commissioners of Public Works in Ireland)

continued to show its Celtic origins. Most people would agree that the
Book of Kells is one of its most perfect examples, with its skilled execution and infinite variety. The Norman-Welshman, Gerald, saw a book
like this at Kildare in the twelfth century. This is how he describes it:

87

(It) contains the four gospels. . . with almost as many drawings as pages, and all of them in marvellous colours. Here you can look upon the face of the divine majesty drawn in a miraculous way; here too upon the mystical representations of the Evangelists, now having six, now four, and now two, wings. Here you will see the eagle; there the calf. Here the face of a man; there that of a lion. And there are almost innumerable other drawings. If you look at them carelessly and casually and not too closely, you may judge them to be mere daubs rather than careful compositions. You will see nothing subtle where everything is subtle. But if you take the trouble to look very closely, and penetrate with your eyes to the secrets of the artistry, you will notice such intricacies, so delicate and subtle, so close together and well knitted, so involved and bound together, and so fresh still in their colourings that you will not hesitate to declare that all these things must have been the result of the work, not of men, but of angels.[9]

In the seventh and eighth centuries the old Celtic and the new Christian-Latin ways of looking at things joined together. Because that happened we today can study the Old Irish law tracts and enjoy the Old Irish tales; because of that, Irish artists gained a new vision, and yet interpreted the Christian message in their own individual style. So we have what is often called the Irish golden age. No doubt there was hardship – we know very little of what simple people thought – but on the whole Irish society must have been comparatively prosperous and there was much of beauty to be seen. The Irish did not keep all this to themselves. Bede, the English historian, tells us how St Aidan went from the monastery of Iona to convert the heathens of Northumbria. Monasteries and schools were set up in England, and, for a time, some English students came to Ireland for further education. Speaking of these students, Bede tells us that the Irish welcomed them all kindly, and, without asking for any payment, provided them with books and teachers. Irish monks took their own books to Northumbria, and taught the scribe's art to their English pupils.

While northern England had still been pagan, the Irish were already masters of a fine script. A psalter, known as the Cathach (Fig. 24), attributed to St Colum Cille, was written about 600, and shows features which later became typical of Hiberno-Saxon manuscripts. In it the scribe provides headings with a series of decorated initials which diminish in size until they are brought into the body of the text. This was a favourite device of Irish scribes, and can also be seen in manuscripts from Bobbio. It is used again, with much greater elaboration, in the Book of Durrow, which was written a generation or two later. Some modern scholars argue that this book was produced in Northumbria, others say it was written in Ireland or Iona. But wherever it was produced, it was created under the direction of a man who had received an Irish training. If it was written in Northumbria it demonstrates how much the Irish had taught their converts. Every good teacher learns from his pupils, and Irish illuminators had borrowed from the designs of English jewellers, perhaps even from the work of Pictish sculptors or from Roman remains still to be seen in Britain. But Irish masters left their stamp on English monasticism, so that even after 664 (when many Irishmen left Northumbria) their disciples continued to produce books which showed strong Irish influence, in marked contrast to the new styles in book decoration which were now coming into England from the Continent.

We know a lot more about the Irish in England, because Bede, a great historian, wrote about them: on the Continent in the later seventh and eighth centuries we have to trace them by a series of less satisfactory clues. They helped to evangelise the pagan tribes of Germany, though their work was largely superseded by English missions. Irishmen on the Continent thought of and prayed for those at home. At Salzburg, where an Irishman named Fergil was abbot and bishop, the list of persons, living and dead, for whom the community undertook to pray includes the abbots of Iona, from Colum Cille, the founder, down to the fifteenth abbot, who was Fergil's contemporary. There are also Irish names in the litany written for Fergil's German successor in the bishopric of Salzburg, saints whom Fergil himself had most probably remembered in his prayers, among them the abbess of Clonbroney who would have been in middle age when Fergil was a boy. Fergil, and others less distinguished, whose names are now forgotten, had an eagerness of mind and intellectual curiosity not common in the eighth century. The writings of seventh- and eighth-century Irishmen, preserved in continental libraries often under false names, can still be identified by their style, idiom, and special

33 Page from Book of Kells, *c*. 800: arrest of Christ (Trinity College, Dublin)

interests.

So the Irishman's love of learning, fostered by centuries of pagan tradition, combined itself with the art of writing and the Latin books brought by Christians to Ireland. Irish artists learned to decorate the manuscripts they wrote with old patterns and new designs. Irish smiths turned their ancient skills to glorify the Christian church. Irishmen went out in pilgrimage, 'seeking salvation and solitude', but they also evangelised pagan peoples; they built up libraries on the Continent, wrote works of scholarship and helped to make ready for the flowering of learning which was to follow in ninth-century Gaul.

THE AGE OF THE VIKING WARS

(9th and 10th centuries)

by Liam de Paor

The noblest share of earth is the far western world
Whose name is written Scottia in the ancient books;
Rich in goods, in silver, jewels, cloth and gold,
Benign to the body in air and mellow soil.
With honey and with milk flow Ireland's lovely plains,
With silk and arms, abundant fruit, with art and men.

Worthy are the Irish to dwell in this their land
A race of men renowned in war, in peace, in faith.[1]

These are lines from a Latin verse written by Donatus of Fiesole, an Irish bishop living in Italy in the ninth century. He was describing Ireland in her golden age — a land which had not been invaded since prehistoric times and which had been Christian for more than three centuries.

The eye of exile is fond, and Donatus perhaps paints too rosy a picture. All was not perfect in early Christian Ireland, and there are many signs that her monastic culture was already in decline by the end of the eighth century.

Yet the grandfather or great-grandfather of the poet could have known the artists who worked on such triumphs of the metalworker's craft as the Tara brooch or the Ardagh chalice. Donatus himself could have known the men who worked on the Book of Kells, the extraordinary masterpiece which marks the culmination of early Irish art. This book is unfinished — perhaps because of the disasters which befell many of the Irish monasteries at the end of the eighth century.

Some scholars believe that the Book of Kells was written and painted at the Irish foundation of St Colum Cille on the island of Iona off the Scottish coast. Iona is open to the sea on all sides and it was from the sea that, suddenly, disaster came. In 795, long low ships, with patterned sails, appeared from the ocean and ran their prows up on the beach. From them came helmeted warriors, armed with heavy swords and iron spears, who ransacked the monastic village for valuables and slaves, taking as trinkets the jewelled shrines and ornaments of the altars. Raiders were back again in 802, and yet again in 806, when they murdered no less than sixty-eight of the monks. After this visitation the abbot, Cellach, moved to Ireland with the survivors, carrying with him the precious relics of Colum Cille. He was given land at Kells in the territory of the southern Uí Néill, where he founded a new monastery. One can imagine the Book of Kells, its ornamentation cruelly interrupted by the murderous raids, being carried back to the home country and housed with other valuables and relics in the building constructed at that time which is now known as Colum Cille's House at Kells. In gospel books as such the raiders had no interest, for they were illiterate, and pagans.

The flight of Cellach and his monks was to be but one of many such flights in the coming years. In the very year of the first attack on Iona, raiders – probably indeed the same ships' crews – attacked Lambay off the Dublin coast, and for the next forty years or so the pagans from the sea struck again and again at the monasteries all around the shore of Ireland, even such lonely sanctuaries as the bleak Skellig eight miles off the Kerry coast. Most of those who so fiercely attacked our shores came from the fjords of western Norway, sailing west to Shetland, then south to Orkney, along the Atlantic coast of Scotland, and so to Ireland. From other parts of Scandinavia at this time raiding parties went out, not alone seafarers who could negotiate coasts and rivers in their ships, but horsemen as well, who would make long journeys overland. The Danes ravaged the Friesian coast and also eastern England, and tested the defences of Charlemagne's empire. The Swedes crossed the Baltic and penetrated deep into Russia. In time the Scandinavian ships were to appear off Cadiz and in the Mediterranean – even at the gates of the great

34 Viking ship, Gokstad, Norway, 9th century (Universitetets Oldsaksamling, Oslo)

imperial city of Byzantium itself.

What sort of people were the vikings? — to use the name by which the Scandinavian raiders are commonly called. They have received what is nowadays called a 'bad press', for most of the contemporary records of them come from the very monasteries which had good reason to fear and dislike them. In a violent time their heathenism and their indifference to sanctuary struck horror into the monks. An Irish monk of the time, listening thankfully to the howling of a storm one night, wrote in the margin of his manuscript:

> The wind is rough tonight
> tossing the white-combed ocean;
> I need not dread fierce vikings
> crossing the Irish Sea.[2]

93

They came from the valleys and fjords of western Norway, and at home were farmers and seamen, skilled in many crafts. Their way of life was not very different from that of the Irish of the period, except that they were still pagans, worshipping the old gods. Before the raids began, they had colonised the islands of Shetland and Orkney where their settlements have been excavated. Here they lived a simple rural existence in farm villages like that at Jarlshof, where their long houses have been found. Their technology was advanced and they had a keen eye for business and trade.

The Nordic peoples had developed great skill as carpenters and had gone through an intensive period of development in the design and construction of ships. They lavished great care and elaborate ornament on the vessels of kings and great leaders especially. One of these ships is described by a Saxon chronicler: 'with a golden beak and a purple sail furnished within a close fence of gilded shields'. Some of these have survived, for a dead viking chief was buried in splendid style with his ships, his weapons and his goods, and such burials have been excavated. The Gokstad ship – a true viking long ship – shows well the low raking lines, the clinker construction of overlapping planks, and the curved prow which made these shallow-draught vessels seaworthy and yet suitable for inshore waters, estuaries and rivers. With the development of sails, which can be followed on Swedish stone-carvings, the vikings were equipped for venturing out on the dangerous and unknown Atlantic.

Their courage and skill brought them not only on the southward course to Ireland, but also on the northward passage to the Faroes, Iceland, Greenland, and even the foggy coasts of the North American continent. Some went looking for new lands to colonise, for the Scandinavian populations were growing too big for the amount of farmland available at home. Others went to trade or to make what profit they could from piracy. New trading routes and merchant centres were coming into being in northern Europe and these provided a stimulus for the Scandinavians with their command of the waterways.

About the time of the earliest raids the vikings for the first time began to build towns, commercial centres such as Kaupang, Birka, and Hedeby at strategic points on the shipping routes. The towns were defended with earthen palisaded ramparts and wooden towers – traces of the ramparts still remain in Hedeby in Denmark and other sites. Inside the ramparts were houses of timber or wattle-and-daub construction, and the size of the population no doubt fluctuated considerably, swelling for the winter and summer markets. The voyages, whether for trade or loot, or both, began to be organised on a larger scale, and fleets rather than single ships or small groups of ships plied the seaways. Such fleets appeared in Irish waters in 837, and with them the Norse attack changed its character.

There were sixty ships in the Boyne mouth that year and sixty on the Liffey. Legendary history tells of one Turgesius who 'assumed the sovereignty of all the foreigners in Ireland', and records begin to tell of conflict between various Irish kings and the newcomers. The Norse were now trying to set up permanent bases in Ireland. The first was set up at the Liffey mouth, and from here large-scale expeditions were mounted deep into the interior of the country. Monasteries throughout the island were raided, but the chief viking effort was probably directed at the seizure of land for settlement, following the pattern of ninth-century viking activity elsewhere. The fleets rode at anchor on the Shannon lakes in the heart of Ireland.

The Norse apparently built their first fortified settlements in 841, one at Linn Duachaill (now Annagassan) on the Louth coast, the other at the Liffey mouth. The name 'longphort' which the Irish gave to these defended bases indicates that they began with the building of a stockade around the ships. The longphort on the Liffey was thereafter to play a central part in Irish history: this was the foundation of the city of Dublin.

Dublin indeed supplies us with a good deal of information about the Norse in Ireland at this time, for its ninth-century cemetery was accidentally discovered a hundred years ago when the railway cutting for the line from Kingsbridge was being made near Islandbridge. The Norse town itself would have been quite small – not much more than the present day High Street. The *Thingmote,* or assembly place outside the town, was still there in the seventeenth century when it was referred to as 'the fortified hill near the college'. The *Haugen* or burial-mounds nearby gave

95

35 Round tower and St Kevin's Church, Glendalough, *c.* 900 (photo. Commissioners of Public Works in Ireland)

their name to Hoggen Green, later known as College Green. The Haugen have long since been removed, but from the Islandbridge graves have come warriors' weapons: typical ninth century Norwegian swords. These swords often had triangular pommels, sometimes with silver patterns hammered into the iron. There were also rarer and more costly Frankish swords, made by continental armourers who signed their products, and iron spear-heads, and specimens of that favourite Norse weapon, the iron axe. Some of the burials had a more pacific character, tools rather than weapons being buried with the dead – knives, hammers, forge-tongs and sickles. Women were buried wearing their distinctive Norse 'tortoise brooches' or with their household gear – linen smoothers and spindle whorls. One of the chief occupations of the vikings is attested by a number of sets of folding bronze scales which were used by these first

96

citizens of Dublin in striking their bargains.

In the meantime, what of the Irish? What were they doing all these years and why did they not put up a better resistance to the invaders?

It must be remembered that in ninth-century Ireland there was no one responsible for the defence of the island as a whole. There were many small kingdoms, and a traditional division of the island into two halves: Leth Cuinn, dominated by the Uí Néill of Tara, and Leth Moga, dominated by the Eóganachta of Cashel. At the time of their rise to power, centuries before, both these paramount dynasties had taken lands from the Laigin, or Leinstermen. The Laigin had never really or fully acquiesced in the overlordship of either the Uí Néill or the Eóganachta, and their province in the south-east really formed a third, and crucially important, division of the country.

As the Norse crisis reached its peak, the Eóganachta and the Uí Néill began to come into conflict for the first time on a large scale. The career of Feidlimid mac Crimhthainn, king-bishop of Cashel, who challenged the kings of Tara and perhaps destroyed more churches than any of the Norse, is a symptom of the mounting anarchy in Irish affairs. He died in 847. From 850 onwards we have accounts in the annals of Irish alliances with Norse bands in the incessant warfare of the time, and we hear too of battles – often at sea – among the Norse themselves. A leader named Olaf founded a kingdom of Dublin, which remained a separate small state, within the general Irish polity, but with extensive overseas connections. The Norse were now drawn more and more into Irish affairs, playing their own parts in the complex and shifting alliances of the little kingdoms. From the confused welter of battles within kingdoms and battles between kingdoms in the second half of the ninth century, there did emerge a gradual strengthening of the power of the kings of Tara. The vikings in the northern half of Ireland were gradually brought under control. Raids, sometimes on a large scale, continued, but the Norse policy of making fortified settlements was checked. Dublin remained a strong state. It played a large part in the affairs of the vikings in Britain, since its rulers had dynastic interests in York. The Dublin Norse are frequently found allied with the Leinstermen or with the newly powerful

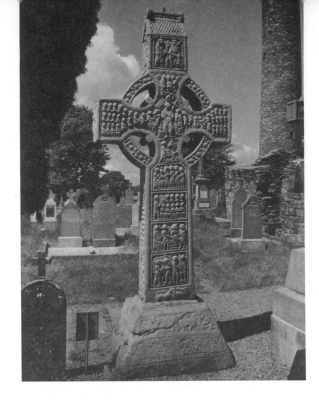

south midland state of Osraige under its king, Cerball.

As the ninth century drew towards its close there was a slackening of Norse activity in Ireland, while the conflict between the most powerful dynasties of the north and the south came to a climax. Finally, in a great battle at Belach Mughna in Leinster, Flann Sinna, king of Tara, defeated Cormac mac Cuilennáin, king-bishop of Cashel, in 908. Cormac and many of the leaders of the Eóganachta were killed, and the power of the ancient Cashel dynasty suffered a decline from which it was never fully to recover.

What effect had all these raids and wars on Irish life and culture in the ninth century? Apart from the writings of annalists and chroniclers we have an abundance of other kinds of evidence of the looting and destruction. Almost every Irish church of the time must have contained little silvered and enamelled caskets for holding relics. Most of those which still survive are finds from western Norway. Indeed the Irish

37 Detail from Muiredach's Cross, Monasterboice: the arrest of Christ (photo. Commissioners of Public Works in Ireland)

archaeologist who visits the museums of Oslo, Bergen, Stavenger, and Trondheim can fill his notebook with drawings of Irish metalwork found in the graves of vikings who had returned to die at home with the loot of their expeditions to far-off Ireland. Often mountings or ornaments from reliquaries are found re-used to make brooches for the vikings or their ladies. As a Scandinavian scholar puts it, 'it would be possible to reconstruct the viking expeditions to Ireland on archaeological evidence alone, even if every literary record were lacking'.[3]

In Ireland itself similar material has been found from time to time – Irish-style metalwork used as harness mounts in a horse burial at Navan, pieces of metalwork of Irish manufacture re-used as ornamental mounts for a set of viking weights from the Islandbridge cemetery. From the contents of the Dublin graves one can easily picture the raiders riding back from the Irish midlands with enamelled and gilt trinkets, to be traded to the ships which had put in at the quayside from Norway or the

Isles, perhaps in exchange for new Frankish swords.

Irish manuscripts at St Gall and other places on the Continent testify to another kind of movement of valuables out of Ireland: the books, carried off not as prey but for safe keeping by monks and scholars to the courts and monasteries of Europe. Some of the earliest examples now known of writing in the Irish language – usually explanatory notes on Latin books — have survived just because they were brought to the Continent in this manner. The number of manuscripts which were destroyed – 'drowned' as the chronicler picturesquely puts it in lakes or sea – can never be calculated.

If then we were to summarise the ninth century as a grim and barbarous period we would have a good deal of evidence to support us. Yet it is easy to exaggerate the effect of marauding raids and small-scale wars and to forget that medieval chroniclers, like modern journalists, appreciated a good story and could find a ready market for sensationalism. Life went on. What is more surprising, we have much evidence for new developments in art and scholarship at this time. It is impossible to be precise about dates here, but it was in the time of the viking wars that stone churches built with mortar began to replace wooden buildings in Ireland. Not many have survived the centuries, but we can in outline trace the development from timber prototypes to stone-roofed churches like St Kevin's at Glendalough. And in the same period of warfare and destruction the building of the elegant bell-houses also began. The models for these were almost certainly early belfries in Italy, but a very distinctive Irish type was soon evolved which still adds grace to our landscapes. They were soon adapted to serve a secondary purpose as places of refuge, which is why in most of the round towers the doorway is raised some distance above the ground. From the top windows a small hand-bell rang out to tell the hours, or to warn of sudden danger. All too often, however, as happened for example at Monasterboice, those who took refuge in a monastic belfry perished by fire together with the books and valuables they had with them, since the tower by its design served as an excellent chimney.

The development of stone sculpture throughout the viking period in

38 Irish enamelled bronze mounting from
Viking grave, Myklebostad, Norway,
8th century (Bergen Museum):
wash drawing by Liam de Paor

Ireland is more remarkable. The cross of Patrick and Columba at Kells
was carved at this time, probably shortly after the community of Iona
settled in Ireland. It is an early example of a series in which we can watch
new schemes of figure-carving – mainly scenes from the scriptures – being
worked out throughout the century. The chief centre of the early figure-
carving school was the valley of the river Barrow, especially at Castledermot and Moone. The carvings are influenced by the revival of art in
the Carolingian empire, although there the work was chiefly in media
other than stone. There is nothing in Europe of the time to compare with
the elaborated schemes of imagery which were finally worked out by the
Irish artists on great monuments like Muiredach's cross at Monasterboice
or on the Cross of the Scriptures at Clonmacnoise, erected early in the
tenth century by the same Flann Sinna, king of Tara, who at the battle of
Belach Mughna triumphed over Cormac mac Cuilennáin, king-bishop of
Cashel. Cormac was renowned in Irish tradition as a patron of learning
and a scholar in his own right. Scholarship too survived the early viking
wars, but a great deal of our evidence for it comes from the Continent.

Irishmen played a considerable part in the revival of learning in Europe under and after Charlemagne, and many of their writings have survived. Sedulius Scottus and Johannes Eriugena are only two of the eminent names of those of them who made their contribution in the main European tradition. At home, as we know from many sources, the process of fusion of the native and Latin traditions of literature and learning was carried on vigorously in the ninth and tenth centuries.

Ireland, however, was not to be allowed a very long breathing space for the pursuance of her cultural traditions. New large-scale viking incursions began in the tenth century. In 914 a great fleet sailed into Waterford harbour and established a base there. From the new settlement of Waterford the Scandinavians mounted expeditions deep into Munster. Some years later another Norse settlement was made at the head of the Shannon estuary – the beginning of the city of Limerick. Later chroniclers, looking back on this period, speak of 'immense floods and countless sea-vomitings of ships'[4] in Munster, but the chief development of the time was the foundation of trading towns. The most important of these was Dublin, apparently established on a new basis at this time near the ford which crossed the Liffey above its mouth.

Excavations at Wood Quay have shown that Dublin was a ramparted or walled town, in close contact from the tenth century onward with England, and certainly trading farther afield. A city of wooden streets and wooden houses and workshops, it soon became a major centre of crafts and manufacture as well as of commerce. Its products influenced the hinterland in many ways, as did those of Limerick and Waterford. The towns, especially Dublin and Limerick, changed the Irish economy and set in train new developments: the market had arrived.[5]

While the rulers of Dublin and Waterford for a good part of the first half of the tenth century were occupied by their interests in York, in alliance with the Scots, until they were finally driven out by the English of Northumbria, the Norse met with steadily stiffening resistance in the northern half of the country: the quarrelsome kings were even from time to time impelled to patch up their own differences to deal with them. They did not found market towns in the north. In the south, viking

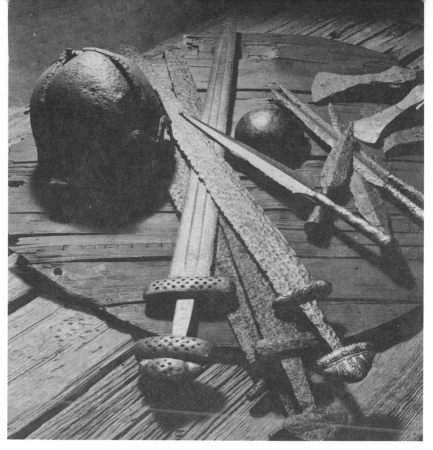

39 Viking weapons, Norway, 9th century (Universitetets Oldsaksamling, Oslo)

settlements, although small, were comparatively successful. The declining Eóghanachta seemed unable or unwilling to hinder them.

In the second half of the tenth century a new aggressive power emerged in Munster, through the expansion of a hitherto obscure petty kingdom of East Clare, Dál Cais, whose leader Mathgamain captured Cashel from the Eóganachta in 964. Shortly afterwards he defeated the Norse of Limerick at the battle of Sulchoid and sacked their city. The description of the sack of Limerick in the O'Brien tract, *Cogad Gaedel re Gallaib,* gives an impression of the wealth of a viking port town:

They carried off their jewels and their best property, and their saddles beautiful and foreign, their gold and their silver; their beautifully woven cloth of all colours and of all kinds. The fort and the good town they reduced to a cloud of smoke and to red fire afterwards. The whole of the captives were collected on the hills of Saingel. Every one of them that was fit for war was killed, and every one that was fit for a slave was enslaved.[6]

Mathgamain himself was killed in 976 but his brother Brian Bóruma (otherwise Boru) within a few years brought first Limerick, then all of Munster, under his control. From Cashel he systematically set about building up power for himself.

In the meantime, the Norse of Dublin also suffered a disastrous defeat, at the battle of Tara in 980. The victor was Máel Sechnaill son of Domnall, who became king of Tara in that year. In 981 he besieged and took the city of Dublin, carrying off a great prey from the Norse and imposing a heavy tribute on them.

The Norse from now on were reduced to playing subordinate roles in the renewed struggle for power between the rulers of the northern half and the southern half of Ireland. Máel Sechnaill, representing the ancient northern dynasty of the Uí Néill, showed considerable energy in this struggle, but Brian, representing the usurping southern dynasty of Dál Cais, showed the greater ability. He thought in terms which extended beyond the limited traditional Irish concept of kingship. The decisive event in the struggle was the battle of Glen Máma in 999, when Brian defeated the king of Leinster and the Dublin Norse, after which he plundered the city. Three years later Máel Sechnaill, without a battle, yielded to him at Tara, and Brian became, in effect, king of Ireland, or, as he styled himself, emperor of the Irish.

He still had, in the next twelve years, to suppress various dissident northern kings, but the most dogged resistance came from the kingdom of Leinster. Máel Mórda, king of Leinster, allied himself with the Dublin Norse again, and these in turn gathered in viking allies from overseas for a final trial of strength at Clontarf in 1014. In the words of the Icelandic saga:

Swordblades rang on Ireland's coast,
Metal yelled as shield it sought,
Spear-points in the well-armed host.
I heard sword-blows many more;
Sigurd fell in battle's blast,
From his wounds there sprang hot gore.
Brian fell, but won at last.[7]

Clontarf is conventionally taken as marking the end of the viking wars. There were occasional viking expeditions afterwards, but they were irrelevant to the dynastic wars which followed the death of Brian.

The Irish had learned from the vikings. The mobility with ships and horsemen which had initially given the Norse an advantage had now become a feature of Irish warfare. Their superior weapons – the heavy swords, the iron spears, the helmets and mail – were now used by the Irish too. At Clontarf both sides fought with similar weapons. The vikings in their towns were now largely Christian and were an established element in Ireland, influencing the Irish and being influenced by them. They were making silver brooches and other objects, of Irish type but with their own traditional patterns of ornament. Their styles of ornament in turn were being adapted by the Irish – who later were to embody Scandinavian animal-patterns in such works as the cross of Cong and the carvings of Romanesque doorways.

Even before Clontarf, Dublin had begun to mint silver coins, the first ever in Ireland, and these continued to be issued until the time of the Norman invasion. In this we can see one of the most important effects of the viking invasions on Ireland: their influence on the hitherto very simple economy of the country. With the establishment of the towns Ireland ceased to be wholly rural, and the traffic of the ports opened her up to the outside world in a new way, as was to be shown by the important part the Norse towns played in the beginning of the church reforms of the eleventh and twelfth centuries.

The Norse left many permanent marks on Ireland. Words from their language were borrowed into Irish – especially words concerned with

105

40 Viking ship in full sail: reconstructed drawing by Liam de Paor

ships and trade. Norse words or forms also appear in many of our place-names (Wicklow, Waterford, Wexford, Leixlip, Lambay, etc.). The word Ireland itself is of Norse origin. In some place-names Irish words are used, but in a Norse construction, as in the modern names of the provinces, where *Lagins-tír,* for example (literally, the country of the Lagin) has become Leinster. Other place-names, while purely Irish in vocabulary and form, refer to the presence of viking colonies – Fingal in County Dublin is the 'country of the foreigners' and Baldoyle is the 'place of the dark foreigners', while a barony on Waterford harbour again preserves in its name the description *Gall-tír* – 'country of the foreigners'.

Perhaps the most enduring effect of the vikings on Irish life was to shift the social and political centre of gravity once and for all from the midlands to the east coast – indeed one might say to the Irish Sea.

7
IRELAND IN THE ELEVENTH AND
TWELFTH CENTURIES
by Brian Ó Cuív

In three notable ways the eleventh and twelfth centuries were an age of renaissance and progress in Ireland. Cultural activity and the arts, which had suffered a set-back during the height of viking power, came into their own again revealing new and interesting trends. Religious reform, which was sorely needed after a period during which many abuses had crept in and moral standards had dropped, was not only undertaken but was carried through to the point where the church in Ireland, in full communion with the pope, had a basic diocesan organisation which could look to the pastoral care of its flock. In the political sphere the accession of Brian Bóruma (otherwise Boru) to the high-kingship marked a break with the past. It paved the way for a strong central monarchy, and, in spite of considerable strife among the various dynasties, Ireland seemed to be moving in that direction when the Anglo-Norman invasion occurred and changed the course of history.

> Fearann cloidhimh críoch Bhanbha;
> bíodh slán cáich fá chomhardha
> go bhfuil d'oighreacht ar Fhiadh bhFáil
> acht foirneart gliadh dá gabháil.

(The land Ireland is sword land; let all men be challenged to show that there is any inheritance to Fiadh Fáil except of conquest by dint of battle.)

With those words of encouragement to a descendant of a Norman lord a sixteenth-century poet[1] voiced a thesis which had been put forward long before his time – that the Norman conquest of Ireland was justifiable on the grounds that there was no people from time immemorial who had taken Ireland otherwise than by force. Diplomacy required such reasoning, for the professional poets had to praise both Irish and Anglo-Irish chieftains. At any rate if the poets had to choose between such a justification for the Norman invasion and that advanced by Henry II, king of England, they would undoubtedly have rejected Henry's case as being incompatible with the facts. For Henry had sought from Pope Adrian IV permission 'to enter the island of Ireland in order to subject its people to law and to root out from them the weeds of vice', 'to enlarge the boundaries of the church', and 'to proclaim the truths of the Christian religion to a rude and ignorant people'.[2] The poets, with their long tradition of native learning, knew how unfounded was the description 'rude and ignorant people'. They knew that in the very century in which Henry came to Ireland the leaders of their own profession had reorganised their craft and had laid the basis for a prescriptive grammar of Irish, the first such grammar of a western European language.[3] They knew of a revival of learning which had taken place in the eleventh and twelfth centuries in the great monastic schools and of which they had seen material evidence in the form of manuscripts in Irish and in Latin. They knew that old artistic forms had been blended with new in the illumination of manuscripts and in the decorative metalwork of the period. And they knew of a great activity in church building during the course of which Romanesque and Gothic styles of architecture were introduced to Ireland.

In the monastic schools in the pre-invasion period interest was no longer directed mainly towards Latin learning. Irish traditions had come into their own and we still have three remarkable manuscripts of the twelfth century which are clear evidence of this. One of them was compiled in the great monastery of Clonmacnoise about the year 1100, another probably somewhere in Leinster about the same time, and the third in the monastery of Terryglass in Tipperary between 1150 and 1200.[4] As we turn the pages of these manuscripts we can picture a monk sitting in the writing-room copying pagan epic tales of the Ulster heroes such as 'Táin bó Cuailnge' or the poem composed in praise of Colum Cille by the leader of the poetic profession at the end of the sixth century, or the genealogical lore by which the Irish kings and chieftains laid great

108

41 Entry referring to Brian Bóruma in Book of Armagh (Trinity College, Dublin)

store, or the Christian vision-text 'Fis Adamnáin' which is one of the forerunners of Dante's 'Divine comedy'. Much of this material was handed down from earlier times, and these manuscript compilations were now ensuring its safe transmission. We can hear the voice of the monk as he transcribes unceasingly:

> Is scíth mo chrob ón scríbainn;
> ní dígainn mo glés géroll;
> sceithid mo phenn gulban caelda
> dig ndaelda do dub glégorm.
>
> Sínim mo phenn mbec mbráenach
> tar áenach lebar lígoll
> gan scor, fri selba ségann
> dían scíth mo chrob ón scríbonn.

(My hand is weary with writing; my sharp great point is not thick; my slender-beaked pen jets forth a beetle-hued draught of bright blue ink.

I send my little dripping pen unceasingly over an assemblage of books of great beauty, to enrich the possessions of men of art, whence my hand is weary with writing.[5])

There are other manuscripts more restricted in scope, such as the two eleventh-century or early twelfth-century copies of the 'Book of Hymns' of which one is in Trinity College, Dublin, and the other in the Franciscan House in Killiney. Here we see clear evidence of the survival of the art of illumination, and we are reminded of the Welshman, Sulien, who came to study in Ireland about 1045 and who apparently acquired not only a knowledge of our literature but also a familiarity with the techniques of illumination.[6]

We think, too, of the new literature produced in these two centuries: tales and historical poems; lives of saints, sermons, biblical history and other religious texts, and fine devotional lyrics; the 'Vision of Mac Con Glinne' which is a wild goliardic satire on the monks of the time; and the Irish versions of the stories of Troy and Thebes, and 'the Civil War of the Romans'; and we recall that there, too, Irishmen were innovators, for not even the oldest French version of the Troy story is as old as ours.

When we turn to the surviving specimens of ornamental work in stone and metal we get another glimpse of the versatility of Irish craftsmen and their readiness to adopt new patterns and techniques. Here on stone crosses, such as those of Kilfenora and Dysert O'Dea, there are artistic motifs for which a Scottish origin has been suggested. And on crosiers and reliquaries, and on the magnificent processional cross of Cong which was commissioned by Toirdelbach Ua Conchobair, king of Connacht, about 1123 to enshrine a relic of the True Cross, we see motifs which suggest Scandinavian influence, and we are reminded thereby of the viking contribution to the making of Ireland in these centuries. For it has been pointed out that the gift of the Norsemen to Ireland was her own coast-line, her sea-port towns, the beginning of her civic communities, and her trade.

In ecclesiastical architecture the story is similarly one of development and innovation. A continuation of the tradition seen in the bee-hive huts of earlier times is shown in the stone-roofed churches such as those at Killaloe, Devenish, and Kilmalkedar. In Cormac's chapel in Cashel, which was built by Cormac Mac Carthaig, king of Munster, and was consecrated in 1134 in the presence of the great assembly of dignitaries of the church and of royal persons, we have an exotic stone-roofed building which may owe something to German influence. Already the Romanesque style had been introduced, and it flourished throughout the twelfth century producing such buildings as Saint Fingin's church in Clonmacnoise and others whose magnificence we can guess at from what remains of them, such as the doorway of Clonfert cathedral and the chancel arch at Tuam. The Gothic style, too, had appeared and its influence was reflected in the transitional architecture which can be seen, for example, in Cistercian abbeys such as that at Boyle which was probably commenced shortly after 1161 and not completed until 1218.

Cultural activity reflects the age and people to whom it belongs. On the basis of what we have seen, we would hardly concede that in the eleventh and twelfth centuries the Irish people were all rude and ignorant. But let us turn from this evidence and all that it tells us to what we know of the

42 Irish missal, 12th century, from Corpus Christi College, Oxford, now in the Bodleian Library (photo. Oxford University Press)

people of the time, and especially the rulers through whose patronage so much of this cultural activity was made possible, and the churchmen who secured the support of the kings, not only in this matter of culture and church-building, but also in the more important matter of religious reform.

Our period opens with the accession of Brian Bóruma to the Irish high-kingship. This was a break with a long tradition and provided an example which other provincial rulers were not slow to follow. The earlier tradition was that the king of Tara was the chief king in Ireland, and the Uí Néill of Meath and Ailech, from whom the Tara rulers were drawn, could look back upon a period of over five hundred years during which their rule had rarely been seriously challenged. Even in Munster the Dál Cais, to whom Brian belonged, were a minor people whose rise to supreme power took place in little over half a century. Following the

112

expansionist designs of his father, Cennétig, and of his brother, Math-gamain, Brian first established himself as king of Munster in the place of the traditional Eóganacht king of Cashel. Then he extended his power until finally in 1002 his supremacy was acknowledged in the northern half of Ireland by Máel Sechnaill, king of Tara, who had been high-king since 980.

Not satisfied that the submission to him of the reigning high-king demonstrated his own supreme authority, Brian made expeditions to the north in 1002 and 1005 in order to take hostages from the northern states. In the following years he made further expeditions to the north and took more hostages and thus showed himself to be undisputed king of Ireland. It was during his second expedition in 1005 that Brian visited Armagh where he made an offering of twenty ounces of gold to the church and confirmed to the apostolic see of Saint Patrick the ecclesiastical supremacy over the whole of Ireland. The decision was recorded in Latin on a page of the ninth-century Book of Armagh in the presence of the high-king by his scribe who concluded the entry with the words (Fig. 41): 'Ego scripsi, id est Calvus perennis, in conspectu Briani imperatoris Scotorum et que scripsi finivit pro omnibus regibus Maccriae.' (I, Máel Suthain, have written this in the presence of Brian, emperor of the Irish, and what I have written he has determined for all the kings of Cashel').[7]

With Brian the Irish high-kingship became a reality. He was about sixty years of age when he attained it, and in the twelve years of his reign he consolidated his position in the political and military spheres, while at the same time, according to the twelfth century text 'Cogad Gaedel re Gallaib' ('The war of the Irish with the foreigners'), initiating a rehabilitation of religious and learned institutions, as well as restoring communications by building bridges and roads. There may be exaggeration in this old account, but we have seen evidence of a renaissance in the eleventh and twelfth centuries and it would be less than just not to give some of the credit of this to Brian.

For most of us the name of Brian Bóruma calls to mind the battle of Clontarf, which has always caught the imagination of the Irish people. The events which led to it were many, but fundamentally the issue

43 Head of crozier
of the abbots of
Clonmacnoise, late
11th century
(National Museum
of Ireland)

involved was Brian's claim to rule all Ireland, including the Norse towns. So when the former high-king, Máel Sechnaill (otherwise Malachy), appealed to him for help against the Leinstermen and the Dublin Norse, Brian marched on Dublin. The result was the pitched battle on 23 April 1014 which we call the 'battle of Clontarf' but which in Irish tradition is sometimes called 'Brian's battle'. It was, indeed, Brian's battle, for the support that he had from the other provinces on that Good Friday was relatively meagre, and, as we know, the men of North Leinster fought against him along with the Norsemen. The decisive victory lay with the Irish, and the final blow was given to viking hopes of establishing their domination over Ireland as they were to do two years later in England under Canute. In Ireland they contented themselves henceforth with developing the towns which they had founded at Dublin, Wexford, Waterford, Cork, and Limerick, and the eastern ports were to prove of great importance in the early years of the Norman invasion. The triumph at Clontarf was a sad one, for the losses on the Irish side included Brian

44 Cross of Cong
c. 1123, detail
(National Museum
of Ireland)

himself, and his eldest son Murchad, as well as many other royal persons and nobles. Neither of Brian's other sons, Tadg and Donnchad, was powerful enough to take his father's place as king of Ireland, so it fell to the erstwhile king, Máel Sechnaill, to resume the rule of the whole country, now truly high-king until his death in 1022.

Some idea of the political organisation of Ireland in the eleventh century is got when we consider that the country then consisted of between one hundred and two hundred kingdoms of varying size and importance together with the Norse towns. When we see the names of the more important local kingdoms, we recognise several which are familiar to us as barony or territorial names, such as Corcu Baiscinn, Corcu Duibne, Múscraige, Uí Echach of Munster, and another kingdom of the same name in Ulster which we know in the form Iveagh. At a higher level Ireland was still a heptarchy of states – Munster, Leinster, Connacht, Meath, Ailech, Airgialla, and Ulaid. As a result of Brian's successful intervention the Uí Néill no longer shared solely among themselves the right of succession to the high-kingship, which had now become a prize to be fought for by rival provincial kings. A new term appears in our records – *rí co fresabra* ('king with opposition'), which was applied to a provincial king who aspired to the high-kingship but who did not gain the submission of all the other provinces – and few of the claimants can be rated higher than that. In fact Airgialla and Ulaid did not count in the struggle for the high-kingship, and even Meath was kept out of the running through the political manoeuvring of the other contestants. Indeed one of the noticeable features of the period, and one of the factors making for a lack of stability, is the interference of provincial kings in the affairs of other states or provinces. We see new political alignments which led to the advancement of certain kingdoms and the decline of others. We note with surprise that among the kings of Dublin between 1070 and 1130 were two Leinster kings, two Munster kings, and a Connacht king. Even more surprising is an annalistic statement that Domnall Ua Briain, a great-grandson of Brian Bóruma, took the kingship of the Hebrides in 1111. According to the Chronicles of the kingdom of Man and the Isles the people of Man had asked Muirchertach Ua Briain, then king of Ireland, to give them a ruler and he sent them Domnall. All these dynastic movements were part of the political evolution of Ireland which was halted so completely by the Norman invasion.

Through our annalistic records we can trace events in this evolution during the century and a half from the death of Máel Sechnaill to the coming of the Normans in 1169. The picture that they give is one of violence, confusion, and turmoil. We read of quarrels between kings and between chieftains, of the mutilation of rivals by blinding or in some other way, of military hostings, of burnings of dwellings and church buildings, of forays and battles, and of violent deaths. Yet in many ways conditions were not very different from what they had been in preceding centuries, nor was Ireland particularly unstable as compared with Wales or Scotland or England. In one respect, however, there was a remarkable development, that is in the organisation of the church. It is worth considering this, in view of Henry's claim about the need to 'proclaim the truths of the Christian religion' to the Irish people of which he so fully convinced the pope that he was given in 1155 the authority he sought to invade Ireland.

It is well known that between the introduction of Christianity in the fifth century and the time of Brian Bóruma the church in Ireland had for the most part met the religious needs of the Irish people from within. Though in communion with Rome, it was to a large extent self-governing and self-renewing and, when circumstances required it, self-reforming. When we come to the eleventh century we find that many of the old monasteries founded by the early saints and their followers were still in existence and flourishing, and that they were spread throughout the country. Many of them, as we know, were centres of learning, but they were primarily religious centres, and we may suppose that from them and from others of which we know nothing the spiritual welfare of the people was looked after to some extent. Moreover the *Schottenklöster* or 'Irish monasteries' of Ratisbon, Würzburg, Mainz, and other places in Germany, remind us that even in the eleventh century Ireland was sending missionary sons abroad, for those German foundations date from this later era when John of Ireland, Marianus Scottus, Marianus of Ratisbon, and others were preaching the gospel or leading lives of asceticism in Europe.

We might suppose that, with numerous religious houses throughout Ireland and the missionary movement under way again, the moral well-being of the people was assured. Unfortunately this was not so, for after the long centuries of the viking wars and consequent upheavals there was spiritual and moral laxity. Deeds of violence were frequent, even against priests and nuns and against church property. The sacraments were neglected, there was a reluctance to pay tithes, and the marriage laws of the church were disregarded. The laxity about marriage, it is true, may have been due to the brehon law which differed from the rules of the church in this regard. However, there was clearly a need for a spiritual renewal, and with it reform of the church itself, for part of the trouble lay in the organisation of the church which was monastic rather than diocesan, a feature which resulted in a lack of priests engaged in pastoral work. Another

45 Dysert O'Dea Cross, county Clare,
mid-12th century (photo, Commissioners
of Public Works in Ireland)

characteristic of the Irish church was that there was hereditary succession to certain church benefices and that these were frequently held by laymen. Of course to a people accustomed to the principle of hereditary succession in other walks of life, including poetry, this would not have seemed strange.

At any rate reform was needed, and it came. Through the renewed contacts with Western Europe, established by the latest wave of Irish missionaries, and also through Irish pilgrims who found their way to Rome, Irishmen at home became aware of the vast church reform which was taking place on the Continent. The fact that the Norse towns had become Christianised and from early in the eleventh century looked to Canterbury for episcopal consecration was an important factor. Among the earliest reformers were Máel Ísa Ua hAinmire, who was consecrated bishop of Waterford by Saint Anselm of Canterbury in 1096, and Gilla Espaic, or Gilbert, who had been a monk with Anselm in Rouen and who was made bishop of Limerick about 1106 and was appointed papal legate. Gilla Espaic put forward a plan for a diocesan and parochial organisation for Ireland and a uniform liturgy. In the south these reforming clerics had the support of Muirchertach Ua Briain the high-king. Armagh had already joined the movement in the person of Cellach Ua Sínaig who inherited the position of abbot in 1105. Cellach was the seventh in a series of members of the Ua Sínaig family who held the position without taking

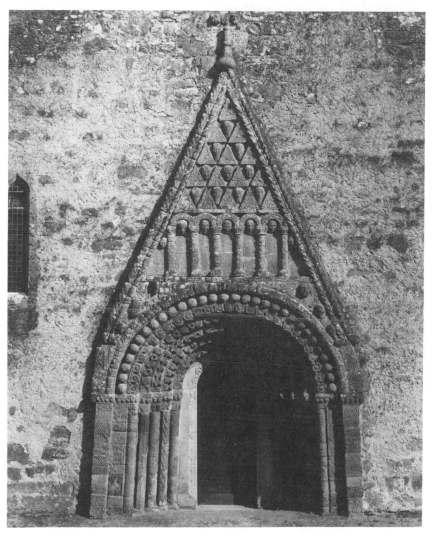

46 Doorway of Clonfert Cathedral, county Galway, 12th century (photo. Commissioners of Public Works in Ireland)

119

holy orders, and several of whom were married,[8] but before long he was consecrated as bishop while he was visiting Munster as 'comarba Pátraic' or 'heir of Patrick'. So now, for the first time in many years, Armagh, chief see of Ireland, was under the rule of an 'heir of Patrick' who was also a bishop, and Cellach was recognised as primate. In 1111 a national synod at Ráith Bresail, near Cashel, presided over by Cellach and the high-king, divided Ireland into twenty-four sees thus replacing the old monastic organisation.

Forty years were to pass before reorganisation was brought to a successful conclusion. In the meantime a younger man, Máel Maedóc, whom we know as Saint Malachy, had succeeded to Cellach and it fell to him to conduct the necessary negotiations with the pope. On his journeys to Rome he stayed with Saint Bernard at Clairvaux, and he poured forth to him his concern about the state of Ireland. He was so impressed with what he saw in Clairvaux that he introduced the Cistercians to Ireland, where their first settlement was begun at Mellifont in 1142 on land given by the king of Airgialla. On its completion in 1157 this fine abbey was consecrated in the presence of an assembly of bishops and kings. Among the royal gifts to the church on the occasion were a hundred and sixty cows and sixty ounces of gold and a townland – all given by the high-king –, and sixty ounces of gold given by the king of Airgialla, and another sixty ounces given by the wife of Tigernán Ua Ruairc who is better remembered today for her unfortunate escapade with Diarmait Mac Murchada, the king of Leinster. Though there had been Benedictines in Ireland early in the twelfth century, it was with the coming of the Cistercians that the era of the old Irish monasteries came to an end.

Saint Malachy died at Clairvaux in 1148 on his second journey to Rome, but his design for the Irish church bore fruit four years later when, at the synod of Kells, Ireland was divided into thirty-six sees with four archbishoprics, and the *pallia* were distributed by the papal legate, Cardinal Paparo, to the archbishops of Armagh, Cashel, Dublin and Tuam. So in 1152 the legate could report to the pope that the church in Ireland had now the basic organisation to look to the pastoral care of its flock. The reports which led to Pope Adrian's strange grant to King

Henry II three years later were either deliberately false or were based on a misunderstanding of the true state of affairs in Ireland.

Had the political evolution of Ireland towards a strong national monarchy proceeded as satisfactorily as the ecclesiastical reform, the *Laudabiliter* grant might never have been used by Henry II. Unfortunately the rivalry over the high-kingship did little to promote a sense of national unity. In fact, the position with regard to the kings of Ireland, whether 'full' or 'with opposition', in the period 1022-1169 is far from clear, and there are some periods for which no king is named – periods of 'joint rule' as they are called. However, we can compile from various sources, including the twelfth century 'Book of Leinster', this list of kings for whom the supremacy was claimed:

> Donnchad, son of Brian Bóruma, of Munster
> Diarmait, son of Máel na mBó, of Leinster
> Toirdelbach Ua Briain of Munster
> Muirchertach Ua Briain of Munster
> Domnall Ua Lochlainn of Aileach
> Toirdelbach Ua Conchobair of Connacht
> Muircheartach Mac Lochlainn of Aileach
> Ruaidrí Ua Conchobair of Connacht.

The list shows how things had changed. Only two of the eight kings are of the old stock, the Uí Néill; three are of the line of Brian; and Leinster and Connacht have now joined in the competition. For the first hundred years or so the descendants of Brian Bóruma maintained fairly successfully their claim to supremacy. In the twelfth century the northern Uí Néill asserted themselves for two short periods. But the O'Connor star really appeared to be in the ascendant, for Toirdelbach Ua Conchobair was one of the most outstanding of all the kings since Brian Bóruma and when his son Ruaidrí took the high-kingship in 1166 it looked as if the O'Connors might succeed in establishing a feudal-style hereditary kingship which would be comparable to the dynasties in other countries. This dream was shattered, however, by the action of the king of Leinster, Diarmait Mac Murchada, or 'Diarmait of the foreigners' as

47 Cistercian abbey, Boyle, County Roscommon, 12th and early 13th century (photo. Commissioners of Public Works in Ireland)

he is called. It is perhaps significant that the Leinstermen always resented and resisted the central authority – that of Tara in prehistoric and early historic times, that of Brian Bóruma before the battle of Clontarf, and now that of Ruaidrí Ua Conchobair. The matters at issue between Diarmait and Ruaidrí were not so vital, but they culminated in the banishment of Diarmait from Ireland. Another king might have accepted the judgement, and perhaps gone on a pilgrimage to Rome where Brian Bóruma's son, Donnchad, had died in 1064 after being dethroned by his nephew. Instead Diarmait hied off to Bristol and thence to France where he appealed to Henry II for aid to regain his kingdom of Leinster. The resultant Norman landing in Wexford and all that followed form another chapter in the history of Ireland. It is sufficient at this point to say that were it not for the unforeseeable consequences of Diarmait na nGall's action in seeking help abroad the political evolution which, as we have seen, was a feature of the eleventh and twelfth centuries might have continued to the point of producing a strong central native monarchy. As it was, the Gaelic hegemony in Ireland came to an end with Ruaidrí Ua Conchobair. The last entry in the Book of Leinster list of kings of Ireland from time immemorial is 'Ec in Ruadrí sin 'na ailithre i Cunga' (That Ruaidrí died as a pilgrim in Cong). That was in 1198. Ruaidrí was buried in Clonmacnoise near the spot beside the high altar where his father Toirdelbach Mór had been buried in 1156. An epoch in our history had ended.

122

THE NORMANS: ARRIVAL AND SETTLEMENT
(1169–c. 1300)
by F. X. Martin

Ireland, more than most countries, cannot escape her past. The Norman settlement – over eight hundred years ago – has left an indelible mark on the face and character of the country, on its seaports, highways, and bridges, its castles, churches, and towns. The songs, the literature, the very faces of the people today pay tribute to those fearless Norman knights who came and saw and conquered, and settled in the country. No other event except the preaching of the gospel by Saint Patrick and his companions has so changed the destinies of Ireland.

And yet the coming of the Normans began as a casual, almost an accidental affair. If we compare it with the Norman invasion of England in 1066 the contrast is revealing. William the Conqueror planned and executed the invasion of England on a grand scale; recruits flocked to his banner from France, Germany, and other parts of Europe. He had some claim to the English throne, and his fleet sailed from Normandy with the blessing of Pope Alexander II. His conquest of England was systematic, ruthless, and complete.

The story of why the Normans came to Ireland begins as a personal drama, with two warrior kings, Dermot MacMurrough of Leinster and Tiernán O'Rourke of Breifne, pitted one against the other; it is a tale of raids and counter-raids, of bravery and brutality, of the abduction of O'Rourke's wife, Dervorgilla, of the undying resentment of O'Rourke, of the overthrow and exile of MacMurrough. And so the drama continued, but now as a one-man show, with MacMurrough pleading his case successively in England, France, and Wales. And even when the Normans came, almost reluctantly as we shall see, they rarely acted on an organised plan. Nevertheless they came to stay.

Between 1156 and 1166 the struggle for political supremacy in Ireland lay between Murtough MacLochlainn of Ailech in the north, the most powerful king in Ireland, and Rory O'Connor, king of Connacht. MacMurrough supported MacLochlainn, and O'Rourke cast his lot with O'Connor. The struggle swayed forward and backward, from Ulster to Leinster, to Connacht, to Munster, with endless campaigns, cattle-raids, burnings, and atrocities, so that in the words of the annalist 'Ireland was a trembling sod'.[1]

O'Connor was content, once he defeated MacMurrough, to take hostages from him and reduce his power to a small kingdom centred around Ferns in Wexford. But O'Rourke was implacable in his resolve to destroy MacMurrough. His burning resentment went back fourteen years, to his humiliation before all the men of Ireland in 1152 when his wife, Dervorgilla, had been abducted by MacMurrough. Yet she proved the old adage that a man chases a woman until she catches him, for according to both the Irish and Norman accounts it was she who arranged the abduction. An Irish historian, Keating, relates how she sent MacMurrough a message urging him to seize her:

As to Dermot, when this message reached him he went quickly to meet the lady, accompanied by a detachment of mounted men, and when they reached where she was, he ordered that she be placed on horseback behind a rider, and upon this the woman wept and screamed in pretence, as if Dermot were carrying her off by force; and bringing her with him in this fashion, he returned to Leinster.[2]

Neither Dervorgilla nor Dermot could be accused of acting in the folly of youth – he was then aged forty-two and she was a ripe forty-four. O'Rourke recovered her the following year but he was determined to get even with MacMurrough, and now in 1166 he had his opportunity, MacMurrough's supporters and followers were melting away; his great ally, MacLochlainn of Ailech in the north, was dead; O'Rourke, O'Melaghlin, and the north Leinster tribes were massing on his frontier; the Norsemen of Wexford were prepared to attack him in the rear. When Ferns was captured and his stone palace destroyed he decided there was nothing for it but flight. He sailed away secretly with a few followers from Ireland in August 1166. He landed at Bristol, then the main port for

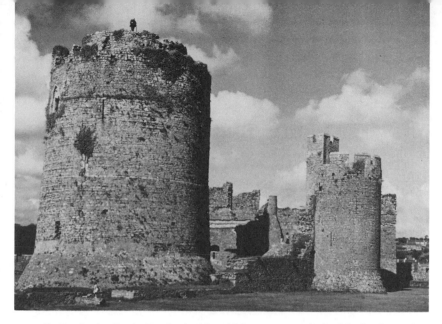

48 Pembroke Castle, Pembrokeshire, 12th century: typical of the border society
from which the Anglo-Norman invaders of Ireland came

commerce with Ireland, and thence went to France in search of Henry II,
king of England. Dermot was determined to recover his inheritance in
Ireland and was seeking for allies.

King Henry was French rather than English. He was born in
Normandy, reared in France, and spoke Norman French, not English;
most of his life was passed on the Continent, and England was only part
of his empire, the Angevin empire which embraced England, Normandy,
Anjou, Maine, Poitou, and Aquitaine, with sovereign claims over
Toulouse, Wales and Scotland.

He was a restless man, always on the move throughout his wide
dominions, and Dermot, after travelling from city to city, deeper and
deeper into the south of France, finally found him in a distant part of
Aquitaine. Henry was already interested in Ireland; in 1155, when he was
but one short year on the throne he considered an invasion of Ireland, but
the project was postponed. His advisers sought the blessing of the papacy
for a marauding expedition, just as William the Conqueror did when
invading England a century earlier. In 1155 the pope was Adrian IV, the
only Englishman ever to sit on the papal throne. It is fairly certain,
though some historians have queried it, that he issued a bull *Laudabiliter*

commissioning Henry to enter Ireland and set about its religious reform, but the king was too busy then to divert his forces to that mysterious and warlike island in the west.

In 1166, however, the problem became alive again when Dermot stood before him, an impressive figure and personality as described by a contemporary, Gerald of Wales (Giraldus Cambrensis):

Diarmait was tall and well built, a brave and warlike man among his people, whose voice was hoarse as a result of constantly having been in the din of battle. He preferred to be feared by all rather than loved. He treated his nobles harshly and brought to prominence men of humble rank. He was inimical towards his own people and hated by others. 'All men's hands were against him, and he was hostile to all men.'[3]

Dermot stated his case and made his offer:

> Hear, noble King Henry,
> Whence I was born, of what country.
> Of Ireland I was born a lord,
> In Ireland acknowledged king;
> But wrongfully my own people
> Have cast me out of my kingdom.
> To you I come to make complaint, good sire,
> In the presence of the barons of your empire.
> Your liege-man I shall become
> Henceforth all the days of my life,
> On condition that you be my helper,
> So that I do not lose everything,
> You I shall acknowledge as sire and lord,
> In the presence of your barons and earls.[4]

Henry, a man of boundless energy, high intelligence, and rapid decision quickly summed up the situation: he himself was too busily engaged in his many territories to lead an expedition to Ireland but he had nothing to lose by encouraging this exiled king. He accepted Dermot's offer of fealty, promised to help him as soon as possible, and loaded him with presents. More welcome to Dermot, however, was an open letter in which Henry invited his subjects, English, Norman, Welsh, and Scots, to rally to Dermot's assistance. Dermot returned to Bristol, but found that even with the king's letter to his credit there was no rush of recruits for an expedition to Ireland. He decided that the most likely place to find volunteers was across the Severn, along the Welsh border, where Normans were continually engaged in warfare with the native Welsh.

These Normans were French in speech and origin, restless members of the finest fighting stock in Europe. Many had intermarried with the Welsh nobility, but their children were without any special allegiance to England, Wales, or France. They were ruthless and cunning, experts as sailors and horsemen, builders of castles and churches, men with an instinct for discipline and order. They were tough, intelligent, and land-hungry. Ireland, already famous in Welsh stories and legends, was beckoning to them across the water.

Dermot shrewdly sought interview with one of the great Norman leaders in Wales, Richard FitzGilbert de Clare, the earl of Strigoil, better known as 'Strongbow'. Here was an experienced war-leader, descendant of a powerful Norman family, but now a discontented man, without wife, out of favour with Henry II, and therefore likely to seek fame and fortune in some new field such as Ireland. Strongbow was a hard bargainer. Eventually he agreed to lead an armed force to Ireland and restore Dermot to power, but on condition that Dermot give him his eldest daughter, Aoífe (Eva), in marriage and the right of succession to the kingdom of Leinster.

Dermot then set off along the Welsh coast road to St David's securing along the way and on his return journey promises of help from a number of Norman-Welsh knights whose names were to become part of Irish history — FitzHenry, Carew, FitzGerald, Barry. Before leaving Wales he also visited Rhos in Pembrokeshire. Here he got promises of support from the vigorous Flemish colony which had come from Flanders sixty years previously – their names were to figure prominently in the invasion of Ireland — Prendergast, Fleming, Roche, Cheevers, Synott.

Dermot could no longer restrain his impatience to return to Ireland

127

49(a) Norman knights, from the Bayeux tapestry, late 11th century *(Vetusta monumenta, vi, 1819)*

49(b) Norman foot-soldiers, from the Bayeux tapestry, late 11th century *(Vetusta monumenta, vi, 1819)*

and sailed back with a handful of Normans, Flemings, and Welsh, in 1167. He recovered his local power around Ferns, but O'Connor and O'Rourke attacked him once again and he submitted after a short fight. He even paid O'Rourke one hundred ounces of gold in reparation for the abduction of Dervorgilla. There the matter seemed to rest, but Mac-Murrough was only biding his time, and sent urgent messages to Wales, promising plunder, riches, and land for those who would come to his support.

> Gold and silver, I shall give them
> A very ample pay.
> Whoever may wish for soil or sod,
> Richly shall I endow them.[5]

The first formidable contingents of invaders ran their flat ships in on the sandy beach at Bannow Bay early in May 1169, altogether, it is claimed about six hundred of them, led by Robert FitzStephen, Hervey de Montmorency, and Maurice de Prendergast. There were mounted knights in mail, foot-soldiers, and archers on foot, 'the flower of the youth of Wales', with their deadly bows. Dermot promptly joined them with several hundred men, and the combined force marched on Wexford.

The Norsemen, the inhabitants of the town, sallied out to meet Dermot's army but received a shock when they discovered they were not dealing with a brave array of Irish warriors, lightly-clad, armed with axes, swords, slings, and javelins. Instead they were faced with serried ranks of foot-soldiers and archers, flanked on either side by a squadron of horsemen, armed with long lances, kite-shaped shields, glittering helmets and coats of mail. Behind them massed Dermot's army, impatiently waiting for battle and the kill.

The Norsemen were driven back pell-mell into Wexford, and next day the town capitulated. O'Connor and O'Rourke, alarmed at Dermot's activity, marched against him once again, but after some skirmishing near Ferns they came to terms. They were willing to recognise him as king of Leinster south of Dublin, and he was to rid himself of his foreign

129

allies. O'Connor's main interest was to see that he himself was recognised as high-king. Once MacMurrough had made his submission O'Connor marched away unaware of the danger from the Normans.

MacMurrough wrote urging Strongbow to hasten, assuring him that Ireland was there for the taking. Strongbow was now prepared to come in person, and as an advance guard he sent a daring young nobleman, Raymond Carew, styled 'le Gros' ('the Fat'), one of the FitzGeralds, with ten knights and seventy archers. Raymond landed his men and horses at a rocky headland called Baginbun on the coast of Wexford, between Bannow Bay and the Hook. Here they threw up earthen ramparts which are still to be seen. The attack came only too soon. An army, calculated in later Norman records, almost certainly with gross exaggeration, as three thousand strong, of Norsemen from Waterford city and Gaelic Irish from the Decies, Ossory, and Idrone, marched on the entrenched force of less than a hundred Normans and Flemings. The battle was short and decisive. An old jingle runs:

> At the creek of Baginbun
> Ireland was lost and won.

A herd of cattle, collected by the Normans behind the ramparts was suddenly driven forth against the oncoming troops. This wild rush of horned beasts bore down the foremost Norse and Irish, and while confusion reigned the Normans charged and overthrew their opponents. Seventy of the leading townsmen of Waterford were taken prisoner on the battlefield. No mercy was shown to them; their limbs were broken and their bodies thrown over the cliffs.

Before Waterford could recover from this disaster worse befell it. On 23 August Strongbow and his army – said to have been two hundred knights and a thousand other troops – landed at Passage, near where the Suir and the Barrow meet. He was joined by Raymond, and two days later the Normans swept on to the assault of Waterford. The Norse and the Irish within the walls now knew how merciless were the attackers and twice the Normans were beaten off, but the indomitable Raymond le Gros breached the walls at one weak point and led a fierce attack through

50 Motte and bailey, Tipperary Hills, county Tipperary, 12th century (photo. Commissioners of Public Works in Ireland)

the gap. Reginald's Tower, which still stands, witnessed some of the bloodiest fighting. When night fell the city was in the hands of the Normans.

Strongbow summoned MacMurrough, who came gladly, bringing his daughter, Aoife, to fulfil in part the bargain made in Wales two years previously. Popular tradition, and a well-known fresco in the precincts of the British House of Commons, depict the marriage taking place at the close of the battle, with the dead, the dying, and flaming houses in the background. This is not historically accurate since MacMurrough did not arrive for at least some days after the battle. But it is symbolically true since the marriage was part of the Norman victory.

What manner of man was Strongbow, this new power in the land? Gerald of Wales has described him:

He had reddish hair and freckles, grey eyes, a feminine face, a weak voice and a short neck, though in almost all other respects he was of a tall build. He was a generous and easy-going man. What he could not accomplish by deed he settled by the persuasiveness of his words. . . When he took up his position in the midst of battle, he stood firm as an immovable standard round which his men could re-group and take refuge. In war he remained steadfast and reliable in good fortune and bad alike. In adversity no feelings of despair caused him to waver, while lack of self restraint did not make him run amok when successful.[6]

Strongbow was not impetuous, but he was daring. He and MacMurrough now proposed to march on Dublin, which was a semi-independent kingdom under the control of the Norsemen, with its Norse-Irish king Askulv. Dublin was in alliance with King Rory O'Connor who hurried with his army to its defence; with him came another army led by Mac-Murrough's old enemy, O'Rourke of Breifne. O'Connor lay in wait at Clondalkin, on what was then the only main highway from Wexford to Dublin, and also sent bands of soldiers to guard two narrow defiles, one near the Wicklow coast, the other at Enniskerry. We must remember that Ireland was then covered with dense forests. MacMurrough outwitted O'Connor and O'Rourke, leading the Normans by a series of paths over the Wicklow and Dublin mountains down by Rathfarnham and arrived in front of the city walls.

The Norsemen, nonplussed at the turn of events, began to sue for peace, utilising the archbishop of Dublin, St Laurence O'Toole, as their mediator. O'Connor and O'Rourke, indignant that the Norsemen were parleying with the Normans and MacMurrough, marched away in disgust. While negotiations were still proceeding two young Norman knights, Raymond le Gros and Milo de Cogan, with a band of their followers suddenly burst into the city, cut down the guards and within a short time were masters of Dublin. Askulv and many of the Norsemen fled to their ships and sailed away to their kinsfolk in the Hebrides and the Isle of Man, vowing to return as avengers. Dublin fell to the Normans on 21 September 1170.

The Normans were only some months settled in the city when disaster threatened them from all sides. MacMurrough died about 1 May 1171, leaving Strongbow successor to a turbulent kingdom. The Leinster tribes revolted and rallied to support Murtough, nephew of Dermot Mac-Murrough. While Strongbow was visiting the dying MacMurrough at Ferns an assault on Dublin by the Norsemen, led by Askulv, the deposed king of Dublin, tested the Norman fighting skill to the utmost. The Norsemen came in a fleet of ships from Norway, the Hebrides, and the Isle of Man, carrying, it is claimed, a thousand men. Gerald of Wales described them:

They were warlike figures, clad in mail in every part of their body after the Danish manner. Some wore long coats of mail, others iron plates skilfully knitted together, and they had round, red shields protected by iron round the edge. These men, whose iron will matched their armour, drew up their ranks and made an attack on the walls at the eastern gate.[7]

They advanced on foot in a solid phalanx against the eastern gate of Dublin, swinging that terrifying weapon, the broad battle-axe, but were met by a charge of Norman knights on horseback. The phalanx was broken in a fierce fight, and the Norsemen were cut down. Askulv was taken prisoner and tried in the hall of his own palace in Dublin, but any hope of mercy was extinguished by his proud defiance and open threats to his captors. He was beheaded there and then in the hall.

Stongbow returned to Dublin to meet a greater danger from the Gaelic Irish. Rory O'Connor arrived near Dublin with a large army, as did O'Carroll from Ulster, Murtough MacMurrough from southern Leinster, and the inevitable O'Rourke from Breifne. The sea approach was cut off by a fleet of thirty ships manned by Norsemen from the Isle of Man and the Hebrides.

The Gaelic Irish had no knowledge of siege warfare and therefore had to try and starve out the Normans. After two months thus beleaguered the Normans grew desperate for want of food, and secretly decided to attack. Three companies, each of two hundred men, under Strongbow, Raymond le Gros, and Milo de Cogan, slipped out of the city, made a detour and then a sudden attack on Rory's camp at Castleknock. The attack was unexpected. O'Connor was bathing in the river Liffey with many of his men; over one hundred of them were killed while O'Connor barely managed to escape. Many more of the Irish in the camp were slain and all their supplies were captured. This lightning victory ended the siege and established the Norman supremacy in arms over both Norse and Gaelic Irish.

Strongbow's worries were far from finished. The next threat came not from the Irish or Norse but from Strongbow's own royal master. Henry II had been quite willing to allow his subjects in Wales, the Normans and the Flemings, to gamble their lives and fortunes in a risky adventure to

51 Carrickfergus Castle, county Antrim, early 13th century (photo. Bord Fáilte Éireann)

Ireland, but now that they had succeeded he had no intention of seeing a strong kingdom under Strongbow arising on England's flank. So, he arrived at Waterford in October 1171 with a well-equipped army of knights, foot-soldiers, and archers. His journey up through the country was a triumphal progress. The Normans, the Irish, the Norse all did homage to him. The bishops assembled at Cashel – St Laurence O'Toole, archbishop of Dublin, was one of them – and they likewise made submission to Henry II. Only the princes of Cenél Eógain and Cenél Connaill gave him no welcome; this was not due to any active hostility on their part but because those north-westerly parts of the country were too remote and too embroiled in their own disputes to interest themselves in the coming of the foreign king.

At this point it seemed as if a peaceful solution might be found for the Norman domination of Ireland. By the treaty of Windsor in October 1175 Rory O'Connor pledged himself to recognise Henry II as his overlord and to collect annual tribute for him from all parts of Ireland, while Henry agreed to accept Rory as ard-rí (high-king) of the unconquered areas. The scheme broke down for two reasons – Rory was ard-rí in name only; he found it hard to enforce authority even in his own territory in Connacht. Secondly, Henry could not restrain his barons in Ireland from seizing more Irish land, and he himself made several grants of large areas without consulting Rory or the Irish kings.

The Norman conquest of the remainder of Ireland was never undertaken in a systematic fashion. The kings of England were too busily engaged in continental wars to give any serious attention to Ireland, and it was left to the barons in Ireland to pursue it in a haphazard fashion. As a general rule the Normans contented themselves with the plains, the coasts, and the riverways; they left the hill-country, the woods, and the boglands to the native Irish.

Henry reserved to himself Dublin with its hinterland, and the coastal land from Bray down to Arklow. Also Wexford, and Waterford, and the adjoining district as far as Dungarvan. Most of Leinster was held by Strongbow as a vassal of the king, while the kingdom of Meath was given to Hugh de Lacy as a counter-balance to Strongbow.

The organising of the 'kingdom of Meath' was one of the notable achievements of the Normans. The kingdom included what are now the counties of Meath, Westmeath, Longford, with parts of Offaly and Cavan. The success was largely due to the masterly talents of Hugh de Lacy. He established his chief castles at Trim and Drogheda, and studded his territory with castles and manors as de Courcy was doing in Ulidia. The castles were occupied by his vassals and fellow-knights – the Plunketts, the Nugents, Daltons, Barnewalls, and others – while they attracted back the Gaelic Irish to till the land and herd the cattle.

The conquest of north-eastern Ulster was a remarkable adventure, and was the work of one daring Norman; John de Courcy. This tall, fair, muscular young knight was modest in private life but fierce in battle. Early in 1177 he collected about three hundred soldiers from the discontented garrison at Dublin and Irish troops in addition. Under the eagle standard of the de Courcy family, they invaded Ulster and captured Downpatrick, the capital of Ulidia. The native king, MacDunlevy, gathered an army but was defeated. He retired, called upon MacLochlainn,

135

the king of Cenél Eógain, and the two kings returned with a still greater army, a flock of clerics, two bishops, and a collection of relics. This great Ulster rally was broken in battle in June 1177, and de Courcy became lord of Ulidia, which he ruled for twenty-seven fruitful years. Under his firm guidance, Norman genius left a permanent heritage to Ulster. Centres were established at Downpatrick, Dromore, Newry, Dundrum, Carlingford, Carrickfergus and Coleraine. But these were no mere garrisons: around ˙each centre a town grew up, the surrounding countryside was tilled, and monks and canons regular built abbeys.

Despite the treaty of Windsor, to which he had put his name in 1175, Henry II now began to sign away the lands which still belonged to the Gaelic Irish. To himself he reserved the city states of Cork and Limerick, but the MacCarthy 'kingdom of Cork' stretching from Mount Brandon in Kerry to Youghal was given to Robert FitzStephen and Milo de Cogan, while the O'Brien 'kingdom of Limerick', which embraced present-day north Kerry, Limerick, Clare, and Tipperary was granted to Philip de Braose. It will come as a surprise to many to find that Munster, under Norman influence, became one of the most French of countries outside of France.

The Norman advance progressed steadily in the north, west, and south. A castle was built at Coleraine and the advance began along the coast towards Derry. Another castle at Clones brought a whole sweep of territory to the Normans. Fortresses at Roscrea, Clonmacnoise, and Athlone brought the Normans to the Shannon. A line of fortresses sprang up along the coast from Cork to Bantry Bay, and across Kerry from Castlemaine to Killorglin and Killarney.

Perhaps the greatest demonstration of Norman arms was the conquest of Connacht. It was an act of treachery since the O'Connors, kings of Connacht, had continued as faithful allies of the kings of England. But the young Norman-Irish barons, the de Burgos, the de Lacys, the Fitz-Geralds, could not be restrained. An impressive feudal array of Norman Ireland, knights with their foot-soldiers, archers, and retainers, crossed the Shannon in 1235 and bore down all before it. The army moved forward irresistibly, from Athlone to Boyle to Westport, brushing aside all opposition. What are now counties Roscommon and Leitrim were left to the Gaelic Irish , while the rest of the province was divided up among the Normans, the Welsh, and the Flemings. Towns made their appearance in Connacht – Galway, Athenry, Dunmore, Ballinrobe, and Loughrea. Galway and Athenry in particular became prosperous walled centres, but there were never sufficient Normans in Connacht for the province to become a feudalised area as did Leinster and large areas of Munster.

By the year 1250 – within eighty years of the invasion – three quarters of the country had been overrun by the Normans. Nobody has ever accused the Gaelic Irish of lack of courage, yet how can one account for the success of the Norman forces in Ireland? They were far less in numbers than the Irish, they were fighting far from their homes in England and Wales, they had little or no support from the king of England. It was each Norman for himself.

The Normans were not only a race of warriors but those who came to Ireland were seasoned fighters against the Welsh, whose tactics and weapons were much the same as those of the Irish. The Normans advanced into battle on an organised plan, unlike the Irish who bravely charged in disarray. The Normans, superior in their weapons – the long sword, the lance, the iron helmet, the hauberk of mail covering body, thighs and arms – contrasted with the Irish soldier carrying his axe and short sword, and clad in a linen tunic. One of the most feared groups of the invaders were the Welsh archers with their long bows; the Irish spear, javelin, and sling-stones, hitherto so effective, were no match for the far-flying arrows of the Welsh. What Irish army could stand the shock first of a shower of deadly Welsh arrows, followed by a charge of armed Norman knights on horseback, completed by an onslaught from disciplined lines of Flemish foot-soldiers?

Norman success did not end with victory on the field. Their fortresses ensured that they would hold the territory they conquered. Their first fortresses were not of stone. They began by building motes – they threw up a mound of earth, anything from twenty to forty feet in height, with very steep sides, and a flat space on the summit from thirty to a hundred feet across. Around the summit was a loop-holed wooden palisade

137

52 Cistercian Abbey, Dunbrody, county Wexford, 13th century (photo. Commissioners of Public Works in Ireland)

crowned by a battlemented tower of wood. Around the base of the mote they dug a wide ditch; beyond the ditch was the enclosure or courtyard where soldiers' quarters and workshops were built. This circular courtyard was ringed around with an earthen rampart surmounted by a wooden palisade. Sometimes there was a further ditch dug and another rampart beyond that. Altogether the mote was a formidable obstacle for the Irish, and their only hope to overcome it was to make a surprise attack and set the wooden structures on fire. After the year 1200 the Normans, by then well established, began to substitute stone for wood, and their castles became in most cases impregnable against Irish attacks.

It is too often assumed that the Normans brought only war and division to the country, but this is to look at the later centuries when the Norman-Irish colony was in decline. Let us instead see what was accomplished by the Normans during the first century and a half of their time in Ireland.

The Normans were the first to give Ireland a centralised administration. Much of the credit for beginning the work must go to King John (1199-1216) a most exasperating and unfortunate monarch. Thanks to him, Dublin Castle was built and an active government established; coinage for Ireland was struck; the jury system introduced. Sheriffs were appointed, and by 1260 there were, apart from Dublin, seven counties – Louth, Waterford, Cork, Tipperary, Limerick, Kerry, and Connacht; besides, there were the liberties of Meath, Wexford, Carlow, Kildare,

Kilkenny, and Ulster. The summoning of parliament in 1297 with elected representatives from each county and liberty was the first step on the long road to democracy.

It would be a mistake to think of Norman Ireland as engaged in continuous deadly warfare with the Gael. Once an area was occupied by the Normans it gained peace and order, where previously there had been raids and counter-raids between warring factions of the great Gaelic families. It is true that war continued in the border areas between the Gael and the Gall, but that was no fiercer than the clash of arms within the Gaelic territories between different Gaelic families or various members of the same family. Contrast the organised 'land of peace' in Leinster, Meath, and much of Munster with the turbulent condition of Connacht under the O'Connors.

This peace and order was not bought at the price of exterminating or expelling the ordinary Irishman from his land. In fact, the Normans strove hard to ensure that the Gaelic Irish would remain to herd cattle and till the soil, as they had been doing under their native chieftains. Now for the first time Ireland knew systematic agriculture and estate management. The only people to be displaced were the Gaelic nobility, as the Anglo-Saxon aristocracy had been in England, and this was not because of any anti-Gaelic policy but represented a struggle for power between two groups of aristocrats, the Norman and the Gaelic. The Normans undoubtedly came to conquer and transform, but also to adapt themselves to the country as they did in England and Sicily. They were willing to consider the Gaelic chiefs as their social equals. Several of the great leaders were married to daughters of the native princes – Strongbow to Aoife, daughter of MacMurrough; de Courcy to Affreca, daughter of the king of Man; de Lacy to Rose, daughter of Rory O'Connor, the high king; William de Burgo to the daughter of Donal O'Brien, king of Thomond.

The towns were one of the lasting Norman gifts to the country. It is no exaggeration to state that the vast majority of the existing towns and villages in Ireland owe their origin to the Normans. Though the Norsemen established Dublin, Wexford, Waterford, Cork, and Limerick, they made few permanent settlements inland. But wherever the Normans

139

settled, a mote, a manor, or a castle was established, then a mill, work-shops, houses for the officers, artizans and retainers, then a church, and very often a monastery or a friary. A regular market was held, and often an annual fair. And so gradually a town took shape. Sometimes, as at Athenry, New Ross, and Drogheda walls were built to enclose the town. The Gaelic Irish never took kindly to the towns, and for this reason the roll-calls of the towns list names which were almost invariably Norse, Norman, Welsh, and English – Le Decer, Lawless, Keppok, Golding, Forster, Newton, Bodenham, Hollywood, and the like, but you will rarely find the Os and Macs among them.

The growth of towns meant the growth of trade, both inland and foreign. One clear proof of this is that the Normans were the first to make general use of coins in Ireland. The Irish kings had no mint of their own, and the Norse made very limited use of their silver coin. New Ross near where the Nore and the Barrow meet is an example of how towns formed part of normal Norman life. It was founded early in the thirteenth century by William Marshal, son-in-law of Strongbow, as a port for his extensive estates in Leinster. A bridge spanned the river to the road leading to Marshal's principal castle at Kilkenny. The ruins of a church at Ross, in early English style, bear witness to the taste and piety of the townspeople. A poem written in Anglo-French to celebrate the enclosure of the town in 1265 shows that many trade guilds were already there, and a few years later we have abundant details of over five hundred separate properties in the town. It was a flourishing town for the export of wool and hides, and we know that large quantities of wheat, cheese, and other provisions went through Ross to the Norman armies in Wales. It became a rival of Waterford. In five years the customs duties on wool and hides alone brought the equivalent of a huge sum in modern money into the royal treasury.

The Norman invasion also produced a new wave of religious activity in the wake of Norman arms. The religious orders in particular benefited from Norman advance. For instance the magnificent Cistercian abbeys of Dunbrody and Tintern in County Wexford, the extensive priories for canons regular of St Augustine at Kells, County Kilkenny, and Killagh,

County Kerry, the Benedictine abbey at the Ards in Down. The Normans, who were always quick to seize on what was new, practical, and progressive, also welcomed the friars to Ireland in the thirteenth century – Dominicans, Franciscans, Augustinians, and Carmelites. These were the new religious orders, men dedicated to preaching, to popular religion, beloved of the people. Wherever the Normans went, clusters of friars followed; their churches and friaries sprang up throughout the Norman territories; they even penetrated ahead of the Normans into Gaelic territory where they were also welcomed.

In France and England it was the Normans who built so many of those breath-taking medieval cathedrals – Beauvais and Rouen in France, Canterbury and Durham in England. Everything in Ireland was on a more modest scale, but here too it is to the Normans that we owe practically all our medieval cathedrals – such as St Patrick's in Dublin, St Mary's in Limerick, St Canice's in Kilkenny. Symbolically Strongbow was buried in Christ Church Cathedral, Dublin, which he helped to rebuild.

For a variety of reasons the impetus of the Norman drive in Ireland had begun to slow down by the middle of the thirteenth century. The sparse Norman population outside of Leinster and parts of Munster, lack of male heirs for their principal ruling families, no direct supervision of Irish affairs by the kings of England, the absence of any organised plan to subjugate the country as a whole – all these took their toll. Besides there was the drainage of men and supplies from Ireland to the wars in Scotland and Wales, as well as the fatal attraction which the wars against France on continental soil were beginning to have on the kings of England. Equally important was a toughening of native Irish opposition to the Norman power, which manifested itself in a striking way in the battles of Callan (1261) and Áth in Chip (1270).

By 1232 north Kerry was under Norman control, was ringed with castles, and was functioning as a county under the sway principally of the FitzThomas branch of the Geraldine family. The MacCarthys, hemmed into the south-west extremity of Ireland, struck back against the increasing Norman pressure. FitzThomas summoned the feudal forces of Munster to his aid, and was also joined by an army under the king's

141

justiciar, William de Dene. The Irish and colonial armies locked in a fierce battle at Callan, near Kenmare, in 1261, and the Norman-Irish were decisively otherthrown. FitzThomas, as well as his son and a host of followers, was killed in the fighting. Thereafter the Norman-Irish were restricted to the upper half of Kerry, while the MacCarthys and O'Sullivans held the south-west corner of Ireland as their own.

An equally momentous battle determined the fate of the north-western part of the country. The royal justiciar, Ralph d'Ufford, backed by the powerful Walter de Burgo, had regained control of Sligo, then Roscommon, and in 1270 these two leaders marched through Roscommon to Carrick-on-Shannon, 'and all the foreigners of Erin with them', say the Irish annals. They came to a bloody stop at the ford of Áth in Chip, where the Irish armies led principally by Aedh O'Connor, displayed not only their customary courage but unexpected military skill. The Norman-Irish were routed, leaving arms and suits of mail scattered on the field of battle; in the words of the annalist, 'no greater defeat had been given to the English in Ireland up to that time'. The gallowglasses, those magnificent fighters of Norse-Scottish stock, protected by mail and carrying their long axes, had come to join the forces of the O'Connors some years previously, and the Irish now had an effective answer to the Norman military superiority in battle.

No less important than these battles were two political events, signs of the change in the native Irish outlook. In 1258 Tadhg O'Brien, son of the king of Thomond, and Féilim O'Connor, son of the king of Connacht marched to Caeluisce (Belleek), on the river Erne, and there acknowledged Brian O'Neill of Cenél Eógain as king of Ireland. The agreement was short-lived but it was a revolutionary step for the Irish kings to reach unity by free choice. Equally significant was the invitation in 1262-3 from a number of Irish chiefs to King Haakon of Norway, then with his fleet off the coast of Scotland, asking him to become their leader against the Normans. The invitation came to nothing, but Ireland was for the first time turning for help to other powers in Europe, a feature which was to become part of the pattern of Irish history.

The tragedy of the Norman invasion was not the conquest of Ireland –

53 Map of Ireland, *c*.1150-*c*.1250, by Liam de Paor

for that never took place – but the half conquest. The Normans never came in sufficient numbers to complete the conquest; and the kings of England, on whom rested the responsibility for the peace and progress of Ireland, were either unwilling to assist their barons in Ireland or too distracted by dangers in England and wars on the Continent to turn their minds seriously to the Irish problem. If the conquest had been completed as in Normandy, England, and Sicily, a new nation would have emerged, combining the qualities of both peoples.

Instead, by the year 1300 there was a drawn battle, with the Normans controlling most of the country, but the tide was already beginning to turn against them. The Irish question had become part of the heritage of Ireland and England.

9

THE MEDIEVAL ENGLISH COLONY
(13th and 14th centuries)

by J. F. Lydon

It is found by the jury that, whereas William Bernard, on the Sunday after the Nativity of St John Baptist last, in the town of Newcastle of Lyons, was playing at ball with men of that town and the ball was struck in the direction of John McCorcan, who was standing near to watch the game, John ran towards the ball, which William was following in pursuit, and met him so swiftly that he wounded William in the upper part of his right leg with a knife which he, John, had upon him, which knife unfortunately without John's knowledge pierced its sheath and so injured William, to his damage of five shillings. And the jurors, being asked if John did this from ill-timed zeal or ran against William from malice aforethought, say that it was not so, but that it was for the purpose of playing that he ran towards him to hit the ball. Therefore it is considered that William recover against him his said damages.[1]

This was the judgement in a typical case which came before the court of the justiciar in Dublin in 1308. It is just the sort of case which might be heard in a district court today and it is a useful reminder of how much we owe to the settlers from England and Wales who colonised a large part of Ireland in the twelfth and thirteenth centuries. Our legal system and our courts of law are in large measure inherited from them. So too is our legislature (the oireachtas), which is directly descended from the parliament that developed in medieval Ireland. Indeed the very idea of representation, by which the representatives elected by local communities (now our parliamentary constituencies) have the power collectively to bind through legislation the communities which elected them, is one of the great principles which we have inherited from medieval Ireland. Initially parliament had been composed of the great secular and ecclesiastical lords. But gradually it became more representative of the whole community with the election of delegates from the counties and towns, and of proctors (as they were called) from the lower diocesan clergy as well. Representatives of counties were elected to the parliament of 1297, of the towns in 1299, and of both in 1300. During the fourteenth century it became increasingly the practice to summon the commons to parliament, and before the end of the century they had established their right to be present. By then parliament had assumed the representative character it was to retain right down to the present day.

Our civil service and the system of administration through which it works, though greatly enlarged and much more complex, is still in essence a system devised in the thirteenth century. The medieval exchequer, presided over by the treasurer, with its higher officials and clerks, its complicated records (in Latin and French) and methods for keeping accounts, its control over state income and expenditure, is not completely dissimilar from the Irish exchequer as it exists today. Local government, too, shows many ties with the middle ages. While sheriffs have now disappeared, coroners survive. And the continued existence of mayors and corporations, town clerks and town councils, provides in many cases a direct link with a period when municipal authority was in its infancy in Ireland. The first list of freemen of Dublin comes from the last quarter of the twelfth century. The earliest Dublin charter, the first municipal charter in Ireland, was granted by Henry II as early as 1171-2, and on this was based the charters granted later by John after he became 'lord of Ireland'. These in turn were the models for other municipalities as they developed in Ireland.

The part of Ireland which was colonised by settlers from England needed a code of law and a system of efficient central and local government if order were to be maintained and lawlessness suppressed. This was supplied in the thirteenth century, which was a great period of expansion and development in every sphere of life. Through the English colony new links were forged with the world outside Ireland and new contacts were established with a European civilisation at the height of its development during what one writer has called 'the greatest of centuries'.

54 Charter of Dublin, 1171/1172 (Muniments Room, City Hall, Dublin)

The advent of the friars, and especially the Dominicans and Franciscans, brought a whole new world of learning to Ireland. Through the colony the medieval papacy was brought into closer contact with the Irish than ever before. Because the early upper-class settlers spoke French and were the products of a French-orientated civilisation, they brought with them a code of chivalry and a vision of courtly love which was to leave its mark on the Gaelic literature of the period. This can best be seen in the new form of Gaelic love poetry which was born — the *dánta grádha* based on the *amour courtois* –

> There are two within this house tonight
> Whose looks of love betray their secret;
> Tho' lips may neither speak nor kiss,
> Eyes – pinpointed – are fiercely meeting.[2]

At the same time the English settlers were developing their own literature, of which very little has survived. But enough remains to show that Anglo-Irish poetry, probably because of a close contact with Gaelic poetry, could be surprisingly in advance of the English poetry of the day. For example there is the famous poem of Friar Michael of Kildare, written in the early fourteenth century, called 'The land of Cokaygne':

> Here there is a right fair abbey
> Both of white monks and of grey.
> Here are bowers and high halls,
> And of pasties are the walls
> Of flesh and fish and of rich meat,
> All the best that men may eat.
>
> Flour-cakes, the shingles all
> Of church and cloister, bower and hall,
> Pins there are of puddings rich,
> Meat that princes can bewitch.
> Men may sit and eat it long,
> All with right and not with wrong.[3]

In the towns the beginnings of drama can be discerned with morality and miracle plays in places like Dublin and Kilkenny, performed by the local craft guilds – the carpenters, the tailors, the bakers, and the rest.

The feudalised part of Ireland, then, the areas settled by the colonists, was a part of a wider community – the feudal world of western Europe – and was benefiting from that contact. It was a land of manors and villages, with broad fields tilled in strips; a land of castles and small cottages, markets and fairs, parish churches, abbeys, and friaries. Great progress was made everywhere in the arts of peace. Forest was cleared, and more land was ploughed as new methods of agriculture were introduced. Commercial life expanded and trade boomed. New walled towns, like Athenry and Nenagh, sprang up everywhere. Old ports were developed such as Dublin and Waterford, or new ones created like Drogheda, Galway, and New Ross.

One of the most interesting survivals from the literature of this period, composed in Ireland, is a poem in French which describes in a long narrative how the town of New Ross was enclosed by walls in the thirteenth century. The citizens were afraid that, lacking walls, the town would be at the mercy of warring factions in the vicinity. And so, the poem tells us:

> Commons both, and leading men,
> Gathered in the council then,
> What for safety to devise,
> In shortest time and lowest price;
> 'Twas that around the town be thrown
> Walls of mortar and of stone.

Masons and workmen were hired, to mark out and build walls.

> Yet small advance these fellows made,
> Though to labour they were paid.

So the town council met again and passed a law that all citizens must help in building the walls:

> Vintners, drapers, merchants, all
> Were to labour at the wall,
> From the early morning time,
> Till the day was in its prime.

Each day they came to labour, even the priests:

> And the priests, when mass was chanted,
> In the foss they dug and panted;
> Quicker, harder, worked each brother,
> Harder, far, than any other;
> For both old and young did feel
> Great and strong with holy zeal.

Finally on Sunday even the ladies arrived to join in the work:

Then on Sunday there came down
All the dames of that brave town;
Know, good labourers were they,
But their numbers none may say.
On the ramparts there were thrown
By their fair hands many a stone.
Who had there a gazer been,
Many a beauty might have seen.
In all the lands where I have been,
Such fair dames working I've not seen.[4]

And so the walls were completed, sufficiently strong to keep out the most determined enemy. Secure within, the town prospered and trade expanded.

The life of the town was very like that in similar towns in England, and this similarity was reflected in the buildings and art of the colony. The large parish church of St Mary's, New Ross, for example, perhaps the earliest fully Gothic church in Ireland, was built by William Marshal in what is known as the Early English style. In the details of its ruined choir and transepts we can see the first transplantation to Ireland of the flourishing English Gothic of the time, which was to appear a little later in the design of the thirteenth century cathedrals – like that of Cashel – of southern and eastern Ireland.

Great developments of this kind were taking place all over the colonised area. Everywhere one discerns progress. Everywhere, seemingly, stability reigned. In this 'quiett and welthie estate', as a sixteenth-century writer called it, the whole colony was to share. The records of the great lordship of Carlow show that the lord enjoyed a total revenue of about £450 from his lands there annually – at a time when the income of the Dublin exchequer was about £6,000. The great prosperity of the colony is also shown by the large sums of money which English kings like Henry III or his son Edward I were able to draw from the colony. It was this prosperity which made possible the lavish endowment of the church with land, and the building of abbeys and friaries which sprang up everywhere and whose magnificent ruins may still be seen in the Irish countryside.

149

55 The medieval
court of exchequer,
late 14th century,
from the Red Book
of the Exchequer
(J. T. Gilbert (ed.),
*Facsimiles of the
national manuscripts
of Ireland, iii, 1879)*

Prosperity meant leisure and the desire for education. Many of the Franciscan and Dominican houses had schools attached; so too had some of the cathedrals, like St Patrick's in Dublin. In 1320, the archbishop of Dublin, Alexander Biknor, founded a university in the city, though it did not outlast the troubled years which followed later in the century. For the most part students preferred to go abroad to universities, to Paris, for example, and above all to the schools at Oxford. Probably the most famous of all these was Richard FitzRalph, one of the great scholars of his time, who preached before the pope at Avignon, became chancellor of the University of Oxford and finally archbishop of Armagh. He was a well-known preacher and in a sermon that he preached on 25 March 1349, in the Carmelite church in Drogheda, he exhorted his people to put their trust in Mary who would deliver them from their present distress. Their distress was caused by the great plague which struck the country in the winter of 1348-9, the black death, which had already swept through Europe and in the process killed more than one third of the population. A Franciscan from Kilkenny, Friar Clyn, gives a vivid description of this

150

plague and the ravages it caused in Ireland. According to him the cities of Dublin and Drogheda were almost completely depopulated within a few weeks. In Kilkenny, he tells us, 'there was hardly a house in which only one had died, but as a rule man and wife with their children and all the family went the common way of death'. He expresses the shock and the horror the huge number of deaths caused and he recounts the common belief that the plague was going to sweep everyone away and bring the world to an end. He himself, an educated man, shared in this belief. The last words he wrote in his chronicle are poignant and moving:

Among the dead expecting death's coming, I have set [these deeds] down in writing, truthfully as I have heard them and tested them; and lest the writing should perish with the writer and the work fail with the worker, I leave parchment to carry on the work, if perchance any man survives or any of the race of Adam may be able to escape this pestilence and continue the work I have begun.

Shortly after this the chronicle stops suddenly and another hand added the words: 'it appears that the author died here'.[5] Friar Clyn himself fell a victim to the plague.

The plague and its effects caused panic in the colony and created havoc among the settlers. Many fled from outlying districts to the towns, and from there they fled back to England. Manors and villages were left deserted and fields untilled. The forest crept back into land which had been cleared. But this migration from Ireland and decay of the colony was not only the result of the black death. It had been going on for some time as a result of a remarkable Gaelic revivial which was threatening the colony everywhere. Already by the end of the thirteenth century a distinction was made between *terra pacis* and *terra guerre,* the land of peace and the land of war. By 1297 an Irish parliament found it necessary to legislate on how peace was to be maintained and on how war (when there should be war) was to be fought. We read of expeditions mounted against Gaelic Leinster, or against an O'Brien or a MacCarthy. There was, in fact, recurrent war. But it must be seen in its proper perspective. For most people in the colony, or for that matter in the Gaelic areas, the war was usually far away and never touched them. True, they might be expected to make a contribution towards the war effort, by providing

56 Trim Castle, county Meath, early 13th century (photo. Commissioners of Public Works in Ireland)

money to finance it or food to feed the armies. And as always in time of war there were financiers (usually Italians), merchants, shipowners, and middlemen of all kinds who were only too ready to turn a war to profit. Indeed it could be argued that the market towns, and especially the ports, prospered from the wars. And of course the landless knights, the gentlemen of leisure of the age, found employment in the wars. It would be hard, therefore, to argue that the wars that were fought in the thirteenth century were a very serious matter which vitally impaired the prosperity of the settlers or even severely retarded the development of the colony.

Nevertheless one thing is quite clear. The Gaelic chieftains as a whole were never conquered or forced to come to terms. All over Ireland there were enclaves of independent Gaelic Irish, from which attacks could be mounted on the colony. Some of these, like the area controlled by Mac-Carthy of Desmond, were able to put up a successful resistance against the Anglo-Irish and beat them in open battle. The battle of Callan in 1261, one of the first great Gaelic victories, virtually secured the future independence of the great lordship over which the MacCarthys ruled for the remainder of the middle ages. The O'Donnells of Donegal similarly consolidated their independence around the same time at the battle of

152

Credran (1257) when they halted Geraldine expansion into the north-west. Before the end of the thirteenth century, then, the tide had turned. The expansion of the colony was halted and gradually its frontiers were pushed back.

One of the most spectacular aspects of this Gaelic revival was the attempt to revive the old high-kingship. At a famous meeting at Caeluisce on the river Erne in 1258, the sons of the kings of Thomond and Connacht and the leading nobility met together and there, as the annalist puts it, 'gave supreme authority to Brian O'Neill'. But we must not make too much of this or think that there was a new national spirit, conspicuously absent in the past, now evident in Ireland. Brian O'Neill's closest neighbour in Ulster, O'Donnell of Donegal, refused to acknow-ledge the authority of O'Neill. And the man who was at this very time mounting the most successful resistance against the expanding colony, MacCarthy of Desmond, was not present at the meeting nor, so far as we know, did he endorse the new sovereignty of O'Neill. In any event the whole thing came to a sorry end afterwards, when Brian O'Neill was defeated and killed at the battle of Downpatrick (1260). Three years later, in 1262-3, another abortive attempt to restore the high kingship resulted in an offer to King Haakon of Norway; but he died before he could land in Ireland. The most successful attempt at revival followed when in 1315, Edward Bruce, brother of King Robert of Scotland, was invited to Ireland and in 1316 crowned high king. For three years, before he was killed at the battle of Faughart in 1318, Bruce created havoc in the colony and rocked the settlement to its foundations. But notwithstanding this he failed in the end, and with him the attempt to create a kingdom of Ireland and drive out the settlers ended. From then on the Gaelic revival failed to find a national leader. Its impulse remained local down to the end of the middle ages; its success was measured in the innumerable battles fought by local chieftains or confederations of chieftains. So while everywhere the Gaelic recovery of lost territories was remarkable, there was never any serious attempt made to unite Gaelic Ireland or to bring about the downfall of the English government in Ireland and the end of the colony.

153

This great revival was manifested in other ways, not least by the new impulse given to Gaelic institutions and the Gaelic way of life. An expanding Gaelic area provided more patrons from the aristocracy for the poets, historians, lawyers, and leeches. Many of the greatest books in Irish date from this period – great compilations like the Leabhar Breac or the Yellow Book of Lecan (with its curious imaginative drawing of the banqueting hall at Tara). These were essentially traditional in their content. Indeed, great volumes like the Book of Ballymote were almost one-volume libraries of Irish learning, story and verse, gathered together for the use of the leading Gaelic families. From this period of revival, too, come many of the commentaries on the old Irish law tracts, written by lawyers for the schools of law which they conducted, like the famous school of the Davorens in County Clare. And it is at this time too that the earliest medical treatises in Irish (mainly translations from Latin) were written down, or curiosities like the earliest astronomical treatise.

Without patrons the poets and scholars of the period would have found it difficult to survive, and naturally enough they looked in the first place to the Gaelic noble families for this patronage. But it is clear that the Anglo-Irish nobility also patronised the Gaelic men of letters, even as early as the thirteenth century. And not only that, but some of them took to writing poetry in Irish themselves, displaying occasionally a skill which equalled that of the professionals. When Jenkin Savage died in 1374, the annalist records that 'he left poetry an orphan'. But the outstanding example without a doubt is the third earl of Desmond (d. 1398), a man who at one time was head of the English colony in Ireland, but a man who also won fame for the quality of the poetry he composed in Irish. He is a perfect example of the process of cultural assimilation by which many of the settlers were to become, in a time-worn phrase, 'more Irish than the Irish themselves'. The fact is that from the very beginning many of the settlers married into Gaelic families. From Gaelic mothers and cousins they quickly picked up the Irish language, so that for many of them it became their first language. And from that it was but a short step to the adoption of Gaelic customs like fosterage.

Even by the end of the thirteenth century the government in Dublin

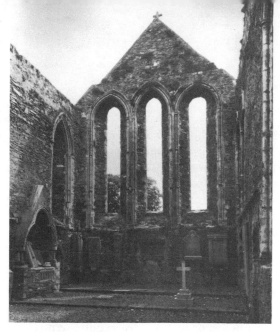

57 St Mary's Church, New
Ross, county Wexford,
1220–35: east window (photo.
Commissioners of Public
Works in Ireland)

had become alarmed by the degree of assimilation which had already taken place. Its answer to the problem was a series of parliamentary enactments designed to keep the 'races' apart – what we in a race-conscious age would call a policy of apartheid. This legislation, some of it incidentally sent over from England, found its most famous expression in the statutes of the Kilkenny parliament of 1366. A great deal of nonsense has been written about these statutes in an attempt to show that they were anti-Irish in their purpose. But in fact the main target of the statutes and of similar legislation before and after was the Anglo-Irish settlers in the land of peace. In spite of all the attempts of the government, however, the settlers were being swamped culturally in most parts of the country. Numerically inferior and lacking a real cultural tradition of their own, assimilation in some degree was inevitable. For some of them it meant being almost wholly absorbed by Gaelic Ireland. Here the classic example are the de Burghs who became the Burkes of Connacht, almost indistinguishable in the eyes of the government from their Gaelic neighbours.

The Gaelic revival posed a more serious problem to the government in military terms. In the fourteenth century in particular it proved impossible to maintain a sufficient defence against the resurgent Gaelic chieftains, even in regions dangerously close to Dublin like Wicklow.

With the help of the gallowglasses, who were mercenary soldiers from Scotland, and their own new-style armies and weapons, the Gaelic leaders were able to cancel out the military advantages which the settlers had enjoyed in the early days of the colony. In addition it was soon discovered that the financial resources of the colony, greatly reduced by loss of territory to Gaelic Ireland and by the migration of settlers from Ireland, were not adequate to maintain an army large enough to carry on a regular and successful war against the Gaelic chieftains everywhere. In the end the colony was forced to fall back on help from England, which for a time was readily available. But England had her own problems to face in her wars with Scotland, and above all in the long struggle with France which we know as the hundred years war (1338-1453). It was not easy to turn badly-needed revenues aside to meet Irish requirements. But for most of the fourteenth century financial help was more or less readily made available to the Irish government, and expeditions were mounted in England to help to control the Gaelic revival. An outstanding example of this was the expedition of Edward III's son, Lionel, duke of Clarence, in the 1360s. But none of these military interventions from England provided more than a temporary answer to the problem, and the Gaelic revival continued. England began to feel that this heavy financial outlay on Ireland was too much of a burden on her already overstrained financial resources. And the outlay was heavy, even by English standards. As long as the war with France continued it proved increasingly difficult to find enough money for the Irish wars. Finally, before he died, Edward III decided that the time had come when the colony in Ireland must fend for itself and bear most of the cost of its own defence.

At the very end of the fourteenth century, however, peace with France and a truce with Scotland gave Richard II a wonderful opportunity to intervene decisively in Irish affairs. He did not hesitate, and in the autumn of 1394 he came himself, the first king to do so since 1210, at the head of a mighty army such as Ireland had never seen before. He waged a successful war in Leinster and forced the great Art MacMurrough to come to terms and promise to vacate Leinster altogether. Soon all the great Gaelic leaders came to the king and made their submissions in

58 Meeting between Art MacMurrough and the earl of Gloucester, June 1399, from British Museum, Harleian MS 1319 (J.T.Gilbert *Facsimiles of the national manuscripts of Ireland*, iii, 1879)

magnificent ceremonies and with great pomp. It looked as if at last the Gaelic revival had been checked, and the king sailed back to England confident that Ireland would present no problem in the future. Within a few months, however, war had broken out again. The king's own heir, Roger Mortimer, was killed in battle. Richard II came back, in terrible anger, in 1399. But by then the whole situation had changed. In Leinster Art MacMurrough had learnt a hard lesson and now proved impossible to pin down. And while the king was waging war in Leinster, his great enemy, Henry of Lancaster, landed in England and seized the throne. Richard II, it could be said, lost his throne in Ireland, and because of the Gaelic revival. And so he had to return to England suddenly, leaving the Irish problem unsolved. Never again in the middle ages did an English king come to Ireland. The colony continued to shrink as the Gaelic area continued to expand. The new Lancastrian dynasty in England, beset by a series of crises which it found difficult to overcome, had little time and less interest to spare for Ireland. It was left to go its own way, the Gaelic and Anglo-Irish elements learning to live together, until the original colony had shrunk to the Pale.

10

THE GAELIC RESURGENCE AND
THE GERALDINE SUPREMACY
(*c.* 1400–1534)

by Art Cosgrove

Richard II's expedition to Ireland in 1399 had failed to achieve a settlement of the country; and its most striking consequence was the overthrow of the king himself. For while Richard sought in vain to come to
grips with Art MacMurrough amid the Leinster forests, Henry
Bolingbroke, his rival for the English crown, had mustered the forces
necessary to replace him as king of England and lord of Ireland. The
responsibilities of that lordship lay lightly on Richard II's successors. No
other monarch was to visit Ireland during the middle ages in an attempt
to invest the title 'lord of Ireland' with practical significance. England's
involvement in an expensive war against the French left her with neither
the men nor the money to meet effectively the oft-repeated requests for
assistance from the English colony. And from the mid-fifteenth century
England herself was gravely weakened by the struggle for the crown
between the Lancastrian and Yorkist factions, known as the 'wars of the
roses'.

In this situation Ireland could not be completely ignored; for she
became a factor of real importance in English politics, first by her
espousal of the Yorkist cause, successful in 1461, and then after 1485, by
the threat she presented to the Tudor dynasty through her support of
Yorkist pretenders. It became apparent that Ireland's fate might determine the course of English history; if she had contributed in 1399 to the
overthrow of one king, she might now provide a starting point for the
making of another. More particularly there emerged the truth of the
warning quaintly phrased by the author of the *Libelle of Englysche
polyce,* written about 1436:

Nowe here beware and hertly take entente,
As ye woll answere at the last jugemente. . .
To kepen Yrelond, that it be not loste,
For it is a boterasse and a poste
Undre England, and Wales is another,
God forbede but eche were other brothere,
Of one ligeaunce dewe unto the kynge.[1]

Only when Ireland appeared as a threat to England's security was the English government prepared to attempt a reconquest of the country.

Inside Ireland, where the soldiers of the Gaelic chiefs were now a match for the colonists, the diminution of the land under English control, the attacks on the colony by the Gaelic Irish and the hibernicisation of the Anglo-Irish all continued with only sporadic interruptions throughout the fifteenth century.

In 1435 the Irish council requested the English king to consider

How that his land of Ireland is well nigh destroyed and inhabited with his enemies and rebels, in so much that there is not left in the nether parts of the counties of Dublin, Meath, Louth, and Kildare, that join together, out of the subjection of the said enemies and rebels scarcely thirty miles in length and twenty miles in breadth, thereas a man may surely ride or go in the said counties to answer the king's writ and to do his commandments.[2]

And even the small area of the English Pale was beleaguered by attacks from the Gaelic Irish, so much so that the colony was constrained at one stage to request the king to complain to 'our. . . most holy father the pope. . . with a view to having a crusade against the said Irish enemies'.[3] To the English colonists the Gaelic Irish appeared little better than infidels or heretics!

But without financial support from England the colony could do little to stem the Gaelic advance. Resort was had to 'black rents', bribes to the Gaelic chieftains, which brought a temporary cessation in their attacks, or else armies to fight the Gaelic Irish were supported by the local population who were forced to find provisions for men and horses and quarters for the troops. This system of raising an army was known in Ireland by the term, 'coign and livery'. Whether used by Gaelic or Anglo-

59 Clara Castle, county Kilkenny: a typical tower-house of the late 15th century (photo, Commissioners of Public Works in Ireland)

Irish leaders or by English chief governors it cast a heavy burden on those who sought to earn a peaceful living from the soil. Archbishop Swayne of Armagh summed up the evil effects of such a policy in 1428:

All the lieutenants that have been in this country, when they come thither, their soldiers live on the husbandmen, not paying for horse-meat nor man-meat and the lieutenant's purveyors take up all manner of victuals i.e. corn, hay, beasts and poultry, and all other things needed for their household, and pay nothing therefore but tallies, so much so, as it is told to me, there is owing in this land by lieutenants and their soldiers within these few years £20,000.[4]

Outside the Pale area the country was divided up into a patchwork of individual supremacies with varying degrees of loyalty to the English crown. The Gaelic chieftains conducted affairs inside their areas according to their own laws and traditions with little reference to the English administration. And straddling the country in a rough diagonal between Dublin and Cork were the three great Anglo-Irish lordships, the Butler earldom of Ormond and the Fitzgerald earldoms of Desmond and Kildare. And these earls, too, were caught up in the complex world of Gaelic Irish politics through their alliances with and antagonisms towards their Gaelic neighbours.

Into this situation there came as lieutenant in 1449 Richard, duke of York. Thirty-seven years of age and a veteran of the war in France, the duke was seen as a possible focus of opposition to the weak and pietistic Henry VI as king of England. And his appointment to Ireland was designed to divert his attention from this role at a time when the pattern of the conflict between Lancaster and York was already taking shape.

Richard arrived at Howth in July 1449. Accompanying him was his wife Cicely Neville whose renowned beauty had earned for her the title, the 'rose of Raby'. The pair received an enthusiastic welcome. A Gaelic history records:

> He was received with great honour, and the earls of Ireland went into his house, as did also the Irish adjacent to Meath, and gave him as many beeves for the use of his kitchen as it pleased him to demand.[5]

Through his descent from the de Burgh and Mortimer families the duke had hereditary claims to the earldom of Ulster and the lordships of Connacht, Trim, and Leix. And he was accepted not only as a member of the Anglo-Irish aristocracy but also as an answer to the oft-repeated demands of the colony for the appointment as chief governor of a lord of noble birth from England. For the colony believed that

> the people will more favour and obey (a lord of noble English birth) than any man of Irish birth, for men of the English realm keep better justice, execute your laws and favour more the common people there. . . better than ever did any man of that land or is ever like to do.[6]

The Gaelic Irish, too, were impressed by this mighty prince from across the sea. So numerous were the submissions made to him by the Gaelic chieftains that a contemporary observer was brought to express the over-optimistic hope that 'ere twelve months come to an end, the wildest Irishman in Ireland shall be sworn English'.[7]

In October 1449 a son, George, afterwards duke of Clarence, was born to the duke and his wife; amid scenes of enthusiasm he was baptised in Dublin with the earls of Ormond and Desmond as sponsors at his font. By the time of his departure from the country in August 1450, Richard had effectively forged the link between Ireland and the Yorkist cause which was to last for over forty years. And when the Yorkist forces were routed at Ludford Bridge in September 1459, it was to Ireland that the duke fled for refuge. Here he was received with open arms, and the Irish parliament took steps to legalise his position as chief governor of the country and to protect him against the charge of treason made by the

finally triumphed in England with the accession to the throne in March 1461 of the duke's son, Edward IV. And the possibility of a more lasting division between England and Ireland was thus averted.

Not that Ireland was without Lancastrian sympathisers. The Butlers of Ormond had not joined in the general sympathy for the Yorkist cause, and Sir John Butler attempted to revive Lancastrian hopes inside Ireland. But in 1462 his forces suffered a defeat at the hands of Thomas Fitzgerald, son of the seventh earl of Desmond, at the battle of Pilltown near Carrick-on-Suir. The Annals of the Four Masters record that 'there were four hundred and ten of the slain of his people interred, besides the number who were devoured by the dogs and birds of prey'. And among the spoils of victory taken by Desmond was a manuscript which was in part a copy of the great Irish codex known as the Psalter of Cashel.

That an earl of Desmond should interest himself in works in the Irish language was not surprising. The growing gaelicisation of the Desmond earls had been a feature of the previous hundred years. Gerald, the third earl of Desmond, on his death in 1398 was praised by the Annals of Clonmacnoise as a 'witty and ingenious composer of Irish poetry', and some of his verses survive in the Book of Fermoy. Thomas himself is described in a Gaelic source as

the most illustrious of his tribe in Ireland in his time for his comeliness and stature, for his hospitality and chivalry, his charity and humanity to the poor and the indigent of the Lord, his bounteousness in bestowing jewels and riches on the laity, the clergy, and the poets.[8]

The victory at Pilltown had established this man as the most powerful lord inside Ireland. And in March 1463 when he had succeeded his father as eighth earl of Desmond, the Yorkist king, Edward IV, appointed him chief governor of the country, though he warned him at the same time against the adoption of Gaelic Irish law and customs.

During the four years of his rule, Desmond, through his connections with Anglo-Irish and Gaelic Irish leaders, exercised authority over a much wider area than his immediate predecessors in the office.

The county of Cork was represented in parliament in 1463 for the first time in many years. In the same parliament a relaxation was made in the laws against intercourse with the Gaelic Irish so that the citizens of Cork, Waterford, Limerick, and Youghal might legally trade with their Gaelic Irish neighbours.

Outside the Pale area, the towns, in general, remained English in language and sympathy long after the countryside around them had reverted to the Gaelic Irish. But they could not exist in isolation. As a statute of 1463 pointed out, 'the profit of every market, city and town in this land depends principally on the resort of Irish people bringing their merchandise to the said cities and towns'[9]. Nor was it easy for the towns to communicate with one another or with Dublin. Travelling by land in fifteenth-century Ireland was a difficult and hazardous business. The mayors of some towns were excused the duty of coming to Dublin to take the oath of allegiance to the crown because of the dangers presented by the journey. Attendances at parliament were depleted for the same reasons. And the journey from the Pale into the interior of the country became even more hazardous after the town of Castledermot fell to the Gaelic Irish. As was pointed out afterwards, the town

was one of the keys of Leinster for the king's liege people dwelling therein and thereabout and a safeguard and a good harbourage to the king's people that should pass from those parts and the east parts of Ulster, and from the counties of Louth, Meath, Dublin, and Kildare to the parts of Munster. . . (But) the said town was utterly destroyed by the said enemies and never recovered since, to the final destruction of all the parts thereabout.[10]

The towns that survived remained as walled enclaves of the English interest. Waterford, though captured by Sir John Butler in 1462, withstood a ten-day siege in 1495 when the Yorkist pretender Perkin Warbeck renewed his bid for support inside Ireland.

During Desmond's period of office some attempt was made to provide a centre of higher education inside Ireland. In the absence of any local university, Anglo-Irish and Gaelic Irish students repaired to the English universities at Cambridge and Oxford. But many of these emigrants did not settle happily in this strange environment. And in 1422 the English parliament introduced legislation against those called 'wild Irishmen' who were accused of fomenting disturbances in Oxford. Limitations were placed on the entry of Irishmen into the university and Irish scholars, forbidden to live in a hall of their own, were ordered to dwell among their English fellow-students. Even at this stage Irish emigrants did not easily integrate into English society. In Ireland, Desmond's project to set up in Drogheda a university 'in which may be made, bachelors, masters, and doctors in all sciences, as at Oxford' unfortunately came to nothing; but he did found at Youghal in 1464 a college dedicated to the Blessed Virgin which was modelled to some extent on All Souls, Oxford.

Desmond's close connections with the Gaelic Irish eventually incurred for him the hostility of the Pale residents led by the English bishop of Meath, William Sherwood. He was accused of extorting coign and livery to support his forces; and at the time of his appointment the English king had warned him to repress 'the extortion and oppression of our true subjects there and especially that damnable and unlawful extortion and oppression used upon them called coign and livery'.[11] And in his campaign of 1466 when he was captured by his brother-in-law, O'Connor Faly of Offaly, he cannot have been readily distinguished from the Gaelic chieftains with whom he was allied or against whom he was fighting. These considerations led Edward IV to despatch to Ireland in 1467 Sir John Tiptoft, earl of Worcester, who was to replace Desmond as chief governor. Tiptoft was an English nobleman renowned for his scholarship and the cold ruthlessness he displayed towards his enemies. The use of summary methods of execution against the king's enemies earned for him the unenviable title of 'the butcher'. Shortly after his arrival in Ireland, both the earl of Desmond and his brother-in-law, the earl of Kildare, were accused of treason on the ground of their connections with the Gaelic Irish. When Desmond came to Drogheda to answer the charge, he was taken and beheaded on 14 February 1468.

The execution of Desmond is described with an air of shocked surprise in the Gaelic histories.

A great deed was done in Drogheda this year, to wit, the earl of Desmond. . . was beheaded. And the learned relate that there was not ever in Ireland a foreign youth that was better than he. And he was killed in treachery by a Saxon earl. . .[12]

61 Carved figures from the cloister of the Cistercian abbey of Jerpoint, county Kilkenny, 15th century (photo. Commissioners of Public Works in Ireland)

The immediate reaction to the earl's execution was a rising of both Gaelic and Anglo-Irish lords with which Tiptoft had not the forces to cope. An agreement was therefore reached whereby Kildare was received back into favour on condition that he would make the Irishmen of Leinster to be at peace, according to his power. Subsequently Tiptoft returned to England, there himself to meet death during the brief Lancastrian restoration of 1470, when his execution had to be postponed for a day because of the mob which wished to lynch the infamous 'butcher'.

The failure of Tiptoft's mission demonstrated the real difficulties involved in any attempted settlement of Ireland. To achieve a reconquest of the country demanded the expenditure of resources far beyond what any English king was prepared to spend. The only alternative, therefore, was to entrust the government of Ireland to Anglo-Irish lords like Desmond and Kildare who, through their close connection with the Gaelic Irish, could rule the country more effectively and less expensively than any man sent from England. But there was also the danger inherent in such a policy that an Anglo-Irish governor might use his position to enhance his own power independently of the English crown. One of the accusations made against the executed earl of Desmond, though never sustained, was that he had wished to make himself king of Ireland.

The alienation of the Desmond family and the eclipse of the house of Ormond paved the way for the rise of the Kildare earls, situated much nearer Dublin in their strong castle of Maynooth. And in 1478 there succeeded to the chief governorship, Garret More Fitzgerald, famous as 'the great earl'. The power of the great earl did not depend solely on his position as chief crown representative in Ireland. By his first marriage he had six daughters, all of whom 'married well'. And he thus established connections with a number of the chief families, Anglo-Irish and Gaelic Irish, in the land. A particularly close link was forged with the O'Neills of Tyrone; for the earl's sister Eleanor married Conn More O'Neill and their son, Conn Bacach O'Neill, earl of Tyrone, in turn married his cousin Alice, the earl's daughter.

In the tradition of the Fitzgeralds, the earl displayed an interest in both the languages and cultures of Ireland. The breadth of his interests can, to some extent, be gathered from his library which contained works in Latin, French, and Irish. And drawing to himself the loyalty of both Gaelic and Anglo-Irish, the earl came closer than anyone else to embodying a spirit representative of the whole of Ireland. Clearly the earl was a potential threat to English rule in Ireland. But in the event he used his power not to make himself an independent ruler but to support the Yorkist cause, to which he remained attached.

Thus when the Lancastrian Tudor, Henry VII, succeeded to the English throne, Ireland was once again involved in Yorkist plots. In 1487 Lambert Simnel, the Yorkist pretender, was received in Ireland as the nephew of Edward IV and on 24 May, was crowned Edward VI of England in the presence of a large gathering of Irish nobles and prelates. And the earl's brother, Thomas Fitzgerald, accompanied the army which invaded England in support of the boy pretender and which was

167

defeated at Stoke in June 1487. Simnel was captured and made a servant in the king's kitchen. Again in 1491 a second Yorkist pretender, Perkin Warbeck, was received in Cork as Prince Richard. Both the earls of Desmond and Kildare were implicated in the plot to place him on the English throne, though Warbeck departed from Ireland again in the spring of 1492.

Henry VII could not allow the continuance of the threat which Ireland now presented. Accordingly in 1494 he sent over to Ireland Sir Edward Poynings, a capable soldier and administrator who had shared the king's exile and had been knighted after Henry's victory at Bosworth in 1485. He was to reduce the country to 'whole and perfect obedience' and thus prevent Yorkist pretenders from again using Ireland as a base. If we can trust the testimony of the northern chief, O'Hanlon, the earl of Kildare also recognised Poynings' ability. For he warned O'Hanlon:

Do not attempt anything against the deputy that you would not attempt against me myself, for he is a better man than I am, but enter into peace with him and give him your son as surety.[13]

The acts of the parliament which Poynings summoned to Drogheda in December 1494 form the best known legislation of the medieval Irish parliament.

The division between the four counties of the Pale (Louth, Meath, Dublin, and Kildare) and the rest of the country was clearly recognised by the ordinance which required the inhabitants on the border of this area to build a double ditch six feet high to repel Gaelic Irish invaders. In a similar defensive vein it was laid down that the chief castles of the land, those of Dublin, Trim, Athlone, Wicklow, Greencastle, and Carrick-fergus should have as constables men born in England.

The statutes of Kilkenny in 1366 had attempted to proscribe the use of the Irish language, laws, and customs. These were now confirmed with the significant exception of the regulation forbidding the use of the Irish language. Clearly in the period since 1366 the use of the Irish language had become so widespread that any attempt to check the speaking of it was futile. As early as 1394 the most English of the Anglo-Irish

62 King Henry VII, 1485–1509, by
an unknown Flemish artist
(National Portrait Gallery, London)

magnates, the earl of Ormond, was able to act as interpreter in the dealings between Richard II and the Gaelic chiefs. Only the Pale area and some of the towns now retained the English language.

In general the Kilkenny statutes had failed to check the Gaelic resurgence. Even in the matter of hair-style and dress Gaelic usages predominated and were again prohibited in 1537, when it was laid down

that no person or persons, the king's subjects within this land. . . shall be shorn or shaven above the ears, or use the wearing of hair upon their heads, like unto long locks called 'glibes', or have or use any hair growing upon their upper lip, called or named a 'crommeal'. . .

At the same time people were forbidden 'to wear any mantles, coat, or hood made after the Irish fashion'.[14]

The dress of the people in this period varied, as always, according to wealth or rank. The poorer inhabitants of the bogs and mountains usually went bareheaded, with little other covering than an Irish cloak. More prosperous men favoured a mantle of frieze or cloth and a wide linen tunic gathered into numerous pleats with wide-hanging sleeves, generally dyed saffron colour. On their heads were conical caps of frieze and their legs were encased in close-fitting hose called 'trews'. The women were fond of brightly-coloured skirts, kilted, and embroidered with silk and many ornaments, while on their heads they wore a hood of folded linen. In this sphere, as in the case of language and law, the attempt of the English 'to teach us their ways' had not proved successful.

169

The standard of housing also varied. The tower houses were the typical dwellings of Anglo-Irish gentry and Gaelic chiefs at this time, and these impressive constructions of several storeys provided defence against the marauding raids of enemies as well as hospitality and entertainment for friends. On the other hand, observers reported to the pope from the dioceses of Ardagh and Clonmacnoise in 1516-17 that many of the Irish lived in fields and caves with their cattle and that the few houses that did exist were poor constructions of timber and straw.

The most celebrated enactment of the parliament of 1494 was that afterwards known as Poynings' law down to its virtual repeal in 1782. Under its terms parliament was to meet in Ireland only after royal permission had been granted and after the king and council in England had been informed of and had approved the measures which it was proposed to enact. Though variously interpreted in the three centuries that followed, its main purpose at the time was to prevent a chief governor from using parliament to the detriment of the king's interests, as Kildare had done when in 1487 he had caused it to give official recognition to a pretender to the English throne, Lambert Simnel.

Poynings' parliament had taken place against the background of a revolt provoked by the arrest of the Great Earl, whom Poynings suspected of treasonable alliance with the Gaelic Irish chiefs of the north. But he was restored to power by Henry VII in 1496 and remained in control of the country until his death in 1513. Though often termed 'the all-but-king of Ireland', he made no attempt to set himself up as the independent ruler of the country. Freed of his Yorkist sympathies he remained loyal to the Tudor monarchy, though the power he exercised inside the country was amply demonstrated by his victory over the Clanrickard Burkes at the battle of Knockdoe in 1504. Combining under him a large force of both Gaelic and Anglo-Irish leaders, Kildare crushed a similar confederation under Burke's leadership, thus ending a conflict which, according to some reports, was sparked off by Burke's ill-treatment of his wife, the earl's daughter, Eustacia. The Tudor kings, for their part, were content to have Ireland ruled for them by a loyal subject.

This policy of non-intervention from England was continued for some

170

years after Garret Oge succeeded his father both as earl of Kildare and chief governor in 1513. But in 1519 the powerful Henry VIII decided to take a more active interest in Irish affairs. Kildare was summoned to London and the earl of Surrey, a nobleman respected for his ability both as soldier and statesman, was despatched to Ireland with a small force to reduce the land to good order and obedience.

Surrey found the task beyond his powers. And in 1521 he reported to the king his belief that Ireland could only be reduced by conquest and that this would require an army of six thousand men supported by artillery and munitions from England. Fortresses would have to be built to control each section of the country successively occupied. And since military occupation alone could not endure unless accompanied by a large plan of colonisation, it would be necessary also to bring in English settlers to occupy Irish lands. But Henry VIII was not prepared to meet the cost of such a thorough policy, and Surrey was recalled in 1522.

Surrey had also been enjoined to bring about the unification and anglicisation of the Irish church. This was to be done under the authority of the English Cardinal Wolsey who had risen from humble origins to become the king's chief adviser and the effective head of the English church. But this task, too, presented Surrey with insuperable obstacles.

The church in Ireland mirrored the divisions of secular society. The archdiocese of Armagh itself was split between the Pale residents of the south and the Gaelic Irish of the north; and the archbishop was able to exercise little jurisdiction over his flock 'among the Gaelic Irish', as he commonly lived not at Armagh but in his castle at Termonfeckin, County Louth. During the fifteenth century English bishops appointed to dioceses in the Gaelic Irish area were usually absentees, and if they did reside in their dioceses were unable to understand either the language or traditions of their flocks. John Kite, an English official and a servant of Wolsey who was appointed to the archbishopric of Armagh, complained bitterly to his master about the 'barbarity' of both the Gaelic and Anglo-Irish committed to his charge. In many other dioceses the bishopric had become the preserve of particular Gaelic Irish families and a number of bishops were of illegitimate birth. Preoccupied with secular and military affairs, prelates even neglected the repair of their churches. According to reports in 1516-17 both the cathedrals of Clonmacnoise and Ardagh were in ruins; in the latter, the writer relates:

. . . hardly the walls are left. In it there is only one altar, exposed to the open air, on which mass is celebrated by one priest only, and that rarely. There is no sacristy, bell-tower or bell, but only the bare requisites for the celebration of one mass kept in a cupboard in the church.[15]

Another observer reported on the state of religion in the country in 1515:

For there is no archbishop, nor bishop, abbot nor prior, parson nor vicar, nor any other person of the Church, high or low, great or small, English or Irish, that is accustomed to preach the word of God, saving the poor friars beggars. . .[16]

It was with justification that the friars beggars, the observant or reformed branches of the Franciscan, Dominican, and Augustinian orders, were excepted from this general condemnation. The growth in the number of their houses throughout the country testifies to the strength of the movement. It was these men who, through constant preaching and administration of the sacraments, kept religion alive in Ireland during this period and stiffened Irish resistance to the religious innovations of Henry VIII when he broke with Rome after his marriage to Anne Boleyn in 1533.

In the same year Garret Oge was summoned to England for the last time. When he departed in February 1534 he entrusted the government of the country to his eldest son, Thomas, Lord Offaly. On 11 June 1534 Offaly galloped into Dublin with a band of armed men each wearing a silken fringe on his jacket, the decoration which gave to Offaly the name, Silken Thomas. In the council chamber in St Mary's Abbey he flung down the sword of state and declared to the astonished councillors that he was no longer the king's deputy but his enemy.

Traditional accounts of the rebellion have tended to attribute it solely to the youthful impetuosity of Thomas himself. More recent research, however, suggests that Thomas acted with both the knowledge and approval of his father. The objective of the rebellion was to persuade the king that he could not afford to abandon his reliance on the Kildare earls in the government of Ireland. The demands put forward by Silken

63 Ireland, *c.* 1500, showing the Pale and the great lordships, after the map in E. Curtis, *A history of medieval Ireland*, 1938

Thomas make this clear. He wanted a royal pardon for the rebellion and permission to hold the chief governorship of Ireland for life.[17]

Silken Thomas's revolt had not been inspired by his opposition to Henry VIII's religious policy, though he attempted to gain support for it on these grounds. But religion was to become the burning question in Ireland as elsewhere in Europe. And when a difference in religion was added to the differences already existing between England and Ireland in language, culture, and tradition, the reconquest of the country from England's point of view, became not just desirable but a pressing political necessity.

173

11
THE TUDOR CONQUEST
(1534-1603)

by G. A. Hayes-McCoy

King Henry VIII, who succeeded to the throne of England in 1509 and became king of Ireland in 1541, occupies a position in time almost half way between the Norman invasion and the cessation of British rule in this part of Ireland. Henry's arrogant and well known figure is, however, as far as the history of this country is concerned, something more than a half-way mark.

His reign saw a new departure. Before it, and particularly in the century before it, the English crown was powerless in most parts of Ireland; but Henry and his successors pushed their affairs so well that Henry's daughter Elizabeth was in due course able to pass on to her successor – that is, to James VI of Scotland, who became James I of England – something unique: the undisputed rule of the entire island. Between them, four sovereigns of the house of Tudor, Henry VIII, Edward VI, Mary, and Elizabeth, completed the conquest of Ireland. Not only did they bring the whole country for the first time under the control of a central government, but they ensured that that government would be an English one.

The principal motive which inspired the Irish undertakings of these sovereigns was self-protection. The first Tudor, Henry VII, had seized power in England and he and his successors were determined to retain it. They feared that domestic rivals or foreign enemies might use Ireland as a base for operations against them. Irish recalcitrancy was, from their point of view, a danger which increased as the sixteenth century progressed and as they became more deeply involved in the European struggle for power and in the religious warfare of the age. Just as, towards the end of the century, the English were to aid the Dutch rebels against Spain, the Spaniards might – in fact did – aid the Irish rebels against the English. If the Tudors were to continue to rule England they must rule Ireland as well.

A further motive for the Tudor conquest of Ireland was provided by what later ages would call imperial expansion. England was jealous of the great power of Spain, and she became increasingly preoccupied with the necessity of extending her own dominion – and her trade – overseas. England's first steps to empire were taken within these islands. Ireland was the first field for English enterprise and colonisation. Sir Walter Raleigh, Sir Humphrey Gilbert, Ralph Lane – the leaders of the early English colonies in North America – all gained their first experience in Ireland, and England learnt to establish herself beyond the Irish Sea before she leaped the Atlantic.

Such consideration led in Henry VIII's time to the abandonment of the earlier English policy of keeping the Anglo-Irish and the Gaelic Irish apart. Soon, aggression took the place of defence. By 1534 Henry could dispense with much of the assistance of the Anglo-Irish lords upon which he and his predecessors had formerly relied and could undertake a more direct and a more forceful control of Irish affairs. The power of the king's Irish council, which met in Dublin, increased steadily, and a new kind of English official, the forerunner of very many generations of skilled and loyal servants of the crown who were to manage Ireland for England, had begun to make his appearance.

The rebellion of Thomas Fitzgerald, the son of the ninth earl of Kildare, who was a leader of the Anglo-Irish and who is famous in our history as Silken Thomas, was quelled with a ruthless severity. Sir William Skeffington, the king's representative, attacked the Fitzgerald stronghold of Maynooth castle with his artillery. Guns were, of course, no novelty in the Ireland of that time, but Skeffington – for, as he said, 'the dread and example of others'[1] – used his weapons to a new purpose. When he had battered their fortifications and forced Silken Thomas's garrison to surrender, he gave the survivors 'the pardon of Maynooth' – that is, he executed them. It was an action without precedent in the Irish wars, which up to then, although they had been frequent, had not been bloody – and it was a foretaste of what was to come. The Tudor period in Irish history was one of violence. The rebellion completed the downfall of the house of Kildare; from that time forward the viceroy was to be an Englishman – one whom few Irish lords could oppose – and until 1922 there was always to be an English army in Dublin.

Six years after the downfall of the Fitzgeralds, in 1541, Henry acquired a new crown. The Irish parliament declared him king of Ireland. If we except Edward Bruce, who was crowned in 1316 but who never reigned, Henry was the first monarch to bear this title. He assumed it because it matched his Irish ambition better than the medieval title, lord of Ireland, which his royal predecessors had borne. And it was a natural step for one who had broken with Rome to take. Many people believed that the pope was the king of Ireland and that the lordship which the kings of England exercised was 'but a governance under the obedience of the same'.[2] Now they were disillusioned. Henry adopted a new symbol to suit his new authority. As his coinage shows, he introduced the harp as the emblem of Ireland.

Henry had neither the inclination nor the money (despite his new coinage) to continue the military offensive that had given him such a victory over the Leinster Fitzgeralds. Although his authority was much less in other places than it had been in rebellious Kildare, he soon abandoned Skeffington's spectacular methods and proposed to control Ireland by other means.

Outside the towns and the area of the English Pale, which was not 'above twenty miles in compass', Ireland was at that time largely inhabited by the two classes whom contemporary Englishmen called 'English rebels' and 'Irish enemies'. The 'rebels' were the Anglo-Irish lords who had fallen away from their allegiance and had adopted many of the ways of Gaelic life, that is, the Fitzgeralds of Desmond, the Roches, Barrys, Powers, and others in Munster; the Butlers, Dillons, Tyrrells, and many more in Leinster; the Burkes and others in Connacht; and a few families like the Savages in east Ulster. The 'Irish enemies' were more numerous. There were sixty or more Gaelic lords or captains, some of them descen-

64 King Henry VIII, 1509–47, after
Holbein (National Portrait Gallery,
London)

65 Irish groat of Henry VIII (National
Museum of Ireland)

dants of the provincial kings of old, each of them a ruler of high or low degree and all of them independent of England – O'Neill, O'Donnell, Maguire, MacMahon, O'Reilly in Ulster; Kavanagh, O'Byrne, O'More, O'Connor in Leinster; MacCarthy, O'Brien, O'Sullivan in Munster; O'Connor and O'Kelly in Connacht – to name only the more notable of them.

The English had, up to this, looked upon these Gaelic lords as inveterate enemies. They had done so because the system of society under which the Gaelic part of the Irish population lived – their traditions, institutions, laws, and language – was still, although three centuries had elapsed since the Norman invasion, different from the English system. The Gaelic Irish had a cultural and institutional life of their own, a life that their ancestors had lived from time immemorial, and although they and the English lived side by side in Ireland they were, in fact, two different nations. In the centuries when the English had held the Gaelic Irish at arm's length their interests had frequently conflicted to the point of enmity. Soon, when it became clear that the new policy of the Tudors would deny them their distinctiveness and would wipe out their independence, many of the Gaelic lords were to display an even greater enmity than before.

Yet Henry hoped to arrange the affairs of his new kingdom peaceably. He was well equipped for war, but he told his Irish lord deputy in 1520:

We and our council think, and verily believe, that in case circumspect and politic ways be used, you shall bring the Irish lords to further obedience. . . which thing must as yet rather be practised by sober ways, politic drifts, and amiable persuasions, founded in law and reason, than by rigorous dealing. . . or enforcement by strength or violence.[3]

Twenty years later, although in the meantime Lord Deputies Grey and St Leger had been demonstrating the government's strength by a series of expeditions – in reality they were raids – throughout Ireland, Henry was still recommending 'good and discreet persuasions'.[4] And his policy bore fruit. The earl of Desmond submitted to him on his knees; MacWilliam Burke of Galway humbly besought pardon; O'Brien submitted; Conn O'Neill, the greatest lord in Ulster, crossed to England and, speaking through an interpreter, thanked the king for his mercy and swore

66 Irish warriors and peasants, by Albrecht Dürer, 1521 (National Gallery of Ireland)

allegiance to him. These three were ennobled. Burke was made earl of Clanrickard, O'Brien earl of Thomond, and O'Neill earl of Tyrone. By the time of Henry's death in 1547 forty of the principal Gaelic and Anglo-Irish had made their peace and had undertaken to obey English law.

Such of these lords as had been living according to the Irish system gave up their lands to the crown and received them back again as feudal fiefs. All agreed to abandon the old ways and, by learning English and ceasing to wear distinctively Irish garments, to establish uniformity of language and dress throughout the king's dominions. Henry's intention was to bring about a revolution. He wanted to substitute for the 'sundry sorts' of people who made up the Irish population – that is, the Anglo-Irish and Gaelic Irish – one class only, the king's subjects, all of whom would be anglicised. The agreements by which these alterations were promised or effected were like so many treaties entered into by independent powers, and, like treaties, many of them were made only to be broken. But no such wholesale changes – in particular no such inroads on the Gaelic system – had been contemplated before this in Ireland.

Nor was this policy of unification that was to bring about the destruction of the old Gaelic world Henry's only Irish legacy. He also introduced the reformation. Henry clashed with the international

179

catholic church because, in England, he was the self-willed ruler of a national state. The clash speedily became a breach. By 1534 Henry had abolished the English jurisdiction of the pope, had taken the pope's place by assuming the title 'supreme head on earth of the church of England', and had altered the succession to the throne so as to exclude the daughter of the queen whom – in defiance of the pope – he had divorced. Soon the English monasteries were dissolved. The attempt to repeat these changes in Ireland was part of the policy of anglicisation of the country. There was no popular resentment against the church in Ireland such as had become evident in England, and the new protestantism can as yet have had few Irish followers; but it was necessary that Irish religious practice should, in the interest of Tudor absolutism, be made to conform with English practice. When the Irish parliament of 1536 passed – not without opposition – an act which made Henry 'the only supreme head on earth of the whole church of Ireland', their performance was justified by the statement that 'this land of Ireland is depending and belonging justly and rightfully to the imperial crown of England'.[5]

The reformation was at first noticeable only in the towns and in the Pale, in which area, by the end of the reign, nearly all the religious houses had been dissolved. Things were different in the districts under Gaelic rule, where indeed the old church was separately organised. It was said as early as 1539 of the friars and other priests in Ulster that they

do preach daily that every man ought, for the salvation of his soul, fight and make war against our sovereign lord the king's majesty, and if any of them die in the quarrel his soul. . . shall go to Heaven, as the souls of SS Peter, Paul, and others, who suffered death and martyrdom for God's sake.[6]

Ultimately the reformation had little success in Ireland. Edward VI, who succeeded Henry VIII in 1547, attempted to introduce doctrinal changes. He was resisted. His successor, Mary, was a catholic, and she officially restored the old religion. Queen Elizabeth I, the last of the Tudors, sought to establish a uniformity of protestantism within her dominions. The resistance which Elizabeth encountered in Ireland was far greater than that which her father had met. The Irish parliament of 1560 – which, like all the parliaments of the century, represented only the more

67 Hugh O'Neill,
from H. Adami,
La spada d'Orione
(Rome, 1680)

V G O
CONTE DI TIRONE
GENERALE IBERNESE.

anglicised parts of the country – tried to make Ireland protestant by legislation; but the religious conservatism of the people, the fact that the reformed religion was associated with an alien government, and the missionary efforts of the agents of the counter-reformation – the Jesuits and other priests who came to Ireland from the Continent – all combined to entrench catholicism. The old religion, professed by Anglo-Irish and Gaelic Irish alike, soon disclosed itself as a force making for Irish unity, and for resistance to England. As time went on it became increasingly clear that the established church was the church of the new English colony and of the official class.

Henry's successors, Edward, Mary, and Elizabeth, continued their father's civil policy. Although the English determination to control Ireland increased as the century progressed, not even Elizabeth, who was the strongest of the Tudors, abandoned until the very end the hope of achieving her purpose by negotiation.

The first indication that negotiation might be inadequate came from Ulster. Conn O'Neill, who had agreed when he was made earl of Tyrone 'utterly to forsake' the name of O'Neill – that is, he agreed to become the subject of the new king of Ireland and renounced his claim to be an Irish king – died in 1559. The question was, who was to succeed him? If his son Matthew, the heir according to English law, succeeded, the Ulster part of Henry's settlement might have been preserved. But another son, Shane the Proud, claimed that he was the legitimate heir and that, according to the system upon which the O'Neill lordship and all the other Gaelic lordships rested, Conn had been a ruler only for life. Conn had had 'no estate in what he surrendered'; therefore, Shane held, the surrender and the grant of the earldom were of 'no value'.[7]

It was a bold plea – all the more so in that Shane made it in the queen's court in London, where he went at Elizabeth's expense in 1562, accompanied by an escort of gallowglasses, or Scots-Irish mercenaries 'armed with battleaxes, bare-headed, with flowing curls, yellow shirts dyed with saffron, . . . large sleeves, short tunics, and rough cloaks, whom the English followed with as much wonderment as if they had come from China or America'.[8] Strangely – but we must remember that the queen had hope of a compromise – Shane was 'sent home with honour'. He behaved as a king in Ulster for five more years and was in the end (1567) brought down not by the queen, but by his neighbours, the O'Donnells and the Antrim Scots, whom he had 'yoked and spoiled at pleasure'. His head was placed on a spike over one of the gates of Dublin. By tolerating Shane, Queen Elizabeth had accepted, as far as Ulster was concerned, a temporary reversal of the anglicisation project. She tolerated Shane's successor, Turlough Luineach, in the same way. Turlough was no rebel; he cost the English nothing, and he was held in check by his rising rival, Hugh O'Neill. Hugh, the grandson of Conn, had been indoctrinated in England and it was hoped that he might eventually redeem the north.

Elsewhere the queen was quite clearly gaining ground as the century advanced. The establishment in 1570 of presidencies in Munster and

Connacht brought organised English government into the south and into the country beyond the Shannon; and by 1585, when almost all the modern counties had been defined, the queen largely controlled the provinces of Leinster, Munster, and Connacht. Of these, Munster had proved the most difficult to subdue. The Munster lords resisted efforts to curtail their local authority. And they were led to take sides in defence of their religion in the ideological struggle which then split Europe, the struggle of catholic against protestant – a contest heightened in 1570 by the excommunication of the queen. Munster rebelled in 1579. Continental efforts to assist the rebels – in particular, a landing of Spaniards and Italians at Smerwick in 1580 – strengthened the English determination to crush them, and by 1583 the rebellion had been put down with great severity. It was followed by plantation, that is, by the dispossession of the rebellious landholders and their replacement by loyal English colonists. Plantation had already been tried in the midlands and the north, and it was the policy that was in the next century to transform Ulster and to set up the English colonies in America. Although the Munster plantation was not destined to be a success, Munster was quiet in 1585 when Connacht was taken in hand. Connacht presented little difficulty. The lords and great landholders of that province agreed to make a settlement which confirmed them in their estates, introduced money rents instead of the services and contributions in kind of the Irish system, and eventually abolished hereditary local jurisdiction.

So far, from the English point of view, all was well. It appeared that great progress had been made in the anglicisation of Ireland. The towns none of which was of native origin, lent active support to the servants of the crown. When the survivors of the Spanish armada came ashore after their shipwreck on the Irish coast in 1588, these enemies of England were almost everywhere treated as enemies by the Irish as well. And a significant effort in the progress of anglicisation was made when in 1592 Queen Elizabeth founded a university at Dublin. Ireland had diverged from the general pattern of medieval Europe in that all previous schemes to found a university had failed, and thus her first university (and the only one for 250 years) was inevitably identified with the protestant establish-

68   Armagh in ruins,
c. 1600, from a map
by R. Bartlett
(G. A. Hayes-McCoy,
*Ulster and other Irish
maps c. 1600*, 1964)

ment. Trinity College, Dublin, named after its prototype in Cambridge, and invested with all the powers of a university, was intended to be not only a centre of higher learning but also a pillar of the established church. It became a seat of learning, but it had no significant effect on the exodus of young catholics to continental seminaries for their higher education.

There was one outstanding exception in the record of Tudor success in Ireland. Ulster had been for long unaffected by the changes that were so noticeable elsewhere. But the northern lords were uneasy. They distrusted

England. They remembered the attempts to poison Shane O'Neill, the massacre of the Scots in Rathlin, Bingham's breaches of faith in Connacht, the kidnapping of Hugh O'Donnell, the execution of O'Neill of Clandeboye, O'Rourke of Breifne, MacMahon of Monaghan – the list of acts of violence and treachery that Ulster attributed to the queen's agents lengthened as the century progressed. The Ulster lords looked uneasily upon arrangements that were made within their own bounds, in Monaghan, in 1591. Soon they were determined to make no more such arrangements and to keep out a president, sheriffs, provost marshals, and English lawyers – men without sympathy who would, regardless of the consequences to the Gaelic communities, abolish all power that conflicted with the queen's.

The English conquistadores, for their part, accepted this challenge. Ulster was for them the recalcitrant Ireland, a possible point of entry for their continental enemies, a bad example for the uneasily converted, the cajoled, and the coerced of the other provinces. They believed that Hugh O'Neill would aid them and that Ulster, split by feuds, would never unite against them. If necessary, they would do by the strong hand in Ulster what had been done by negotiation in Connacht. They had no conception of the magnitude of their task; they did not foresee that they would have to fight as the English had never fought in Ireland before to prevent Ulster from undoing the Tudor conquest as a whole.

Some of the Ulster lords – in particular, Maguire – had been fighting to uphold their sovereignty and to keep the English out of Ulster since 1593. In 1595 Hugh O'Neill, earl of Tyrone, who had been assisting his more warlike neighbours for some time, openly joined them. From that moment until 1603, when Queen Elizabeth died, everything revolved round the issue of the Ulster war. It was the final contest which would decide the future of the Gaelic institutions and would complete – or make it impossible to complete – the Tudor conquest.

The leading spirit, the man who was so largely responsible for the long series of Irish successes in this struggle, was Hugh O'Neill. This man, who had plotted successfully to overcome his rivals in Tyrone and who claimed (like Shane O'Neill) that he was overlord of the greater part of

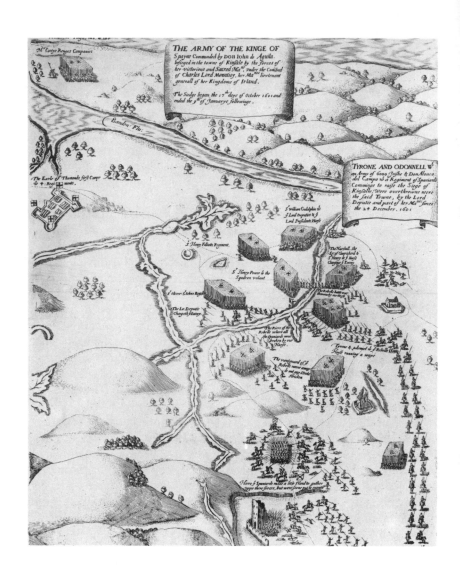

The labels within the illustration read:

Mr Earle Roques Companies

THE ARMY OF THE KINGE OF
Spayne Commanded by Don Iohn de Aquila.
besieged in the towne of Kinsale by the forces of
her victorious and Sacred Ma.ty vnder the Comānd
of Charles Lord Mountioy, her Ma.ties lieutenant
generall of her Kingdome of Irland.

The Siedge began the 17th daye of October 1601 and
ended the 9th of Ianuarye followinge.

Bandon Flu:

TYRONE AND ODONNELL W.th
an Army of 6000 foote & Don Alonzo
del Campo w.th a Regiment of Spaniards
Comminge to raise the Siege of
Kinsale, were overthrowne neere
the said Towne, by the Lord
Deputie and part of her Ma.ties forces
the 24 December, 1601

The Earle of Thomonds first Campe & 4 Regiments.

S.r William Godolphin w.th
y.e Lord Deputies & y.e
Lord Presidents Horse

S.r Henry Follietts Regiment

S.r Henry Power w.th the
Squadron volant

The Marshall, the
L.d of Clangboord &
S.r Henry & y.e Horse
Charginge y.e Enemy

S.r Oliver S.t Iohns Regim.t

The Le: Deputie
Chargeth y.e Enemy

The Rebels battle
beeinge in disorder

The River of the
Rebells where all
the Spaniards were
broken by our
Horse

Tyrone & a squadron of y.e Rebells Comp.t
flinge running a waye

The vantgarde of y.e
Rebells meeninge
to ayd the Strait
flaunke

These y.e Spaniards made a litle stand to gather
vpp there forces, but were forced out to retyre.

69   The battle of Kinsale, 1601, from [Thomas Stafford], *Pacata Hibernia*, 1633

Ulster, was a courageous and a cautious leader. Occasionally emotion overcame him, but ordinarily he was crafty, calculating, and ambitious. He loved power, and the realisation that the queen would not tolerate his continued exercise of it was undoubtedly his chief motive in taking up arms. O'Neill knew that there could be no separate solution for Ulster, and consequently he tried to involve the whole country in the war. The English said that the Irish hoped 'to recover their ancient land and territories out of the Englishmen's hands',[9] to bring all Ireland under Gaelic rule, and to make O'Neill the lieutenant of the pope and the king of Spain – England's ecclesiastical and civil enemies. O'Neill would probably have settled for less, perhaps for non-interference with the Gaelic lords, the employment of Irishmen in offices of state, and freedom for catholicism. But both sides were driven to extremes. The aid of England's national enemy, Spain, became essential for O'Neill, and his acceptance of it increased what was, from the English viewpoint, his guilt. The old Tudor fear became a reality. Queen Elizabeth's enemies were using Ireland to injure England.

Until the end of 1601, when the Spaniards came, the Ulstermen remained on the defensive. They repulsed attacks in the two areas where it was possible to mount attacks against them, over the Blackwater north of Armagh and over the Erne at Ballyshannon. Their hope was to avoid any defeat – which would have broken up their confederacy – and to prolong the war; if they were still in the field when Elizabeth died they might make better terms.

O'Neill fought in the traditional Irish way. He attacked moving columns of the English and laid ambushes, some of which developed – like Clontibret in 1595 – into battles. His soldiers were musketeers, calivermen, and pikemen, like the English, and he did not lack firearms. He was an outstanding organiser and he perfected a system of native mercenaries called bonnachts which provided him with a trained army of almost 10,000 men in 1601.

Until 1597 the English merely marched into the Irish territories and left garrisons in castles or roughly constructed forts. O'Neill's great victory at the Yellow Ford, north of Armagh, in 1598 made them more

187

cautious. After that they tried simultaneous attacks on south-west and south-east Ulster, the entries to O'Donnell's country and to O'Neill's. When Lord Deputy Mountjoy, the best of their soldiers, came in 1600 they multiplied their garrisons, and introduced a policy of frightfulness. They destroyed their enemy's corn in the fields, burnt houses, and carried on the war through the winter. They used their sea power to make a landing behind O'Neill's back at Derry (1600).

Still, the Ulstermen remained unsubdued, and when the Spaniards arrived in Kinsale O'Neill and O'Donnell marched south to join them. But this involved their assumption of the offensive, which was a new departure for them, and when they tried to cooperate with the besieged Spaniards at Kinsale their efforts met with disaster. Despite their years of military success, the Irish were unable to fight the kind of formal battle which their opponents – fully realising their own danger of being caught between the two fires – were quick to force upon them. When Mountjoy showed that he was going to attack them outside Kinsale, the Irish infantry tried to array themselves in the massive formations which had for so long brought victory to their Spanish allies in the great continental battles of the age, but they had never fought in that way before. They were slow and inexpert in their movements, and, to increase their difficulties, their horsemen deserted them. Mountjoy's men came on. They overran the Irish piecemeal, one unwieldy division after another, and very soon all was over. O'Neill and his Ulster, Connacht, and Munster allies were completely defeated. The Spaniards soon surrendered the town of Kinsale and, in due course, the hitherto unsubdued Ulster was overrun. The war ended with O'Neill's submission in 1603.

The battle of Kinsale had decided everything. Mountjoy's victory meant the repulse of the Spanish invasion and the ultimate overthrow of O'Neill, O'Donnell, and their companions. It meant also the downfall of the last of the Gaelic lordships and the end of the old Irish world. Queen Elizabeth was dead by the time of O'Neill's surrender at Mellifont (30 March 1603), but the policy of her house had succeeded. Ireland, despite the resistance of so many of her lords, was conquered.

THE COLONISATION OF ULSTER AND THE REBELLION OF 1641

(1603–60)

by Aidan Clarke

The history of Ireland in the first half of the seventeenth century was rich in event, and perhaps bewildering in the number and complexity of the interests involved. The Irish, the old English, the new English, the royalists, the parliamentarians, and the Scots – each of them played their separate parts in the confusion of events. But what happened at that time can be summarised in a single brief sentence. The land of Ireland changed hands.

When the treaty of Mellifont brought the nine years war to an end, most of the land in every province was in the possession of catholics – some of them the descendants of early English settlers, but most of them the native Irish themselves. By 1660, catholics, whatever their origin, were allowed to own land only to the west of the river Shannon, in the province of Connacht and the county of Clare. Elsewhere, there were new landowners – Scots and English who had come to Ulster in the first decades of the century, and, in Leinster and Munster, more recent settlers who had arrived in the wake of Cromwell's armies in the 1650s.

The Tudor conquest of Ireland had arisen from the need to make a protestant England safe in a Europe divided by religion, but that conquest was not complete. It was a measure of 'the great O'Neill's' achievement that the nine years war ended, not in the punishment of the defeated rebels, but in a negotiated settlement. O'Neill and O'Donnell – earls of Tyrone and Tyrconnell – were allowed to return to their lands and live among their people.

The war had changed many things. Ulster was dotted with forts and garrisons, and no longer beyond the reach of English armies and English law. English authority extended, for the first time, over every part of Ireland, and the old Gaelic ways were withering. But O'Neill was still a force to be reckoned with, and the government had been glad enough to bring the war to a successful end, without insisting upon any compensation for its long and costly effort.

Circumstances quickly changed however: and the opportunity to make a much more profitable use of victory soon presented itself. For O'Neill and many of his followers were unwilling to accept the new order of things – unable to settle down as ordinary landlords where they had lately been independent princes. After four resentful years of subjection to the English crown, O'Neill took ship, at Rathmullan in Lough Swilly (3 September 1607), and went into voluntary exile on the Continent. With him went O'Donnell and more than ninety of the leading men of Ulster.

The 'flight of the earls' left Ulster leaderless, and the government jubilant. There was no longer any need for caution or conciliation in Ulster. The exiles had left their people defenceless, and presented the government with an ideal opportunity to solve the problem of Ireland's chief trouble spot. The ideal solution had been known for generations. It was, in a word, plantation. The idea of plantation was straightforward. Land was the source of wealth and the basis of power. To take it from the catholic Irish and give it to protestant immigrants would at once weaken resistance to English rule and bring into being a protestant community sufficiently numerous, and sufficiently powerful to keep the peace in Ireland. If the Irish would not become protestant, then protestants must be brought to Ireland.

Under the Tudors, the idea had been experimented with only in the most half-hearted way, and the small groups of settlers 'planted' in Leix and Offaly in the 1550s and in Munster in the 1580s had made little difference to the balance of power in Ireland.

What was planned in Ulster after the 'flight of the earls' was much more ambitious and much more systematic. In each county to be planted the native Irish were to be segregated in defined areas, so that a network of new, entirely protestant, communities could be created. Preparations

70 Donegal Castle: a Jacobean mansion added *c.* 1615 to an O'Donnell tower-house (15th–16th century) by the English 'servitor', Captain Basil Brooke, to whom the house and adjoining lands were granted under the plantation scheme (photo. Bord Fáilte Éireann)

went ahead rapidly. Much of the land was confiscated in the six counties of Armagh, Cavan, Coleraine, Donegal, Fermanagh, and Tyrone, and then granted out again in lots of from one to two thousand acres at easy rents, on condition that those who received it should bring in protestant tenants to cultivate the soil and build defences – a castle and a bawn – for the safety of the settlement. The region between the Foyle and the Bann was treated as exceptional: for it the city of London was enlisted as collective 'undertaker', with special obligations (including the rebuilding of the ruined city of Derry), and special privileges. Hence Derry was renamed Londonderry, while the former county of Coleraine, augmented by territory hitherto part of Tyrone, became the county of Londonderry.

In the years after 1609, the plantation gradually took shape. Settlers arrived in Ulster – many of them from England, many more from the lowlands of Scotland. With them they brought their own traditions, their own institutions, and their own familiar way of life. They levelled the forests and devoted themselves to arable farming, rejecting the pastoral ways of the Irish. They built towns and villages of neat timber-framed

71 Magherafelt and Salterstown, county Londonderry, in 1622: plantation villages
built by the Salters' Company of London, from Sir Thomas Phillips's survey
(D.A. Chart (ed.), *Londonderry and the London companies, 1609–29*, 1928)

houses and thatched or slated stone cottages, carefully sited, and laid out
as fortified frontier posts. They established markets and local industries,
built churches and schools, and introduced the ordinary amenities of life
to which they had been accustomed at home – and some, indeed, which
were unusual, as in Moneymore in County Londonderry where the residents were provided with a piped water supply. The changes which these
numerous and socially diversified protestant newcomers wrought in
Ulster were dramatic and far-reaching. A whole new society was created,
one which was not only entirely alien to the native traditions of the area,
but also entirely different in character from every other part of Ireland. It
was not just the protestantism of the planters that made Ulster distinctive, but their whole way of life. Nonetheless, the colony did not go completely according to plan, for there were not enough settlers to exploit the
resources of the province in full. The segregation plan was not carried
out; the native Irish remained, as tenants and labourers, but were gradually forced by economic pressure to move to the worst lands. As a result,
the supposedly protestant area was riddled with native Irish catholics –

embittered and degraded, waiting their chance to strike back.

In the years in which the plantation was being established, however, little attention was paid to the native Irish, and they, in their turn, remained relatively quiet. The government took it for granted that they were disloyal, and suspected that the chief among them were in constant communication with England's enemies on the Continent. In many cases, the government was right. Ireland had its place in the reckonings of catholic European statesmen. When the catholic archbishop of Armagh died in 1625, for instance, the choice of a new primate assumed an international significance: both France and Spain sponsored candidates. The candidate of Spain, which was at war with England and hoped to have the Irish as allies, was successful.

But the significant link between Ireland and Europe was religious, not political. It was not Spain which was of the first importance, but Rome, for these were the years of the counter-reformation – of the catholic church's drive to recover the ground lost to protestantism. At its most spectacular level, the counter-reformation was concerned with politics, but it also involved a sustained organisational effort to improve the routine administration of the church's affairs and some of Rome's attention was devoted to making provision for the regular servicing of the church in Ireland. Arrangements were made to ensure a constant supply of clergy, to encourage the expansion of religious orders, and to create educational facilities in Europe for young men from Ireland who wished to enter the priesthood. Throughout the early seventeenth century, this work of organisation and invigoration was going steadily on, and the position of the church in Ireland was being consolidated. Bishops were appointed to sees which had long been vacant, the religious orders – and the Franciscans in particular – recruited members widely and set up many new houses, and a steady stream of young men crossed to the Continent, to enter one or other of the twenty Irish colleges which prepared them for the Irish mission, or to become, like Luke Wadding, statesmen of the church, and advisers to the papacy. And this intimate and continuous contact with continental catholicism was the lifeline of the faith in Ireland.

Within Ireland itself, the government had quickly found that to defeat the Irish was not to defeat catholicism – for there existed in Ireland a large and influential group which was, though catholic in religion, English by descent, the group called the 'Old English'. They no longer, of course, controlled the government of Ireland, as they had in the past, but they still owned one-third of the country's land, and they were still loyal to the English crown. But they were seriously disturbed by the fear that England no longer valued their allegiance, that the government tended to assume that all catholics were disloyal and would no longer be prepared to distinguish between the native Irish and themselves. If this were so, then the government might be expected to accept remorselessly the first opportunity to deprive them of their land. For some years political interest centred upon their attempts to persuade the government to renounce any such intention, and to allow an act of parliament to be passed giving them full security.

The government was not, in fact, disposed to trust them, but necessity compelled it to act as if it did. When Charles I came to the throne in 1625 and launched into a war against Spain, financial difficulties prompted him to grant concessions to the Old English in return for a large sum of money. In the 'Graces', which he granted in 1628, he promised them the guarantee which they had asked for – and in doing so, he seemed to be recognising that their position was indeed unique, and that they were entitled, though catholic, to special consideration. But when the war came to an end, and the money was spent, his promise was broken, and the Graces repudiated.

It took skill and ruthlessness to weather the effect of this breach of faith. They were provided by a new lord deputy, Viscount Wentworth, who arrived in 1633 and set about the task of making Ireland self-supporting and rescuing its government from the local pressures which his predecessors had been unable to resist. Within six years, he achieved his aims, building a strong, efficient, and independent administration which fearlessly attacked the interests of every important group in Ireland. To the Old English it was his treatment of the Irish parliament that was the most ominous. Tradition had long accustomed them to regard that parlia-

72 King Charles I, 1625–49, by Daniel Mytens, 1631 (National Portrait Gallery London)

ment as embodying their right to participate in the business of government from time to time, and to be consulted about matters of policy. The first breach in that tradition had come with the plantation in Ulster, which had naturally led to a considerable increase in the number of protestant members of parliament. Nonetheless, when parliament met in 1613, the Old English were still sufficiently powerful to frustrate an attempt by the government to introduce anti-catholic legislation. But the very fact that such an attempt was made revealed clearly that if the Old English were to maintain their position in Ireland they must continue to control parliament. When Wentworth convened a parliament in 1634, however, it became evident that they had failed to do so. Wentworth exploited the occasion adroitly. By refusing to allow parliament to deal with any business other than that presented to it by the government, he made constructive opposition impossible. And by arranging for the election of a group of government officials, who held the balance of power in the house of commons, he was able to play catholic against protestant to secure approval of a government policy which included the repudiation of the more important of the Graces. The Old English, who looked upon parliament as a means of protection against the government, discovered that in Wentworth's hands it had become another weapon against them.

195

73 Thomas Wentworth, 1st earl of Strafford, after Van Dyck (National Portrait Gallery, London)

It was this success in exploiting the Irish parliament that made it possible for the lord deputy to disregard local interests entirely in the years following. One quarter of catholic land in Connacht was confiscated, and for the first time no distinction was made between Irish and Old English. Many of the planters in Ulster were penalised for failing to fulfil the conditions on which they had received their grants, and proceedings were taken against the presbyterian practices which the Ulster Scots had brought with them from Scotland. The members of the protestant establishment were cold-shouldered and deprived of the influence and the profits of government to which they had been accustomed. While Wentworth was in Ireland, there was no effective opposition to him: but as soon as he was called back to England in 1639, all those whom he had antagonised made common cause against him in the Irish parliament.

It was at this point that the turn of events in England began to have a decisive influence upon what happened in Ireland. Wentworth had been recalled because religious disagreements between the king of England and the presbyterians in Scotland had ended in open war. In the summer of 1640, the Scots were victorious. When Charles asked the English parliament for help, it turned upon him and used his difficulties to demand a series of reforms which stripped him of much of his power.

At first, all this seemed very much to the advantage of discontented groups in Ireland. The Old English, the planters in Ulster, and many of

196

74   Sir Phelim O'Neill: contemporary
print (British Museum, Department of
Prints and Drawings)

the protestants in other parts of Ireland joined together in the Irish
parliament to destroy the inconveniently powerful system of government
which Wentworth had created. Exception was taken to almost everything
he had done in Ireland. Even his largely ineffectual attempts to promote
economic enterprises were held against him, and he was alleged to have
harmed Irish trade – though its seems clear that it was during his rule that
the Irish economy fully recovered from the setbacks which it suffered
from the Elizabethan wars. The attack upon Wentworth was not
confined to Ireland. The Irish parliament cooperated enthusiastically
with the English parliament in preparing a charge of treason against him:
together, they succeeded in bringing about his execution in 1641. At the
same time, the Old English were able to use the king's troubles in
England to persuade him to grant, once again, the Graces, and to agree
to abandon the idea of planting Connacht.

Experience showed, however, that promises were not enough. The
Old English were convinced that they could not safely continue to enjoy
their property and their freedom of worship unless they could establish
firmly their right to use the Irish parliament to protect themselves against
future changes in government policy. They tried, therefore, to persuade
Charles to allow parliament to play a more independent and influential
role in the government of Ireland. Charles, however, who had already
found ·it impossible to resist similar demands from the English
parliament, was not prepared to agree to any reduction of his authority in
Ireland, and the Old English were forced to rest content with his
assurances of good will. But even while some in Ireland were doing their

197

best to take advantage of the position in which the king's difficulties in England had placed him, others were beginning to realise that that weakness might prove very much to the disadvantage of catholics in Ireland. For the English parliament was militantly and intolerantly protestant, and so were its allies, the Scots. If either of the two should use their new power to take a hand in Irish affairs, there was every reason to believe that their policy would be to suppress the catholic worship which Charles permitted, and to extend the area of plantation.

The fear that this would sooner or later happen, was one of the motives which prompted some of the Irish, particularly in Ulster, to begin to think in terms of an armed rising. It was not the only reason. The Irish in Ulster had never reconciled themselves to English rule nor to the plantation: they had always hoped to recover the property and the social position which had been taken from them. In 1641, they saw their chance to profit from English divisions. Their plan was to seize Dublin castle, to capture the principal members of the government, and at the same time to take possession of the chief strongholds in Ulster in a series of local risings.

If they had succeeded, they might very well have found themselves, overnight, in a position to dictate terms to the king and parliament of England. But they did not succeed. On 22 October, the eve of the day appointed, a drunken indiscretion led to the discovery of their plan. The key men were captured, and the attack on Dublin castle never took place. But the local risings in Ulster went according to plan, and the movement spread rapidly and widely under the leadership of Sir Phelim O'Neill. O'Neill and his followers denied that they were rebels. They insisted that they had risen in arms to defend themselves and to protect the king from the English parliament. To attract support, O'Neill went to the trouble of forging instructions from Charles ordering the Ulstermen to rise in his defence. And each of his followers was required to take an oath of loyalty to the king.

At first, the Ulster Irish met with only local resistance. It was not until they had established themselves in control of most of Ulster and marched south into Louth and Meath, that they had their first engagement with

75 Plan of Drogheda in 1657, by Robert Newcomen (John D'Alton, *History of Drogheda*, 1844). A good example of a medieval walled town – or rather pair of towns, as there were originally separate boroughs north and south of the river Boyne, each with its own walls and gates. The barbican of St Lawrence's gate (A) is the most impressive remnant of the thirteenth-century fortifications. The Magdalene tower (B) is part of a Dominican friary, where Richard II held court in 1395. A century later, Poynings held his famous parliament in the town. When Cromwell stormed Drogheda in 1649 he broke in at St Mary's churchyard (C) in the south-east corner. The steep height of Millmount (D) was then seized and the defenders put to the sword. Another place of refuge, the steeple of St Peter's church (E), was burned by Cromwell's orders, and a ruthless slaughter of garrison and townspeople followed

199

government troops. At Julianstown Bridge, not far outside Drogheda, they defeated a small detachment marching to the relief of the town. Almost immediately afterwards, as they laid siege to Drogheda, they were joined by the Old English of the area, and the combined forces began to call themselves the 'Catholic Army'. The Old English made common cause with their Ulster fellow-catholics because they too were suspicious of the English parliament's intentions, because the government in Ireland had made it clear that it did not trust them and would not defend them, and because they were satisfied that the northern Irish remained loyal to the king. In the early months of 1642, the movement spread throughout Ireland, and success seemed near. Then, reinforcements began to arrive from England and the government began to recover ground. By April, the northerners had been pushed back into Ulster, and many of those in arms were anxious for peace. But the government was not prepared to negotiate. It was determined to seize the chance to subdue Ireland once and for all. The English parliament, indeed, had already begun to borrow large sums of money on the security of the land which it expected to confiscate in Ireland.

It had become obvious that this was to be a fight to the finish. So, at the prompting of the clergy, arrangements were made to set up a central organisation to direct the war. It was agreed that a representative assembly should meet in Kilkenny in October 1642. By the time it met, the situation had changed in two important ways. The king and parliament of England had finally gone to war with one another: and exiles had begun to return from the Continent to lend a hand in Ireland, many of them experienced professional soldiers, and among them Colonel Owen Roe O'Neill and Colonel Thomas Preston.

For some seven years thereafter the situation was extremely confused. The king maintained an army in Ireland under the command of the earl of Ormond, but his sole desire was to come to terms so that he could concentrate his resources upon the civil war against parliament in England, if possible with Irish help. The English parliament gradually built up an army in Ireland, but made little real effort to prosecute the war since it regarded the defeat of the king in England as its first priority.

76   Maps by J.G. Simms
showing
the proportion of land
owned by catholics in
Ireland according
to counties, in 1641,
1688 and 1703. The effect
of the Cromwellian
confiscation, as modified
at the restoration,
is indicated by the first
and second maps, the
effect of the Williamite
confiscation by the
second and third maps

201

The Scots also kept an army on foot in Ireland, but it was active only in defence of the planters in Ulster. The Confederate Catholics, as they called themselves, had adopted a hopeful motto – 'Ireland united for God, king, and country' – but they were, nonetheless, divided. On the one hand were the Old English, who had little to gain and much to lose, and who were prepared to agree upon moderate terms with Charles. On the other hand were the Irish, led now by returned exiles and by an Italian papal nuncio, Archbishop Rinuccini. These men, knowing little of the circumstances in which the war had begun, and paying little attention to the danger of Charles being defeated by parliament, insisted upon seizing the chance to demand the full recognition of catholicism and the restoration of confiscated lands to the Irish. No agreement proved possible, and the war dragged on, distinguished only by a masterly victory over the Scots won by O'Neill at Benburb on the Blackwater in 1646. It was not until the English civil war came to an end with the trial and execution of Charles in 1649, that events in Ireland took a decisive turn. The years of opportunity had been wasted in haggling and bargaining with Charles while the really formidable enemy, the English parliament, had built up its strength.

When that parliament had disposed of Charles, and abolished the monarchy in its own favour, it turned its attention to Ireland. Its ingrained distrust of catholicism was inflamed by exaggerated reports of the brutality with which the Ulster planters had been treated in 1641. And when Oliver Cromwell landed at Dublin with a puritan army in 1649, his mission was not only conquest but also revenge. The indiscriminate inhumanity with which that revenge was exacted upon the royalist garrison and many of the townspeople of Drogheda, and upon the defenders of Wexford, became indelibly impressed upon the folk memory of the Irish. So too did the severity of the settlement which followed the overcoming of Irish resistance. But that severity was not indiscriminate. Not many were executed for their part in the rebellion. Men in arms were treated leniently enough: they were allowed to emigrate to the Continent, and more than 30,000 took advantage of the opportunity. The poor were left undisturbed: a general pardon was issued, and they were able to resume their ordinary lives without fear of punishment. It was the wealth of the land of Ireland that the government of England was interested in. And it reserved its special fury for those who owned that land. It divided catholic landowners in Ireland into two groups – those who had been guilty of involvement in the rebellion, and those who had not. The first were to lose all their estates, and all their property rights. The second were to be allowed to own a proportion of the amount of land which they had held. But it was not to be the same land. Ireland, also, was to be divided into two parts. The first part was to consist of Connacht and Clare, to which all who had established their innocence were to be transplanted and in which they were to receive the land to which they were entitled. The second part was to be the remaining twenty-six counties, in which confiscated land was used to pay the government's creditors – the adventurers who had lent money or provided supplies for the army, and the officers and soldiers who had served without adequate pay.

Though some of the ordinary soldiers did settle on the small pieces of land which they were given, most sold out their interest and returned to England. Those of the officers and adventurers who had received substantial grants were more apt to stay. In fact, the arrangements made for the settlement of Irish land under Cromwell never approached the thoroughness intended by those who had planned the earlier plantation in Ulster. No organised attempt was made to establish protestant communities, except in the towns. What was changed was the people who owned the land, not the people who lived and worked upon it. The Cromwellian settlement was not so much a plantation, as a transference of the sources of wealth and power from catholics to protestants. What it created was not a protestant community, but a protestant upper class.

Though dramatic changes were to come in the years following, when Charles I's son was restored to the English throne, the newcomers managed to hold on to a great deal of what they had gained. And just as James I's plantation had permanently altered the character of Ulster, so Cromwell's settlement transformed the character of the landowning aristocracy of Ireland.

13

THE RESTORATION AND THE JACOBITE WAR

(1660–91)

by J. G. Simms

In 1660 the English commonwealth collapsed and Charles II was called home. Catholics had fought for the royalist cause in Ireland and many of them had followed Charles into exile. They now looked forward to toleration of their faith and recovery of their lands. The king himself was sympathetic, but he had been recalled by the commonwealth army, and it insisted that Cromwell's land settlement should be maintained. Charles made promises to both sides. Cromwellian soldiers and adventurers should keep what they had; catholics should get back what they had lost for the sake of religion or support of the king. It was impossible to satisfy everyone. As Ormond, the lord lieutenant, remarked: 'there must be new discoveries of a new Ireland, for the old will not serve to satisfy these engagements'.[1]

An act – the act of settlement – was passed by an all-protestant parliament to give effect to the king's declaration. Innocents – the term was strictly defined – and a number of specially named royalists were to get their lands, and the Cromwellians were to be compensated with other lands of equal value. But such lands were not to be found, and it was necessary to pass a second act to explain the first one. This laid down that most Cromwellians should give up one-third of their lands so that some catholics could be restored. About five hundred catholics had been declared innocent before the court closed down. Most of them and a number of influential individuals got back at least some of their former property. Many claimants were left unsatisfied, and the Gaelic Irish came off worst of all. Cromwellians resented having to give up even part of

77 James Butler, 1st duke of Ormond, by Sir Peter Lely (National Gallery of Ireland)

their estates, and recovery was a slow and troublesome business, even for those catholics who recovered something. Many who failed to do so, turned 'tory', took to the hills and woods, and raided the new settlers. Redmond O'Hanlon in Armagh and the three Brennans in Kilkenny were famous tories of this time.

When stock was taken of the restoration settlement, catholic land-owners were better off than they had been under Cromwell, but they had recovered only a fraction of their original estates. In 1641, before the war began, they had owned about three-fifths of the land. At the end of the restoration period they owned little more than one-fifth. They resented the settlement as a breach of faith, and were ready to take the first chance of upsetting it. In later years Dean Swift was to sum up their attitude:

The catholics of Ireland. . . lost their estates for fighting in defence of their king. Those who cut off the father's head, forced the son to fly for his life, and over-turned the whole ancient frame of government. . . obtained grants of those very

205

estates the catholics lost in defence of the ancient consitution, and thus they gained by their rebellion what the catholics lost by their loyalty.[2]

A catholic bishop denounced the settlement as repugnant to God and nature. The poet Ó Bruadair lamented the purgatory of the men of Ireland and railed at the low breeding of the Cromwellians:

Roughs formed from the dregs of each base trade, who range themselves snugly in the houses of the noblest chiefs, as proud and genteel as if sons of gentlemen.[3]

Religion was the other great question of the reign, and there were many ups and downs in the fortunes of the catholic church. Ormond was willing to grant toleration in return for an unquestioning acknowledgement of the state's authority and a denial of the pope's right to depose a king. He demanded that catholics should sign a declaration to this effect – the remonstrance drawn up by the Franciscan, Peter Walsh. But its terms were unacceptable to the church, and no concordat was reached. In practice the church was tolerated for much of the time, but there were often changes in the official attitude, and the hysteria of the 'popish plot' in England had its counterpart in Ireland. Archbishop Peter Talbot died in prison; Archbishop Oliver Plunkett was martyred on the scaffold.

The twenty-five years of Charles II's reign were in many ways a period of frustration and anxiety for catholics, and of uneasy dominance for protestants. But they were also a period of unusual peace and economic expansion in Ireland, in spite of restrictions imposed by English trading policy. The export of Irish cattle was banned, and Irish wool was reserved for England. But a flourishing butter and meat trade developed; Irish wool found a ready market in England and was often smuggled to the Continent. The population grew, and by the end of the reign Ireland had nearly two million inhabitants (three-quarters of them catholic). Dublin was the second city in these islands and its population was estimated at over 60,000. Cork and Limerick were prosperous sea ports. Protestants, besides owning most of the land, held a dominant position in administration and commerce. But there remained a nucleus of catholic nobility and landed gentry, lawyers, and traders, who could form the basis for a catholic revival if a favourable opportunity should arise.

78 Richard Talbot, duke of
Tyrconnell (National
Portrait Gallery, London)

That opportunity came in 1685, when Charles died and was succeeded
by his catholic brother, James II. Catholics in Ireland now hoped for a
new deal; the alteration of the land settlement and the recognition of
their church. But James was king of England: the land settlement and the
established Church of Ireland were regarded as essential props of English
rule, and James was committed to maintaining them. Protestants were
anxious for the future, but took comfort from the king's assurances and
from the appointment of his protestant brother-in-law, Lord Clarendon,
as lord lieutenant. Clarendon's first speech was a life-line for protestant
landlords:

I have the king's commands to declare upon all occasions that, whatever
imaginary. . . apprehensions any men here may have had, his majesty hath no
intention of altering the acts of settlement.[4]

207

But it was soon clear that the real power lay with Richard Talbot, brother of the dead archbishop; he had long been James's intimate and had shown himself an able and forceful advocate of catholic claims. He was made earl of Tyrconnell and head of the Irish army, which he proceeded to reorganise by dismissing many protestants and appointing catholics instead. Clarendon was soon recalled and Tyrconnell took his place as viceroy. The appointment of the first catholic viceroy for over a hundred years was welcomed by Irish catholics and lampooned by an English protestant:

> Ho, brother Teig, dost hear de decree,
> Dat we shall have a new deputy;
> Ho, by my soul, it is a Talbot,
> And he will cut all de English throat.[5]

Catholic judges and privy councillors were appointed, and more and more key posts in the administration were filled with catholics. The Church of Ireland was not disestablished, but there was a marked unwillingness on the part of catholics to pay dues to protestant ministers. Church vacancies were left unfilled, and the income used to give subsidies to catholic bishops.

Protestants took fright; merchants called in their stocks and pessimists left for England. Everything seemed to turn on the land settlement, and there was a growing demand by catholics for its repeal. Judge Rice said he would drive a coach and six through the act of settlement. Counsellor Nagle in the famous Coventry letter argued that, if James died without a son, catholics would have no security unless they were entrenched as landed proprietors: the settlement must be altered while the going was good. The Cromwellian mapmaker, Sir William Petty, and his friend Southwell compared the settlement to a ship in a stormy sea, and to St Sebastian shot through with arrows. Preparations were made for a parliament in which the protestant monopoly of Charles II's reign should be replaced by an overwhelmingly catholic membership. Town charters were revoked and the new corporations were mainly catholic.

Two catholic judges went over to England to get the king's approval to

79 Patrick Sarsfield, earl of Lucan (Franciscan House of Studies, Killiney, co. Dublin)

a bill for the alteration of the settlement. They were greeted by a London mob carrying potatoes stuck on poles and shouting 'make way for the Irish ambassadors'. The parliament that Tyrconnell planned to hold threatened to bring about a reversal of the long-standing protestant predominance in Ireland and to put a catholic predominance in its place. The situation seemed ripe for a catholic take-over, supported by the full weight of government influence.

But revolution in England again frustrated the hopes of Irish catholics. James II's policy of favouring his co-religionists had aroused the opposition of English protestants, and the birth of a son to him gave the prospect of a continuing catholic dynasty. In 1688 seven English notables invited Wiliam of Orange, husband of James's protestant daughter, to invade England and drive out his father-in-law. The king's cause quickly collapsed in England, and he took refuge in the France of Louis XIV. But Tyrconnell held out for him in Ireland, and could count on the willing help of the catholics, who saw in James the only hope for their land and their religion. Protestants grew still more alarmed: migration assumed panic proportions, and the Ulster colonists prepared for armed resistance. In March 1689 James landed at Kinsale with French money and arms. His chief interest in Ireland was as a stepping-stone to the recovery of his throne, and he was unwilling to weaken the English hold on Ireland. The Irish were chiefly interested in James as a means of getting the land settlement altered and the position of the catholic church secured. James was forced to summon the parliament that a later generation was to call the 'patriot parliament' because it asserted its independence of the parliament of England. The declaratory act laid down the principle of the sovereignty of the 'king, lords, and commons' of Ireland a century before Grattan and the Volunteers. After much wrangling the land settlement was reversed and the property of the Williamites as rebels was declared to be confiscated. Liberty of conscience was decreed; tithes were to be paid by catholics to their priests, by protestants to their ministers. Irish trade was to be freed from the restrictions of English law, and a ban was placed on the import of English coal.

The proceedings of the parliament represented, though not completely, the aspirations of the 'Old English' – catholics of English stock – rather than those of the Gaelic Irish. Had James won the war, its legislation would have replaced a protestant oligarchy by a catholic oligarchy; it would not have undone the English conquest or restored Gaelic rule. James insisted on the maintenance of Poynings' law to ensure Ireland's subordination to the English crown, and the protestant Church of Ireland was not officially disestablished. Catholics were disillusioned by the king 'with his one shoe English and his one shoe Irish', who appeared bent on appeasing his protestant subjects. The parliament was in any case ill-timed, as its effectiveness depended on a Jacobite victory, and its debates distracted attention from the conduct of the war, which was the real business in hand.

The war that followed was a major crisis in our history. In Irish it is called 'Cogadh an dá rí', the war of the two kings, *Rí Séamus* and *Rí Liam,* but it was much more than that. It confirmed the change of kings in England and established a protestant succession. But in the European context it was an important theatre of a war between France and a league

80   James II landing at Kinsale, 12 March 1689; contemporary Dutch print
(National Gallery of Ireland)

of lesser powers – a league that crossed religious boundaries. The Holy
Roman Emperor and the catholic king of Spain were William's allies, and
the pope himself was no friend to Louis XIV, the patron of James. Both
sides fought with international armies, and Irish battles made headlines
in several countries of Europe. In the Irish context the war was a struggle
between protestant and catholic, the newer settlers and the older
inhabitants. It was more closely balanced than any previous contest.
Both sides were proud of their achievements and have enshrined them in
their folklore. Catholic memories of Sarsfield and Limerick are matched
by protestant pride in Derry, Enniskillen, and the Boyne.

211

The conflict began with the armed resistance of the Ulster colonists in Derry and Enniskillen. Derry endured the greater hardship and got the better publicity. They found a forceful leader in the Rev. George Walker, whose diary of the three-months siege is a memorable record of courage and suffering. Derry was at the point of starvation when the relief ships broke through the boom and brought supplies to the beleaguered city. The Inniskillingers showed dash and military skill, and their victory at Newtownbutler was a major success. James's failure to reduce the north was fatal to his cause. His army retired and the way was clear for a Williamite landing under the veteran Marshal Schomberg.

Next year — in 1690 – the French sent 7,000 troops, but demanded that as many Irish troops should be sent to France in their place. Soon afterwards William himself came over to Ireland. It was a risky step, for England was threatened by France and he had not command of the sea. While he was in Ireland the French defeated the English and Dutch fleets at Beachy Head, and the way seemed clear for a French invasion of England, which, however, did not take place.

The two kings met at the Boyne, where James had drawn up his Irish and French troops on the southern bank. William had the larger army – about 36,000 as compared with James's 25,000. William's troops included Dutch, Danes, Germans, and Huguenots as well as British. He was not a great general, but showed himself a brave and reckless soldier. The day before the battle he was wounded by an Irish shot, and reports of his death got as far as Paris, where bells were rung and bonfires were lighted. It was only a flesh-wound, and with the phlegmatic remark 'it's well it came no nearer' he resumed his reconnoitring. The battle took place on 1 July by the old calendar, (12 July new style) and its centre was the ford at Oldbridge about three miles above Drogheda. There was sharp fighting at the river crossing, and William at the head of the Inniskillingers had a difficult passage. The Irish cavalry fought well, but at the end of the day James had fled, his army was in full retreat, and William was clearly the winner. In a military sense it was not a decisive victory; the Irish losses were small and their army lived to fight another day. But it was reported all over Europe, and it had a great psychological effect. *Te deums* were sung in the catholic cathedrals of Austria for the victory. Dublin and eastern Ireland fell to William, and the Jacobites made a disordered retreat to the Shannon. William thought that all resistance was over, and demanded unconditional surrender. Tyrconnell and the French took much the same view of the situation.

But the Irish had a spirited leader in Patrick Sarsfield, who inspired the defence of Limerick and contributed to it by blowing up William's siege train at Ballyneety (11 August 1690). The walls of Limerick were breached, but fiercely held, and William had to go back to England with his work half done. Tyrconnell and the French troops left for France. Sarsfield remained in effective command till the following year, when Tyrconnell returned and the French commander St Ruth arrived. French soldiers did not return and for the rest of the war the Jacobite army was predominantly Irish.

The war dragged on into 1691, when Ginkel, the Dutch general, crossed the Shannon at Athlone, where the bridge was the scene of desperate struggle. This was followed by 'Aughrim's dread disaster', the major battle of the war. St Ruth, the French commander, had chosen a strong position on the slopes of Kilcommodon hill. Ginkel's army floundered in the bog that separated the armies, and St Ruth called on his men to drive the enemy to the gates of Dublin. Then at a critical stage of the battle St Ruth was killed; a causeway through the bog was betrayed to Ginkel's men and confusion set in on the Irish side. Their losses were heavy, and Ginkel won an impressive victory.

William was anxious to bring the war in Ireland to an end as soon as possible, so that he could transfer his army to the Continent where it was badly needed for the defence of Holland. On his behalf Ginkel had been bargaining with the Irish catholics, offering toleration for their religion and security for their property in return for surrender. After Aughrim, Galway accepted the terms. The townsmen and the garrison were given guarantees for their property; priests and people were to be allowed the private practice of their religion.

Limerick was now the last place of importance to hold out. The Irish had little prospect of successful resistance, and their chief thoughts were

81   The battle of the Boyne, 1 July 1690,

of what bargain they could strike with Ginkel. The French officers urged them to hold on as long as possible, so as to keep William's army in Ireland for another campaigning season. They promised aid from France, but the Irish were disillusioned with Louis XIV, who had given them much less help than they had expected. They had no wish to be

214

by Theodore Maas (National Library of Ireland)

expended in the interests of French long-term strategy. Tyrconnell died and Sarsfield, who had in the year before been the mainstay of resistance, now thought it useless to go on. He decided to make terms with Ginkel, and after more than a week of bargaining the treaty of Limerick was signed (3 October 1691). It was agreed that as many of the Irish soldiers

215

as wished should be given liberty and transport to go to France and fight on there. Sarsfield and some 14,000 others left Ireland, the forerunners of the 'wild geese' who in the eighteenth century made a name for themselves at Fontenoy and on many other European battlefields. Sarsfield himself had little longer to live; in less than two years he was fatally wounded at the battle of Landen. But he had made a remarkable reputation, and his memory has been preserved in Irish songs and folklore.

For those that stayed behind, the Limerick terms seemed not ungenerous. Catholics were offered such rights of worship as they had enjoyed in Charles II's reign or were consistent with the laws of Ireland. Those who were in Limerick or other garrisons that resisted to the end were promised their property and the right to practice their professions. Sarsfield insisted that this guarantee should extend to those under the protection of the Irish in some counties of the west. Ginkel agreed, but when the treaty reached London the clause was missing, and a lengthy argument resulted in the protestant Irish parliament refusing to ratify it.

The treaty of Limerick was of great advantage to William, as it ended a troublesome side-show in Ireland and allowed him to transfer his troops to Flanders, where he was hard pressed by the French. But his protestant supporters in Ireland thought the terms of the treaty were foolishly generous, and their opposition resulted in the treaty giving catholics much less than they expected. A number of individuals were allowed to keep their property and the confiscation of land that followed the war was much less drastic than Cromwell's had been. Many were protected by the treaty, and the missing clause proved less important than catholics had feared. There was confiscation of the property of those who had gone to France, of those who had died, and of some of those who had surrendered prematurely. The catholic share of the land was in this way reduced to about one-seventh. But all catholics were soon subjected to new penal laws, and the century that followed was the classic age of protestant ascendancy.

14

THE AGE OF THE PENAL LAWS
(1691–1778)

by Maureen Wall

The treaty of Limerick in 1691 marked the third great defeat for the catholic cause in seventeenth-century Ireland. This time the victory seemed to be decisive, and the Irish parliament, now entirely protestant, soon set about buttressing protestant ascendancy in all walks of life. Members of the Church of Ireland were restored to their position as first-class citizens; protestant nonconformists and catholics were again made liable for payment of tithes to the established church, and a comprehensive series of new anti-catholic measures was passed. These laws, like all Irish legislation since 1494, had the prior sanction of the king and his council in England; for the parliament in Dublin throughout the eighteenth century was but a colonial-type parliament, subordinate to the government in London. Moreover in 1720 the right of the Westminster parliament to legislate for Ireland was formally declared by an act of that parliament (6 George I, c. 5). British policy for Ireland simply aimed at maintaining the connection between the two countries and ensuring that Ireland should not compete with the mother country in matters of trade. For centuries, restrictions had been imposed on Irish trade by the Westminster parliament, and now in 1699 Ireland's export trade in manufactured woollen goods was virtually destroyed. It was useless for men like William Molyneux to challenge the right of that parliament to legislate for Ireland; for, however much Irish members of parliament might resent the fact that the kingdom of Ireland was being treated as a colony, they realised that they were an isolated minority, surrounded by a potentially hostile catholic population, and dependent on the military strength of the mother country for protection against invasion by a foreign foe, or rebellion by the catholic majority in which they could lose everything.

To maintain the land settlement, therefore, and the protestant settlement in church and state, the Irish parliament enacted what came to be called the 'popery code', which would, they believed, keep the catholics in a state of permanent subjection. The Irish executive, headed by the lord lieutenant was not controlled by the Dublin parliament, and thus the British government, while being a party to the making of anti-catholic laws for Ireland, was also in a position to mitigate the severity of their enforcement; and so, by balancing one religious group against another, was able to use the age-old 'divide and rule' system to maintain its hold over the country.

It is important to remember that these laws were enacted against the background of a major European war in which Ireland had already been made the catspaw of the contending powers. Great numbers of Irish soldiers were in the army of Louis XIV of France, and might form the spearhead of an invasion force to which the Irish catholic population would certainly rally to restore the Stuarts to the throne. These soldiers of fortune were the famous 'wild geese'. It is not surprising, therefore, that members of an all-protestant parliament should have done everything in their power to retain for protestants their privileged position. Ruling minorities have done the same before and since in many parts of the world. Of course the persecution of protestants in France, Spain, and in the Empire was cited to justify the savage laws now passed against Irish catholics, but in these countries the members of the persecuted sect formed only a small minority, while Ireland was unique in Western Europe in that the persecuted formed the majority of the population.

Ostensibly the aim of the anti-catholic laws was to eradicate the catholic religion in Ireland, but in fact, apart from sporadic outbursts of persecution, the penal laws against religious worship were largely allowed to fall into desuetude from about 1716. Indeed, in the conditions prevailing in the eighteenth century their general enforcement would have proved an impossible task. The penal laws which were enforced, however, or which were automatic in their operation, were those which debarred catholics from parliament, from holding any government office

82 An Irish cabin, from
Arthur Young's *Tour in
Ireland* (1780)

– high or low – from entering the legal profession, and from holding commissions in the army and navy. This comprehensive exclusion was achieved by prescribing for all these offices and professions, qualifying oaths, which no catholic would take – oaths which contained such statements as the following.

I do solemnly and sincerely, in the presence of God, profess, testify and declare, that I do believe, that in the sacrament of the lord's supper there is not any transubstantiation of the elements of bread and wine into the body and blood of Christ, at or after the consecration thereof by any person whatsoever: and that the invocation, or adoration of the virgin Mary, or any other saint, and the sacrifice of the mass, as they are now used in the church of Rome, are superstitious and idolatrous. . .[1]

Great numbers of barristers and lawyers went over to the established church early in the century, including John Fitzgibbon, father of the future earl of Clare, chief architect of the act of union.

These qualifying oaths successfully closed all avenues of advancement to catholics in public life, though they were free, to a great extent, to amass wealth in trade and industry. Protestant supremacy could never be completely secured, however, while catholics retained any sizeable proportion of landed property. Even after the Williamite confiscation catholics

219

83 A wooden cross of the penal era
(National Museum of Ireland)

still owned about 14 per cent of Irish land. A system was devised, by acts passed in 1704 and 1709, which forbade catholics to buy land at all, or take leases for longer than 31 years, and which at the same time brought so many pressures, inducements, and prohibitions to bear on catholic land-owners, that by 1778 scarcely 5 per cent of Irish land was left in catholic hands. In the meantime, for one reason or another most of the catholic landlords – Viscount Fitzwilliam, Browne of the Neale, the earl of Antrim, Martin of Ballinahinch, French of Monivea, Lord Kingsland, Lord Mountgarrett, Lord Dunsany, and many others – had gone over to the established church, so that by 1778 catholic proprietors owned but £60,000 a year of the total rental of Ireland, then calculated at £4,000,000.

At the other end of the scale was the mass of the catholic peasantry, whose general condition of poverty and wretchedness was not due to the penal laws, and to whom it mattered little whether their landlords were catholic or protestant. As catholics their main grievance was the tithe payment to the established church; but in general the century witnessed a fall in their standard of living due largely to the rising population, which brought with it keen competition for farms, and pushed up the already high rents. The trade restrictions and the lack of mineral wealth and of business initiative in the country condemned the bulk of the population to depend on agriculture for a livelihood, and to depend more and more on the potato for food. The great famine of the 1840s is proof that their condition continued to deteriorate long after most of the penal laws had been repealed.

Jonathan Swift, dean of St Patrick's, bitterly attacked the society which tolerated the terrible condition of the poor. In 1729 he published *A modest proposal. . .* , a savage satire in which he offers for public consideration a scheme for killing off year-old children, whose flesh will make 'a most delicious, nourishing, and wholesome food'. George Berkeley, protestant bishop of Cloyne, also directed attention to the social and economic evils of Ireland in *The querist*, first published in the 1730s. In it he asks hundreds of questions, for some of which answers have yet to be found:

Whether there be any country in Christendom more capable of improvement than Ireland?

Whether my countrymen are not readier at finding excuses than remedies?[2]

There is plenty of contemporary evidence of the wretched state of great numbers of the rural population at the time. For instance Arthur Young, who toured Ireland in the 1770s, wrote:

The cottages of the Irish, which are called cabbins, are the most miserable looking hovels that can well be conceived. . . The furniture of the cabbins is as bad as the architecture; in very many consisting only of a pot for boiling their potatoes, a bit of a table, and one or two broken stools; beds are not found universally, the family lying on straw.[3]

It would of course be wrong to think of the life of the peasantry as one of unmitigated sadness and despair, though there were terrible visitations like the famine of 1741. But in normal times, when weather and harvests

221

84 Catholic chapel, James's Gate, Dublin, built in 1738–49; with minor alterations,
including the addition of a bell, it remained the parish church till 1853
(reproduced from *Catholic emancipation centenary record*, ed. M.V. Ronan,
1929, facing p.33; see also Nicholas Donnelly, *Short histories of Dublin
parishes*, pt lx, 1911, pp 230–32)

were good, they led a carefree enough life. The arts of the shanachie,
singer, dancer, and musician were widely cultivated and appreciated; and
these people, though poor in the world's goods, had a rich treasury of
folk culture, much of which has been preserved by their descendants
even to our own day. The year saw a succession of religious feasts or
pilgrimages to the well of the local saint. The pilgrimage to Lough Derg
flourished, and the pilgrims brought home crosses (nowadays known as
'penal crosses') as souvenirs, inscribed with the date of their visit.
Pilgrimages were, it is true, forbidden by law, but newspaper references
and travellers' tales indicate that this fact cast no undue gloom over the
proceedings. Indeed the chief opposition to them came from some of the
catholic bishops and clergy, who had been educated in the university
cities of Europe, and who viewed some of these native manifestations of
piety with considerable disapproval, and were, for instance, severe in
their condemnation of festivities on May Day and of levity at wakes and
patterns.

    Although many bishops and hundreds of the regular clergy had left the
country after the banishment act was passed in 1697, and had been
forbidden to return under penalty of incurring death for high treason,
about a thousand diocesan priests had been permitted to remain; and
gradually, during the first two or three decades of the century, despite the
savage laws on the statute book, the catholic church was reorganised and

222

reformed; and before the middle of the century the hierarchy had been restored to its full strength for the first time since the reformation. Priests and bishops naturally fell under suspicion during periods of war between England and France, and when invasion threatened they were sometimes forced to go into hiding; but by and large, during peace time, they went about their duties with little fear of molestation by the authorities so long as they inculcated, or tried to inculcate, in their flocks respect for their rulers and private property, and reminded them, as they so often did in published catechisms and sermons, that they must be subject to the temporal authority because all authority came from God. This was the only possible line for them to follow at the time, if they were to remain in the country with the connivance of the government. (Even after their position had been legalised in 1782 the catholic clergy of Ireland did not dare to speak out against injustice by the ruling class until after the union of 1800, when bishops such as Doyle of Kildare and Leighlin, who denounced the peasants for their crimes against the property-owners, at the same time denounced those who were demanding rack rents, tithes, and taxes from a poverty-stricken people.) Their admonitions to their flocks to obey the laws in the pre-1782 period, however, lost much of their force because the people knew that the bishops and many of the clergy were themselves breaking the law by their very presence in the country.

Not the least of the problems confronting bishops was the indiscipline of some of their clergy. Priests whom they censured sometimes denounced them to the civil authorities, and some became converts to the established church. The lament of Father Dominick O'Donnell's

223

mother, said to have been composed when he became a protestant clergyman in Donegal in 1739, is one of the best known songs from the penal law period:

Crádh ort, a Dhoiminic Uí Dhomhnaill,
Nach mairg ariamh a chonnaic thú;
Bhí tú 'do shagart Dia Domhnaigh,
'S ar maidin Dia Luain 'do mhinistir.

Pill, pill, a rúin ó,
Pill, a rúin ó, is ná h-imthigh uaim;
Pill ort, a chuid den tsaol mhór,
Nó chan fheiceann tú 'n ghlóir mur' bpille tú.

Thréig tusa Peadar is Pol,
Thréig tú Eóin, 's an bunadh sin,
Thréig tú bain-tiarna an domhain –
Ó 'sí bhíos i gcónaí ag guí orainn.[4]

(Woe to you, Dominick O'Donnell,
Alas for anyone who ever saw you;
On Sunday you were a priest
And on Monday morning a minister.
Come back, come back, love,
Come back, love, and do not leave me;
Come back, my share of the world,
For unless you come back you'll not see the eternal glory.
You abandoned Peter and Paul,
You abandoned John and their kindred,
You abandoned the queen of the universe
Though it is she who is constantly praying for us.)

Despite the penal laws, most of the cities and towns outside Ulster had their catholic chapels, and new ones were being erected from early in the century. Only the places of worship of the established church could legally be dignified by the name 'church', and all the old churches and monasteries and cathedrals, which had escaped destruction at various

86 Scene after open-air mass at a scathlan, Bunlin Bridge, county Donegal, 1867
Despite its date, this illustration may be taken as applicable to the period
surveyed in the present chapter (*Sights and scenes in Ireland* [1896])

times since the reformation, and indeed all the original church temporalities, were the property of the established church. Many of the Dublin
chapels were at first merely converted stables and storehouses, but by the
beginning of the second quarter of the century new chapels were being
built, almost all of them close together in the lanes and back streets along
the Liffey. These were St Mary's in Liffey Street, St Michan's in Mary's
Lane, St Paul's in Arran Quay, St James's in Watling Street, St
Catherine's in Dirty Lane, St Nicholas's in Francis Street, St Audeon's in
Cook Street, St Michael's in Rosemary Lane, and St Andrew's in Hawkins Street, all in charge of the diocesan clergy. The religious orders had
their chapels also. The Franciscan chapel, at first in Cook Street, later
moved to Merchants' Quay where it was popularly referred to as Adam
and Eve's, from the sign of a nearby tavern. The Dominicans were in
Bridge Street, the Carmelites at Wormwood Gate and Ash Street, the
Augustinians in John's Lane, and the Capuchins in Church Street. The

225

Dominican nuns were in Channel Row, the Poor Clares in King Street, the Carmelites at Arran Quay, and the Augustinians at Mullinahack.

In rural Ireland chapels were often simple thatched structures, such as that at Arles in County Leix, but in many parts of the country, particularly in the north, it was often difficult to obtain sites for chapels from protestant landlords. Moreover some parishes were so large and scattered that they could not be served by one chapel, and mass was often said in private houses and at mass rocks in the open fields, or in 'scathlans' – little shelters where the priest and altar were at least partially protected from the elements. Sometimes too the people assembled for worship in the ruined shells of ancient abbeys such as Ballintubber and Graignamanagh. The harsh realities of conditions for catholic worship in eighteenth century Ireland are well illustrated by a story handed down in the family traditions of a prominent Fermanagh family. The story goes that Sir John Caldwell, the local squire in the period 1714-44,

although a staunch protestant, always treated the Roman Catholics with humanity and tenderness; in particular, one stormy day, when it rained very hard, he discovered a priest, with his congregation, at mass under a hedge; and, instead of taking that opportunity of blaming them for thus meeting so near his house (and having the priest hung, as he might have done), he ordered his cows to be driven out of a neighbouring cow-house, and signified to the priest and people that they might there take shelter from the weather, and there finish their devotions in peace.[5]

Indeed few of the protestant propertied or professional class in Ireland wished to see the masses of the people converted to protestantism, since it was to the material advantage of the ruling class to keep the privileged circle small. Nor was there any display of missionary zeal on the part of the majority of the bishops and clergy of the established church. Protestant nonconformists were granted legal toleration of their religion in 1719, but they were still compelled, like the catholics, to pay tithes to the established church, and they continued to be excluded from all offices under the crown. Their property rights, however, were never withdrawn or restricted, as were those of catholics, and they continued to enjoy the right to carry arms, to vote in elections and to sit in parliament. During the first three quarters of the century the members of the established church could afford to discriminate against protestant nonconformists with impunity. There was no danger whatever they might make common cause with the catholics, and in the event of invasion or rebellion they could be relied on to stake their lives and property in defence of protestantism and the English connection.

Soon after the middle of the century a catholic party began to emerge from the ghetto into which they had been driven by the popery laws. Their spokesmen were Charles O'Conor of Belanagare, whose ancestors had been high kings before the Norman invasion, and John Curry, a Dublin doctor. These men, by their historical writings and pamphlets, sought first to disprove the charge so often made by British historians, that the Gaelic Irish were a barbarous people; and the charge made by contemporary protestant polemical writers that the catholics were still only waiting for an opportunity to embark on a massacre of protestants. These had for long been stock-in-trade arguments to justify the continuance of the popery laws. Curry and O'Conor, together with Thomas Wyse of the Manor of St John in Waterford, next sought to organise the rising catholic middle class of the towns, who had largely escaped the net of the popery laws, into a delegate committee (founded in 1760) to act as a channel of communication between the catholic population and the government, in an effort to secure some measure of relief from the penal laws. At the same time Lords Trimlestown, Gormanston, Fingall, and Kenmare, spokesmen of the now sadly depleted catholic aristocracy, continued to regard themselves as hereditary leaders of Irish catholics. These two groups differed on the question of leadership, but they were all agreed in accepting the English conquest and the Hanoverian succession, and there was none among them who wished for a Stuart restoration, still less for the re-emergence of a Gaelic state. The case they offered for consideration was that catholic allegiance to the pope did not prevent their being loyal subjects of the king; that their record for seventy years had been one of unswerving loyalty to the established order; and that they deserved to be restored to some, at least, of the rights of which they had been deprived.

During the seven years war (1756-63) the catholics of Dublin and of other cities presented loyal addresses to king and parliament, insisting on their complete devotion to the British connection, and their willingness to assist in repelling any attempt at invasion by a foreign power. In 1762, when England was confronted with a Catholic coalition of France, Austria, and Spain, a scheme was under discussion between the catholic leaders and the government for recruiting Irish catholic regiments to fight in the army of England's ally – Portugal. But the members of the Irish parliament objected so violently to the arming of papists, that the whole project was hastily dropped. Unfortunately, the proposal was immediately linked with an outbreak of agrarian violence in Munster. These Whiteboy activities in Munster were paralleled by similar agrarian disturbances among the Hearts of Oak and Hearts of Steel in Ulster, and were directly caused by grievances regarding enclosure of commonages, forced labour, unemployment, rack-rents and tithes – grievances for which they were refused redress in the law courts. Because he had expressed sympathy with the peasantry in their distress, Father Nicholas Sheehy was convicted on a trumped-up charge of murder, in the town of Clonmel in 1766, and was hanged, drawn and quartered. His grave in Shandraghan soon became a place of pilgrimage, and his death provided later generations of Whiteboys with a patron saint.

The proposals to enlist catholic regiments, and an attempt to introduce a bill in parliament in 1762 to permit catholics to take mortgages on land, awakened the fears, real or simulated, of many protestants; and it suited the leaders of militant protestant ascendancy to insist that the Whiteboy disturbances in Munster were a popish rebellion, fomented by the French. They called on influential protestants to close their ranks and to defeat all efforts by catholics, and by the administration, to alter in the smallest degree the system so wisely devised by their ancestors for their protection.

Had statutory reform of the tithe and the land system been carried through at this time, it might have considerably changed the course of Irish history. Instead, the year 1766 saw the introduction of the first act against the Whiteboys – one of the most significant events in the history of this country – for, although it was not apparent at the time, coercion as

87 Charles O'Conor of
Belanagare (National
Library of Ireland)

CHARLES O'CONOR of BELANAGARE.

*Lucem redde tuæ, dux bone, patriæ!
Instar veris enim, vultus ubi tuus
Affulsit populo, gratior it dies,
Et Soles melius nitent. Hor*

*Restore, blest patriot, to thy Country light —
By Craft parricidal? in gloom oppress'd;
At sight of thy bright Countenance the night
Retiring, all in gladdening Spring is drest.*

applied then, and during the subsequent hundred and fifty years, was an admission that Ireland was in a state of smothered war. Coercion served only to encourage in the masses of the rural population a spirit of non-cooperation with the ruling authorities, and a total lack of faith in legal methods and institutions as a means of redressing their wrongs. In spite of admonitions, denunciations, and even excommunication by their own clergy, oathbound secret societies continued to exist, and, particularly in times of distress, the people obeyed the local Whiteboy code instead of the law of the land.

It should not be forgotten that the Gaelic poets of the eighteenth century were the pamphleteers and journalists of the Gaelic-speaking multitude. Many a song was sung at a fair or in a tavern or around the firesides satirising a local convert, or a tithe proctor or land agent, or denouncing local injustice, or reminding the people of their national identity; and

229

prophesying, rather unrealistically, a utopian future, with the Irish language and the catholic religion high in favour again, when, with the aid of Louis of France, the Stuarts would return to the throne. These songs served to build up a public opinion of which the ruling class of the day, and even English-speaking well-to-do catholics, were largely unaware. The Stuarts, for the most part, had never brought anything but disaster and disillusionment to Ireland, but to these simple country people, uninstructed in the realities of politics, any change, it seemed, was bound to be for the better and they probably visualised the revolution, which they hoped would follow a Stuart return, much in the same way as an oppressed and exploited people today might think of communism as a panacea for all their ills.

From hundreds of such Jacobite songs one might perhaps choose: 'Rosc Catha na Mumhan':

> D'aithníos féin gan bhréag ar fhuacht
> 'sar anaithe Thétis taobh le cuan,
> Ar chanadh na n-éan go séiseach suairc
> Go gcasfadh mo Shésar glé gan ghruaim.
> Measaim gur subhach don Mhumhain an fhuaim
> Is dá maireann go dubhach de chrú na mbuadh
> Torann na dtonn le sleasaibh na long
> Ag tarraingt go teann 'nár gceann ar cuaird.[6]

(I knew well by the cold and the stormy sea by the shore and by the tuneful and cheerful singing of the birds that my bright prince would return without sorrow. I think that for Munster and for our fine folk who are now dejected the noise of the waves against the sides of the ships drawing steadily near us is a joyful sound.)

Eventually towards the end of the 1760s when the hue and cry against the Whiteboys had died down, the catholic upper and middle classes began to hope once again for some relaxation of the penal laws. At this time a growing opposition group in the Irish parliament, led by such men as Henry Flood and the earl of Charlemont, was increasingly advocating resistance to British interference in Irish affairs. As a result the British government tended to adopt a sympathetic attitude towards the catholics as a counterpoise to the assertion of Irish protestant nationalism, and in order to restore the balance in the age-old game of 'divide and rule'. Some supporters of the administration, such as John Monk Mason and Sir Hercules Langrishe, sponsored bills in parliament in the years between 1762 and 1778 that would have enabled catholics to take mortgages on land and to take leases for longer than 31 years, but the forces of militant protestant ascendancy rallied their supporters each time to defeat these measures.

However, the war of American Independence brought about a new situation and when France declared war on Britain in 1778 and rumours of invasion began to circulate once more, the British government decided to force the issue of catholic relief, on the grounds that wartime strategy and the security of the empire demanded it. Not only was it deemed expedient to conciliate catholics in case of invasion, but catholic recruits were urgently needed for the army. The British government set the good example by passing a relief act for English catholics early in 1778. Nevertheless, when Luke Gardiner introduced a bill in the Irish parliament permitting catholics to take leases for 999 years, and restoring full testamentary rights to catholic landowers, it met with a concerted and sustained opposition. In the end, after long and acrimonious debates, sometimes lasting far into the night, this first catholic relief bill was steamrollered through the Irish parliament, because British statesmen believed that it was necessary for the safety of the empire at the time.

Those protestants who had fought so long and so tenaciously to prevent any relaxation of the laws, had always contended that once the popery code was relaxed in the smallest degree it would be the signal for unlimited demands by the catholics in the future. The prognostications were naturally proved correct. Catholic leaders regarded the act of 1778 as but a beginning, and the years from 1778 to 1829, or indeed until the beginning of the present century, saw the emergence of a pattern now familiar in other countries: first the struggle for complete equality or for integration as we would call it today, and when that failed, a struggle for political supremacy between the privileged minority on the one hand and the underprivileged majority on the other.

15
THE PROTESTANT NATION
(1775–1800)
by R. B. McDowell

The war of American independence profoundly and dramatically influenced Irish politics. There were significant resemblances between the
position of Ireland and the North American colonies within the imperial
framework. Each colony had a representative assembly just as Ireland
had its more venerable and decorative parliament. Yet the Westminster
parliament claimed the right to legislate for both the colonies and Ireland
alike. So when the American colonists defied the British parliament, they
were fighting Ireland's battle. Many Irishmen appreciated this and
openly sympathised with the colonists, their sympathy being intensified
by the fact that many of the colonists were emigrants from Ireland, more
especially from Ulster. But the government secured the support of the
Irish parliament for its American policy, and as the war went on military
units maintained at Ireland's expense were sent overseas. The result was
that, when in 1778-9 France and Spain, taking advantage of their old
rival's transatlantic difficulties, entered the war on the American side,
Ireland, stripped of troops, lay open to invasion. Faced with this danger
Irishmen, or at any rate the Irish protestants, sprang to arms. All over the
country groups of neighbours or public-spirited landlords formed volunteer corps. Volunteering soon became the fashion. The corps were
numerous and splendidly uniformed. Reviews and parades were frequent.
Gentlemen proudly used their volunteer rank, and Ireland soon
abounded with captains and colonels. Volunteering not only provided an
outlet for patriotism and opportunities for conviviality, but it also
generated political activity. A corps easily became a debating society.
And not only was political Ireland better organised than ever before but

it soon became obvious that a drastic shift in power had taken place. Armed force – the ultimate arbitrator – was no longer controlled by the government but by the politically-minded public.

All this coincided with a growing awareness of Ireland's grievances, commercial and constitutional. The dislocation of trade caused by the war strained a weak economy. By 1778 the commercial restrictions were being vigorously denounced as the source of Ireland's economic ills. The Volunteers paraded in Dublin with a cannon, having round its neck a placard with the words 'Free trade or this!' The British government, caught between British businessmen determined to maintain their privileges and angry Irishmen, fumbled, uncertain what was best to do. And when at last in 1779 it decided to conciliate Ireland by abolishing the commercial restrictions, it was too late to gain gratitude. By then a new agitation was gaining force – an agitation directed against the limitations on the powers of the Irish parliament imposed by Poynings' law, and the act of 1720 declaring the right of the British parliament to legislate for Ireland.

This movement had a great and eloquent leader in Henry Grattan, who after entering parliament in 1775, speedily established himself as a superb orator – nervous, high-flown, romantic. With generous enthusiasm he demanded that Ireland should be granted its rightful status, that of an independent nation, though he always insisted that Ireland would remain linked to Great Britain by a common crown and by sharing a common political tradition. In a series of powerful speeches he expounded his case, but the government, retaining a majority in parliament by the use of patronage, successfully repulsed his attacks. Outside parliament, however, the situation was growing critical. In the autumn of 1781 Lord Cornwallis, at the head of a large British force, hemmed in at Yorktown, Virginia, by an American army and a French fleet, surrendered. Then in February 1782 delegates from a number of Ulster Volunteer corps gathered at Dungannon in the parish church and pledged their support to resolutions in favour of legislative independence. The old empire was crumbling with defeat in America, there was a loss of confidence, and in Ireland an absence of force. Shortly after the Dungannon meeting, Lord

North, the British prime minister whose government had been struggling to maintain the old imperial system, was driven from office and the whigs who took his place were anxious to conciliate Irish opinion by abolishing the restrictions on the Irish parliament. The declaratory act was repealed and in the following year the British parliament specifically renounced its claim to legislate for Ireland. And Poynings' act was so drastically modified that the only control over Irish legislation retained by the crown was the right to veto bills. Also it was agreed that Ireland should have an annual mutiny act and that the Irish judges should be irremovable except by deliberate parliamentary action.

Ireland was now in form an independent kingdom sharing a monarch with the neighbouring island. For the moment there was a great upsurge of satisfaction and pride. Signs of sovereignty appeared in many directions. An Irish post office separate from that of Great Britain was started, the Bank of Ireland was founded, the Custom House and the Four Courts were built. Rutland Square and Merrion Square were completed. The Dublin which Malton at this time depicted was undoubtedly and self-consciously a capital city.

The sense of national unity manifested itself in the removal of a number of the religious, social, and economic disabilities which in the past had been imposed on the Irish catholics, though it should be quickly added that generosity was checked by caution. Only extreme liberals were prepared to allow catholics a share in political power. There was also an optimistic feeling about the economic future. Agriculture, as the famous Arthur Young noted when he toured Ireland, was improving, though by rapidly advancing English standards there was plenty of room for further improvement. Irish industry was expected to benefit from the availability of cheap labour and abundant water-power. The Irish parliament was ready to assist with tariffs and bounties, though keen protectionists sensed an unwillingness to go too far against English interests, and we still have a reminder of the economic optimism of the period in the great canals linking Dublin with the Shannon – impressive and extravagant eighteenth-century engineering feats.

It was soon seen however that constitutional forms did not correspond

88 James Caulfield, first earl of
Charlemont, by William Cuming
(National Gallery of Ireland)

with political realities. Ireland was legally an independent country. But
the king of Ireland was represented by a lord lieutenant nominated by the
British government, and the lord lieutenant selected and controlled the
Irish executive, which in turn controlled the patronage – peerages,
places, and pensions – that influenced the outlook of many M.P.s.
Behind the façade of independence, the British government continued to
exercise control over Irish affairs. There was an obvious remedy – to
reform parliament so that it should more accurately mirror public
opinion. And in the early eighties liberals in England and Ireland were
vigorously discussing schemes of reform. In Ireland the Volunteers took
up the question, and after provincial conventions made up of delegates
from different corps had agreed that the house of commons must be
made more representative, it was decided to hold a national Volunteer
convention in Dublin which would prepare a plan and submit it to
parliament to be turned into legislation. The delegates gathered at the
Rotunda on 10 November 1783 under the chairmanship of Lord
Charlemont, the general of the Volunteers, noted for his refined taste as
a patron of architecture, in politics a very cautious liberal. The most
conspicuous of the delegates was Hervey, bishop of Derry and earl of
Bristol, a magnificent prelate, a mighty builder of mansions, and at this
time a strong radical. The most influential delegate was Henry Flood, a
man with a strong political intellect and a severe oratorial style. Flood
dominated the convention, and its plan of reform reflected his views. It
was presented to the house of commons but that body, refusing to be
overawed by armed men, summarily rejected it. The M.P.s had gauged
the situation correctly. The Volunteers were far too respectable and law-
abiding to employ force against parliament. When what they believed

235

was a reasonable plan was turned down, they had no idea what to do next. In fact they went home quietly.

From then on, reformers were face to face with a major problem. What was to be done if a majority in parliament, determined not to lose their privileges and confident that the system in practice worked very well, simply refused to alter existing arrangements? At first, reformers seem to have believed that the pressure of public opinion, if it were mobilised and displayed to its fullest extent, might shame or frighten the house of commons into reforming itself. And shortly after the Volunteer convention dissolved, the radicals of Dublin, led by Napper Tandy, an exuberant and at times absurd orator and a very shrewd political organiser, attempted to assemble a reform convention. It was to be made up of delegates from the counties and parliamentary boroughs who, having been chosen by the people, were to gather in Dublin and frame a plan of reform. It was a complete failure. Only a comparatively small number of delegates arrived (25 October 1784), and their deliberations attracted very little attention. In fact Irish radicals were taught another lesson. In the absence of success, the momentum behind a movement can slacken as the public lose interest.

Indeed during the middle eighties Irish politics were remarkably placid. But it was the quiet that precedes a storm. Events in France – the meeting of the states general, a great representative assembly, and the fall of the Bastille – were to start off a great political seismic disturbance. It is impossible to sum up the significance of the French revolution in a phrase. But it might be said that its driving ideas can best be expressed by the words liberty and equality. Liberty meant in the first place that the individual was protected against the arbitrary use of power by the government and in the second place that the nation – or at least those who were considered fit for the vote – should control the government. Equality meant that no section of the community should be legally privileged. Furthermore all institutions were to be ruthlessly examined, judged by the criteria of liberty, equality, and efficiency, and, if condemned, completely reshaped. It was the first time that a great European community had attempted to reconstruct the whole of its constitutional and admini-

89 Volunteer parade in College Green, 4 November 1779, by Francis Wheatley (National Gallery of Ireland)

strative machinery. Of course many of the principles the French were enunciating were, it could be argued, the commonplaces of British and Irish political thinking. But whereas in the British Isles they were used to justify the revolution of 1688, in France they were being employed to open up a new era. The relics of the past were being swept away, and European man, or at least the middle classes, were taking over control of their destiny. Liberals all over Europe were exhilarated at the prospect of reshaping society.

There were many links, commercial, cultural, religious, and family between Ireland and France, and the Irish newspapers provided abundant coverage of French happenings. And just at the very time the French revolution was getting under way, Irish politics had for local reasons begun to stir. Six months before the states general met, George III, king of Great Britain and Ireland, went out of his mind. It was agreed that the regent of Britain and Ireland should be the prince of Wales. But a great debate broke out over the method by which he should be installed in office. Grattan and his friends stressed that it should be made clear that the British regent did not automatically become regent of Ireland. The king's recovery put an end to the debate, but by then an Irish whig or liberal opposition led by Grattan, the Ponsonbys, and Curran, a great advocate who could fuse indignation and humour in his speeches, had come into existence. It demanded not the reform but the 'purification' of parliament by the drastic scaling down of the pension list and by limiting the number of the office-holders permitted to sit in parliament. The whigs denounced in scathing terms the government's methods of maintaining a majority. At the same time Grattan's fervent belief in the British connection was shown in the summer of 1790. There was a possibility of war between England and Spain when their claims clashed on the west coast of North America. Grattan emphasised that the interests of England and Ireland were inseparable. His attitude angered a young protestant barrister, Theobald Wolfe Tone, who was beginning to take an interest in politics. He promptly published a pamphlet in which he argued that Ireland had no quarrel with Spain, and that 'the good of the empire' was a specious phrase. About a year later he developed his views at greater length in his famous publication, *An argument on behalf of the catholics of Ireland*. Tone argued that Ireland had 'no national government', its government being under British control, that the only way to counteract British influence over Irish affairs was by parliamentary reform, and that parliamentary reform could only be won if two underprivileged groups, the Irish catholics and the protestant radicals, cooperated in a reform programme that included catholic emancipation.

Tone's views greatly impressed the Belfast liberals. Belfast, at this time a town of about 20,000 inhabitants, was pulsating with economic and political life. It was the centre of the linen trade, the importance of which was symbolised by the recently opened White Linen Hall, and Ritchie was about to open his new shipyard, a step that marked the beginning of a great industry. At the same time the inhabitants were intensely interested in voluntary organisations for charitable and educational purposes – the Belfast Society for the Promotion of Knowledge, for which Tone's friend, Thomas Russell, a dreaming soldier, was the first librarian; the governors of the Academy, who managed a successful grammar school; and the Belfast Charitable Society which in the Poor House took care of the sick poor and set sturdy beggars to work at spinning and weaving. The typical Belfastman of the period, a presbyterian businessman, was bound to be critical of the ruling world of episcopalian landlords and to suspect

90 Theobald Wolfe Tone, *c.* 1792,
(National Library of Ireland)

that his economic interests were being ignored. Tone was invited to Belfast in the autumn of 1791. He was one of the few Irish politicians who found himself at home both in Belfast and Dublin, and during a fortnight of conversation and conviviality the Belfast Society of United Irishmen was founded (14 October). Immediately afterwards Tone got into touch with Napper Tandy, that experienced municipal politician. And as a result of Tandy's efforts the Dublin Society of United Irishmen came into existence in November. These societies were middle-class debating societies which strove to mould public opinion. The Dublin society published numerous manifestos, including a plan of parliamentary reform which appeared in 1794. This plan suggested that Ireland should be divided into 300 parliamentary constituencies equal in population, and that every man should have a vote (one prominent member of the society considered it logical that women should have the vote too, but admitted that the idea was impractical).

How did the United Irishmen hope to secure reform? Apparently at first they still trusted to persuasion, to the pressure of public opinion. Volunteer corps and political clubs passed resolutions in favour of reform, and early in 1793 Ulster reformers held a representative convention at Dungannon, the delegates pledging their support to parliamentary reform. It was hoped that later a national convention could be held at Athlone. To radicals parliamentary reform was the first step towards a just and efficient administration of Ireland. They looked forward to the abolition of tithe, a reduction in government expenditure, lower taxation, the encouragement of trade, and help for primary education.

But the pressure group which was successful during 1792 and 1793 was

239

91 The parliament house and Trinity College, Dublin, *c.* 1793, by James Malton
(National Library of Ireland)

a catholic body. In 1791 the catholic committee began to bestir itself. Strengthened by the loss of its more moderate members who wished to leave the question of concessions to the government, the committee presented a petition to parliament asking for further relaxation of the penal laws. The result was the meagre relief act of 1792. When the catholic question was being debated in the house of commons, some M.P.s sneered at the committee's claim to represent the catholics of Ireland. The committee, led by a number of energetic and successful Dublin businessmen, of which the most prominent was John Keogh, reacted vigorously. They engaged Tone as their assistant secretary, thus both advertising their belief in toleration and obtaining a very efficient employee. And they decided to prove that they represented catholic opinion by asking parish delegates to choose representatives from the counties and towns all over Ireland to meet in Dublin.

The catholic convention assembled in Dublin in December 1792 and agreed to ask for the abolition of the remaining penal laws. A delegation was chosen to go to London to interview the prime minister, by-passing the Irish government. The lord lieutenant and his advisers were convinced that the protestant ascendancy should not be tampered with at a time when the established order all over Europe was threatened. Concessions might set the country on a slippery slope. Fitzgibbon, the lord

240

chancellor, a hard-headed, outspoken conservative, was to argue that catholic emancipation would lead to parliamentary reform and that a reformed parliament would break the connection with Great Britain – a connection which was essential to British safety and Irish social stability. In fact his arguments almost completely reversed Tone's.

But the British government, facing the certainty of a war with revolutionary France, was desperately anxious to conciliate Irish opinion. And Burke, the great intellectual opponent of the revolution, was urgently eager to win over the Irish catholics to the conservative side by granting them the concessions they were morally entitled to. The British government put pressure on the Irish government and the result was the relief act of 1793 which swept away most of the disabilities and gave the catholics the vote. But the catholics were still excluded from parliament, from the judicial bench, and from the higher offices of state. At the same time the government agreed to some other concessions to Irish public opinion. Some pensioners and placeholders were excluded from parliament. Cottages were exempted from the hearth tax, the powers of juries in libel cases were extended. But at the same time Volunteering was suppressed, a paid home-defence force – the militia – under government control, was formed, and a convention act was passed forbidding assemblies to meet which claimed to represent a large section of Irish opinion.

By concession and repression authority was preparing to meet a time of crisis. Abroad Britain was now at war with France; at home there was much agrarian discontent, directed against tithe and rent. And in Ulster, competition for land led to rural rioting between catholics and protestants, rioting culminating in the 'battle of the Diamond' and leading to the formation of the Orange Society (September 1795). The whigs or liberals led by Grattan were in favour of further concession to the catholics. Complete catholic emancipation and a moderate parliamentary reform bill, stopping well short of manhood suffrage, would, they believed, satisfy the country at large. In January 1795, after a wartime coalition government had been formed in Great Britain, Fitzwilliam, a whig and a friend of Grattan's, became lord lieutenant and for the moment it looked as if the Irish whigs would be in control. But Fitzwilliam was inexperienced

241

92 The Custom House, Dublin, *c.* 1793, by James Malton (National Library of Ireland)

and impetuous. The British cabinet thought that in agreeing to complete catholic emancipation he was exceeding his instructions. Fitzwilliam was recalled – a decisive disappointment to those who hoped to carry out reforms by constitutional methods.

Meanwhile the radicals were growing impatient. Their impatience expressed itself in two forms. They began to organise themselves on military lines and tried to obtain help from revolutionary France. In the spring of 1794 William Jackson, a French agent, visited Dublin. Tone gave him a paper on Irish conditions which suggested that a French invasion would be welcomed. Jackson had brought with him to Ireland an old acquaintance who steadily informed the government of his doings. In the event, Jackson was arrested and on being convicted of treason dramatically committed suicide in the dock on 30 April 1795.

Tone was in an awkward position since it was clear that he had had dealings with Jackson. But the legal evidence against him was thin and he was personally well liked by some influential conservatives. So in the end he was permitted to emigrate to America. Using America as a stepping stone he reached France at the beginning of 1796. There, speaking on behalf of the Irish radicals, he started to press for a French invasion, and in the summer his requests were reinforced by Arthur O'Connor, a young M.P., who had shocked the house by expressing radical views. Since the beginning of the war the French had been considering an

242

invasion of the British Isles, and Ireland was an obvious target. The very fact that it lay so far to the west rendered it easier for a French expedition to avoid the blockading squadrons. And if the French secured control of the Irish ports it was clear that British trade would be seriously impeded and the whole west coast threatened. Moreover, as Tone especially emphasised, in Ireland the invader would meet with a friendly reception. In Paris he put the case forcibly to Carnot 'the organiser of victory', and in December a French fleet carrying a force of 14,000 men, under the command of Hoche, one of the most brilliant of the young revolutionary generals, set out from Brest for Ireland. Everything went wrong for both the British and the French. The British fleet was badly placed and sluggishly led. The French, delayed by dockyard deficiencies, sailed as the winter storms set in. The fleet was scattered, Hoche's ship was carried far into the Atlantic, and the units which reached Bantry Bay, after tossing for some days in wild weather off the coast, failed to make a landing.

That the French should come so very near to success was most alarming to the Irish government, particularly as it was well aware that discontent at home was becoming effectively organised. In 1794, about a year after the war began, the Dublin Society of United Irishmen had been constrained by the authorities to suspend their meetings. Soon after, some of the middle-class reformers, acting along with urban workingmen and countrymen long accustomed to agrarian conspiracy, began to build up a widespread, secret, oath-bound society, pledged to obtain emancipation and reform. The organisation was based on innumerable small committees which sent representatives to local committees, which sent their representatives to county committees, which in turn sent representatives to provincial committees, the system culminating in a national committee.

The government took vigorous counter-measures. It encouraged the formation of yeomanry corps by conservatives, eager to defend the existing order, suspended the habeas corpus act, and passed an insurrection act which in a 'proclaimed district' imposed a curfew and gave the magistrates extensive powers to search for arms. And in 1797 Lake, a heavy-

93 Belfast from Cromac Wood, *c.* 1780 (Ulster Museum). Note the shipping in the harbour, the rural setting of the town, and, in the background, Cave Hill with MacArt's Fort (where Tone and his friends spent a memorable day in May or June 1795)

handed soldier, set to work by systematic raiding for arms to disarm Ulster. Soon throughout Ireland the desperate efforts of the government to check conspiracy produced a steady succession of incidents and outrages. The United Irishmen were determined to win catholic emancipation, radical reform, and independence. The upholders of the existing order were equally determined to preserve law and order, maintain the connection with Great Britain, and to resist French aggression. Neither side was prepared to yield and each charged the other with being ultimately responsible for the unhappy condition of the country.

One practical consideration influenced the radicals. As time went on and their organisation was extended and improved the danger grew that the government might regain the initiative and smash it. And the government had one valuable asset, its intelligence system. Early in 1797 Thomas Reynolds, who had a house in County Kildare, joined the United Irishmen. He was made a member of the Leinster provincial directory and shortly afterwards he decided to supply the government with information. As a result, in March 1798, the Leinster directory of the United Irishmen, meeting at Oliver Bond's house in Bridge Street, Dublin, were all arrested. Lord Edward Fitzgerald, an experienced soldier and a fervent revolutionary, managed for some weeks to evade arrest but on 19 May his hiding place was discovered, and he was captured, mortally wounded. When therefore a few days later the United

244

Irishmen rose in rebellion, their efforts were badly coordinated, and the rebellion from a military point of view was a series of isolated struggles. There was skirmishing in the counties round Dublin, which was firmly held by the authorities. In the south-east there was a widespread rising in the counties of Waterford and Wexford. Having secured control of their own counties the rebels tried to drive west and north but were halted at New Ross and Arklow. Finally military columns converged on Vinegar Hill beside Enniscorthy, where the rebels had pitched their main camp, and after a fiercely fought engagement the United Irish force was dispersed. In the north there were risings in Antrim and Down. But Lake's operation in the previous year had seriously weakened the United Irishmen in Ulster. Moreover the government forces kept control of the strategic centre of the area, Belfast. At Antrim the rebels under Henry Joy McCracken and at Ballynahinch under Henry Munro were decisively defeated.

A few days before the rebellion broke out, Napoleon sailed for Egypt, which he had decided should be the main French overseas objective. So with the forces available only minor French expeditions could be sent to help the Irish rebels, and in fact these expeditions arrived after the rising had been suppressed. In August a small French force under Humbert landed at Killala and was joined by many Irishmen. Humbert's campaign was exciting but short. Having defeated a force of yeomanry and militia at Castlebar, he was surrounded by Cornwallis, the viceroy, at the head of a much larger force and compelled to surrender at Ballinamuck in County Longford (8 September). A week or so after Humbert surrendered, another small French expedition set sail for the north of Ireland. Off Lough Swilly it was met by a superior British squadron and most of the French ships were captured (October). On board the flagship was Wolfe Tone, serving as a French officer. He was brought before a court martial in Dublin, found guilty, and before he could be executed, committed suicide (19 November).

The rebellion had one important consequence. It demonstrated unmistakably that Ireland presented an urgent political problem. To William Pitt, the British prime minister, Ireland constituted a challenge. Pitt had

A.Lord'ion'2ake his horse shot under him
B. Earl of Ancrum and Lord Roden,
there Gallant Charge Cavalry.
C. Royal Artillery, Capt.ʳBlomfield
commanding the British And Capt.ᵗ
Crawford the Royal Artillery.

The BATTLE of VINEGAR HILL in IRELAND
Fought June 21.ˢ 1798,by the Kings forces against
When after an hour & a half fierce Fighting the
Troops gaind a compleat Victory, & took the Reb-
ers side Arms, Camp Batt Brass 9 Inch brass
6 Metal 1 pounr.ˢ no Draw times Metal

94   The battle of Vinegar Hill, Enniscorthy, 21 June 1798: contemporary print
(National Library of Ireland)

a powerful, creative intellect and he was prepared to tackle a major question by producing a bold, long-term solution. In the eighties he had planned to make Great Britain and Ireland a great free trade area, but had been beaten by the suspicions and prejudice of vested interests. Now in 1798 he decided on a union of the two parliaments – the British and the Irish. This, he argued, would ensure coordinated activity in an emergency, encourage British capitalists to invest in Ireland, thus raising Irish living standards, and, by transforming the position of Irish protestants from that of a minority in Ireland into a majority in the United Kingdom, remove their fears of catholic emancipation. Pitt's approach to politics might be described as mathematical. He found it hard to comprehend the importance of a force such as nationalism in which emotional factors play

95 Robert Emmet (National Library of Ireland)

a major part. When his proposal came before the Irish parliament, a body which always appreciated high-spirited rhetoric, a number of members, led by Grattan, emphasised with passionate intensity Ireland's separate identity among the nations, and asserted that Ireland possessed a national individuality which demanded political expression in the form of a separate parliament. After a strenuous and exciting debate in 1799, the government's proposal was rejected by a majority of five. The government then set to work to obtain a majority, partly by propaganda and persuasion, partly by trying to gratify the crudely personal objectives of many peers and M.P.s. By these methods it secured a majority for the union in both houses; the act of union was passed during the session of 1800 and on January 1801 Ireland became part of the United Kingdom.

The enactment of the union coincided with the end of the first phases of Anglo-French conflict, and within a few months of the act receiving the royal assent Cornwallis was in France negotiating a peace. But the treaty of Amiens (27 March 1802) only provided a breathing space. By the summer of 1803 Great Britain and France were again at war, and the undismayed remnant of the United Irish leadership began to plan a new effort against the authority in Ireland. They again hoped to secure French help, but Napoleon was intent on a direct invasion of England, and the rising organised and led by Robert Emmet, a younger brother of one of the radical leaders of the nineties, ended in a scuffle in the streets of Dublin on the night of 23 July 1803. Emmet was captured, and after a trial in which he made a dramatic confession of his political faith, he was executed. Ireland settled down to a period of peace punctuated by agrarian disturbance and catholic agitation.

16

THE AGE OF DANIEL O'CONNELL

(1800–47)

by J. H. Whyte

This chapter covers roughly the first half of the nineteenth century, and we are calling it the age of Daniel O'Connell. The title is appropriate because there is probably no other half-century of Irish history which is so dominated by the personality of one man. Daniel O'Connell, born in 1775, was the son of a small landlord in County Kerry. He was called to the bar in 1798 – being one of the first catholics to enter the legal profession after catholics were permitted to do so in 1792 – and he rapidly became one of the most successful barristers in Ireland. He soon began to pursue a political career as well as practising at the bar, and from about 1814 until his death in 1847 he can be considered the most prominent politician in Ireland.

Before we embark on an examination of his career, however, a word should be said about the political situation in which he had to work. The act of union had been passed in 1800, and Ireland was now subject to the parliament at Westminster. The failure of the union was not inevitable. Indeed there might have been great advantages for Ireland in being linked with what was then the richest country in the world. But the destiny of Ireland was now no longer decided by Irishmen. Of the 658 members of the house of commons, only 100 represented Irish constituencies. Clearly, then, the success or failure of the union would depend on the attitudes taken to Irish problems by the M.P.s from Britain who formed the great majority.

For Irish problems existed in plenty. The most serious of these problems, we can now see on looking back, was the question of the land. The land of Ireland was simply not sufficient to feed all those who were trying to get a living off it. Population was increasing rapidly. This led to competition for land, and drove up rents, thus reducing still further the people's resources. Things could have been better if farming methods had improved, but, except in Ulster, most farmers had no security of tenure, and they had learnt by experience that, if they improved their holdings, the landlord was quite likely to put up the rent. And so the problem continued, getting worse year by year, until the famine of 1845-8, in the most terrible possible manner, reduced the population to more manageable proportions.

However, although, on an objective view, the land problem seems to have been the worst problem of early nineteenth-century Ireland, it is fair to say that it was not the problem that most preoccupied politicians until the great famine made it impossible to ignore it. In earlier years, both British ministers and Irish politicians were more concerned with other and more immediate problems. Catholics and presbyterians resented paying tithes to the established church. Local government was controlled by small oligarchies in each borough. There was no provision for relief of the destitute. Many Irish industries were declining, under competition from large-scale industry in Britain.

The most prominent issue of all, in the early years of the union period, was the catholic demand for full emancipation. Most of the penal laws had, it is true, been repealed in the 1780s and 1790s. Catholics could now maintain schools, join the professions, and vote at parliamentary elections. But they were still debarred from all the more important offices in the state. They could not sit in parliament, and they could not be judges, or colonels in the army, or captains in the navy, or be ministers in the government, or hold any except the most junior offices in the civil service. These restrictions naturally galled catholics, all the more as Pitt had virtually promised, when he carried the union between Britain and Ireland in 1800, that it would be followed by complete emancipation for the catholic body. But opposition from the king, and from Pitt's fellow ministers, proved too strong, and the plan was dropped.

O'Connell's long career was a packed and many-sided one, and we shall here be concerned with what were undoubtedly the two most important movements associated with it: the successful struggle for catholic emancipation in the 1820s, and the unsuccessful struggle for repeal of the union with Britain in the 1840s.

In the first twenty years of the nineteenth century, the catholic agitation for full emancipation was carried on by a coterie of landlords, merchants and professional men. They had no claim to speak for the mass of Irish catholics. And they also quarrelled continually among themselves. So, although their doings took up plenty of space in the newspapers, it is not surprising that successive British governments found it unnecessary to take notice of them.

The real struggle for catholic emancipation began with the forming of the Catholic Association by O'Connell in 1823. O'Connell had taken a prominent part in the ineffectual catholic politics of the previous decade, and he had learnt from experience. There was an important difference between his association and previous attempts at catholic organisation. The association was not confined to a clique of well-to-do catholics. It aimed at a mass membership, which was to be secured in two ways.

Firstly, the association called in the aid of the catholic clergy. The clergy had not played much part in the catholic movement so far, but – distributed as they were all over the country, knowing their people, and trusted by them – they were splendidly placed to be the local leaders of the agitation. Secondly, and perhaps more important, the association inaugurated what was known as the 'catholic rent'. This was a subscription of a penny a month, a sum so low that even the poorest could pay it. As a result thousands joined the association, and it soon had a larger income from the pennies of the poor than previous catholic bodies had ever obtained from the subscriptions of the rich. Just as important as the income brought in by the catholic rent was its psychological effect. To pay a subscription to a movement increases one's interest in it, and now many thousands of catholics, in all walks of life, were identified with the Catholic Association. Contemporary observers noticed the improved morale and corporate spirit of the catholic body. As a Church of Ireland bishop, Dr Jebb of Limerick, noted:

96 Daniel O'Connell
(National Library of
Ireland)

There is what we of this generation have never before witnessed, a complete union of the Roman Catholic body. . . In truth, an Irish revolution has, in great measure, been effected.[1]

It was not long before this new vitality in the catholic body began to make itself felt. A general election was held in the summer of 1826. Catholics could not sit in parliament, but they had the vote, and in most of the Irish counties they formed a majority of the electorate. Most of these voters were tenant farmers, and hitherto they had generally voted for their landlords' nominees. In some counties this had meant that opponents of catholic emancipation had been returned to parliament by a largely catholic electorate. But a stop could be put to this if once the

251

Catholic Association could persuade these electors to vote according to their religion and not according to their landlords' wishes.

In the general election of 1826 this was done. In four counties – Waterford, Westmeath, Louth, and Monaghan – sitting members who opposed the catholic claims were turned out, and replaced by new members who, though of course protestants themselves, were supporters of catholic emancipation. The victory was due to the organising power of O'Connell and the association. The catholic rent provided the money. The local clergy canvassed the electors and led them to the polls. When some of the voters were victimised by their landlords after the election, the Catholic Association compensated them out of its funds. The association had only to perfect its organisation, and at the next general election it would be able to chase the opponents of catholic emancipation out of almost every Irish county.

But before the next general election occurred, the association had won a still more spectacular, and, as it proved, decisive triumph: the famous Clare election of 1828. In those days M.P.s who were appointed to ministerial office were obliged to stand for reelection in their constituencies, and the election in this case was caused by the appointment of one of the M.P.s for Clare, Vesey Fitzgerald, to a post in the British cabinet. Vesey Fitzgerald's position in Clare was a strong one. He had been the sitting member for the last ten years. He was a resident landlord, with, apparently, a good reputation among his tenants. He was himself friendly to catholic emancipation. But he had taken office in a government opposed to the catholic claims, and the Catholic Association was bound by resolution to oppose every member of such a government.

The association at first tried to find a friendly protestant to stand as its candidate against Vesey Fitzgerald. But Fitzgerald was so strongly entrenched in Clare that it proved impossible to find an opponent. It was at this point that the idea was broached that O'Connell himself should oppose Fitzgerald. As a catholic, O'Connell could not sit in parliament, but there was no law forbidding him to go forward as a candidate. O'Connell accordingly announced his candidature, and went down to Clare. There, he was supported by the now well-tested electioneering

97 'Catholic petitioners, or symptoms of a peaceable appeal': cartoon of the Clare election, 1828, showing O'Connell at the head of a band of roughs (Radio Times Hulton Picture Library, H 60004)

machinery of the Catholic Association. The electors were canvassed by their priests and by officials of the association. When polling began, they were led to the booths in Ennis by their priests, in disciplined bands. Something of the atmosphere of disciplined enthusiasm can be caught even from the dry pages of contemporary newspapers. Here, for instance, is the account of one reporter:

Tuesday morning

Eight o'clock. Between 300 and 400 of John Ormsby Vandeleur's freeholders are now passing up the street to the Court House, preceded by colours, every man with a green leaf in his hand, and amidst the loudest cheering from the townspeople. They are western men from Kilrush, and brought in by their clergy to vote for O'Connell. Along the road the general cry of these men was – 'Here's Kilrush, high for O'Connell, high for our priest'. Mr O'Leary the priest of Kilrush, came with them and the town is full of catholic clergy. There are fifteen booths opened for the polling.

Ten o'clock. Mr M'Inerney, the priest of Feakle, is just passed in at the head of a number of freeholders from that parish, carrying green boughs, and music before them.

Eleven o'clock. Another large body of men has passed in, preceded by a green silk flag, Shamrocks wreathed in gold – 'Scariff, and civil and religious liberty' in gold colours.

Mr O'Connell has been chaired to the Court House, and at the door implored the people to be true to their religion and their country.

Mr Maguire is moving about the streets and addressing every group of free-holders. The qualification oath is required, and magistrates are now administering it at the office of Mr Henry the sub-sheriff. This will retard the election if persevered in.

Twelve o'clock. Rev. Mr Murphy of Corofin, is come in with Mr Staunton Cahill, at the head of at least 500 men decorated with green branches and walking in ranks. Mr Murphy stood up in his gig, and was hailed with the loudest cheering.[2]

The organising skill of the Catholic Association had its inevitable effect. The gentry and the big farmers stood by Fitzgerald, but the small farmers deserted him almost *en masse*. O'Connell was elected by 2,057 votes against 982.

The British government at this time was headed by the duke of Wellington, the great soldier of the Napoleonic wars. The next most important member of the government was Sir Robert Peel, the home secretary. Both Wellington and Peel had been opposed to catholic emancipation, but neither of them was completely inflexible on the matter. They recognised that the Clare election had produced a new situation. The excitement among Irish catholics after their victory was so intense that there was no telling what might happen. Although O'Connell sincerely declared that he wished to win catholic emancipation by peaceful means only, it was not certain that he could control his followers. And, with large numbers of catholics in both the police and the army, the government could not count on the loyalty of the forces if a collision should occur.

There was another consideration which weighed with Wellington and Peel. Even if they wanted to pursue a policy of holding down the catholics, they could not be sure that they would be supported by a majority in parliament. For there was already a strong body of opinion in parliament which felt that emancipation ought to be granted. A series of divisions in the eighteen-twenties showed that the house of commons was almost evenly divided on the question, with as a rule, a slight majority in favour of emancipation. Only in the house of lords was there a substantial majority against. Thus a policy of repression, while it might be supported in the house of lords, would probably be defeated in the house of commons.

254

To Wellington and Peel these arguments were decisive. Though they did not like emancipation, no other course now seemed possible, and in the parliamentary session of 1829 they introduced a catholic emancipation bill. Their arguments did not convince everybody, and a minority contested the bill to the end. But they carried with them enough peers and M.P.s to ensure a safe majority in both house, and on 13 April 1829 the catholic emancipation act became law. By its terms, all the important remaining restrictions on catholics were removed. True, catholics were still debarred from the lord lieutenancy of Ireland and from the lord chancellorships of England and Ireland. But they could be M.P.s, cabinet ministers, judges, generals, admirals. And even if the number of catholics who could aspire to any of these positions was very small, the whole body gained in morale from the removal of the taint of inequality.

It was a great victory for O'Connell, and for the Catholic Association which he led. It seemed to show, also, the power of organised public opinion. Once the people of Ireland were sufficiently organised, it seemed, the British government must give way to their demands. There was no need to use violent means. There were, however, special advantages for O'Connell in this agitation. He was not facing resolute opponents. He was facing fairly moderate-minded ministers and a divided house of commons. If the situation had been different, even the formidable organising power of the Catholic Association might have been insufficient to force a change.

The winning of catholic emancipation left O'Connell as the hero of the great mass of the Irish people. His influence with them was higher than ever before, and he was the head of a small band of Irish members in the house of commons. For twelve years after emancipation, he used his influence generally to support the English liberal party. This, he felt, was in Ireland's best interest. The liberals, he considered, were a good deal better than the conservatives, and besides he was able to win from them a steady trickle of reforms for Ireland. More people were given the vote; municipal government was cleaned up; the police was made into a more impartial force; and tithes were converted into a rent charge.

In 1841, however, the liberals were defeated in a general election, and the conservatives returned to power. Their prime minister was Sir Robert Peel, the man who had so long opposed catholic emancipation and who had in the end conceded it only when it was no longer possible to do anything else. O'Connell had always hoped some day to restore to Ireland her own parliament, and now that her enemies had returned to office, there seemed no point in delaying his ambition any longer. He forthwith launched the second great agitation of his career – the campaign for repeal of the union between Ireland and Britain.

In this agitation, O'Connell could count on the sympathy of the bulk of the people of Ireland. Their instinctive national feeling, their admiration for him personally, and the programme of practical reforms which he promised once repeal was won – all these drew them to his side. He set about organising them in the same way as he had during the campaign for catholic emancipation. He founded a Repeal Association (1840) which was run on the same lines as the Catholic Association had been. He collected a repeal rent which realised much larger sums than the catholic rent had ever done. He secured the help of most of the catholic clergy, whom he was able to use as local organisers.

The most characteristic device of his campaign for repeal was the monster meeting. Mass meetings had been held during the catholic emancipation campaign, but they now took place on a much greater scale. During 1843 – when the agitation had reached its climax – more than forty such meetings were held, each at a site selected so as to be central for the people of a large surrounding area. As demonstrations of the disciplined ardour of a people, these monster meetings surpassed even the Clare election of 1828. The attendance at them was enormous. At several it was estimated as being into the hundreds of thousands. No less impressive than the numbers were the earnestness and orderliness of the people. Some idea of the atmosphere of these meetings can be given by reading a contemporary description of one of the most successful, that at Tara (15 August 1843):

At nine o'clock in the morning a small train of private carriages containing O'Connell and a dozen friends, set out from Merrion Square. They passed

98 Davis, Duffy and Dillon in the Phoenix Park, planning the foundation of the
Nation, 1842, by J.F. O'Hea (C. Gavan Duffy, *Young Ireland*, 2nd ed., 1896)

through some of the chief thoroughfares of Dublin, and the windows and pavements were already occupied by eager spectators. Carriages containing members
of the corporation in their robes of office, and other notable citizens, fell in
silently at various points, and in the suburbs a long line of vehicles, chiefly the
famous Dublin jaunting cars, crowded with citizens, was waiting to join them,
and the *cortège* became a procession. The route lay through a succession of ham-
lets, villages, and towns, and in every hamlet, village, or town the entire population was afoot in their holiday dress, and the houses were decorated with banners
or evergreens. The local muster headed by its local band immediately took its
place in the procession, on horseback or in vehicles. Wagons, capacious 'floats'
brought from the city, and the country carts used in agriculture, were all
employed and were all found barely sufficient to accommodate the people. It was
afterwards ascertained that toll was paid at Cabra, Phibsborough, and Blanchards-
town on thirteen hundred vehicles. The horsemen could not be strictly computed,
but it was estimated that the number in attendance on O'Connell did not fall short
of ten thousand. Before the procession had arrived within a dozen miles of the
historic hill large crowds were discovered who had come from distant places
during the night, and bivouacked in the green pastures of Meath, under a genial
August sky. A little later the repealers of Kells, Trim, and Navan, the chief towns
of Meath, joined the procession. They had more leisure and more inducement to
aim at organisation, and they presented a striking appearance. Each town was

257

preceded by its band in the national uniform of green and white, and by banners with suitable inscriptions. They were mustered by mounted marshals, distinguished by badges, horsemen four deep, footmen six deep, and the men of each parish marched, O'Connell afterwards declared, 'as if they were in battalions'. Three miles from the hill the vehicles had to be abandoned; from the immensity of the attendance there was space only for footmen. The abandoned vehicles were drawn up in line to wait the return of their occupants, and it is one of the wonders of this wonderful era that they were found at the day's close without appreciable loss or injury. Around the base of the hill the bands and banners were mustered. The bands amounted to forty, an equipment sufficient for an army; the banners were past counting.

The procession however was but a river discharging itself into an ocean. The whole district was covered with men. The population within a day's march began to arrive on foot shortly after daybreak, and continued to arrive, on all sides, and by every available approach, till noon. It was impossible from any one point to see the entire meeting; the hill rose almost perpendicular out of the level plain, and hill and plain were covered with a multitude 'countless as the bearded grain'. The number is supposed to have reached between 500,000 and 750,000 persons. It was ordinarily spoken of as a million, and was certainly a muster of men such as had never before assembled in one place in Ireland, in peace or war.[3]

What did O'Connell hope to gain by organising these tremendous meetings? The answer seems to be that he thought that the demonstration of the will of the Irish people would itself be enough to ensure the conversion of the British parliament to repeal. He put the point clearly when he launched the repeal agitation:

The actual mode of carrying the repeal must be to augment the numbers of the Repeal Association, until it comprises four-fifths of the inhabitants of Ireland. . .

When such a combination is complete, the parliament will naturally yield to the wishes and prayer of an entire nation. It is not in the nature of things that it should be otherwise.

Such a combination as I have spoken of was never yet resisted by any government, and never can. We are arrived at a stage of society, in which the peaceable combination of a people can easily render its wishes omnipotent.[4]

In support of this claim he could point to his success in 1829. Catholic emancipation had been won by such means. There had been no need to

99 Repeal meeting at Tara, 15 August 1843 (*Illustrated London News*, 26 August 1843)

fire a shot. The British government had given way as soon as it realised how powerful feeling in Ireland had become. But O'Connell seems to have overlooked vital differences between the situation of 1829 and that of 1843. In 1829, as we have seen, he already had much influential support on his side. About half the house of commons, and a substantial minority even in the house of lords, were already convinced of the wisdom of emancipation. It needed only the conversion of Wellington and Peel to turn this body of opinion into a decisive majority in both houses of parliament. In 1843, however, parliament was almost solidly opposed to repeal. In the house of commons, O'Connell had only his own handful of supporters – about twenty members – while liberals and conservatives were united against him. In the house of lords, he probably had no support at all. And not only were the numbers of his opponents much greater in 1843, but so was their determination. As we have seen, many of those English politicians who disliked catholic emancipation were prepared to withdraw their opposition rather than face a war in Ireland. But on the question of repeal, they were ready to go all lengths rather than yield. On 9 May 1843, the prime minister, Sir Robert Peel, made this clear in language about as emphatic as he could find:

100 The affray at the widow McCormack's house on Boulagh Common, near Ballingarry, county Tipperary, 29 July 1848 (*Illustrated London News*, 12 August 1848)

There is no influence, no power, no authority which the prerogatives of the crown and the existing law give to the government, which shall not be exercised for the purpose of maintaining the union; the dissolution of which would involve not merely the repeal of an act of parliament, but the dismemberment of this great empire. . . Deprecating as I do all war, but above all, civil war, yet there is no alternative which I do not think preferable to the dismemberment of this empire.[5]

The last and biggest of the monster meetings was scheduled to be held on 8 October 1843, at Clontarf, the scene of Brian Boru's victory over the Norse on the outskirts of Dublin. A bare few hours before the meeting was due to begin, the government banned it. Parties were already on the move towards the meeting-place from distant districts. But O'Connell, true to his principle of always keeping within the law, complied with the government's order and called off the meeting.

This did not mean the end of the repeal agitation. The Repeal Association continued to meet. The repeal rent brought in almost as much in 1844 as it had in 1843. But O'Connell's retreat at Clontarf is generally, and rightly, seen as the turning-point. For the government, by forbidding the meeting even at the risk of provoking bloodshed, had proved the falsity of O'Connell's basic assumption. It was not true that what he called 'the peaceable combination of a people' would necessarily prevail. After the failure of his monster meetings, O'Connell did not seem to know what to do next. Slowly the movement lost impetus, dissensions broke out in the Repeal Association, and long before O'Connell's death in 1847 it was clear that he had failed.

Has the repeal movement any permanent significance, then, in Irish history? The answer is that it undoubtedly has, but in ways rather different from those which O'Connell had anticipated. To the historian, the permanent effects of the repeal movement are to be found not in O'Connell's own activities, but in those of a group of ardent politicians which his movement called into being – Young Ireland. This was the name given to a group of men, mostly in their twenties, who were associated with the *Nation*, a weekly newspaper founded in 1842 to assist O'Connell in his repeal campaign. Between them, this group worked out ideas that were to prove important in Irish politics for the rest of the nineteenth century and sometimes down to the present day.

The most gifted of them was a Dublin protestant barrister, Thomas Davis. He did most to express the group's concept of Irish nationality, as embracing everyone who lived in Ireland, regardless of creed or origin. This idea did not begin with Davis – it can be found in Tone and in O'Connell himself – but it was expressed more fully and more generously by Davis than by anyone before him.

Hardly less influential than Davis was the editor of the *Nation*, a catholic journalist from County Monaghan, Charles Gavan Duffy. He was responsible for working out the tactical theory of how an Irish parliamentary party should function in the house of commons – the theory of remaining equally independent of both English parties, and in particular of rejecting all appointments from British governments of any colour. His ideas influenced, in varying measure, all subsequent leaders of Irish parliamentary parties during the period of the union. A later recruit to the group was John Mitchel, a unitarian solicitor from County Down. Mitchel was the one who most explicitly made the case for complete separation from England, and who was most ready to advocate the use of physical force. By doing so he revived a tradition in Ireland that had subsided since the failure of the United Irishmen, but which remained continuously alive from his time, through the Fenians, to the men of 1916.

A figure on the fringe of the group who deserves to be mentioned was James Fintan Lalor. Lalor, the crippled son of a farmer in County Leix, was unknown personally to most of the Young Irelanders, but he made his impact by published letters in the *Nation* and other papers. He stressed the importance of the land question. To him, national independence was an abstract idea which by itself would never fire the rural masses of Ireland. What mattered to them were the immediate evils of the land system – the high rents, the lack of security. The national question, he claimed, would never secure the full attention of the people of Ireland until it was linked with the land question. Parnell and Davitt were to operate on the same principle in 1879-82.

In the short run, the Young Irelanders failed much more ignominiously than O'Connell himself. From being among his most devoted supporters, they became, after 1844, first his critics and then his opponents. Having broken away from him, they quarrelled among themselves, then plunged into an unplanned and completely unsuccessful insurrection in 1848, and nearly all ended up as either convicts or refugees.

But in the long run they were very far from failures, for they left behind them what they had written, and it is probably safe to say that no other group has had so great an influence on the thinking of later generations of Irishmen. More of the effects of this thinking will be seen in subsequent chapters. But it seems reasonable at this point to claim that the calling forth of this group was the greatest, if unintended, effect of O'Connell's repeal movement, just as the greatest effect of his leadership of the emancipation movement had been to arouse the political consciousness of the Irish catholic masses.

17
THE GREAT FAMINE
(1845–50)
by E. R. R. Green

The tempestuous course of Irish history in the nineteenth century often seems to resemble a mountain torrent in flood, where foam and swirling water hide the rock and boulders. The excitement of politics is like the rush and roar which so easily hold our attention. But what of the rocky channel which is the cause of all the turmoil? The fundamental conditions of economy and society are the channel down which the stream of history flows, and to write of one without the other is mere description without explanation.

Although there is no need to go any further back than the eighteenth century, there are a few general considerations which must first be taken into account. To begin with, there are certain limitations placed by nature on the economic potential of our country. We lack the mineral resources which are a guarantee of industrialisation, particularly the coal without which it was hardly possible in the nineteenth century. We do not lie at any of the great crossroads of international trade. Perhaps our greatest natural asset is the rich pasture produced by a mild and humid climate, but this favours a type of agriculture which provides only limited employment opportunities. Now, it is possible for societies as for individuals to achieve surprising success with limited resources, but we conspicuously lacked the kind of ordered and secure society which might have made this possible. A strong neighbour deprived us of independence at an early date but left the job of conquest no more than half finished. The energetic Tudor monarchs would probably have put this to rights except that their determination to be done with over-powerful noblemen coincided with a tragic schism in Christendom and precipitated a century and a half

101 Searching for potatoes during the famine (*Illustrated London News*, 22 December 1849)

of dynastic and religious conflict.

This struggle ended with the failure of James II to regain his throne and was followed by nearly a century of peace, about the longest Ireland has ever known. The eighteenth century is a remarkable period in our history, far from well known and not at all easy for us to understand. It was not just a time of peace from exhaustion as historians have often assumed. The country benefited from even a limited participation in Atlantic trade as witnessed by the prosperity of the ports. Much was done to improve communications by the building of roads and canals. The linen industry was the conspicuous success in an industrial sector which

264

became increasingly vigorous. Ireland too, had retained her parliament, and it became important as a focus of patriotic sentiment.

Ireland was far from being the most distressful of European countries in the eighteenth century. On the contrary, her prospects for a time seemed on the whole rather bright. What went wrong, then? We can best find this out by subjecting the economy and society of eighteenth-century Ireland to a somewhat closer scrutiny. There were important weaknesses in both. The standard of life of the landlords was set in the main by their far richer brethren in England which meant that too many of them were living beyond their means. In consequence, they cared little about what went on in their estates so long as they yielded the maximum money income. The tenants of such men could not hope to receive any help in investment or even to reap benefit from their own improvements.

In consequence, irresponsibility at the peak of Irish society bred the same vice at the bottom. Commercial and industrial prosperity were threatened by the disparity between English and Irish resources of every kind, a threatening situation which was aggravated by the political subordination of the one country to the other.

There were danger signals which might have been perceived and overcome but for the distortion of the Irish economy caused by the great war with France, a war which lasted over twenty years. The price of grain rose rapidly in wartime and more and more Irish grassland was broken up. A shift from pastoral to tillage farming created a demand for more labour as well. It was a situation which might have been exploited to their own advantage by tenant farmers and labourers but for the fact that the need for land was so great in a country with a rapidly increasing population. Ireland had been sparsely populated at the beginning of the eighteenth century, but conditions favoured a rise in numbers. To begin with, armies were no longer killing people or destroying their crops. Most important of all, the Irish people had assured themselves of abundant, healthful food by adopting a potato diet. Not only is the potato almost an ideal food, especially if supplemented by milk, but the produce in potatoes of a given area of ground is much greater than that for any grain crop.

265

102 Cork Society of Friends' soup kitchen (*Illustrated London News*, 16 January 1847). The man on the left is collecting tokens on a stick.

Wartime emphasis on tillage completed the triumph of the potato. It enabled the farmer to produce grain purely as a cash crop and incidentally to offer a higher rent. Nor did he need money to pay labourers; they were satisfied with a patch of ground on which to grow potatoes. Those who were fortunate enough to possess sizeable leaseholds set up as landlords themselves by creating under-tenancies. Fathers subdivided their holdings to provide for sons. Landless men reclaimed the mountain and the bog, and colonised them.

Peace came in 1815, but there was no halting the forces released during the war. Although the economy was virtually stagnant, population continued to leap ahead. It was estimated that there were 5 million people in the country in 1800; by 1821 there were said to be over 6½ million, and in 1841 there were over eight million. Although not of a kind familiar to us now, Ireland after 1815 was faced with an unemployment problem on a gigantic scale. Emigration, both to Great Britain and to North America, developed steadily but the effect was barely visible. The figures of the 1841 census reveal the appalling insecurity of Ireland's vast population.

103   A famine funeral (*Illustrated London News*, 13 February 1847)

Only 7% of holdings were over thirty acres in size, 45% were under five. In Connacht the holdings under five acres went as high as 64%. Again, while Armagh was the most thickly populated Irish county, Mayo came second, and the most thinly populated counties were Meath and Kildare. Clearly, density of population and size of holdings bore little relation to the fertility of the soil.

Over two-thirds of the Irish people were dependent on agriculture for a livelihood in 1841, but the condition of the other third was far from enviable. The growing efficiency and scale of British industry struck hard at the smaller Irish manufacturer. In a United Kingdom there was no longer any use in invoking the aid of the government; not that protection could probably have done much in any case. Irish business was also severely hit by the policy of monetary deflation pursued by the authorities until the exchequers were amalgamated in 1826. The steamship and the railway had a similar effect to the removal of tariff protection by lowering transport and handling costs and striking at the livelihood of Irish manufacturers and wholesalers.

The survival of a vast impoverished population depended on the recurring fruitfulness of the potato and on that alone. The potato too, is perishable and cannot be held in store to relieve scarcity like grain. In such circumstances, if anything were to happen to the potato harvest disaster would occur on a scale which Ireland would be unable to control and for which the British government was unprepared. Dark and gloomy though the prospects of Ireland might have been, the disaster when it came was more sudden and complete than anyone could have imagined. There was a long spell of wet weather in July of 1845, which did no apparent harm to a promising potato crop. Then in August came news of a strange disease attacking the crop in the south of England. It was potato blight. The crop all along the eastern seaboard of the United States and Canada had been ravaged in 1842, but this was its first appearance in Europe. In September, blight was observed in Waterford and Wexford, and then spread rapidly until about half the country was affected.

Although partial potato failures were nothing new in Ireland, the authorities took prompt action. Sir Robert Peel, the prime minister, appointed a scientific commission to investigate the new disease. It unfortunately failed to discover that blight is actually a fungus growth and not a disease of the potato itself, and in consequence none of the suggested remedies were appropriate. Peel's relief measures on the other hand were prompt, skilful, and on the whole successful. His immediate concern was to prevent soaring food prices in Ireland, and he accordingly purchased some £100,000 worth of Indian corn and meal in the United States early in November with which he hoped to be able to control the market. A relief commission was set up to cope with distress and the formation of local committees was encouraged. Local voluntary contributions were supplemented, usually to the extent of two-thirds, by government grants. Relief works, of which the government paid half the cost, were also set up to provide employment, for it was proposed to sell food rather than give it away. The various schemes undertaken gave work to about 140,000 people at one time. The government also expended some £365,000 in 1845-6 and provided as much again in loans.

Peel decided against prohibition of exports of food from Ireland. Far

104 Charles Edward Trevelyan, assistant-secretary to the treasury, London, 1840–59 (Radio Times Hulton Picture Library, P 48257)

more serious in his mind were the tariffs imposed on imported grain in the interests of the English farmer. Peel, therefore, took the momentous decision to repeal the corn laws as they were called. Agricultural protection had been a burning issue in English politics for years, and had become symbolical of the struggle for power between the landed class and the business men. Peel persisted, although he knew that to do so was to bring down his government and to tear the tories apart. A whig government came in under Lord John Russell. The change boded ill for Ireland, for the whigs were much more wedded to current beliefs about the economic system. These were the days when *laissez faire* was the creed of intelligent and up-to-date people, all of whom were convinced that not only was it wrong for the government to meddle with economic laws but futile. Charles Trevelyan, who as permanent head of the treasury had been in control of relief, was very much in sympathy with these ideas. He could not have found a more congenial superior than the new chancellor of the exchequer, Charles Wood, a firm believer in economy and non-intervention. It was decided at once that in the event of a second failure of the potato crop there would be no government buying; the supply of food was to be left exclusively to private enterprise.

There was a second failure, in 1846, and this time it was complete. The prospect of an appalling disaster caused no modification in the government's plans. Relief was to be limited to public works. Nor was the government any longer to meet half the cost, which was to be borne entirely by the rates. The idea, of course, was to force the Irish landlords to bear the cost. The whole burden fell on the Irish board of works. Now

269

winter set in, not a normal winter, but the harshest and longest in living memory. There was no food left, and panic began to seize the famished people. Hungry mobs roved the country, but above all they poured in on the relief works. The numbers employed leapt from 30,000 in September, to 150,000 in October, to 285,000 in November, and finally reached nearly half a million in December.

In the new year the government had to admit defeat; the board of works was spending nearly £30,000 a day and its staff had risen to over 11,500. The decision was taken in January 1847 to abandon public works and extend direct relief. It should be realised just how momentous this must have seemed to the English official mind. The basic principle of the great English poor law reform of 1834 was that relief should be given only in workhouses, and it was orthodox belief that any departure from the rule resulted in population increasing faster than the means of subsistence. To begin with, an act was passed providing for the establishment of kitchens and the free distribution of soup. The most dramatic result of this measure was the expedition of Alexis Soyer, the famous chef of the London Reform Club, to set up his model kitchen where soup could be made according to the same recipe as that which he had devised for the London poor.

Government relief measures were augmented by voluntary effort. Fund-raising groups were formed in Ireland, Britain, America, and elsewhere, which provided the resources for feeding many of the worst sufferers, especially in Connacht. The Religious Society of Friends (Quakers) took a leading part in this work, and the reports of its agents from all over Ireland did much to inform public opinion in Britain on the nature of the catastrophe. One such report was from William Edward Forster, who was later to be chief secretary for Ireland (see below, p. 287).

The situation in Ireland had reached its worst by February 1847. Great gales blew and the country was covered in thick snow. Starving people crowded into the towns and flooded to the public works which the government was proposing to close. A fever epidemic now spread like wildfire through the country. What people called 'famine fever' was in fact two separate diseases, typhus and relapsing fever. Nor was this the

105 A post-famine eviction scene (*Illustrated London News*, 16 December 1848)

only scourge. Dysentery was to be expected among people who had been eating raw turnips or seaweed or half-cooked Indian meal, and it too often led to the fatal bacillary dysentery, the 'bloody flux', which now also became epidemic. Scurvy became general among those who were forced to resort to Indian meal, which is lacking in vitamin C. 'Famine dropsy' or hunger oedema, to give it its proper name, was widespread, and resulted from starvation pure and simple. It is hardly relevant to ask how many died of starvation; there were many ways in which terrified and under-nourished people exposed to the bitter winter and to infection in soup kitchens and workhouses or on public works could perish.

People everywhere were now seized by a panic to get out of Ireland. Emigration was limited to the spring and summer, so that the effect of the partial failure of the potato crop in 1845 did little to increase the numbers that year. It was a different story in July and August of 1846 when universal failure brought the new spectacle of heavy autumn emigration. The poor cottiers went first, and then in the early weeks of 1847 the small farmers began to forsake the country in droves. Six thousand emigrants sailed from Liverpool alone in January. So great was the demand for passages that direct sailings began from Ireland. It was mainly from smaller Irish ports that the notorious 'coffin ships' sailed, old and overcrowded craft whose owners had been drawn into the traffic in the hope of high profits. Liverpool was the first city to be invaded by what was virtually an army of refugees. The population of the port at that time was about a quarter of a million, and in one January week of 1847 over 130,000 people had to be given poor relief. By June, it was reckoned that 300,000 destitute Irish people had landed in the town. A very high proportion of them, of course, soon sailed for North America, but a residue of the most poverty-stricken inevitably remained. More than 100,000 emigrants sailed for Canada in 1847 (the most economical way to the United States at that time being by this indirect route), of whom it is estimated that at least a fifth perished of privation and disease.

Meanwhile, the government having set up the soup kitchens, proceeded to the next part of its plan for handling famine in Ireland. The poor law extension act of June 1847 proposed to dispose neatly of the whole problem by thrusting responsibility on the Irish poor law, thus leaving Ireland to bear the whole cost through the poor rates. The immediate sufferers were to be the Irish landlords whom the whigs blamed by and large for the disaster that had taken place. Inevitably, to reduce the burden of rates, the landlords became more determined in their efforts to evict pauper tenants. The process of clearance was helped by the 'quarter-acre clause' of the act which excluded anyone who held more than one rood of ground from relief. An intolerable burden was placed on the Irish poor law unions whose workhouse accommodation was already grossly overcrowded. Even so, they managed to increase the maximum number of inmates from around 100,000 to 300,000 within four years. In 1849 the staggering number of 932,000 people were maintained in the workhouse for some period. There could hardly be more poignant

106 Emigrants leaving [Cork] for Liverpool on the *Nimrod* and the *Athlone*
(*Illustrated London News*, 10 May 1851)

evidence of the beggary to which Ireland had been reduced.

Black '47 had by no means seen the end of the famine. Blight struck less hard in the autumn of that year, and there was a return of confidence. In 1848, it returned with full virulence. But we know enough already of the horror of those years, and it is time to attempt a summing up of the consequences of the famine. To begin with, we need to be clear in our minds that this was primarily a disaster like a flood or earthquake. The blight was natural, no one can be held responsible for that. Conditions in Ireland which had placed thousands upon thousands of people in complete dependence on the potato are another matter. Yet the historian, if he is conscientious, will have an uneasy conscience about labelling any class or individuals as villains of the piece. The Irish landlords held the ultimate responsibility, but on the whole they were as much involved in disaster as their tenantry. The ministers of the crown who had to accept responsibility once the disaster occurred were callous, parsimonious, and self-righteous. Yet these are the very qualities which Charles Dickens, for instance, found so distasteful in men of their class, and they were exhibited as much to the English as to the Irish poor.

The potato blight had destroyed the ramshackle economy which had grown up during the French wars. A staggering problem of unemployment was liquidated in the most terrible sense of that word. In 1851 the population was 6½ million, 2 million less than the estimated population of 1845. Something like a million had succeeded in getting away and another million had perished. Yet if we turn to the agricultural statistics we find that, despite the loss, Irish production had increased rather than diminished. The area under cultivation had increased by over a million acres. The loss of population was paralleled by a decline in the number of holdings. Holdings of not more than five acres had fallen from 45% of the total to just over 15%. Holdings of over thirty acres were now 26% instead of 7%.

The pattern of modern Irish agriculture was beginning to emerge from the ruin caused by the potato blight – a family farm engaged in mixed tillage and livestock production, with the stock rather than grain increasingly providing cash income. The halt to subdivision, of necessity, brought fundamental social changes in Ireland as well. Gone were the days of early marriage and a countryside thronged with young people and children. For many the price of holding together the family farm was to remain unmarried. For many others there could be no staying in Ireland, and their energies went to the building of the United States or other new lands across the seas. Against the economic improvement must be set a worsening of political conditions. The resentment in Ireland against English handling of the famine crisis was deep and slow to heal. Worse still was the bitter hostility between landlord and tenant which boiled over into a great agrarian conflict when falling farm prices caught the farmer in the late seventies. Change in such conditions was necessarily slow, and even today it might be argued that we still have much to do to repair the damage that the Irish economy suffered in the early nineteenth century and to heal the scars that the famine left on our society.

18

FENIANISM, HOME RULE, AND THE LAND WAR

(1850–91)

by T. W. Moody

The forty-odd years between the famine and the fall of Parnell are dominated by two great questions, the land and national independence. The struggle of the tenant farmers for security in their holdings and the national struggle for independence each expressed itself in two ways, the one constitutional and parliamentary, the other revolutionary and conspiratorial. The constitutional tradition is represented in this period by Gavan Duffy's Irish Tenant League of the fifties and by Isaac Butt's home rule movement of the seventies. The revolutionary tradition is represented by the sporadic violence of agrarian secret societies, by the Young Ireland rising of 1848, and above all by the Fenian movement of the sixties. Neither of the two methods of action proved effectual when used separately. But in 1879, in face of an upsurge of agrarian distress that threatened to match that of the great famine, a common front between constitutional and revolutionary nationalists was achieved through the transcendent political genius of Charles Stewart Parnell and the passion for social justice of Michael Davitt. The struggle for land and the struggle for independence became merged in a mass movement without precedent in Irish history. Two resounding successes were achieved – for the cause of the tenant farmers, in the so-called 'land war' of 1879-82, and for the cause of home rule, in 1886, when the British liberal party under the leadership of Gladstone acknowledged the justice and the necessity of giving Ireland self-government. Though the land question was far from being settled by 1882, though Gladstone's home rule bill of 1886 was defeated in the house of commons, and though the whole national movement was disrupted by the tragic fall of Parnell in 1890-91, the consequences of the 'new departure' of 1879 were to have profound and lasting influence on the whole future of Ireland and of Anglo-Irish relations.

Post-famine Ireland was an exhausted, dispirited, and divided country. In six years – 1845-51 – the population had been reduced by about two millions. The upward trend of the preceding half-century was reversed. The population decline was accompanied by a gradual increase in the size of agricultural holdings and in gradually rising standards of rural living. But relations between landlords and tenants grew more embittered than ever as the tenants' demands for security grew more insistent and the efforts of landlords to get rid of unwanted tenants were redoubled. In the fifties the mass of the people, preoccupied with the struggle for survival, had neither energy nor spirit to struggle for national independence. O'Connell's repeal movement had already collapsed before the great famine began. At the height of the famine James Fintan Lalor had made a white-hot appeal to the tenant farmers to save themselves from starvation and at the same time to overthrow British authority by a general strike against rent. The message had fallen on deaf ears. The desperate attempt of the Young Irelanders in 1848 to win self-government by armed insurrection had begun and ended in the futile affray at Ballingarry. But if the spirit of resistance to British rule now burned very low, Ireland's population was more deeply divided than ever between the minority, largely protestant, who supported the union, and the majority, almost entirely catholic, who were alienated from it.

To the majority of Irishmen the union was now identified with hopes disappointed, grievances unremedied, liberties denied, with poverty, backwardness, and above all with the catastrophe of the great famine. On the other hand a substantial minority regarded the union as justified by its results and were determined at all costs to maintain it. They included the landowning aristocracy throughout Ireland and, in Ulster, a closely knit protestant community composed of all social classes from landowners to factory workers. For unlike the rest of Ireland, the north-east experienced during the first half of the nineteenth century an industrial revolution that brought increasing prosperity to the region and transformed Belfast into a great centre of linen manufacture, shipbuilding, and engineering. This industrial development, for which the capital was provided by Ulster protestants, had its vital connections with industrial Britain and was a powerful vested interest on the side of the union. In another way also, economic conditions in Ulster were exceptional: for in many areas, the tenant farmers enjoyed a degree of security in their holdings – the 'Ulster custom' – unknown anywhere else in Ireland.

So, then, the maintenance of the union was regarded as a vital interest not only by Great Britain but also by an important element within Ireland itself. Yet the idea of a united, self-reliant, and independent Irish nation was firmly established. On the eve of the great famine the Young Ireland leader, Thomas Davis, had given classic expression to this idea: the Irish nation was a community in which Irishmen, whatever their creed or class or ancestry, were called upon to work together for the common good in mutual affection, mutual respect, and political freedom. Davis's noble vision was to be cherished by every generation of Irish nationalists down to our own day, but was far removed from the realities of post-famine Ireland. It was in these circumstances that Charles Gavan Duffy, who had been one of Davis's closest colleagues, tried to reanimate the national spirit through the formation, in 1850, of an all-Ireland league of tenant farmers.

The aim of the Irish Tenant League was the 'three Fs' – fair rent, fixity of tenure, and freedom for the tenant to sell his interest in his holding – to be achieved through an independent Irish party in parliament. Such a party seemed to have emerged when, in the general election of 1852, about 40 professing supporters of tenant right were returned to parliament out of a total Irish representation of 103. But the party quickly disintegrated. There were various reasons for its failure, but what most struck the public was the conduct of some of its leading catholic members, Keogh, Sadleir, and others, in advancing their own careers through the championship of catholic interests with complete disregard for the interests and principles of the Tenant League. Nicknamed 'the

277

107 James Stephens (John Devoy,
Recollections of an Irish rebel,
New York, 1929)

108 John O'Mahony (John Devoy,
Recollections of an Irish rebel)

Irish Brigade', they are better known in Irish history as 'the pope's brass band'. The collapse of the league brought deep despondency and deep distrust of constitutional methods. The next phase of the national movement saw a fierce repudiation of constitutionalism and a fanatical reliance on physical force alone.

The Irish Republican Brotherhood, (I.R.B.) or the Fenian organisation, founded simultaneously at Dublin and New York in 1858 by a number of spirited men, nearly all of whom had been connected with the 1848 rising – James Stephens, John O'Mahony, Charles Kickham, John O'Leary, Thomas Clarke Luby, Michael Doheny. Jeremiah O'Donovan Rossa and his Phoenix society of Skibbereen were the first notable recruits to the new movement. While fully accepting Thomas Davis's doctrine of Irish nationality, the Fenians believed that Britain would never concede independence except to physical force, and they therefore prepared by secret military organisation for an armed uprising to be launched when Britain should be at a disadvantage. They concentrated on a single aim, independence, and insisted that the pursuit of any other aim, even reform of the land system, was a dangerous deviation. Yet, unlike previous revolutionary leaders, they made their converts almost entirely among working men – small farmers and labourers, clerks, shop assistants, and artisans. By 1865 there were thousands of such men enrolled as Fenians and prepared for action, though numerically Fenians never amounted to more than a small minority within the national movement.

109 John O'Leary (John Devoy,
Recollections of an Irish rebel)

110 Thomas Clarke Luby (John
Devoy, *Recollections of an Irish rebel*)

The social composition of Fenianism, combined with its secret organisation, was the basis of the charge frequently made against Fenians,
especially by the catholic clergy, that they were communists. But a crucial
fact about the Fenian movement is that its thinking was simply
nationalist; it had no specific social programme for the Irish republic of
its dreams. Nearly all its members were catholics, but they firmly withstood the disapproval of their church and believed in complete separation
of church and state. It differed from all previous national movements in
that it drew its support not only from the Irish at home but also from the
new Ireland that emigration had created in Britain and the U.S.A. The
special function of the American body was to aid the home organisation
with arms and officers. Considerable numbers of American officers,
trained in the civil war, came to Ireland in 1865 when that war ended; and
it was only because, owing to a conflict of view among American Fenians,
the promised arms did not also arrive, that the rising intended for 1865
was postponed. If a rising had been launched in 1865, with relations
between Britain and the U.S.A. distinctly strained, it would probably
have been a serious, though hardly a successful, challenge to British rule.
When a rising was at last attempted, in 1867, the government had the
conspiracy well in hand and nearly all the Fenian leaders were in prison.
The Fenian rising of 1867, like the Young Ireland rising of 1848, was no
more than a gesture.

Fenianism seemed to have shot its bolt in 1867. But its spirit was not

279

111   Charles Joseph Kickham (John Devoy, *Recollections of an Irish rebel*)

daunted by failure; new men arose to take the place of the imprisoned leaders, the secret organisation was quickly overhauled and improved, and a representative council was established to exercise the supreme authority hitherto vested in James Stephens. Thus reconstituted, the I.R.B. settled down to the heart-breaking task of trying to keep itself in fighting condition until the day for action should come. It had to wait nearly 50 years, during which the successes of constitutional nationalism seemed to have rendered Fenianism irrelevant as well as repugnant to the main stream of Irish politics. In the eyes of unionists Fenianism seemed to be a kind of disease that had infected the rabble of Ireland; but to those who understood it and those who believed in it Fenianism was a flame, the 'phoenix flame', that went on burning, sometimes brightly, more often dimly, in the hearts of ordinary Irishmen. The I.R.B. survived to take a leading part in 1916 in an insurrection of the kind it had aimed at in 1865.

The demonstration of national spirit afforded by the Fenians had profound effects both in Britain and Ireland. In Britain it reacted decisively on the mind of W. E. Gladstone, the greatest British statesman of the age, impelling him to embark upon a programme of 'justice to Ireland' to which he continued to give his best efforts for the rest of his life. His conscience had long been troubled on the subject of Ireland, but he confessed that it was the Fenian rising that had awakened him to a sense of 'the vast importance of the Irish question'.[1] His first administration (1868-74), marked a new era in the history of the union both by the spirit in which he sought to solve Irish problems and by two great measures of reform. First, his church act of 1869 disestablished and disendowed the

112 Jeremiah O'Donovan Rossa
(John Devoy, *Recollections of an
Irish rebel*)

anglican Church of Ireland, whose privileged position had been regarded as an unshakeable part of the union itself. So far as law could do it, all religious denominations were placed on a footing of equality. The Church of Ireland was freed from its long connection with the state, and as a self-governing community entered, bitterly protesting, on a new, more challenging, but happier phase of its history. Second, Gladstone's land act of 1870 marked the first attempt of the British parliament to intervene in the land question on the side of the tenants. It proved ineffective for its purpose of protecting them against eviction, but it was the first step in that direction and as such was a landmark in British legislation. A third problem tackled by Gladstone was that of catholic claims in the field of higher education, which Sir Robert Peel had tried, unsuccessfully, to satisfy by his institution of the Queen's Colleges in 1845. Gladstone's university bill of 1873 was a bold, ingenious, and far-sighted scheme, centring on the concept of a great new University of Dublin, with many colleges and associated institutions throughout the country. In fact the bill antagonised the principal interests involved, both catholic and protestant, and its failure fatally weakened the government. The general election of 1874 resulted in the defeat of the liberals and the return of the conservatives to power under Disraeli. It was Disraeli who, in his last year of office, laid the foundation of a new university, the Royal University of Ireland, which, from 1880 to 1908, served as a working compromise between the claims of the catholic hierarchy and the views of the British parliament.

While Gladstone was endeavouring to solve the Irish problem by reforms, a new effort to win independence by constitutional means was

281

launched in Ireland. This was the home rule movement, founded in 1870 by Isaac Butt, the leading Irish barrister of the age, a man of large and colourful personality, a protestant and formerly a unionist, who had been converted to nationalism by his experience of Irish suffering in the great famine and by the courage and integrity first of the Young Irelanders and then of the Fenians. The objective of the new movement – a subordinate parliament with control over Irish domestic affairs – fell far short of the independence sought by the Fenians. But that now seemed so remote a possibility that a number of influential Fenians, notably Patrick Egan and John O'Connor Power, chose to help Butt win an instalment of independence rather than to remain inactive indefinitely. So an essentially moderate and conservative movement, whose main support came from the catholic middle classes, was started with the goodwill of extreme nationalists. For the Fenians this was a 'new departure', which soon led to deep division among them.

In the general election of 1874, the first to be fought under conditions of secret voting in accordance with the ballot act of 1872, Butt's new party won more than half of all the Irish seats. For the next five years Butt advocated the home rule case in parliament with the utmost persuasiveness, patience, and respect for the traditions of the house of commons. But his claim to separate nationhood for Ireland was not taken seriously by either British party. Soon there arose within the Irish party a small group who held that Butt was quite wrong in trying to conciliate and convince the house of commons. The right policy was to attack and exasperate both British parties by using the ancient procedure of the house of commons for the purpose of obstructing its business. The pioneers of this

114 Isaac Butt, by John B. Yeats
(National Gallery of Ireland)

policy of obstruction, Joseph Gillis Biggar and John O'Connor Power, both of them Fenians, were joined in 1875 by a newly elected M.P., Charles Stewart Parnell, a young protestant landowner of County Wicklow. He had inherited the seeds of Irish nationalism both from his Irish father and his American mother, who was of Irish descent. Though a poor speaker he perfected the technique of obstruction and made himself the best-hated man in the house of commons. This brought him into conflict with his leader, Butt, to whom the activities of the obstructionists were utterly obnoxious. A struggle for mastery between the elderly leader and the youthful new recruit began. By the middle of 1877 Parnell was obviously a rising, Butt a setting, star. Parnell had a matchless genius for leadership. His aloofness and his self-restraint concealed a passionate nature of exceptional intensity and strength of purpose. Conservative in temperament and social outlook, pragmatic and clear-eyed in his approach to every problem, he concentrated his attention on achieving for Ireland the minimum of change that he judged necessary to solve the vital problems while always conveying an impression of dangerous and exciting extremism.

In August 1876 the supreme council of the I.R.B. formally condemned continued cooperation with the home rule movement, but the new policy continued to make converts among Fenians. The Fenian movement in America, as organised in the Clan na Gael, was showing keen interest in it and in Parnell's potentialities as a nationalist. Parnell welcomed Fenian support, and from 1877 onwards was never without it, but regarded any alliance with Fenians as unrealistic and likely only to hinder him in his chosen field.

This was Parnell's position when there entered into Irish politics a striking new personality, Michael Davitt, released from prison in December 1877, after seven years of penal servitude. The previous careers of Parnell and Davitt, both born in 1846, at the height of the famine, present a dramatic contrast. Parnell, the son of a country gentleman, was born in Avondale House, a comfortable country mansion in lovely surroundings in the heart of Wicklow. Till he entered parliament in 1874 he had lived an easy, affluent, aimless life, very much conforming to type. Davitt was the son of an evicted small tenant, exiled in 1850 from Mayo to Lancashire where he spent a hard though not unhappy boyhood in the cotton town of Haslingden. At the age of nine he was working twelve hours a day in a cotton mill. He was just over eleven when in 1857 he lost his right arm in a machine he was minding. This led to four years of unexpected schooling and employment with the local postmaster. A life of comparative security seemed to be opening up when in 1865 Davitt threw himself into the Fenian movement. His Fenian activities earned him in 1870 a sentence of 15 years penal servitude, of which he served seven years, mainly in Dartmoor. His release on ticket-of-leave in December 1877 was the outcome of a long and persistent agitation for amnesty for the Fenian prisoners, in which Butt, Parnell, and others took a leading part. He emerged from prison a far more formidable enemy of Britain than when he went in. He was still a Fenian but critical of Fenian methods and Fenian dogmatism. Passionate and proud, he was also self-critical and self-disciplined. A catholic who had been taught by a Wesleyan schoolmaster, he accepted religious diversity as a social fact and not a ground of estrangement among men. Hatred of British domination and of British landlordism in Ireland was in his blood, and yet, an Irishman reared in England, he rather liked the English and had an instinctive understanding of the English working-man. Above all, he had a passion for social justice that transcended nationality.

Parnell and Davitt were quick to respect and to understand each other. Davitt wanted to get Parnell into the I.R.B. and with his help to organise cooperation between Fenians and Parnellites. Parnell was interested but unconvinced. In 1878 Davitt went to America, where in collaboration with John Devoy, the dominant personality among American Fenians, he formulated a new policy for the national movement. The essence of this second 'new departure', which was endorsed by the Clan na Gael, was an alliance of revolutionary and constitutional nationalists on the two great issues of self-government and the land.

Both the supreme council of the I.R.B. and Parnell refused to accept the new policy. But a rather different 'new departure' was launched by Davitt with spectacular success in 1879. This was his response to an economic crisis that, in the winter of 1878-9, threatened the rural population with a disaster comparable with that of the great famine. As the combined result of falling prices, crop failures, and exceptionally wet weather, a multitude of small farmers were facing bankruptcy, starvation, and eviction. Here was a crisis that dwarfed in importance all immediate political considerations; and Davitt threw all his energies into the task of promoting concerted action for self-defence among the tenant farmers. In April 1879, he joined with James Daly, editor of the *Connaught Telegraph*, and a number of local Fenians in organising a land meeting at Irishtown, in his native Mayo, that precipitated a general agitation in the west. It was clear to Davitt that the one man who could successfully lead the new movement was Parnell, who, after Butt's death in May 1879, was unquestionably marked out as the eventual leader of the home rule party. Parnell agreed to speak at the great land-meeting at Westport on 8 June, and there he gave a headline to the whole ensuing agitation: 'hold a firm grip of your homesteads and lands'.[2] Four months later, when Davitt founded the Irish National Land League to provide the agitation with a nation-wide organisation, Parnell agreed to become its president.

The partnership of Parnell and Davitt in the Land League was essential to the success of the ensuing struggle – Parnell preeminent as the leader to whom all sections of national opinion rendered allegiance, Davitt the league's inspiring genius and principal organiser. The league combined in one great agrarian movement nationalists of all kinds, from moderate home-rulers to extreme republicans. The most combative element was provided by Fenians, though they acted without the approval of the I.R.B. The Clan na Gael gave the league timely financial help, which

115 Charles Stewart Parnell, *c.* 1880
(John Devoy, *The land of Éire*,
New York, 1882)

116 Michael Davitt, *c.* 1880 (John
Devoy, *The land of Éire*)

quickly broadened out into powerful backing from all sections of Irish
nationalist opinion in America. The catholic parish clergy were for the
most part solidly behind the league, and so were a number of the catholic
bishops. In part the league served as a relief agency, augmenting the
work of the voluntary relief-organisations through which, during the
winter of 1879-80, the catastrophe of a second great famine was averted.
But the league's essential task was to organise resistance to the landlords
for the immediate purpose of preventing eviction and securing a
reduction in rents, and for the ultimate purpose of transforming the
tenant farmers into owners of their holdings. The so-called 'land war' of
1879-82 was the greatest mass-movement of modern Ireland. An elaborate system of 'moral-force warfare' was developed: process-serving and
evictions were made the occasion of great popular demonstrations;
families evicted for non-payment of rent were sheltered and supported;
an embargo was placed on evicted farms; persons involved in prosecu-
tions because of their league activities were defended and the families of
those sent to prison were cared for; and the terrible weapon of social
ostracism, the boycott, was perfected as the ultimate sanction of the
league against all persons who violated its code. For the first time the
tenant farmers as a class stood up to the landlords. The passions roused
by the agitation inevitably erupted into violence and outrage, but it was
just because the Land League was technically a lawful organisation that
the government had so much difficulty in coming to grips with it.

In the midst of this upheaval a general election, held in April 1880, put

an end to Disraeli's conservative administration and brought Gladstone
back to office. In Ireland the election was fought on the land issue; and
Parnell, with all the prestige that leadership of the land agitation gave
him, won his first electoral triumph and became head of a militant Irish
party in parliament. Gladstone entrusted the government of Ireland to
one of his strongest and most dedicated colleagues, William Edward
Forster (see above, p. 270), who accepted the chief secretaryship in a
spirit of good will and conciliation towards Ireland. But his initial attempt
to lessen tension by a temporary measure of protection for the tenants –
the compensation for disturbance bill – was frustrated by the house of
lords (August), and he was left with no alternative but to enforce the
existing land law against the tenants. So while he and Gladstone were
preparing a new land bill, the land war became more embittered than
before. The danger of famine was now past but landlords redoubled their
efforts to evict defaulting tenants. The ordinary law became paralysed,
and the Land League assumed the functions of a rival government,
whose courts – forerunners of the Sinn Féin courts set up in 1920 –
wielded stronger sanctions than those of the state itself. It was during this
phase of the land war that Captain Charles Boycott, of Lough Mask
House, County Mayo, defied the league, and added a new word to the
English language. In September 1880 he and his family were reduced to a
state of isolation and helplessness from which they were rescued only by a
relief expedition of fifty volunteer Orange labourers from Monaghan,
protected by strong forces of troops. Some £350 worth of potatoes and
other crops were thus harvested at a cost of over ten times their value.

The government answered the Land League's challenge by obtaining
exceptional powers of coercion from parliament and applying them with
vigour and severity. Davitt was the first leader to be arrested (3 February).
But at the same time Gladstone carried a new land act, based on the principle of the 'three Fs'. This transformed the landlord-tenant relationship
and introduced a system of dual ownership. A special court was created
to which tenants could apply to have a fair rent fixed for their holdings,
and this judicial rent was to hold good for fifteen years. The full value of
the act to the tenants was not at once appreciated. The Land League,

insisting that peasant ownership and not the 'three Fs' was the only satis-factory principle of settlement, refused to call off the agitation. Gladstone retorted by arresting all the principal leaders – Parnell, Dillon, O'Brien, Brennan, Sexton, Kettle – and eventually suppressing the league itself (October 1881). The direction of the movement was taken over by an auxiliary body, the Ladies' Land League, initiated by Davitt before his arrest and headed by Anna Parnell, Charles's indomitable sister. But the ladies were not able to control the wilder elements in the agitation. The spectacle of Ireland a prey to irresponsible nobodies became as repugnant to Parnell as it was to Gladstone. Taking a realist view of the situation, Gladstone made peace with Parnell in the so-called 'Kilmainham treaty' of March 1882, by which the government agreed to make further concessions to the tenants, and Parnell agreed to call off the agitation. Forster, refusing to be a party to the agreement, resigned, the prisoners were released, the regime of coercion ceased, and Lord Frederick Cavendish was sent to Dublin as chief secretary to inaugurate a new and happier era. On the day of his arrival, 6 May, he and the under-secretary, T. H. Burke, were murdered in the Phoenix Park by members of a secret assassination club, the Invincibles. The deed threatened to destroy all the hopes raised by the Kilmainham treaty. It was followed by a ferocious new coercion act, but it did not prevent Gladstone from ful-filling Irish expectations with regard to the vital question of tenants' arrears, and it did not fundamentally alter Gladstone's attitude towards Parnell and Ireland.

The land war convinced British statesmen of both parties that the land-lord system as it existed in Ireland was no longer defensible. Gladstone's remedy, the land act of 1881, progressively diminished the landlords' interest in the land. The fair rents fixed by the land court in the first three years showed an average reduction of nearly twenty per cent. Landlords began to feel that it would be better to sell out to their tenants on favour-able terms than to share ownership with them. Dual ownership thus pre-pared the way for peasant proprietorship; and by a historical paradox, it was a conservative government that, in 1885, established, by the Ashbourne act, the system of state-aided land purchase which, developed by many later acts – and especially the Wyndham act of 1903 – did eventually abolish the old landlordism and turn Ireland into a land of owner occupiers. This has been the greatest revolution in the history of modern Ireland, even though it was not the revolution that Davitt, the 'father of the Land League', had sought. 'The land for the people', the great watchword of the Land League, meant to the tenant farmers only one thing – that they themselves should become owners of their holdings. But from 1881 Davitt defined the phrase as meaning national ownership. From 1882 he never ceased to advocate this object as the only real solution to the land problem.

From the great famine to the land war the idea of national independence had in practice meant little to the tenant farmers. But the land war was not merely an agrarian movement; it was also a great movement of national self-assertion. Parnell and Davitt had no doubt that the destruction of landlordism would lead to the overthrow of English power in Ireland. Parnell at Galway on 14 October 1880 made the characteristic statement: 'I would not have taken off my coat and gone to this work if I had not known that we were laying the foundation in this movement for the regeneration of our legislative independence'.[3] As soon as the agrarian crisis was over, Parnell withdrew from the agrarian agitation, and steered the national movement firmly towards self-government, to be achieved by act of parliament. The Land League was replaced by a new organisation, the National League, dominated by the parliamentary party and providing it with effective electoral machinery. The discipline of the party was perfected and the whole national movement consolidated under Parnell's leadership in preparation for the next general election. That election, held in November-December 1885, was all the more significant because it was the first in British history to be fought on a comparatively democratic franchise. The result was a liberal victory in Great Britain and an overwhelming Parnellite victory in Ireland, where pledge-bound home-rulers were returned for every seat outside eastern Ulster and Dublin University. To Gladstone this result was decisive: in it he recognised 'the fixed desire of a nation, clearly and constitutionally expressed'.[4] In August 1885, after the defeat of his second admini-

117 Land League meeting at Kildare, 3 January 1881; Michael J. Boyton burning leases of the duke of Leinster on a '98 pike (*Illustrated London News*, 8 January 1881)

stration, he became convinced that home rule was a just cause which he was called upon to champion, cost what it might. Thus in January 1886 he formed his third administration for the purpose of giving home rule to Ireland. He was then in his seventy-seventh year, the most dominating, most astounding, most dauntless figure in British politics.

Gladstone's home rule bill of 1886 contemplated a devolution of authority by the imperial parliament to an Irish parliament comparable with that which was to operate in Northern Ireland from 1921 to 1972. The intention of the bill, Gladstone declared, was to discharge a great historic debt of justice to Ireland, and in that spirit it was accepted in principle, while subjected to criticism in some of its details, by Parnell and his party, and by Irish nationalist opinion at home, in America, and in Australasia, as the basis of a lasting settlement. It involved British recognition of Ireland's claim to nationhood and British repudiation of the policy on which Ireland had been governed for centuries. It implied the application to Ireland of those traditions of British statesmanship that had fostered the growth of free institutions in Canada and other parts of the British Empire. That it was tabled at all was a triumph for Parnell's statesmanship and conclusive evidence of Gladstone's perception of the essential conservatism of Parnell. But to the conservative party the bill was infamous – destructive of the unity of the empire, a betrayal of the loyalist and protestant element in Ireland, a surrender to those who had proved by their duplicity and their crimes that they were unfit for self-government. The absence from the bill of any specific safeguards for protestant interests in Ulster, such as a separate legislature, gave the opposition a valuable debating-point. Gladstone was aware of the Ulster problem but believed that the upper chamber of the proposed Irish legislature, which would be weighted in favour of social status and property, would adequately safeguard minority interests. Militant Orangeism counted for far less with him than the passionate insistence of the nationalists that (in Parnell's words):

We want the energy, the patriotism, the talent, and works of every Irishman to make this great experiment. . . successful. . . We want. . . all creeds and all classes in Ireland. We cannot look upon a single Irishman as not belonging to us.[5]

The opposition of the conservative party could not have defeated the bill, but it was decisively augmented by a defection from the two extreme wings of the liberal party – whigs under Lord Hartington on the right, radicals under Joseph Chamberlain on the left. The revolt of the aristocratic whigs was predetermined by differences on social and imperial policy as well as over Ireland; but that of the radicals might conceivably have been avoided if Gladstone had handled Chamberlain differently – Chamberlain who aspired to succeed him as leader of the party and to be the spearhead of social reform. The bill was defeated by a majority of 30. If it had passed the commons it would, of course, have been killed by the lords, but in that case an appeal to the country could have been made under conditions more favourable than those under which Gladstone had to fight the general election of 1886 – the first to be fought in Great Britain on the issue of home rule. It resulted in a heavy defeat for Gladstone, which he accepted with magnificent courage and with no thought of abandoning the struggle.

This attempt, however unsuccessful, to carry home rule made 1886 a landmark in Anglo-Irish relations. It captured the imagination and won the admiration of Irishmen everywhere. It committed the large majority of the liberal party to home rule, and thus fundamentally altered the conditions of Irish and British politics. Nationalist Ireland could no longer regard Britain collectively as the national enemy, and the Irish party was no longer, as it had been since 1880, an alien 'third force' in the British parliament. But the liberal split proved irreparable. During the next twenty years the liberals held office only once, for just under three years (1892-5). But that was not obvious in 1886, and Gladstone continued to the end of his public career (in 1894), to fight for home rule. He made remarkable progress in winning converts and considered, with good reason, that, if the next general election had occurred in the summer of 1890 instead of in 1892 (as it did), he would have had a handsome majority. His efforts were assisted by the egregious failure of *The Times* newspaper to ruin the reputation of the Parnellites, and with it that of the liberals, by branding them with complicity in outrage and murder during and after the land war. A special commission of three high-court judges appointed to inquire into all the charges of *The Times* found that letters on which the most atrocious of them depended had been forged by a renegade nationalist, Richard Pigott. The judges' report produced a revulsion of feeling in Britain in Parnell's favour; but in less than a year all this advantage was wiped out by the revelation in the divorce court (November 1890) of Parnell's adultery with the wife of W. H. O'Shea, a former member of the home rule party.

The immediate reaction of British nonconformist opinion to the O'Shea case was violent hostility to Parnell's continued leadership of the Irish party. No section of British opinion had responded so ardently as the nonconformists to Gladstone's crusade for home rule as a great moral issue, and no single element was more vital to the existence of the liberal party than the nonconformists, especially since the secession of the whig element. The party was thus threatened with a new and ruinous split. It was this political fact, and not any moral judgment on Parnell, that caused Gladstone to demand his temporary retirement from the leadership. Parnell's ferocious refusal to do so produced a bitter and demoralising split in the party he had largely created. His death a year later (6 October 1891) still desperately fighting for his leadership, did not end the

118 Gladstone introducing the home rule bill in the house of commons, 8 April 1886 (*Illustrated London News*, 17 April 1886)

split, which went on till 1900. Nevertheless Gladstone succeeded in keeping the liberal party firm on the home rule issue, and when the general election of 1892 gave the liberals a majority he formed his fourth and last administration for a renewed effort to carry home rule. His second home rule bill (1893) passed the house of commons but was overwhelmingly defeated by the house of lords. He was then 84.

Parnell's fall deprived the Irish party of a leader whose genius was irreplaceable, and seriously injured the home rule cause among the British public. It was all the more tragic because, in the supreme crisis of his life, Parnell abandoned the stern realism that had hitherto governed all his political conduct and allowed his passion and his pride to overmaster him. His refusal to contemplate even a temporary retirement forced an excruciating decision on a majority of his party.

Yet Parnell's achievement as a statesman, damaged though it was by his fall, was far from being undone; nor has it ever been undone. He brought Ireland's claims home to the British people as no Irish leader had ever succeeded in doing, and he is rightly remembered not by the actual extent of the self-government he was willing to accept from Britain but by the spirit of splendid defiance with which he voiced the Irish demand for independent nationhood. His superb leadership during ten critical years created conditions that prepared the way for the final stages in the struggle for independence.

19

FROM PARNELL TO PEARSE
(1891–1921)

by Donal McCartney

The thirty years between the death of Parnell and the signing of the Anglo-Irish treaty in 1921 flashed with more brilliance, and, at the same time, were riddled with more disappointment, than any comparable era in our history. At the beginning of the period the Irish people seemed content that Ireland should remain part of the United Kingdom, retaining English institutions and the English language. In parliament, national demands went no further than a limited measure of control over domestic affairs, and a continuation of the reform of the land system enabling the tenant farmers to become owners of the land they worked. But in 1921 the demand was for a more definite break with England, and for a more distinct and separate national existence in politics, economics and culture.

What follows is an attempt to account for the change that took place in the outlook of a generation.

In 1891 Parnell was dead. The forces which his leadership had held together in a great unified national movement had split apart, and the result was a decade of political division and ineffectiveness.

The bitter years of the Parnellite split presented a sharp contrast with the days of Parnell's glory; and with the fall of Parnell, the romantic hero, young men retreated from the party politics of home rule and fashioned their dreams in other activities. Small coteries turning away in disgust from the vicious political squabbling of the 1890s built for themselves so many separate little dream-worlds in a nationalistic Tír-na-nÓg, where poetry meant more than politics, and where ideals counted far more than votes.

One of these non-political movements emerging in what was called the Anglo-Irish literary revival was led by the poet, William Butler Yeats. In Yeats's vision the poets and the dramatists and the writers would cater for the intellectual, as distinct from the material, needs of Ireland. For without an intellectual life of some kind, it was argued, the Irish could not long preserve their nationality. Yeats dreamed of the people cultivating a national literature that would be of the highest aesthetic quality. And in this movement he was assisted by a galaxy of literary talent – Lady Gregory, George Russell, Douglas Hyde, T. W. Rolleston, Standish O'Grady, J. M. Synge, George Moore, James Stephens, and others. Between them they revived and romanticised the early legends and history of Ireland. And they sent into circulation the image of a new Irish hero, the legendary Cuchulainn, famed for heroic feats, to replace a prosaic Grattan or O'Connell, the models of the home-rulers. The literary revivalists pictured Ireland as a poor old woman who would become a queen once more only when men became as chivalrous as Cuchulainn and thought her worth dying for. This idea was dramatised by Yeats in *Cathleen Ní Houlihan:*

It is a hard service they take that may help me. Many that are red cheeked now will be pale cheeked; many that have been free to walk the hills and the bogs and the rushes will be sent to walk hard streets in far countries; many a good plan will be broken; many that have gathered money will not stay to spend it; many a child will be born and there will be no father at its christening to give it a name. They that have red cheeks will have pale cheeks for my sake; and for all that they will think that they are well paid.

> They shall be remembered for ever,
> They shall be alive for ever,
> They shall be speaking for ever,
> The people shall hear them for ever.[1]

The nationalistic, and even separatist, impact of Yeats and his friends was profound, but it was limited and confined mainly to fellow poetic natures. However, what the literary revival lacked in popular appeal was supplied by the Gaelic League. The Gaelic League, founded by Douglas Hyde and Eoin MacNeill in 1893, had its own dream – at first to keep

295

119 Pioneers of the Gaelic revival:
(a) Douglas Hyde, by Sarah Purser,
R.H.A. (photo. National Gallery of
Ireland);

(b) Eoghan O'Growney (*Leabhar an
t-Athair Eoghan: the O'Growney
memorial volume*, 1904); .

Irish alive where it was still spoken, and later, to restore Irish as the
spoken language of the country. By giving up our native language and
customs, said Hyde, we had thrown away the best claim which we had
upon the world's recognition of us as a separate nation. Therefore the
task facing the present generation of Irishmen was the re-creation of a
separate cultural Irish nation, and this could only be done by what Hyde
called de-anglicisation – refusing to imitate the English in their language,
literature, music, games, dress, and ideas. Hyde argued that the practical
steps taken by the Gaelic Athletic Association to revive the national
games had done more good for Ireland in five years than all the talk for
sixty. D. P. Moran vigorously developed Hyde's message. Every week in
his influential paper, the *Leader*, Moran relentlessly propagated what he
called the philosophy of Irish Ireland in well-written pungent
commentaries on passing events.

With such publicists as Hyde and Moran, workers like MacNeill and
Pearse, and authors like O'Growney, Dinneen, and An t-Athair Peadar,
the Gaelic League caught hold of the popular imagination. It showed
great potential as an adult education-cum-entertainment movement with
its language, history, and dancing classes, its drama groups, its local
feiseanna and the annual *oireachtas* and *ard-fheis*. The league became
much more than a mere language or literary organisation. It propagated
national self-reliance and self-respect, and campaigned against all forms
of west-Britonism and *shoneenism*. The Gaelic League in fact, became a
well-organised, nation-wide pressure-group, and it could claim among its

296

(c) Eoin MacNeill (Cashman Collection,
Radio Telefís Éireann)

other achievements that it gave Irish a prominent place in every branch of education; closed the pubs on St Patrick's Day; turned that day into a national holiday; and promoted native industry by helping to organise industrial parades.

The Gaelic League appealed even to some unionists. Horace Plunkett, for example, then busily engaged in organising the cooperative movement in Irish agriculture, was impressed by the fact that in 1903 the number of Gaelic League branches, 600, had trebled in a couple of years; within a single year Irish had been introduced to 1,300 National Schools; the sale of its publications in a country which allegedly did not read stood at a quarter of a million for one year; its administrative expenses, collected by voluntary subscription, reached about £6,000 a year; and it was employing full-time some twenty-two people. The league, wrote Plunkett, was invigorating every department of Irish life, and adding to the intellectual, social, and moral improvement of the people.

Although it claimed to be non-political the league had provided the best argument yet for the recognition of Ireland as a separate national entity. More than any other movement the Gaelic League provided the atmosphere for the development in Ireland of the new-look nationalism then powerfully operating in Europe. According to this new nationalism politically independent states should be raised up wherever there existed distinct cultural nations. The Gaelic League was demonstrating that Ireland was a cultural nation; therefore, went the argument, Ireland was entitled to become a nation-state.

120 National
Volunteers in
training, 1913
(Cashman Collection,
Radio Telefís
Éireann)

Among the political groups coloured to a greater or a lesser degree by the Gaelic League's philosophy were Sinn Féin, the I.R.B. and Connolly's socialist movement. Sinn Féin owed its inspiration to Arthur Griffith, who, like so many other Dubliners, had remained stubbornly loyal to Parnell's memory. As in the case of Yeats and Hyde and their colleagues, Griffith, too, rejected the post-Parnellite politics of home rule. In the *United Irishman,* the paper which he edited since its foundation in 1899, Griffith first propounded his policy which was in fact an extension of Parnell's obstruction tactics and an adaptation of the Land League's boycott – or, for that matter, the G.A.A.'s ban on foreign games, or the Gaelic League's policy of de-anglicisation – to the political situation. Griffith's articles were collected, and published in pamphlet form for the first time in 1904, under the title, *The resurrection of Hungary.*

The great attraction of the Sinn Féin policy – as it came to be called – was the sheer simplicity of its logic. Griffith held, as indeed did the leaders of the home rule party, that the act of union of 1800 was illegal. But Griffith drew from this the conclusion that the Irish M.P.s who since 1800 sat in the Westminster parliament were thereby participating in an illegality and helping to perpetuate a crime. They should withdraw from the imperial parliament and together with the elected representatives of the county councils and local authorities set up at home in Ireland a

298

121 Citizen Army
on parade, 1914
(photo. Keogh Bros.,
Dublin)

Council of Three Hundred to take over the government of the country
and to pursue a policy of political and economic self-sufficiency. This was
the policy which had won the Hungarians their independence from
Austria.

What is often overlooked is the fact that Griffith was himself a
separatist, at least when he first formulated his policy, and was for a time
a member of the I.R.B. When therefore he proposed that there should be
a return to the constitutional position of Grattan's parliament with the
crown as the personal link between Ireland and England, he did so
because he held that in the circumstances the principle of a dual monarchy
would win more widespread support in Ireland. Griffith's policy possessed
a certain fascination for the members of separatist societies like Cumann
na nGael and the National Council and Maud Gonne's *Inghinidhe na
hEireann*, all of which had developed out of opposition to the royal visits
of 1900 and 1903, as well as for the Belfast republicans who had founded
the Dungannon Clubs. And these were welded together from 1908 to
become the Sinn Féin organisation.

Sinn Féin had some success at local elections and started its own
weekly paper. But although a young intellectual home ruler like T. M.
Kettle could describe Griffith's policy as 'the largest idea contributed to
Irish politics for a generation',[2] Sinn Féin won little sympathy from home
rule supporters generally. Nevertheless Sinn Féin felt confident enough

299

122 Funeral of O'Donovan Rossa, Glasnevin, 1 August 1915 (Cashman Collection, Radio Telefís Éireann)

to engage in a trial of strength with the Irish party in 1908. A young home-ruler, Charles J. Dolan, M.P. for North Leitrim, resigned his seat and offered himself for reelection as a Sinn Féin candidate. But the parliamentary party retained the seat by a two-to-one majority. Sinn Féin however, although no match for the parliamentary party at the polls in the years when the prospects for home rule were brightening, continued to offer an alternative to parliamentarianism.

Between Sinn Féin and the I.R.B., there existed an affinity based on separatist tendencies in both, and cemented by close personal friendships. The big difference between the two was that while Sinn Féin stood by a policy of passive resistance and hoped by aiming at a dual monarchy to cast a net wide enough to catch most Irishmen, the I.R.B. planned to establish an Irish republic by physical force. After the Parnellite split the I.R.B., small in membership, suffered from its own internal divisions and did not consider rebellion feasible in the circumstances. But, like John Mitchel before them, men in the I.R.B. dreamed of the outbreak of a war which would involve England and thereby provide Ireland with an opportunity.

> You that Mitchel's prayer have heard,
> 'Send war in our time, O Lord!'[3]

300

The growth of two armed camps in Europe, and the crowding of one diplomatic crisis on another increased the possibility of a European war. A frail little man with an indomitable Fenian spirit which 15½ years imprisonment had not broken, and with a single idea in his head – *to get the English out* – was cheered by the prospect of a general war. To ensure that Ireland would be ready to seize its opportunity, Tom Clarke returned from exile in America. His small shop in Parnell Street became the nerve-centre, and his closest friend, the handsome Seán Mac Diarmada, then the paid organiser of Sinn Féin, became the essential link-man, in a revitalised I.R.B.

By 1910 the I.R.B. was publishing its paper, *Irish Freedom*, managed by Mac Diarmada and edited by Hobson, with its motto taken from Wolfe Tone – 'to break the connection with England'. And soon eager young nationalists who, as Pearse put it, had been to school to the Gaelic League, like Pearse himself, MacDonagh, Plunkett, and Ceannt, were being drawn into the I.R.B.

Independent of the I.R.B. another small group, of trade unionists and socialists, were dreaming of a somewhat different kind of revolution. Since the land war of the 1880s a revolution had taken place in the ownership of the land of Ireland. For one of the effects of the land war was that following a series of land acts, the unionist ascendancy landlords were replaced by small proprietors, for the most part catholic and nationalist. The settlement of the land question, together with improved material conditions left the farming classes reasonably well satisfied. In the larger towns, however, conditions were far from satisfactory. In 1911, although it was then held that there had been a 'manifest, material improvement' over the previous eleven years, Dublin had one of the most underfed, worst-housed, and badly paid populations in Europe. 21,000 families lived in single-room tenements. The death-rate at birth of 27.6 per 1,000 was higher than that of any other city in Europe (with Moscow second to Dublin). Pearse wrote in *Irish Freedom* (October 1913):

I calculate that one-third of the people of Dublin are underfed; that half the children attending Irish primary schools are ill-nourished. . . I suppose there are 20,000 families in Dublin in whose domestic economy milk and butter are all but

301

123 Éamon de Valéra addressing anti-conscription meeting at Ballaghadereen, 1918 (Cashman Collection, Radio Telefís Éireann)

unknown; black tea and dry bread are their staple diet. There are many thousand fireless hearth places in Dublin on the bitterest days of winter.[4]

Marx, Engels, and Lenin, who each had kept a close eye on Ireland, had allowed for the fact that when the socialist revolution came to the world, overthrowing the existing social order, it might well be sparked off in this country. Events in Dublin in 1913 encouraged this belief among European socialists.

To improve the conditions of the working class a fiery Jim Larkin, assisted by the more intellectual James Connolly, organised the Irish Transport and General Workers' Union. In August 1913 began a showdown between Larkin and the employers' leader, William Martin Murphy. Murphy organised some 400 employers into a federation and locked out the workers who were members of Larkin's union. By the end of September 24,000 people were locked out. A bitter struggle, protracted over eight months, followed. Dublin witnessed massive rallies, baton charges by the police resulting in numerous injuries and a couple of deaths, riots, arrests, imprisonments, food-ships from English sympathisers, and sympathetic strikes.

Neither side won, but the results were far-reaching. The spirit of militancy that had been aroused played a significant role in extending the revolutionary climate. The Citizen Army, which had been established to protect the strikers, continued in existence after the labour troubles had subsided, to play an important part in the rising of 1916. Connolly, who, as far back as 1896, had founded the Irish Socialist Republican Party, was all his life a nationalist as well as a socialist. In 1913, Connolly the socialist had called on the British working class to show solidarity with their brothers in Dublin and to stage a general sympathetic strike. But after some signs that this might be realised, Connolly was disappointed. For the future he put his trust more and more in the establishment of a republic by the Irish workers themselves. 'The cause of labour,' he wrote, 'is the cause of Ireland, the cause of Ireland is the cause of labour'.[5] Besides, Tom Clarke, Pearse, and *Irish Freedom* had given their backing to Larkin in 1913 and thus had increased the sympathy between the labour movement and the republicans.

Here, then, were a number of small dynamic groups – the literary movement, the Gaelic League, the G.A.A., Irish Ireland, Sinn Féin, the I.R.B., and the labour movement – each concerned not so much with electoral or parliamentary success, but devoted rather to some social, cultural, or political ideal and together acting as a ferment in the mind of a generation. It was the interaction of these forces upon each other that was effecting the change in the mental climate of Ireland between 1891 and 1921.

Pearse at Tone's graveside in 1913, and at O'Donovan Rossa's in 1915, is an excellent example of the synthesis of cultural and political separatist traditions then taking place in individuals. On these occasions Pearse spoke as an I.R.B. man, dressed in 1915 in the uniform of an Irish Volunteer, to honour Tone the father of Irish republicanism and Rossa 'the unrepentant Fenian'. His opening paragraphs on Rossa were in Irish, showing the impact which the Gaelic League – 'the most revolutionary influence that has ever come into Ireland', as he called it – had on Pearse. And when in his oration at Tone's grave he spoke the passage about the sorrowful destiny of the heroes who turn their backs on the pleasant paths for Ireland's sake he might well have been paraphrasing the words which Yeats had put into the mouth of Cathleen Ní Houlihan when she enticed the young man in the play to leave all things fair and follow her down the thorny path of history, or equally Pearse's words might have come from the lips of Cuchulainn defending the gap of the north as romanticised in the books of Standish O'Grady. Pearse admired both Tone and Rossa for reasons which would also have won the approval of the labour leader, Connolly; running through these graveside orations was the defiant and self-reliant note of the Sinn Féin gospel. Thus were the ideals of the literary revival, of the Gaelic League, of the I.R.B., of Sinn Féin, of the Irish Volunteers and of Connolly's socialist republicans becoming part of the psychological make-up of a generation which Pearse represented.

What still made the loudest noise on the political surface, however, was home rule. The liberal party under Gladstone had introduced home rule bills in 1886 and 1893 which were defeated. With the unionists entrenched in office, and the Irish parliamentary party split, home rule did not become an issue again until 1906 when the liberals returned to office and the prospects for home rule brightened. Meantime, the Irish party, reunited under Redmond since 1900, recaptured much of the support and respect which it had gained from the Irish electorate in the days of Parnell. Moreover the reform of county government in 1898, which transferred control over local affairs from landlord-dominated grand juries to popularly elected bodies – county councils, and rural and urban district councils – enabled nationalists to gain experience of local self-government which they looked forward to applying in an Irish parliament.

The general election of 1910, which made the liberal government dependent on the support of the Irish party, brought home rule still nearer. For forty years home rule had embodied the hopes and aspirations of the vast majority of Irish nationalists. The Irish party could claim with some justification that nearly every major reform in Ireland during the past forty years was traceable to its efforts. And during these years there had been a massive commitment on the part of the Irish people to the parliamentary party. The decline in the fortunes of Sinn Féin, after losing the North Leitrim by-election was only one indication of the greatly improved prospects of home rule, and of how close the parliamentary party was considered to have come towards achieving its main objective of a domestic parliament for Ireland. As Erskine Childers put it in 1911 in his book, *The framework of home rule*: 'If the Sinn Féin alternative meant anything at all, it meant complete separation, which Ireland does not want, and a final abandonment of constitutional methods.'[6]

In 1912 Pearse spoke from a home rule platform in Sackville Street. The home rule bill of that same year passed the commons, and because of the parliament act of the previous year the house of lords could not delay its coming into operation beyond 1914. In the interval, however, the unionists, basing their tactics on the fact of the existence of a stubborn Ulster aversion to home rule, mounted a violent agitation.

Edward Carson, a successful Dublin lawyer, aided and abetted by the leaders of the conservative party, led the opposition to home rule with considerable skill and courage. 218,000 pledged themselves to use 'all means' necessary to defeat home rule. The Ulster Volunteers were established (January 1913) and armed by gun-running from Germany; and a provisional government was set up (September 1913) to take control of Ulster on the day that home rule became law. Carson declared: 'I am told it will be illegal. Of course it will. Drilling is illegal. . . the Volunteers are illegal and the government know they are illegal, and the government dare not interfere with them. . . Don't be afraid of illegalities'.[7]

The Orangemen felt assured of the full backing of the British conservatives in whatever they might do, for Bonar Law, the leader of the party, had already publicly announced that he could imagine no length of resistance to which Ulster could go in which it would not have his support and that of the overwhelming majority of the British people.

Home rule had reached an impasse. Both Asquith, the prime minister, and Redmond, his Irish ally, thought that it would be extremely unwise to make martyrs out of Carson and his supporters. Asquith calculated that merely by waiting he would see the unionists damage themselves politically by their unconstitutional antics. Asquith, who had not Gladstone's dedication, and Redmond, who was no Parnell, chose to fight the battle for home rule on the ground where they felt they could win – in parliament and by means of parliamentary majorities. Then, faced with Carson's intransigence, Asquith persuaded his fellow parliamentarian, Redmond, to retreat from his first position, which was home rule for all Ireland, and Redmond agreed reluctantly, and step by step, 'as the price of peace'.

Meantime, the voices off-centre of the stage grew louder in their criticism of the shilly-shallying about home rule. *Irish Freedom* declared that Carson was the only Irish M.P. with any backbone; and in imitation of what he had achieved in Ulster, the Irish Volunteers were founded in Dublin (November 1913).

The outbreak of war in 1914 put the question of home rule into cold storage, but the heat that had been generated over the past few years was not so readily turned off. In 1914 the country contained no less than five armies. First were the official forces, which, as the Curragh 'mutiny' had shown, could not be relied on to enforce a settlement of home rule for all Ireland. Then there were the private armies – the Ulster Volunteers, the Irish Volunteers, the Citizen Army, and the I.R.B.

The Irish Volunteers split when Redmond pledged support to England in the war for the defence of 'small nations'. For this he was severely criticised by the more advanced and sceptical nationalists. A contemporary jingle in Connolly's paper, the *Workers' Republic*, expressed their position:

> Full steam ahead, John Redmond said
> that everything was well chum;
> home rule will come when we are dead
> and buried out in Belgium.[8]

After the outbreak of the war the I.R.B., whose members held controlling

124 Dáil Éireann, 1919 (Radio Times Hulton Picture Library, M 91074). The names from left to right are: *1st row* – L. Ginnell, M. Collins, C. Brugha, A. Griffith, É. de Valéra, Count Plunkett, E. Mac Neill, W. T. Cosgrave, E. Blythe; *2nd row* – P. J. Maloney, T. McSwiney, R. Mulcahy, J. O'Doherty, J. Dolan, J. McGuinness, P. O'Keefe, M. Staines, J. McGrath, B. Cusack, L. de Róiste, M.P. Colivet, Fr M. O'Flanagan; *3rd row* – J. P. Ward, A. McCabe, D. Fitzgerald, J. Sweeney, R. J. Hayes, C. Collins, P. Ó Máille, J. O'Mara, B. O'Higgins, J. A. Burke, K. O'Higgins; *4th row* – J. McDonagh, J. McEntee; *5th row* – P. Beasley, R. C. Barton, P. Galligan; *6th row* – P. Shanahan, S. Etchingham (spelling of names as on back of photograph)

positions in the Irish Volunteers, decided on an insurrection to take place before the ending of the war. They secured the cooperation of Connolly's Citizen Army which was also hoping for a rising. The outcome was the Easter rebellion of 1916.

It was not so much the rebellion of Easter week that completed the change in the attitude of the Irish people generally as its aftermath. Of the ninety rebels condemned to death for their part in the insurrection,

From Parnell to Pearse

Signatories of the proclamation
of the republic (24 April 1916),
by Seán O'Sullivan, R.H.A.
(National Gallery of Ireland).

125 Thomas James Clarke

128 James Connolly

129 Thomas MacDonagh

126 Seán MacDiarmada

130 Éamonn Ceannt

127 Patrick Henry Pearse

131 Joseph Mary Plunkett

309

fifteen, despite a mounting volume of protest, were executed, the first executions being on 3 May and the last ones ending on 12 May. The officials appeared to panic, martial law was imposed, and more people were arrested than had actually taken part in the rising. The pacifist, Sheehy Skeffington, although he had taken no part in the rising, was arrested and shot without trial. The government too, apart from the military, made more mistakes, and the threat of conscription hung over the country. The Irish parliamentary party blundered and lost the initiative. Everything that happened in the next few months played into the hands of Sinn Féin, which made the most of its opportunities.

By the time of the general election in December 1918, the country had moved unmistakably towards Sinn Féin. Sinn Féin won 73 seats, the unionists 26, and the parliamentary party a mere 6. The defeat of the parliamentary party took place in circumstances extremely unfavourable to them. They had been geared to constitutionalism and in fact committed to it under Redmond. Essentially they were a peace-time party, but Ireland in 1918, and possibly since 1912, could hardly be described as at peace. But their defeat in 1918 was not sudden, for their position was being undermined for years past by Ireland's most able propagandists – Griffith in his Sinn Féin papers, Moran in the *Leader*, Connolly in the *Workers' Republic*, the I.R.B. in *Irish Freedom*, and Hyde who creamed off into the Gaelic League some of the best talent in the country. The relentless criticism had a wearing-away effect, and it proved decisive when the electorate was offered an alternative to parliamentarianism in the changed circumstances of 1918. Parnell had shown how forces in Ireland could be harnessed to support the Irish party in Westminster. But where Parnell was capable of making use of the Land League and even of the Fenians, the party without Parnell never gained the confidence of the Gaelic League, the I.R.B., or Sinn Féin. It paid the penalty in 1918.

The victorious Sinn Féin constituted itself as Dáil Éireann, pledged itself to the Irish republic and proceeded to put into operation the policy of passive resistance which Arthur Griffith had outlined for it years before. Eamon de Valera, a senior surviving Volunteer officer, became the head of the Dáil, with Arthur Griffith as his deputy, and Michael

132 1916 memorial: statue of Cuchulainn
by Oliver Sheppard in the General Post
Office, Dublin (photo. Bord Fáilte
Éireann)

Collins from the I.R.B. as the ruthlessly efficient organiser of the military
resistance which opposed British attempts to smash Sinn Féin.

The Anglo-Irish war from early 1919 to July 1921, or the 'troubles' as
the people euphemistically called it, seriously embittered Anglo-Irish
relations. It was a struggle characterised by guerrilla warfare, ambushes,
raids on police barracks, and planned assassinations on the one side; and
reprisals, the shooting-up and burning-up of towns, executions and
terrorising on the other, as the 'flying-columns' of the Volunteers took on
the 'black-and-tans' and Auxiliaries of the British. Eventually public
opinion in America and in Britain demanded a truce, which was arranged
in July 1921. In December 1921, after months of negotiations, a treaty,
which was essentially a compromise, was signed by the British and Irish

representatives. The British conceded dominion status to the twenty-six counties; and the Irish negotiators brought back not the republic but 'freedom to achieve freedom'. Ironically, the unionists of Ulster who had most strenuously rejected home rule had been granted a measure of home rule by the Government of Ireland Act, 1920.

The unhappy legislative union, established in 1800, between Ireland and Great Britain had been finally dissolved, but on terms none had visualised. The years 1891-1921 had been a crowded hour in Ireland's history. Solid achievement and improvement there had been in plenty. Larkin had built up trade unionism, William Martin Murphy a commercial empire, Cusack the G.A.A., MacNeill and Hyde the Gaelic League; while Redmond, Dillon, Devlin, and their friends had brought the people within sight of the promised land of home rule. By a series of land purchase acts initiated before 1891 and continued throughout the period the land question was well on the way to being solved in the interests of the tenants. By the universities act of 1908, establishing the National University of Ireland and the Queen's University of Belfast, the university question of the nineteenth century was to a large extent solved; and the constituent colleges of the National University played a big part in the building of modern Ireland. Legislation had improved housing; old-age pensions had been granted; more money had been invested in education. A congested districts board, a department of agriculture, county councils, and light railways had also been established during these years.

Yet there was also grave disappointment. Gladstone once said that men ought not to suffer disenchantment since ideals in politics are never realised. In Ireland none of the dreams had been fulfilled. Not the Gaelic League's Irish-speaking nation, nor Yeats' literary-conscious people, nor the republic of the I.R.B., nor the workers' republic of Connolly, nor Griffith's economically self-sufficient dual monarchy, nor Redmond's home rule within an empire which the Irish helped to build, nor Carson's United Kingdom. Although all the dreams had to some extent been frustrated, the many dreamers had left their mark. With the signing of the treaty, however, the dreaming gave way to political realities.

312

NORTHERN IRELAND, 1921-66
by J. L. McCracken

The vast majority of the protestants in the north of Ireland were bitterly opposed to home rule. 'Home rule is Rome rule' was their slogan. They believed that under a Dublin parliament in which they would always be in a minority their religion, their way of life, and their economic interests would be endangered. And home rule aroused strong passions in Britain too, so that powerful elements there were ready to encourage and sustain the Ulstermen in their opposition. Gladstone's home rule bills of 1886 and 1893 were angrily received in Ulster: there was rioting in Belfast and the Orange order took on a new lease of life. Lord Randolph Churchill came to Belfast to play the Orange card, as he put it, and coined the rallying cry 'Ulster will fight; Ulster will be right'. By the time the third home rule bill was introduced in 1912 its opponents in Ulster were organ ised for resistance. An Ulster Unionist Council had been set up in 1905, a leader had been found in Sir Edward Carson, and the backing of the British conservative party had been secured. Bonar Law, the conservative leader, vied with the Ulster unionists in the violence of his language.

The Ulster unionists did not confine themselves to words. A day of dedication was observed by protestants throughout Ulster on 28 September 1912, when religious services were held and a solemn league and covenant was signed by over 218,000 men who pledged themselves to use 'all means which may be found necessary to defeat the present conspiracy to set up a home rule parliament in Ireland'. An Ulster Volunteer Force was enrolled for political and military service against home rule, a provisional government was formed to take over the province on the day the home rule bill became law, and a consignment of arms was brought in from Germany – all this with the approval and often active assistance of sympathisers in Britain.

133 Sir Edward Carson addressing anti-home rule meeting *c.*1912 (Public Record Office, Belfast)

Even before this storm had reached its full intensity the liberal government had begun to seek a solution in compromise. A proposal that the Ulster counties might decide by plebiscite to be excluded from the operation of the home rule act for six years was rejected by the unionists. 'We do not want sentence of death, with a stay of execution for six years', said Carson.[1] Instead, at a conference at Buckingham Palace in July 1914, he demanded first the exclusion of the whole of Ulster and then of the present six counties. Redmond, the leader of the Irish parliamentary party, refused to accept either proposal and the question of how long the exclusion should last was never discussed at all.

On the outbreak of the first world war the home rule bill was passed, but the coming into force of home rule was postponed until the end of the war. Long before that the situation was utterly changed by the 1916 rising and its aftermath. The home rule of the 1914 act which the unionists had rejected so violently fell far short of the demands of Sinn Féin. With a guerrilla war raging in the country negotiations between the parties was impossible, so Lloyd George decided on an imposed settlement. The Government of Ireland Act, 1920, provided for the setting up of two governments and two parliaments in Ireland, one for the six counties which were to form Northern Ireland and the other for the rest of the country which was to be called Southern Ireland. As well, Ireland was to have representatives in the British parliament and a council of Ireland was to be constituted from members of the two Irish parliaments. Sinn Féin refused to have anything to do with the act and it was a dead letter so far as Southern Ireland was concerned. The Ulster unionists also disliked it, but they decided to accept it as a preferable alternative to Dublin rule. Sir James Craig became prime minister and the Northern Ireland parliament was opened by King George V on 22 June 1921.

Northern Ireland had been brought into existence but its future was far from assured. The Anglo-Irish treaty of December 1921 which ended the war of independence and set up the Irish Free State applied to the whole of Ireland, but Northern Ireland was given the choice of opting out of the agreement and retaining the status it had secured. This was done without delay. A more formidable threat to the new state was the campaign of violence and the sectarian strife which came near to plunging it into anarchy. In 1922, 232 people, including two unionist M.P.s, were killed, nearly 1,000 were wounded, and more than £3,000,000 worth of property was destroyed. In combating this situation the northern government relied in part on the British army, but it also established a regular armed police force and a special constabulary to form what Craig called 'a defence force against our enemies'.[7] Even after the restoration of law and order the threat of the boundary commission still hung over Northern Ireland. The Anglo-Irish treaty had stipulated that if Northern Ireland opted out of the Irish Free State, a boundary commission should be set up to fix the boundary between the two states. The Irish leaders were confident that the outcome would be the transfer of such large areas to the Free State that Northern Ireland would not be able to survive as a separate state. Craig was well aware of the danger and consequently he refused to cooperate. When the commission was set up in spite of him he toured the border areas, reassuring his supporters with the pledge 'what we have we hold'. On the eve of the commission's reporting the *Morning Post* published (7 November 1925) a forecast of its findings which disclosed that only minor changes were contemplated and those mainly in favour of Northern Ireland. This precipitated a crisis which was resolved by a conference between the three prime ministers at which it was agreed to leave the border as it was. Craig returned to Belfast 'happy and contented'.[3]

134   135   136

But the dilemma created by Lloyd George's solution was still unresolved. The act of 1920 set up a state in which about a third of the population was bitterly hostile. Some took part in the attempt to overthrow it by force; the rest, pinning their hopes on the boundary commission, adopted an attitude of non-cooperation. The nationalists who contested the first parliamentary election in Northern Ireland declared in their election manifesto: 'it is our fixed determination not to enter this north-east Ulster parliament'.[4] Though they changed their minds after the boundary issue was settled, they refused to act as the official opposition, and they were not organised as a party; Joe Devlin, the ablest of them, said he had no ambition to lead anyone. Since their aim was a united Ireland, since in other words they aimed not at the overthrow of the government but at the destruction of the state, they could not play the role of an opposition in the traditional parliamentary manner. Herein lay the dilemma which has vitiated political life in the north ever since. The nationalist attitude enabled the unionists to appropriate loyalty and good citizenship to themselves and to use the national flag as a party emblem. Since the nationalists drew their support exclusively from the catholic part of the population, it led the protestant unionists, or at least the rank and file of them, to identify catholicism with hostility to the state. It justified, in unionist eyes, the arrangement of certain local government constituencies so as to prevent local government bodies falling into nationalist hands. It also detracted from the effectiveness of nationalist criticism of the government even on issues which had nothing to do with the constitutional question, and it encouraged irresponsibility, rashness, and a narrow sectarian approach among some nationalists who could never

316

134 Sir James Craig, later Viscount Craigavon, prime minister of Northern Ireland, 1921–40 (Public Record Office, Belfast)

135 Joseph Devlin, Ulster nationalist leader (Public Record Office, Belfast)

136 John Miller Andrews, prime minister of Northern Ireland, 1940–43 (photo. dated 27 Nov. 1940, J.R. Bainbridge, Belfast)

137 Sir Basil Brooke, later Viscount Brookeborough, prime minister of Northern Ireland, 1943–63 (photo. Leslie Stuart, Belfast)

137

hope to be other than a minority opposition, and who could never look forward to assuming office.

The situation in which the nationalists found themselves, and put themselves, also prevented the development of party organisation. Various attempts were made. In 1928 the National League was formed to achieve the national unity of Ireland, to demand justice for nationalists, and to foster cooperation among all creeds and classes. In 1936 the Irish Union Association was established in Belfast by representatives of all the minorities to bridge the gulf between nationalists, republicans, and Fianna Fáil supporters in the province. In the post-war period there was the anti-partition movement. But all these came to nothing. The truth was that apart from the dissensions over methods within the anti-partition ranks the incentive to organise was lacking. In some areas a nationalist was as certain of winning an election as a unionist was in others. No amount of party organisation was going to win votes outside of those areas. There was no floating vote on the constitutional issue.

The unionists, on the other hand, had every incentive to maintain an effective party machine. The unionist party was a broadly-based one, including within its ranks people of all classes, many of whom, in a different political context, might have had labour or liberal affiliations. Although all the prime ministers were drawn from the landed gentry or large industrialist class, working men and self-made men always figured amongst the leaders. But, while the government was always sensitive to back-bench opinion, it frowned on any deviation from the orthodox unionist creed. This was evident in the period of consolidation which followed the crisis of the early years. In those years various pressure groups had caused embarrassment to the government. In 1925 the parliamentary secretary to the ministry of home affairs lost his seat to a representative of a dissident group called the 'unbought tenants'; the protestant churches and the Orange order were agitating for an amendment to the education act of 1923; and temperance reformers, strongly backed by sections of the protestant clergy, were pressing for a measure of local option. The local optionists even put up candidates in opposition to official unionists in the general election of 1929. These were the groups the prime minister had in mind, and not the nationalists, when he decided to abolish proportional representation in parliamentary elections except for the university seats. In his opinion, 'there are really underlying everything two active, alert, vigorous parties in Ulster. . ., one for the empire the other for an all-Ireland parliament in Dublin'. Proportional representation clouded the issue.

What I hold is, if the people of Ulster are ever going – and pray God they may not – into a Dublin parliament, I say let the people understand that they are voting to go into a Dublin parliament and not go in by any trick of a complicated system such as proportional representation.[5]

The abolition of proportional representation in 1929 made next to no difference to the nationalists; what it did was to prevent splinter groups of unionists from winning seats. From 1929 differences of opinion were usually thrashed out within the party circle, and when a dissident group like the progressive unionists went to the polls in 1938 they were ignominiously defeated. As things were, there was little place for the labour party or for independents. Labour won three seats under P.R. in 1925; in 1965 they won two. As for the two major groups, their representation changed very little over the years. At the first general election in 1921, 40 unionists, 6 nationalists, and 6 republicans were returned; in 1965 the numbers were 36 unionists, 9 nationalists, 2 labour, and 5 others. The rigidity of the political situation in the north was shown in two other ways: the high number of uncontested seats at every general election and the stability of governments. Usually about 40 per cent of the members were returned without a contest and sometimes the percentage was over 60. As for the government, not only was there an unbroken period of

138 Shipbuilding at Belfast, October 1956 (Central Office of Information, London). In the background: Belfast Lough, with White Head to the left

unionist rule but there were very few changes of personnel. Lord Craig-avon was prime minister from 1921 till his death in 1940. His successor, J. M. Andrews, held office only till 1943 but he had been a cabinet minister since 1921. He was followed by Lord Brookeborough who had been a minister for ten years. His spell of office lasted till 1963, when he was succeeded by Captain Terence O'Neill. Other ministers and ordinary members on both sides of the house served for long periods; in 1936 for example, 40 per cent of the members had been in the house of commons since it came into existence 15 years before. Northern Ireland was entitled to 13 seats at Westminster and here too there was the same rigidity: normally all but two of these seats were held by unionists who consistently supported the conservative party.

Basically this situation developed out of the turmoil of the early years, but the course of events subsequently tended to perpetuate divisions and to harden allegiances. As the unionist government found its feet the 'step by step' policy of following British legislation began to take shape. The consolidation of the state was shown in such events as the establishment of an Inn of Court for Northern Ireland in 1926, the opening of the Law Courts Building in 1933, and above all the erection of Stormont. The foundation stone of the building, originally planned on an even grander scale, was laid in 1928. Its opening by the Prince of Wales in November 1932 was the occasion of a great unionist demonstration, but, as a protest against partition, the nationalist M.P.s took no part.

The thirties were years of persistent depression and unemployment in the north. The two great Ulster industries, linen and shipbuilding, were in decline, and agriculture was hard hit by the industrial depression at home and in Britain. The government's efforts to stimulate trade and industry had little effect. Unemployment rose from 13 per cent in 1927 to a peak of 28 per cent in 1931, and was still as high as 20 per cent on the outbreak of war. A by-product of this high unemployment was a resurgence of sectarian strife and a renewal of the campaign of violence. An attack on an Orange demonstration in 1931 set off a series of reprisals. There were disturbances in Belfast and elsewhere in 1932 and in succeeding years, culminating in serious rioting in Belfast in 1935, when a number of people were killed. The campaign of violence was carried on intermittently right into the forties, and provided justification, in unionist eyes, for the retention of the special powers act. Originally passed as a temporary measure at the height of the 'troubles' in 1922, it was made permanent in 1933 and was invoked to deal with each successive outbreak.

Events in the rest of Ireland during these years also helped to keep alive the old issues in the north. The dismantling of the Anglo-Irish treaty after 1932, the new Irish constitution of 1937, and the policy of raising the partition question on every possible occasion heartened the nationalists but confirmed the unionists in their resolve, as Craigavon said, that Ulster's position within the United Kingdom and the Empire must remain unchanged. Éire's neutrality in the war was the final proof of how far the paths of the two Irish governments had diverged.

To the north the war brought a variety of new experiences. Although the British government turned down Craigavon's request that conscription should be applied to Northern Ireland, the people of the north shared the other wartime experiences of the British – high taxation, restrictions, rationing, and in Belfast severe air-raids. Many Ulstermen joined the British forces. Thousands of British troops were trained in the province, new airfields were constructed, and Derry became an important naval base. In 1942 American troops began to arrive in the north. To de Valera's protest at their presence Andrews replied that he had no right to interfere in Northern Ireland's affairs. With the development of wartime industries an unwonted prosperity reigned. People from Éire came to work in the north, but they had to register and obtain permits, and the prime minister made it clear that they would not be allowed to remain and become voters: 'a unionist government must always be in power in Northern Ireland'.[6] There was movement in the other direction too. many people, among them unionist working men who had never before had the means or the inclination to do so, went south on holiday to escape from the rigours of wartime conditions. All these experiences were shared by unionists and nationalists, protestants and catholics alike.

After the war there was a growing emphasis on social and economic problems. Large-scale housing schemes were carried out, not only by local authorities but also by the Housing Trust, an organisation set up by the government in 1945.

Legislation designed to aid existing industries and to attract new ones met with considerable success: world-famous firms like Courtaulds, du Pont, British Oxygen, and Michelin Tyres established themselves in the province and thousands of new jobs were created. Under the stimulus of subsidies and development schemes agriculture made great progress. The 'step by step' policy was maintained as the welfare state developed in Britain, with the result that the educational system, the health service, and unemployment and sickness benefit were far in advance of those available in the Republic. These post-war developments tended to underline the advantages of the link with Britain and the differences between north and south.

On the other hand economic necessity was responsible for a measure of cooperation between the two governments in the post-war era. In 1950 they agreed on a scheme for the drainage of the land around Upper and Lower Lough Erne and for the development of a hydro-electric generating station; in 1951 they assumed responsibility for the running of the Great Northern Railway; and in 1952 they set up the Foyle Fisheries Commission to administer the fisheries jointly acquired from The Honourable the Irish Society of London. These arrangements involved meetings between cabinet ministers and civil servants from the two states.

But the old issues survived into the post-war age. Vigorous agitation against partition and the repeal of the external relations act in 1948 raised the constitutional question again. Unionist representations to the British government resulted in the passing of the Ireland Act in 1949, which provided that Northern Ireland should not cease to be part of the United Kingdom without the consent of its parliament. A new campaign of violence was carried on from 1956 to 1962. There were occasions when nationalist demonstrations were broken up by the police. Nationalists continued to complain of discrimination in the distribution of houses and jobs. Unionists used occasions like royal visits to reaffirm their loyalty to Britain. The two communities pursued their separate ways, with their different outlook and way of life. Yet both were sharing experiences which smoothed the way for some halting steps towards the better understanding for which a few individuals and groups had always worked. Increased prosperity, better housing, greater educational opportunities, the impact of T.V., form the background to such significant developments as the meeting between O'Neill and Lemass in January 1965, and the decision very shortly afterwards of Edward McAteer and his nationalist colleagues to accept the role of official opposition at Stormont. The possibilities of the new situation were summed up by O'Neill in these words:

139 Terence O'Neill, prime minister of Northern Ireland, visits Seán Lemass, taoiseach, 9 February 1965. With them are (left) Jack Lynch, minister for industry and commerce, and (centre) Frank Aiken, minister for external affairs. (photo. Lensmen Ltd, Dublin)

'If a spirit of friendship can be established, then I believe that those sterile forces of hatred and violence which have flourished for so long will at last be crushed by the weight of public opinion.'[7]

323

21

THE IRISH FREE STATE AND THE REPUBLIC OF IRELAND, 1921-66

by Patrick Lynch

A knowledge of contemporary history comes more often from political education than from historical education. The more recent the event the more difficult it is to grasp its full historical significance and implications: the civil war, for instance, aroused on both sides strong feelings which still influence opinions and make impartial judgments difficult.

Objectivity in history is probably unattainable. What follows tries, however, to chronicle with historical detachment a selection of the main events of the forty-five years 1921-66. It also seeks to explain the motives of a few of those responsible for these events, and, diffidently, makes some provisional historical judgments on them.

The Anglo-Irish war closed with the truce of 11 July 1921, and the despatch of Sinn Féin representatives to London for negotiations with the British government. Initially Sinn Féin, led by Griffith and de Valera, were at one in arranging these negotiations. But the outcome of them, in the Anglo-Irish treaty signed on 6 December 1921, divided Sinn Féin between those separatists who wanted the reality of an independence that would enable Ireland to look after its own affairs and those who wanted more, who opposed the treaty for a principle – the republic. There may have been disagreement as to what exactly the republic meant. Those who sought the republic, however, knew what it did not mean – it did not mean accepting a treaty which required an oath of allegiance to a British king.

On the side of the treaty were those led by Arthur Griffith. If the treaty failed to offer the full independence for which so many had fought, it did offer, Griffith suggested, a large measure of Irish control over Ireland's

140 Arthur Griffith (Cashman Collection, Radio Telefís Éireann)

destinies. It offered what Michael Collins called the 'freedom to achieve freedom'[1], and when Griffith persuaded a majority of the dáil to support the treaty, he declared that the treaty settlement had 'no more finality than that we are the final generation on the face of the earth'.[2]

The treaty was approved by the dáil by 64 votes to 57 (7 January 1922). British troops began to withdraw from Ireland by agreement, and Irish troops took over control. The provisional government announced the acceptance of the treaty to the people, and went to the country in a general election to seek support for its stand. De Valera, as president of the republic, and his followers opposed acceptance of the treaty, arguing that the people had no right to do wrong and that the dáil had been persuaded to ratify the treaty against its better judgment. The result of a bitterly fought election (June 1922) endorsed the pro-treaty position: 58 pro-treaty candidates were returned, 36 anti-treaty, 17 labour, and 17 representing farmers, independents, and others.

A civil war, which lasted until May 1923, ended in the defeat of those who, wishing to maintain the republic, had opposed the treaty. In the course of the civil war, Michael Collins was killed in an ambush (22 August 1922). The first head of the Irish Free State government, Arthur Griffith, had died ten days before, and was succeeded by William T. Cosgrave.

With the treaty, Britain believed with mistaken complacency that Ireland at last was taken out of British politics. This was partly because, despite the experience of 700 years, British statesmen had never really understood the Irish problem, and partly because the Irish problem was so complex and difficult. Looking back, one can only try to imagine what

325

may have been in Griffith's mind when he accepted the treaty, knowing that it secured less than many Irishmen aspired to. Perhaps Griffith was influenced by the threats of the British prime minister, Lloyd George, as to the consequences of Ireland's rejecting the treaty. Perhaps he was influenced by Collins's belief that the Irish guerrilla campaign against vastly superior British forces was losing its momentum. The realistic Griffith must have been particularly concerned by the knowledge that the partition of part of Ulster from the rest of Ireland was already accomplished, and that no possible outcome of the negotiations between Sinn Féin and the British government could substantially alter this fact. Under the Government of Ireland Act, 1920, a separate parliament for six Ulster counties had come into existence. This was a parliament subordinate to Westminster to which it sent thirteen representatives. The six counties were selected by Lloyd George as comprising the largest possible geographical area in which a majority of the population in favour of partition could reasonably be expected. This meant home rule of a kind for the partitioned area of Ulster. Griffith must have known ever since the enactment of the Government of Ireland Act that his separatist objective could not now be secured for the whole island. He probably decided to accept what could be secured by the treaty in the knowledge that only time, patience, and endurance could obtain for the separated six counties the status and possibilities that the treaty offered to what was to be the Irish Free State.

Irishmen, who, in the Anglo-Irish war, had held out for a republic, were not impressed by the dominion status which the treaty conferred. They would have preferred de Valera's proposal for external association with the British Empire which would have left Ireland a republic in its internal affairs, yet retaining an association with the British Empire in its external dealing. Even this solution, however, would have had to contend with partition in Ulster.

A consideration, which may have commended the treaty to some Irish people, was the British hint that a boundary commission which was to be set up to determine the geographic limits of Northern Ireland, might help to restore the territorial unity of Ireland by reducing Northern Ireland to

326

an area so small as to be politically and economically unsustainable. This would be achieved by incorporating in the Irish Free State the areas in which nationalists were numerous. The boundary commission when, however, it did report, in 1925, contemplated making no change in the boundaries which existed in 1921. Its report was never published because a leakage of information to the *Morning Post* prompted the government of the Irish Free State to reach direct agreement with the British government.

The treaty gave a degree of autonomy to the Irish Free State that probably few Irishmen ever expected to see realised in their lifetime, even though some Irish naval bases were to be retained by Britain, and in certain circumstances, harbour and other facilities might be sought by Britain for defensive purposes. Griffith had set great store by the advantage and importance of fiscal and financial independence; these the treaty offered. The full possibilities of the dominion status conferred by the treaty were hardly foreseen, even by those who freely accepted the treaty. Many supporters of the treaty, for instance, had regretted that the Commonwealth tie should be a compulsory one. Over the next ten years, however, the Irish Free State was to play an increasingly active and significant part in the events leading to the statute of Westminster in 1931. Such men as Desmond Fitzgerald, Patrick McGilligan, and John A. Costello, working closely with the representatives of the Canadian government, were pioneers in transforming the remains of the old British Empire and reshaping the British Commonwealth by turning it into a free association of self-governing states.

De Valera and his party, Fianna Fáil, remained outside the dáil until 1927. After the general election of that year Fianna Fáil became the largest opposition party. De Valera lost the support, however, of republicans such as Seán MacBride and George Gilmore who refused to recognise the constitution or institutions of the Free State. In March 1932, Fianna Fáil secured seventy seats at a general election and de Valera formed his first government with the support of the labour party. This crucial event consolidated the achievements of Irish political democracy in the Free State, for Cosgrave handed over office to men who a decade earlier had challenged the Free State's very existence. W. T. Cosgrave had been head of the government since 1922. De Valera was to remain in power for 16 years, until 1948.

In 1930 the Irish Free State had been elected to the council of the League of Nations and de Valera was elected president of the council in 1932. The government, formed in 1932 by the Fianna Fáil party declared that it would pursue a republican policy, remove the oath of allegiance to the British crown from the Free State constitution, and promote rapid industrialisation. Soon it decided to withold from Britain the land annuities and some other payments, amounting in all to about £5 million a year. The annuities were twice-yearly instalments payable by farmers in respect of the capital cost of buying out the landlords. As the capital costs had been advanced by the British government the Cosgrave government had collected the annuities from the farmers and forwarded them to London.

Britain retaliated by taxing imports of Irish cattle into Britain, and the

Free State replied with duties on British goods. And so began the 'economic war' which persisted for over six years and which intensified the harmful effects on Ireland of the world economic depression of the 1930s. The farmers were the chief victims, yet by and large the electorate remained solidly behind de Valera. In 1938 the annuity dispute was settled by the payment to Britain of a capital sum of £10 million, and the treaty ports were handed over to the Irish government.

These events took place against a background of turbulence as Ireland, like other European countries at the time, was troubled by private armies – the Irish Republican Army, which armed and drilled throughout the thirties, and the Army Comrades' Association, which, following the continental fashion of the day, adopted a uniform from which its members were generally known as Blue Shirts.

Already in 1937 de Valera had introduced a new constitution to replace that which he regarded as imposed by the treaty. It declared Ireland to be a 'sovereign, independent, democratic state'. In the previous year, on the abdication of Edward VIII, the external relations act in effect made the state a republic, though the British monarch was recognised as an instrument for validating the accreditation of Irish diplomatic representatives to foreign countries. The new constitution was adopted by a plebiscite in 1937. In 1938 Dr Douglas Hyde became the first president under the new constitution.

Whether Ireland remained a member of the British Commonwealth or not after 1937 was still a matter of controversy. A test of membership might have been Irish attendance at commonwealth conferences. From 1937, however, until the defeat of the Fianna Fáil government at a general election eleven years later, in 1948, Ireland was never represented at a commonwealth conference. During most of these years, it is true, Britain was at war and Ireland was neutral, yet for purposes of diplomatic accreditation the British monarch remained a recognised Irish instrument under the external relations act.

Economically the trade agreement of 1938 was very important. Irish goods were to be admitted free of customs duties to the British market with the exception of quantitative regulation of agricultural produce. The

329

142 William Thomas
Cosgrave, president of the
executive council of the Irish
Free State 1922–32, on a visit
to New York in 1928 (Radio
Times Hulton Picture Library,
P 37331)

Irish government guaranteed free admission to Ireland of certain classes
of British goods, yet retained the right to protect Irish industry, a very
important concession to Seán Lemass, the dynamic minister for industry
and commerce.

The war years were difficult for Ireland, but the people endured the
hardships of unemployment, emigration, and shortage of supplies as a
small price to pay for the neutrality which the government under de
Valera maintained with resolute determination. There can be little doubt
that de Valera had the mass support of the Irish people behind him when
he withstood the urgings of President Roosevelt to abandon neutrality
and support the allied cause. Very many Irish people, perhaps most, did,
in fact, morally support the allied cause against Nazi aggression, and
many thousands of them served in the British forces as volunteers. But
they also agreed with de Valera that an Ireland divided by a partition that
was supported by Britain could not without stultifying itself and its aspirations join Britain in a campaign for democratic freedom and national
self-determination. The government's policy was to maintain official
neutrality, and to seek, when it could, to preserve Irish men and women
in Northern Ireland from being conscripted into the war effort. Its deter-

mination to limit the effects of the war and to identify the people in the south with those in the north was symbolically demonstrated when the government sent the fire brigades of Dublin and Dun Laoghaire to the help of Belfast on the night of a German fire-bomb raid on that city (15-16 April 1941). At the end of the war in Europe the British prime minister, Winston Churchill, in his victory speech (13 May 1945) taunted Ireland with having remained aloof from the great struggle from which the allies had just emerged. Rarely did any Irishman speak for so many of the Irish at home and in all parts of the world as did de Valera in his restrained and dignified reply to Churchill three days later.

The first post-war general election was held in 1948, and after sixteen years a majority of the electorate decided in favour of a change of government. Although Fianna Fáil was defeated, it remained the largest party. A government was formed, however, of a combination of parties, united not by a previously agreed common policy but in opposition to Fianna Fáil. The inter-party government, as it called itself, had the task of formulating a policy to which all its constituent groups could subscribe, Fine Gael, Clann na Poblachta, Labour, Clann na Talmhan, and independents. Since the election had given a majority vote to no party and therefore endorsed none of the policies offered, it seemed that the people favoured merely change. In evolving this consensus the new taoiseach, John A. Costello, had to face the fact that the treaty settlement to which his party, Fine Gael, had contributed so much had, since 1932, been dismantled step by step by de Valera's government in a succession of measures approved by the people. By 1948 the treaty was no longer an issue in Irish politics. And so the external relations act of 1936 was replaced in 1949 by an act which declared that the description of the state should be the Republic of Ireland. The taoiseach recommended the Republic of Ireland Bill to the dáil as a means of removing ambiguities in the constitutional position and of taking, as he said, the 'gun out of politics' in the twenty-six counties. The British government stated that it regarded the Republic of Ireland Act as bringing Ireland out of the Commonwealth. It had now been demonstrated that the dominion status conferred by the treaty did, in fact, confer the freedom to achieve freedom.

143 Eamon de Valera, president of the executive council of the Irish Free State 1932-7, taoiseach 1937-48, 1951-4, 1957-9; uachtarán 1959-73 (*Irish Press* photo., taken on the occasion of a Radio Éireann broadcast on 'The nation's food requirements', 3 December 1941)

In 1951 Costello's inter-party government broke up as a result of internal conflict following what was called the 'mother and child health scheme', sponsored by the minister for health, Dr Noel Browne, and condemned by the organised medical profession and the catholic hierarchy. The inter-party government was replaced by a minority Fianna Fáil government under de Valera, supported by some independents. In 1954 there was a second inter-party government with Fianna Fáil in opposition. This second inter-party government, again under Costello as taoiseach, continued to press forward with a heavy programme of capital investment, for the development of a country which in this respect had unavoidably been neglected in war-time. A balance of payments problem arose, however, because of excessive demands for imports of consumption goods in 1956, and the fiscal measures necessary to correct it, courageously introduced by Gerard Sweetman, so reduced the rate of economic growth that high unemployment and emigration followed. De Valera was returned to office again in 1957 and remained head of the government until, on the

332

retirement of Seán T. O'Kelly, he became president of Ireland in 1959 when he was replaced as taoiseach by Seán Lemass.

Even now, it is too soon for an Irish historian to form more than a provisional judgment on the first decades of the Irish state. It would be too much to expect complete detachment from all those who took sides in the civil war, and even many of the next generation were influenced by the strong feelings aroused by it. It is certain, however, that William T. Cosgrave, president of the executive council, laid the foundations of efficient and honest administration, which enabled the country to recover in a surprisingly short time from the physical ravages of the civil war. Indeed, most of his political opponents, those who opposed the treaty, would agree that Cosgrave and his colleagues in the first government of the Free State had a hard and thankless task and that they did very efficiently their duty as they saw it. Opponents of the treaty might argue that the first Free State government decided to do for the country, economically and socially, the same kind of thing that a British government might have done if the Free State had remained part of the United Kingdom. The now Irish civil service modelled itself consciously on what it deemed to be the virtues of the British civil service. Indeed, many of the now Irish civil servants had been transferred from the British service. After 1922 Merrion Street became Whitehall writ small. The Garda Siochána were built up as an example to the world of an unarmed police force. The national army was firmly and loyally under the control of the national government.

One wonders what might have happened had Griffith lived. It is true that the ten years from 1922 to 1932 were years of peace and progress in the Free State; but the government's social and economic programme was a far cry from the glowing and heart-warming spontaneity of the democratic programme that General Richard Mulcahy had so eloquently proposed in the united Dáil Éireann on 21 January 1919. Unlike Griffith, not even the ablest members of Cosgrave's government had a completely coherent economic philosophy, in which both agricultural and industrial development equally fitted. Some of them, Ernest Blythe, Patrick Hogan, and Patrick McGilligan had immense analytical abilities, but they lacked faith in the possibility of really rapid industrial development without damaging the interests of the farmer. Griffith, on the other hand, had had deep ideological convictions on the economic significance of Sinn Féin, on the need for dynamic development of manufacturing industries, and on the use of tariffs. He would almost certainly have seen the first economic task of government as the achievement of an industrial revolution in the Free State of the kind that had been achieved earlier in north-eastern Ulster. The Irish agrarian revolution had already taken place under British rule, thanks to Davitt, Parnell, and Dillon.

There had, of course, been tremendous difficulties facing the new government in 1922. First, the country had to recover from the effects of the civil war. Moreover, the Free State lacked an industrial tradition; the border had cut it off from the heavily industrialised areas around Belfast; industrial skills and training were scarce. In spite of these severe handicaps there were very considerable achievements – the restoration of order after the civil war, better marketing of agricultural produce, the consolidating land act of 1923, the establishment of the sugar beet industry, the setting up of the Agricultural Credit Corporation, the vast undertaking of the Shannon scheme. If Griffith had lived, however, it seems doubtful that he would have been satisfied with government action between 1922 and 1932 in using 'selective protection' as a means of carrying out its programme of industrialisation. The government's industrial policy reflected its lack of an industrialised economic ideology, as well as the influence of civil servants and economists whose background and training had closed their minds to most ideas outside the British liberal and *laissez-faire* tradition. It is, indeed, a nice historical irony, at which, as dialecticians, Marx and Engels would have smiled, that Griffith's protectionist policy for industrialisation had to await implementation until the advent to power of de Valera and Lemass after 1932.

Some of the principal economic advances of the first ten years after 1922 were due more to the imagination and initiative of individual ministers than to the advice of civil servants. The civil service saw its role as administering the system as it existed. The intellectual climate of the civil service was unlikely to promote a spirit of innovation, especially

144 John Aloysius Costello, taoiseach 1948–51, 1954–7 (*Irish Press* photo. taken at the first meeting of the first inter-party cabinet, 19 February 1948)

after the onset of the world economic depression in the early 1930s. The high quality and integrity of the civil service were consolidated by the government's creation of independent commissions for recruiting staff to both central and local public service. It was made abundantly and courageously clear by Cosgrave's government between 1922 and 1932 that self-government did not mean jobs at the expense of the taxpayer for postulants with political influence.

In economic policy Fianna Fáil, when it came to power in 1932, showed itself prepared to pursue a vigorous programme of rapid industrialisation under Lemass, minister for industry and commerce, and willing to face the consequences for agriculture of the means employed to secure industrial development – tariffs which raised costs for the farmers. Like most members of the Cosgrave administration before him, Lemass had no doctrinaire economic position; but he was to commit himself to a course of state intervention in economic activity that gave a leftward direction, in practice, to his economic policies. Where private enterprise failed or was unable or unwilling to provide a necessary service Lemass created a

335

public enterprise. Aer Lingus, for instance, was created in 1936 to provide publicly owned air services, and in 1944 Coras Iompair Éireann took over surface transport services which had run into difficulties under private ownership. Bord na Móna (1946) was one of the most successful creations. After 1932, Lemass became the architect of a new Irish industrial revolution. No Irish political party, not even the labour party, was socialist, yet public or state-sponsored enterprise played a large and crucial part in the economy.

After 1948, when the first inter-party government took office, economic policies were adopted which, in some cases, seemed even more radical than anything that Lemass had sponsored. The minister for finance, McGilligan, for instance, introduced the concept of the capital budget, the first explicit evidence of Keynesian influence in Irish public finance. Under successive governments since then the state capital programme has grown progressively in significance. Lord Keynes, indeed, was seeming in practice to have more influence than Connolly on the Irish economy of the fifties and sixties.

When Fianna Fáil were returned at the general election of 1957 following the severe economic crisis of 1956, there was an unprecedented step in public administration. T. K. Whitaker, secretary of the department of finance and head of the civil service, published, in 1958 with the approval of the government, a survey entitled *Economic development*, which was, in fact, a pointer towards the objectives at which he believed the country should aim if living standards were to be raised and unemployment and emigration reduced. Whitaker's prescription was, necessarily, a complicated one, which would be difficult to summarise and dangerous to simplify; but, by and large, he agreed that the country needed greatly increased capital investment, provided it was the right kind of investment, and by the right kind he meant productive investment that added to the wealth and welfare of the country and not merely redistributed existing wealth. Whitaker's report did not recommend economic planning, as such, but the ends and means which he suggested could, in fact, best be achieved, or provided, by economic planning.

Based on Whitaker's report the government approved and published

145 Irish soldier serving in United Nations forces, by John F. Kelly, R.H.A.

its first *Programme for economic expansion*, towards the end of 1958. It is still contested whether that programme was, really, the cause of the remarkable economic recovery that occurred in the years after 1958 or whether its association with that recovery was fortuitous. In any event, growth during the years after 1958 increased by four per cent a year in contrast to a growth rate of less than half that figure in the preceding years. Since *Economic development* was published the prestige of the civil service has been very high in Ireland in circles that earlier looked primarily to the politician for a lead in economic policy.

In 1963-4 the government, under Lemass, introduced its *Second programme for economic expansion* to cover the seven years from 1964 to 1970. The government had now committed itself to all the trials and rewards that economic planning could produce in a free society. Perhaps, like Costello's government in 1956, Lemass in 1964 was trying to do too much too quickly, and so the country again ran into a balance of payments crisis in 1965. Yet, despite the unpalatable measures necessary to correct these troubles there remained hope that the aims of the *Second programme* could be achieved by 1970 (see chapter 22 below). In the meantime, the taoiseach, Lemass, had begun a series of meetings with Terence O'Neill, prime minister of Northern Ireland, which held promise of closer and more constructive relations between the two parts of Ireland.

The year 1965 opened with a dramatic meeting between Lemass and O'Neill, and ended with a new Anglo-Irish trade agreement which offered hope of more mutually rewarding economic relations between

146 Harold Wilson, prime minister of Great Britain, and Seán Lemass, taoiseach, signing the Anglo-Irish free-trade agreement at 10 Downing Street, 14 December 1965 (photo. Thomson Newspapers, London)

Britain and Ireland than ever before. It now seemed possible that the next step would be for Ireland to join the European Economic Community (see chapter 22 below). Closer economic relations with Britain were dictated by the logic of history and geography. For good or ill, Britain is our nearest neighbour. Most of our trade is with Britain. Most of our emigrants go there to work. Indeed, for many purposes, Britain and Ireland comprise a single market. To many people an Anglo-Irish free-trade area had long seemed inevitable.

In the decades immediately after the treaty, in a mood of disillusion and frustration, it was to be expected, perhaps, that the emphasis should be on the more inward-looking aspects of our culture. In a heady spate of puritanism a riot of censorship banned novels by some of the greatest contemporary Irish writers as well as the work of foreign artists of international repute. This, indeed, was a shameful fruit of political freedom. Yet, at the time, Irish literature of world renown was being created by James Joyce, William Butler Yeats, Seán O'Casey, Seán Ó Faolain, Pádraic Ó Conaire, and others. And, then, in the 1940s the wonderful, Brian Ó Nualláin, *alias* Myles na gCopaleen, *alias* Flann O'Brien, writing in Irish and English, came as a scourge of everything false and pretentious in Irish life and writing.

Nor did the treaty bring revolutionary developments in education. Primary schools, it is true, were required, in addition to their normal educational task, to help more effectively in the revival of Irish and this responsibility has certainly placed a heavy burden on both pupils and teachers.

The state's financial support for education, primary, secondary, and university, was, however, far from generous over the years, but prospects for the future were much brighter. Vocational education, extended in the 1930s, achieved distinctive and valuable results, but only in the 1960s did it approach its potential in the context of the comprehensive schools. Perhaps, internationally, for Ireland the most significant educational or cultural event of the years since the treaty was the establishment, sponsored by de Valera, of the Dublin Institute for Advanced Studies (1940) which has attracted scholars of international distinction, among them Erwin Schroedinger, the theoretical physicist.

In 1960, a commission was appointed to inquire into, and report to the government on, all aspects of higher education. Its report was to herald a new approach to the whole subject (see chapter 22 below).

Socially, too, there were great advances. The Irish Free State inherited in Dublin some of the worst slums in Europe. Even in 1966 a good part of Dublin still needed to be restored, but the slums in the old sense were gone and municipal standards were reasonably high throughout the country. The Irish trade union movement, whose growth had been retarded by internal dissension, was strong, numbering about 390,000 members. The movement was also impeded by partition, till in 1964 the Stormont government recognised the Irish Congress of Trade Unions as a negotiating body.

For many years, successive governments failed to find a satisfactory remedy for emigration; but, in 1966, in spite of temporary economic difficulties, the signs were that it was possible to plan economic growth with a view to increasing living standards, improving social welfare, and eliminating unnecessary emigration. As a nation, however, our greatest failure since the treaty has been our failure to provide jobs at home for those who prefer not to emigrate.

Church and state clashed but once since the treaty – in 1951 on Dr Noel Browne's 'mother and child health scheme', which the catholic hierarchy declared to be against catholic social teaching on the rights of the family and of the church in education. Fifteen years later, in 1966, and after the pontificate of Pope John, it was difficult to imagine the issue of a means test being raised as an objection in principle to a medical service. Indeed, after Dr Browne had left office in 1951 a very similar health scheme was introduced by the new Fianna Fáil government, which satisfied the objections of the hierarchy.

In the twenty-one years since the second world war Ireland had achieved as conspicuous a place in the United Nations Organisation as she had earned in the League of Nations. In Geneva, in 1932, de Valera had made an appeal for justice and peace among nations that was tremendously reinforced by his moral standing as a political figure committed domestically to an apparently inflexible political doctrine. By his re-election in June 1966 as president of Ireland, he continued to remain a world political figure.

Since 1948, Liam Cosgrave first, and later, Frank Aiken, led the Irish delegation to the annual general assemblies of the United Nations and indicated the part that a small nation might play in promoting the cause of international peace. The year which marked the golden jubilee of 1916 seemed particularly appropriate to remember the men of the Irish army who, under General Seán MacEoin, responded to the call of the United Nations to maintain order in the far away republic of the Congo, and the other Irishmen who served in Cyprus. The men who declared the Irish republic in 1916 and those who supported it in arms, as well as the men and women who stood for the treaty and those who opposed it, would

147 Map of Ireland, political

find common ground in saluting the Irish soldiers taking part in a peacekeeping force under the United Nations.

The Republic's economy was being rationalised in an empirical blend of private and public enterprise in preparation for entry to the European Economic Community. But the issue of *Planning a just society* by the main opposition party in 1965 was a reminder that economic growth, however essential, was not enough.

22

IRELAND, 1966-82

by J. H. Whyte

The leading feature of the period 1966-82 in both parts of Ireland was the unprecedented pace of change. In Northern Ireland, change was most obviously political, with turmoil succeeding decades of outward calm; but important social and economic changes occurred as well. In the Republic, change was above all economic and social. I shall discuss Northern Ireland first, since the crisis there affected the course of events in the Republic.[1]

Northern Ireland in 1966 seemed on the way to a brighter future. Economically, it was progressing. True, it suffered from high unemployment and from the steady contraction of its staple industries – linen, ship-building, and agriculture. But its ministry of commerce was energetically attracting new industries, and seemed to be making up for the decline of the old staples. Its greatest success was in man-made fibres: Northern Ireland became one of the main centres in Europe for this booming industry. Meanwhile, the ministry of development was pressing ahead with what was fashionably described as the 'infrastructure' – the framework of roads, utilities, and housing which would make Northern Ireland attractive to the entrepreneur. The first piece of motorway anywhere in Ireland was opened between Belfast and Lisburn in 1962, and a new town (Craigavon), between Portadown and Lurgan, was founded in 1965. The growth rate in the period 1960-73 averaged 4 per cent *per annum*, which was higher than in the rest of the United Kingdom, and equal to that of the Republic.

Politically, too, the atmosphere seemed to be improving. Ever since its foundation, Northern Ireland has been sharply divided between a

148 Ian Paisley (RTE 1973)

protestant majority and a catholic minority. The ethnic boundary was maintained by a lack of intermarriage, by separate education, and, in some places, by residential segregation. Political attitudes largely followed religious adherence, with catholics generally favouring a united Ireland and protestants supporting the maintenance of the link with Britain. Catholics complained bitterly of discrimination in jobs, housing, the enforcement of law and order, and the drawing of electoral boundaries. Protestants retorted that catholics were disloyal to the state. But in 1963 a new prime minister, Captain Terence O'Neill, had come to office, who talked of building bridges between the communities. On the other side a catholic leadership was emerging, which owed its education to the implanting in Northern Ireland of the British welfare state, and which was more prepared than its predecessors to acquiesce in the constitutional *status quo,* provided catholics received a fair deal within it. The I.R.A. (Irish Republican Army), which as late as 1956-62 had tried to overthrow Northern Ireland by force, was in eclipse, and its leaders had taken to pursuing socio-economic issues. In the Republic the taoiseach, Seán Lemass, had shown by his visit to Stormont in 1965 (see above, p. 337) that he favoured better relations. The only sizeable group opposed to conciliation was to be found in the right wing of the protestant community in Northern Ireland, where an eloquent agitator, Rev. Ian Paisley, was gaining influence.

Thus the descent into turmoil was not inevitable. Despite the legacy of resentment and mistrust, the forces making for conciliation seemed as strong as those making for conflict, and even after the troubles had begun, there was more than one point when it seemed possible that Northern Ireland might turn back towards peace. The story is best outlined in four periods: 1966-9, 1969-74, 1974-5, and 1975-82.

1966-9. A sign of the new mood of the catholic community was the growth of the Northern Ireland Civil Rights Association, founded in 1967. This body, unlike previous organisations representing primarily the catholic minority, did not challenge the existence of the Northern Ireland state, but demanded merely the ending of abuses within it. From August 1968, marches and demonstrations in support of this objective were held in various towns. The police and the protestant right wing, however, saw this development as a new attempt to undermine Northern Ireland, all the more dangerous because more insidious than an overt campaign against partition. Successive demonstrations were broken up by police and harassed by protestant extremists. To describe the main confrontations – Derry (5 October 1968), Burntollet (4 January 1969), Derry and Belfast (12-15 August 1969) – would take up disproportionate space. Suffice it to say that by mid-August 1969 disorder had reached such a height that the police could no longer contain it, and the Northern Ireland government was obliged to request the British government to send in troops to restore order. The troops, whose arrival was taken in catholic areas as a sign that the police had been defeated, were welcomed.

The Labour government then in office at Westminster had long been urging reform on the Northern Ireland government, and had already obtained some concessions. It now insisted on the adoption of two packages of reforms (August and October 1969) which between them granted almost the whole of the Civil Rights Association's demands. The exclusively protestant special constabulary was to be disbanded. Electoral boundaries were to be redrawn, housing administered by a non-partisan body, and safeguards introduced against discrimination in public employment. The reforms were bitterly resented on the protestant right wing, and they aroused less gratitude among catholics than they would have done if they had come a year earlier, before the disturbances. None

344

149 James Chichester-Clark (Pacemaker Ltd, 1969)

the less, they made an impact, and it seemed not impossible at the end of 1969 that Northern Ireland might find its way back to peace and stability.

1969-74. The next eighteen months were touch and go. On the one hand, the forces making for confrontation were on the upsurge. The unionist right wing relentlessly criticised what it described as 'sell-out' by the Northern Ireland government, while, at the other extreme, the I.R.A. prepared for a renewed campaign. But on the other hand, more moderate elements seemed to be in the ascendant in both protestant and catholic politics. The Northern Ireland government, under successive prime ministers (Captain O'Neill to April 1969, Major Chichester-Clark from April 1969 to March 1971, Brian Faulkner from March 1971), forged ahead with the reforms announced in 1969. On the catholic side a new party, the Social Democratic and Labour Party (S.D.L.P.), was founded in 1970, which, while its aims included a united Ireland by consent, put more stress on reform within Northern Ireland. If the reforms had been completed quickly, it might have been possible for the S.D.L.P. and the more moderate unionists to converge on some new consensus.

However, the reforms included a complicated restructuring of local government, which could not be completed until 1973. Meanwhile, the

345

150 Brian Faulkner (RTE 1969)

army, now strongly reinforced, had been involved in confrontations with catholic rioters, and the initial goodwill earned by the troops in the catholic areas of Belfast and Derry turned to hostility. Early in 1971, the I.R.A. began its offensive. Soldiers and policemen were killed, and the number of bombings mounted month by month. The unionist government came under increasing pressure from protestants for firm measures.

The obvious firm measure to take was internment – i.e. the holding without trial of suspected I.R.A. members until the trouble was over. This had been successfully used in 1922, 1939, and 1956. In August 1971, Faulkner decided that the time had come to use it again. But the way it was employed on this occasion ensured that it would not achieve the same results as before. Firstly, the scale of the operation was unprecedented, with over three hundred arrested (many of whom had to be quickly released when they were found to be innocent of I.R.A. involvement). Secondly, internment was used exclusively against republicans although extreme protestants had done as much to provoke the crisis. Thirdly and most important, it soon became known that some of the internees had been grossly mistreated.

Internment, consequently, only increased the violence. Recruits flocked to the I.R.A. Many catholics – not just republicans, but moderates like the supporters of the S.D.L.P. – went on rent and rate strike, or withdrew from public bodies. Demonstrations against internment were mounted. At one of these, in Derry on 30 January 1972, thirteen people were shot dead by the British army – the notorious 'Bloody Sunday'. This caused a wave of revulsion across nationalist Ireland, and the British embassy in Dublin was burnt down (2 February).

346

151 William Whitelaw (Pacemaker Ltd, 1973)

However, the very seriousness of the situation increased the pressure for a settlement. At Westminster, where a conservative government had been in power since June 1970, the unhappy consequences of Faulkner's policy were producing disenchantment with his regime. In March 1972 the British government suspended the Northern Ireland government and parliament, and introduced direct rule from Westminster. A new office in the British cabinet was established, that of secretary of state for Northern Ireland, and a man with a gift for conciliation, William Whitelaw (later Lord Whitelaw), was appointed to it.

Direct rule did not produce any immediate improvement. Violence during the spring and summer of 1972 reached its highest level. The I.R.A., encouraged by success, redoubled its bombing campaign. Protestant private armies, the Ulster Defence Association and the Ulster Volunteer Force, emerged. Random murders of catholics became frequent, in retaliation for murders by the I.R.A. A brief truce in June between the British army and the I.R.A. collapsed in recrimination. However, the lowest point was reached when on 21 July 1972 ('Bloody Friday') the I.R.A. overreached itself by letting off a chain of bombs in Belfast which killed nine people and injured 130, and in the ensuing revulsion the army was able to reestablish itself in the catholic areas of Belfast and Derry. After that, violence slowly declined.

Meanwhile, Whitelaw was coaxing the more moderate elements in both communities – Faulkner's unionists and the S.D.L.P. – towards agreement. Unionists were mollified by repetitions of the guarantee that Northern Ireland would remain part of the United Kingdom as long as the majority of its inhabitants desired. The S.D.L.P. was promised a share in executive power, and the development of all-Ireland institutions. At an election for a new Northern Ireland Assembly, held in June 1973, Faulkner's unionists and the S.D.L.P., with associated groups, gained a majority. In November 1973 they agreed, after tough bargaining, on the composition of a joint administration. In December 1973, in a conference at Sunningdale in Berkshire, the British and Irish governments, and members of the executive-designate, agreed to set up a Council of Ireland, with representatives from north and south to administer matters of common interest. On 1 January 1974 the new executive took office, with Faulkner at its head, and Gerry Fitt (later Lord Fitt), leader of the S.D.L.P., as his deputy. Once again, it seemed as if Northern Ireland might be edging back from conflict towards consensus.

1974-5. It soon became clear, however, that support for the new executive was fragile. On the catholic side, the I.R.A. maintained its campaign in the weeks after the executive took office. On the protestant side, Faulkner was repudiated by a majority of the unionist party, and eventually set up a new party of his own. A general election for the Westminster parliament, held on 28 February 1974, produced victories for anti-Faulkner unionists in eleven out of twelve constituencies, and indicated that three protestant voters in four had voted for such candidates. Protestant opposition appeared to be directed, not so much at power-sharing with the S.D.L.P., as at the proposed Council of Ireland, which was widely seen as a device to lure them towards a united Ireland.

On 14 May 1974, an organisation called the Ulster Workers Council announced a general strike against the Sunningdale agreement. Enjoying only limited support at first, it slowly gathered momentum until on 28 May Faulkner and his unionist colleagues on the executive decided that they no longer had sufficient support in the community to remain in office, and resigned. The executive forthwith collapsed. Opinions vary

152 (L. to R.) Oliver Napier, Liam Cosgrave, Edward Heath, Brian Faulkner and Gerry Fitt at the Sunningdale Conference (*Irish Times* photo)

on how far its fall was inevitable. On the one hand, the strike could probably have been crushed if the police and army had moved against it decisively in the early stages. On the other hand, it seems likely that, even if the strike had been faced down, some other episode would have occurred that would have proved too much for the fragile unity of protestant and catholic.

The British government now tried another tack. Instead of pressurising Northern Ireland politicians into accepting a settlement, it left them to work one out for themselves. In May 1975 a convention of 78 members was elected, in which politicians of all shades could seek to agree on the future government of Northern Ireland. Agreement in the convention seemed not impossible. By the end of August 1975 a unionist negotiating team led by William Craig – who had hitherto been seen as one of the most intransigent unionist politicians – was exploring with the S.D.L.P. the possibility of a compromise on 'voluntary coalition', which in effect meant that unionists would concede power-sharing for an experimental period, provided the S.D.L.P. put in abeyance their demand for a Council of Ireland.

1975-82. Once again, hopes of agreement were shattered. At the beginning of September 1975, Craig's proposed compromise with the S.D.L.P. was repudiated by his colleague, Rev. Ian Paisley, and by the bulk of the unionists in the convention. A renewed outbreak by the I.R.A. had something to do with the change; but the most important reason appears to have been a feeling among unionists that to concede even temporary power-sharing would be to yield too much to those whom they regarded as fundamentally opposed to the existence of the state. In the convention's report, completed in November 1975, the unionists insisted on the return of majority rule as it had existed before 1972, with only slightly more safeguards for minorities. The S.D.L.P. and moderate unionists refused to sign this report, which was forthwith rejected by the London government as failing to reflect an adequate measure of agreement between the communities.

From 1975, impasse reigned in Northern Ireland politics. At the end of 1975 internment, which had caused such bitterness when introduced in 1971, was brought to an end; but though violence declined in subsequent years, it did not cease. In 1976 the Peace People gave expression to the war-weariness of large sections of the population by organising giant demonstrations; but, though they gained massive short-term support, they were unable to articulate a programme, and faded into obscurity. In 1977, and again in 1979, British secretaries of state attempted to obtain agreement between the parties on a form of devolved government, but were rebuffed with almost equal vehemence by the S.D.L.P. and the unionists. In 1981, ten republicans held in a Northern Ireland gaol on terrorist offences died on hunger strike in pursuit of 'special status', the first and most notable being 'Bobby' Sands. Though the British government faced down the strike, the courage shown by the strikers gained for the republican movement considerable sympathy, including electoral successes. In 1982 a new secretary of state, James Prior, made yet another attempt at securing agreement between the parties by his scheme of 'rolling devolution', and elections to a Northern Ireland Assembly were held in October. But S.D.L.P. and republicans refused to take their seats, and Prior refused to devolve power to a unionist-dominated assembly.

Stalemate seemed built into the situation. None of the parties was strong enough to impose its views; none was so weak that it felt impelled to alter them. The S.D.L.P. moved away from the search for a settlement within Northern Ireland, and called for a united Ireland by consent; but it found no way of securing the consent which was so manifestly lacking. The I.R.A. sought a united Ireland by coercion; but it was not powerful enough to make coercion effective, and in attempting to do so only made unionists more intransigent. Most unionists sought to restore majority rule in Northern Ireland; but successive British governments rejected this demand because it would enable unionists once again to dominate the catholic minority. Catholics felt no gratitude for this, because they felt that Britain could do much more to influence unionists towards accommodation.

Underneath the political stagnation of the late seventies and early eighties, however, important economic changes were taking place. This was not primarily a result of the violence, which reached its height in 1972, whereas the Northern Ireland economy continued to expand until 1973. From 1974 onwards, however, the economy was in decline. This was partly a result of the poor performance of the United Kingdom economy as a whole, partly because of a reduced readiness by the London government to direct aid towards the poorer regions of the United Kingdom. The violence also had an indirect effect, by discouraging investment. These factors combined to produce what has been described as the 'de-industrialisation' of Northern Ireland. During the period 1970-80, the share of the workforce employed in manufacturing fell from 32 to 23 per cent. Many of the largest factories in the region – especially in the man-made fibre industry, which had once been so prosperous – shed workers or closed down altogether. Unemployment leapt

153 James Prior
(Pacemaker Ltd, 1982)

to 20 per cent of insured workers in 1982. The picture would have been worse had not the service sector expanded as rapidly as manufacturing contracted: the proportion employed in services rose during the period 1970-80 from 41 to 54 per cent. Much of the increase was in the public sector, and was made possible only by subventions from the British exchequer. By the beginning of the eighties, for every three pounds of public money raised in Northern Ireland, five were spent there.

Accompanying these economic changes came an important social change: a slow alteration in the balance of the communities. A higher catholic birth rate, and reduced emigration, meant that the catholic proportion of the population was slowly rising, from 35 per cent in 1961 to somewhere approaching 40 per cent in 1981. Meanwhile, the de-industrialisation of Northern Ireland was hitting protestants even harder than catholics: the latter had always experienced a high unemployment rate, but now protestant towns like Carrickfergus and Antrim had to face the closure of their largest employers. On the other hand, the growth of the service sector with its multitude of white-collar jobs gave opportunities to the increasing number of educated catholics. Too much must not be read into these changes. In 1982 it remained true that the average protestant was richer than the average catholic. Nor did the economic and social changes of the previous few years have any visible impact on political attitudes. But they had long-term political implications. They made it harder for the kind of control that had existed before 1966 ever to be asserted again.

In the Republic, the period 1966-82 was on the whole one of rapidly increasing prosperity. True, there were sharp fluctuations. The *Second programme for economic expansion* (see above, p. 337) had to be abandoned before its completion date of 1970, and a more modest *Third programme,* covering 1969-72, had to be abandoned also. The sharp slump of 1974-5, and the more long-lasting one which began in 1979, hit Ireland as much as the rest of the western world. But the average rate of growth through the sixties and seventies was maintained at four per cent *per annum.*

There seem to have been two main reasons for this achievement. The first was the boost to agriculture given by entry into the European Community in January 1973. Irish farmers at once became eligible for the generous financial support available from the community, and their incomes rose dramatically, reaching a peak in 1978. The second was the performance of Irish industry. Down to the late fifties, Irish industry consisted largely of small, often inefficient, units, producing mainly for a protected home market. The dismantling of tariff barriers (see above, p. 329-30) made that kind of industry obsolete, and during the sixties and seventies the Industrial Development Authority made strenuous efforts to attract new firms, largely from abroad, which would have a good export market. The effort paid off, and Ireland became a centre for several industries with promising futures, such as electronics, chemical and electrical goods. This development had the advantage of diversifying the Republic's export markets, and making it less dependent on the British market which was the most slowly-growing of all developed countries.

With rapid economic change came rapid social change. The most striking development was demographic. After more than a century of decline, the population was rising again. From a low point of 2,818,000 at the census of 1961, it reached 3,440,000 at the census of 1981. Not only was the population larger, it was proportionately younger. In 1979 almost half of it was under twenty-five. While greater Dublin grew particularly fast, all parts of the country were affected: Leitrim was the only one of the twenty-six counties to experience a population decline in the decade

1971-81.

With social change came a change in values. The Republic in the mid-sixties seemed a country where traditional Catholic *mores* were still deeply entrenched. Books were banned for being indecent or obscene, the sale and import of contraceptives was illegal, divorce was unconstitutional, and abortion almost unheard of. In subsequent years, this changed fast. The book censorship was eased as early as 1966, when some thousands of titles were released from the list of banned books. The laws against contraceptives came under increasing attack, and in 1979 a measure was carried permitting their import and sale under certain restrictions. By the early eighties, pressure was beginning for a repeal of the constitutional ban on divorce. Abortion remained illegal, but some thousands of Irish girls went annually to England for abortions. The extent of marital breakdown was causing concern, and numbers of couples were living together without marrying. Homosexuals, who once did their best to avoid drawing public attention, formed a pressure group devoted to securing the repeal of their legal disabilities. To be sure, old customs did not collapse. The great majority of the population still went to church on Sundays, and the strength of long-established loyalties was shown by the enormous welcome given to Pope John Paul II when he visited Ireland in 1979. But the Irish value-system was becoming fragmented: part remaining traditionally catholic, part influenced by ideas coming in from Britain, America and the Continent.

An active women's movement developed during the period. The difference it made to the economic position of women was limited. The Republic continued to have a lower proportion of working women than most countries in Europe, and much lower than Northern Ireland. But legal safeguards for women were improved. Legislation was passed to maintain equality of pay and of opportunity, and the tax structure was altered so as to treat working wives more generously.

Discussion of such issues was facilitated by developments in the mass media. Irish television had begun as recently as the end of 1961, but soon showed a willingness to tackle controversial questions. Irish newspapers became increasingly ready to publish investigative journalism, and Irish publishers offered a market for the findings of the first generation of Irish social scientists.

One area of particularly important change was education. The author of the preceding chapter in this volume, Professor Patrick Lynch, had an important part to play in this. He headed a research team whose report, published in 1966 under the title of *Investment in education,* unsentimentally analysed the deficiencies of the primary and second-level systems. A year later, the report of the commission on higher education (1960-67) provided a matching survey of third-level problems. Spurred on by these and other influences, a succession of energetic ministers and civil servants pressed through a series of changes. New curricula were introduced at primary and post-primary level. Many small schools were replaced by larger and better-equipped units. The most sweeping changes took place at post-primary level, where existing schools were enlarged or amalgamated, new types of school introduced, and, from 1967, education provided free for the vast majority of pupils. The free education scheme proved popular beyond all expectation, and the number of pupils in post-primary schools shot up from 143,000 in 1965-6 to 301,000 in 1980-81. In higher education some of the central recommendations of the 1960-67 commission were put into effect, most notably by the setting up in 1968 of a permanent Higher Education Authority to advise the minister for education on the allocation of funds and generally to further the development of higher education. The universities were expanded, and supplemented by new institutions that emphasised vocational and technological subjects – national institutes for higher education and regional technical colleges. The catholic hierarchy contributed to the new thinking on higher education – in 1970 it removed its long-standing 'ban' on the attendance of catholics at Trinity College, and Trinity became an integral part of the national system of higher education.

Not all the changes in these sixteen years were favourable. Inflation remained at worrying levels. Though most people benefited from growing prosperity, there was an intractable pool of poverty, comprising twenty per cent or more of the population: some observers felt that the affluent majority were growing more callous towards their poorer

154   155   156

neighbours. Crime increased sharply in Dublin and pollution in the countryside. There were complaints, in Dublin particularly, of poor postal, bus, and telephone services, and of endless congestion. A worrying problem was the remorseless rise in population, which meant that more young people were entering the labour market than there were jobs to satisfy, so that unemployment remained high. For good or ill, however, there was no question that Ireland was being transformed, both economically and socially.

Politically, the pace of change was less breakneck than in society as a whole, but even there it was considerable. The sixteen years 1966-82 saw five taoisigh (prime ministers) and five changes in the party or parties in power, as against three taoisigh and three changes of party in the preceding sixteen years. The same three parties – Fianna Fáil, Fine Gael, and Labour – dominated the scene, but they became more professional, better funded, and more equipped to meet the era of television.

The period opened with Seán Lemass securely in office, having gained an overall majority in the general election of 1965. Suddenly, in November 1966, he announced his retirement, and a struggle for the leadership of Fianna Fáil ensued. The initial front-runners were two energetic young ministers, Charles Haughey and George Colley; but ultimately the party agreed on a somewhat older man, Jack Lynch, as a compromise candidate. Lynch, who owed his entry into politics to his prowess in Gaelic athletics, seemed at first a rather indecisive figure. Time was to show that he possessed more steel than appeared at first sight.

In October 1968, the Fianna Fáil government was defeated by almost

154 Jack Lynch (RTE 1972)

155 Liam Cosgrave (RTE 1973)

156 Charles Haughey (RTE 1973)

157

157 Garret FitzGerald (RTE 1978)

60 to 40 per cent when it put to the electorate in a referendum a proposal to abolish proportional representation. It was widely expected that this heralded an electoral defeat, but when the next general election came, in June 1969, it produced a net gain of two seats for Fianna Fáil. Lynch's position within the party was strengthened, which proved important when a few months later what became known as the 'arms crisis' burst upon it. In April 1970 customs officers at Dublin airport seized a consignment of arms which had been secretly imported from the Continent, for use by republicans in the north. In May, Lynch dismissed two ministers, Charles Haughey and Neil Blaney, whom he believed to be implicated, and a third minister, Kevin Boland, resigned in protest against the taoiseach's action. Blaney and Haughey were arrested on charges of illegally importing arms; Blaney was discharged and Haughey acquitted. But Lynch weathered the storm. While Blaney and Boland left Fianna Fáil, only a handful of deputies followed them. Haughey remained in the party, although he was not restored to the front bench till 1975.

In February 1973, Lynch called a general election, which resulted in a defeat as unexpected as his victory in 1969 had been. Fianna Fáil actually gained votes in the election, but lost six seats, thus allowing a coalition of Fine Gael and Labour to take office. The crucial reason for the change was that Fine Gael and Labour made a pact before the election, and supporters of each party followed instructions to cast lower preferences in favour of the other. The new government was headed by Liam Cosgrave, son of the prime minister of 1922-32, as taoiseach.

The new government had to deal with the economic crisis of 1974-5, and with the intractable situation in Northern Ireland. None the less, by-elections showed that the government was maintaining its support, and redrawing of constituency boundaries was generally expected to favour it when the next general election came. The election was held in June 1977. For the third time running, the electorate confounded the pundits. It returned Fianna Fáil with the largest majority ever obtained in an Irish general election – 84 seats, as against 64 for all others. An important factor was Fianna Fáil's election package, containing among other things a promise to abolish rates on private dwellings, and road tax on smaller vehicles.

Following the election, Lynch once again became taoiseach. But his term was not an easy one. Some back-benchers disliked his relatively conciliatory attitude to the unionists and the British over Northern Ireland. In 1979 he had to face the revival of economic difficulties. Finally, in December of that year, he unexpectedly resigned. A contest for the leadership ensued, with the same principal contenders as in 1966 – Charles Haughey and George Colley. This time no compromise figure emerged, and Haughey was elected by 44 votes to 38. He forthwith became taoiseach; but he had to contend with continued opposition to his leadership from within his party.

Haughey declared that he intended to make the solution of the Northern Ireland problem the main object of his premiership. But economic troubles and intra-party divisions kept breaking in. In June 1981 he called a general election, in the hope of strengthening his position. It had the opposite effect. No party was returned with a clear majority; independents and representatives of minor parties held the balance of power. A coalition of Fine Gael and Labour, this time under the leadership of Dr Garret FitzGerald, who had succeeded Cosgrave as leader of Fine Gael in 1977, took office.

FitzGerald saw the main problem facing his government as the economic crisis. Haughey, hoping that the depression which set in in 1979 would be short, had maintained levels of public expenditure by borrowing the necessary funds, much of it from abroad. But the depression continued, and the country's external indebtedness increased by leaps and bounds. By the end of 1981 the total public-sector foreign debt reached

£4,800,000,000, or almost half the gross national product. In January 1982, in an attempt to reduce this enormous load, the government introduced a spectacularly severe budget. Its provisions went too far for one crucial independent deputy, and the government was defeated by a single vote.

A general election was held the following month (18 February 1982). Once again the results were indecisive, with independents and minor parties holding the balance of power. But Haughey was more successful than FitzGerald in winning them over, and he returned to office. His hold on office, however, proved precarious. Divisions within Fianna Fáil continued. A series of bizarre scandals touched several people close to Haughey. The recession bit deeper. Government revenue declined, the foreign debt rose even higher, and the government had to increase taxes yet further. In November a pivotal group (the Workers' Party, with three deputies) voted against Haughey on a motion of confidence, and he was obliged to resign. A general election followed – the third in eighteen months. It at last produced a clear result. Fine Gael and Labour between them had a clear majority over all other parties and groups. They negotiated a coalition and took office, with FitzGerald again as taoiseach.

So far in this chapter I have written about Northern Ireland and the Republic as if they had two distinct histories. This largely corresponds with the realities. However, there were some ways in which they shared a common experience, and I shall close by drawing attention to them.

The most obvious of these was that, on 1 January 1973, both became part of the European Community: the Republic as a member-state, Northern Ireland as part of the United Kingdom. The change did less to bring the two parts of Ireland together than some had expected. The increased support for agriculture available in the Community made much more difference to the Republic than to the north – partly because Northern Ireland agriculture had already been well subsidised under British rule, partly because the 'green pound' (the level at which agricultural

158 Haughey-Thatcher Meeting, 8 December 1980 (Colman Doyle photo)

subsidies were paid) was fixed by the respective national governments at a more favourable rate for farmers in the Republic than in the United Kingdom. Furthermore, when, in March 1979, the Community established a European Monetary System, the Republic joined it while the United Kingdom did not. This meant that the Republic's currency, instead of being tied to sterling as it had been since independence, was now linked to the currencies of continental Europe. It soon fell in value as compared with British currency, the lowest point being reached in February 1981, when the Irish pound was worth only 73.38p sterling. This divergence benefited exporters from the Republic. But it meant that, for the first time, people crossing the border had to go to the trouble of changing their money into a different currency. In the short run, the Common Market had led to a more complete economic division of Ireland than had existed before.

However, in other respects, the European Community brought some shared experiences. In June 1979 elections took place all over the Community for the European parliament, and the two parts of Ireland found themselves, for the first time since 1918, voting in the same election. Thereafter, members from the two parts of Ireland sat in the same parliament, and found that, on non-political issues, unionist and nationalist did not inevitably vote in different lobbies.

A non-political force which affected both parts of Ireland was the ecumenical movement. Starting from small beginnings in the sixties, it became a substantial feature of Irish life in the seventies. Ecumenical conferences were held from 1964, and the Irish School of Ecumenics was founded in 1970. From 1968 the heads of the four main churches (catholic, Church of Ireland, presbyterian, and methodist) were meeting regularly, and on occasions issued joint statements. True, cordiality was less than complete. Catholic regulations on the upbringing of children in mixed marriages continued to give offence to protestants. On the other side, two presbyterian moderators refused even to meet the catholic primate. But on the whole, church leaders and theologians were speaking to each other more freely and frankly than ever before.

Another possible link between the two parts of Ireland opened up when, in December 1980, the then taoiseach, Haughey, secured from the British prime minister, Margaret Thatcher, an agreement that their respective civil servants should examine the 'totality of relationships' between the two islands. The strategy appeared to be that the British government might be induced to encourage closer relations between the two parts of Ireland, in return for the Republic's accepting some common institutions with the United Kingdom. An Anglo-Irish governmental council was set up in November 1981, with the prospect of an Anglo-Irish parliamentary council at some future date.

The rapprochement then came to an abrupt halt. There were a variety of reasons, of which the most important was the displeasure felt in Britain at the Irish government's refusal to support it in its dispute with Argentina over the Falkland Islands, which erupted in April 1982. But though no further progress was made, the agreements already reached were not repudiated. It remains to be seen whether the accords of 1980-81 were a dead end, or whether they were the beginnings of a framework in which a solution to Anglo-Irish problems could be found.

One thing remains clear: the period 1966-82 was one of more rapid change than any preceding period of comparable length in Irish history.

23
IRELAND, 1982–94

by Richard English

In July 1982 United Kingdom (U.K.) Prime Minister Margaret Thatcher argued that, 'No commitment exists for Her Majesty's Government to consult the Irish Government on matters affecting Northern Ireland'. Yet the years under scrutiny in this chapter witnessed the development of formal structures by means of which such consultation became a significant part of Northern Irish political life. In elections for the new Northern Ireland Assembly, held in October 1982, Sinn Féin won 10.1 per cent of first preference votes, while the Social Democratic and Labour Party (S.D.L.P.) gained 18.8 per cent. There was alarm in certain circles at the possibility that the I.R.A.'s political alter ego might come to displace the S.D.L.P. as the party representing the majority of Northern Irish nationalists – a prospect unacceptable both to Dublin and to London. Concern grew when Sinn Féin's Gerry Adams was elected as M.P. for West Belfast in the June 1983 U.K. general election, with his party winning 13.4 per cent of votes cast and the S.D.L.P. winning 17.9 per cent. In fact there was little likelihood of Sinn Féin overtaking the S.D.L.P. among northern nationalists, but there is no doubt that political developments were influenced by the perception that republicans were gaining ground in Northern Ireland.

The Irish government's establishment of a forum for debate among Ireland's constitutional parties provided the basis for a telling set of exchanges in relation to Northern Ireland. The New Ireland Forum, which first met in May 1983, comprised representatives from the main constitutional nationalist parties: Northern Ireland's S.D.L.P. and the

362

Republic's Fianna Fáil, Fine Gael and Labour. Having received a large number of submissions, the Forum offered a final report which examined three options for Northern Ireland: that it become part of a unitary Irish state, part of a federal/confederal state, or be governed under a system of joint authority between Dublin and London. The last of these – according, at least, to the report – would involve giving 'equal validity to the two traditions in Northern Ireland'. This notion of equal validity was to become the leitmotif of much policy – Irish as well as British – in relation to the Northern Irish crisis during our period. Although British reactions to the Forum Report disappointed its architects, British governmental attitudes were shifting significantly in the direction of constitutional nationalist thinking. In November 1984 a joint communiqué, issued after a summit meeting between Margaret Thatcher and Irish Taoiseach Garret FitzGerald, stated that 'the identities of both the majority and the minority communities in Northern Ireland should be recognised and respected and reflected in the structures and processes of Northern Ireland in ways acceptable to both communities'. Soon after this summit, there began the serious drafting of what was to become the 1985 Anglo-Irish Agreement. The Agreement, signed on 15 November, symbolised an attempt at a newly co-operative British-Irish approach to Northern Ireland. Endorsed (emphatically) by the House of Commons and (more narrowly) by the Dáil, the accord saw both governments 'affirm that any change in the status of Northern Ireland would only come about with the consent of a majority of the people of Northern Ireland', 'recognise that the present wish of a majority of the people of Northern Ireland is for no change in the status of Northern Ireland', and 'declare that, if in the future a majority of the people of Northern Ireland clearly wish for and formally consent to the establishment of a united Ireland, they will introduce and support in the respective parliaments legislation to give effect to that wish'. Having sought to reassure unionists that Northern Ireland's place within the U.K. was secure as long as a majority there wanted it to remain so, the Agreement established a British-Irish Intergovernmental Conference which was to meet regularly and which would offer a framework within which matters relating to Northern Ireland could be discussed. This innovative development marked a dramatic change in the governance of the region; the permanent secretariat of civil servants (northern and southern) which underpinned the Conference served to emphasise the seriousness of the consultative role newly allotted to the Republic.

Both governments committed themselves, in the Agreement, to supporting the devolution of powers within Northern Ireland 'on a basis which would secure widespread acceptance throughout the community'. Indeed, the document stated that the Conference would 'concern itself with measures to recognise and accommodate the rights and identities of the two traditions in Northern Ireland', and the thinking behind the whole initiative relied on what might be termed a symmetrical approach. The two sides in Northern Ireland were to be accorded equal respect, validity, and legitimacy in the hope that it would be possible simultaneously to reassure unionists and mollify nationalists. Both Thatcher and FitzGerald – co-signatories to the document – have subsequently expressed disappointment with its impact, and it is important to note two particularly crucial points. First, the accord was implemented without the consent of the majority community in the region to which it referred. Unionist hostility to the Agreement was widespread and often fierce; moreover, while much of the heat has gone out of unionist hostility to the initiative, the Agreement is still perceived by many to be a step in a distinctly unwelcome direction. Thus, in February 1994, Democratic Unionist Party (D.U.P.) leader Ian Paisley described the 1985 Agreement as a condominium 'in embryo', one that would eventually grow into a (dreaded) united Ireland. Second, those nationalists – such as Garret FitzGerald – who have argued for the achievement of Irish unity with unionist consent have failed to demonstrate either, first, signs that such consent is beginning to emerge or, second, an effective explanation of how or why it should do so. The Agreement's suggestion that a united Ireland would be forthcoming if unionist consent were to develop looks rather feeble when set against the fact that no such consent can reasonably be expected to emerge. But British and Irish policy toward the northern crisis was founded on the belief that a symmetrical approach was indeed viable. Attempts to reassure unionists coexisted with claims that nationalist stock was rising. At the time of the Agreement, for example, Garret FitzGerald argued that, 'Nationalists can now raise their heads knowing their position is, and is seen to be, on an equal footing with that of members of the unionist community.'

Those who wished to see the S.D.L.P. gaining strength at Sinn Féin's expense were encouraged by the results of the 1987 U.K. general election. The S.D.L.P.'s share of the vote rose by 3.2 per cent, while Sinn Féin's share fell by 2 per cent. It is debatable how far this resulted directly from the Anglo-Irish Agreement, but it is clear that numerous difficulties were experienced by the republican movement during 1987. Sinn Féin's electoral disappointment was complemented by setbacks involving the Irish Republican Army (I.R.A.). In May 1987 eight I.R.A. men were killed during an attack on Loughgall Royal Ulster Constabulary (R.U.C.) station in County Armagh. In November of the same year an I.R.A. bomb killed eleven people at a Remembrance Day ceremony in Enniskillen, County Fermanagh, and the I.R.A. was drenched in a wave of popular and international revulsion. In March 1988 three I.R.A. members on a mission in Gibraltar were killed by British soldiers in an episode which generated lasting controversy. The three were unarmed and much debate ensued concerning the circumstances of their shooting.

While such incidents have a capacity to attract and sustain considerable attention, more significant developments were also underway. The 1989 Northern Ireland Fair Employment Act aimed both to protect individuals from discrimination and to address the problem of unequal employment opportunities in the region. The persistence of significantly different catholic and protestant rates of unemployment in Northern Ireland was considered a major political issue. In part this was because vociferous campaigners – particularly in the United

States – had managed to build up considerable momentum in their agitation on the subject of catholic disadvantage. Moreover, some observers held that religious disadvantage and/or discrimination lay at the root of Northern Ireland's political conflict. While the other grievances of the 1960s civil rights movement had largely been met by the early 1970s, different employment levels – it was argued – remained a source of considerable tension between the two communities. The new legislation replaced the existing Fair Employment Agency with a (tougher) Fair Employment Commission, and it also made compulsory the monitoring of the composition of the workforce, in terms of perceived religion, in all but the smallest firms. The intention was both to identify areas of disadvantage and to implement action aimed at rectifying it.

Whatever the merits of such intention, the implementation of the project faced significant obstacles. Employment had become a politically charged topic in Northern Ireland, and the very qualities of consensus and equanimity required for the effective pursuit of the proposed project were precisely those whose absence had rendered the project urgent in the first place. Thus the government found itself criticised, on the one hand, for acting with insufficient resolution in redressing the imbalances in employment opportunity and, on the other, for exaggerating the importance of discrimination in producing catholic disadvantage. Certainly, disadvantage and discrimination should not be blurred together, and both the question of economic location and that of the perilous state of the Northern Ireland economy as a whole presented severe problems for those endeavouring to rectify unequal job opportunities. Moreover, while some have argued that employment disadvantage helps to sustain the political conflict, it is also true that the political conflict renders more difficult the task of those trying to eradicate inequality in employment. In this sense Northern Irish religious disadvantage in employment differs from some other forms of structural disadvantage. Racial or sexual imbalances in Britain, for example, are not complicated by the questions of political violence or state legitimacy relevant to catholic-protestant relations in Northern Ireland. Issues such as security force membership or safety at work have proved particularly awkward in the Northern Irish context.

The May 1989 District Council elections witnessed slight gains for the Ulster Unionist Party (U.U.P.) and the S.D.L.P., and setbacks for the D.U.P. and Sinn Féin. Later in the year, Northern Ireland Secretary of State Peter Brooke suggested that the U.K. government would respond flexibly if the I.R.A. abandoned violence, and that the government might talk to Sinn Féin under such circumstances. In November 1990 Brooke declared that Britain had no 'strategic or economic interest' in Northern Ireland, and restated the government's preparedness to accept Irish unification in the (unlikely) event that consent to such a development should emerge. Earlier in 1990 Brooke had asserted that, in his view, enough common ground existed to make inter-party talks between the constitutional Northern Irish parties worthwhile. In what became known as the Brooke initiative, the Secretary of State aimed to build inter-party consensus in order that the 1985 Anglo-Irish Agreement could be transcended by arrangements which would be more broadly acceptable and (therefore) fruitful.

The process was to be three-stranded: strand one would involve the four Northern Ireland constitutional parties (U.U.P., S.D.L.P., D.U.P., Alliance Party): strand two was to involve talks between Dublin and the Northern Irish parties; strand three was to address relations between Dublin and London. Predictably, there were numerous difficulties in implementing this schedule. There were, for example, problems concerning the venue for strand two, and concerning the question of who would chair this second strand of talks. Despite such obstacles, Peter Brooke claimed that the initial talks had indeed provided a useful foundation for further progress, and Patrick Mayhew (who became Secretary of State for Northern Ireland in April 1992) continued the talks initiative.

Beginning formally on 29 April 1992 the Mayhew talks sequence moved swiftly, but the enormous differences which separated the various participants were made painfully apparent. There was, for example, a negative response from the other parties to the S.D.L.P.'s proposal that Northern Ireland be governed by a six-person Commission (to comprise three people elected from Northern Ireland and three nominated, respectively, by the London government, the Dublin government, and the European Community). Indeed the talks became increasingly difficult as they grew more specific, and despite Patrick Mayhew's cautiously expressed optimism it appeared that the talks process had revealed the width of the gap separating the unionist and nationalist outlooks. The tension, during the talks, surrounding the Republic of Ireland's constitutional claim to the six counties of Northern Ireland reflected the basic divergence of opinion, between unionists and nationalists, over the legitimacy of partition. Again, while the U.U.P. had conceded the principle that both power-sharing and some form of Irish dimension had a place in the government of Northern Ireland, the S.D.L.P.'s more ambitious nationalist agenda meant that it was not possible to establish a deal on the basis of devolution plus a Dublin connection.

The April 1992 U.K. general election saw the S.D.L.P. vote increase and that of Sinn Féin decline. Sinn Féin's Gerry Adams lost his West Belfast seat to the S.D.L.P.'s Joe Hendron – a significant and symbolic setback for the republican party – but the explosion of two bombs in the centre of London on 10 April signalled the continuing capacity of the I.R.A. to pursue republican goals determinedly by brutal means. Loyalist violence, too, occasioned understandable concern. In 1992 republicans killed thirty-six people while loyalists killed thirty-nine, and the increasing levels of loyalist activity were complemented by friction between loyalists and the RUC. In the wake of the 1985 Anglo-Irish Agreement there had developed considerable tension between loyalists and the police, the former perceiving the latter to be implementing Dublin-tainted rule. In the early 1990s such friction became, on occasions, more pronounced. In August 1992 the loyalist Ulster Defence Association (U.D.A.) was banned by the government.

In the wake of the U.D.A. proscription some people wondered whether Sinn Féin should also have been outlawed. The republican party's relationship with the I.R.A. made some observers feel that it too should be proscribed if moves were being taken against those involved with or supportive of terrorism. But the U.K. government's approach toward Sinn Féin at this time was one of attempting to coax it into the constitutional arena. If anything, the government was speaking in conciliatory rather than coercive tones when it addressed the republican movement. In a speech delivered in Coleraine in December 1992, for example, Patrick Mayhew asserted that

> There are leading Sinn Féin speakers who voice their wish for a peaceful solution and their desire to follow a constitutional path. Provided it is advocated constitutionally, there can be no proper reason for excluding any political objective from discussion. Certainly not the objective of an Ireland united through broad agreement fairly and freely achieved ... In the event of a genuine and established cessation of violence, the whole range of responses that we have had to make to that violence could, and would, inevitably be looked at afresh.

This message – that if republicans abandoned violence then the government would respond positively – formed the foundation of much British policy in this period. For his part, S.D.L.P. leader John Hume was also endeavouring to bring an end to republican violence and to bring Sinn Féin into constitutional politics. Having met and had discussions together, Hume and Sinn Féin President Gerry Adams issued, in April 1993, a joint statement in which they declared their acceptance 'that the Irish people as a whole have a right to national self-determination' and their view that the exercise of this right was 'a matter for agreement between the people of Ireland'.

When the U.K. Prime Minister (John Major) and the Republic of Ireland Taoiseach (Albert Reynolds) issued a Joint Declaration in December 1993, Hume considered that the conditions supposedly justifying republican violence had been rendered irrelevant. The Declaration, he argued, went through the reason traditionally offered by the I.R.A. in an attempt to justify their violent campaign: 'It makes

159 John Hume
(Cork Examiner)

160 Gerry Adams
(Sinn Féin)

very clear that the British government have no selfish or strategic interest or economic interest in Ireland ... And the second major reason given for the use of physical force is that (the British) are preventing the people of Ireland from exercising the right to self-determination and the Declaration is very clear on that'. Indeed, the December 1993 Joint Declaration did see the U.K. government agreeing 'that it is for the people of Ireland alone, by agreement between the two parts respectively, to exercise their right of self-determination on the basis of consent, freely and concurrently given, North and South, to bring about a united Ireland, if that is their wish'. While republicans might resent the document's acceptance of Northern Ireland's right to block such a development, there is no doubt that the Declaration did mark a significant concession to the language and framework of Irish nationalist argument.

The two governments' attempt to reconcile the competing aspirations of Ulster unionists and Irish nationalists, however, ran up against the same problem – that of starkly divergent assumptions – which had plagued the inter-party talks process. It remained difficult, for

370

161 Albert Reynolds
(Cork Examiner)

162 John Major
(Cork Examiner)

example, to see how one could reconcile unionist attachment to the U.K. with the statement of an I.R.A. representative, published in the latter part of 1993, that, 'The obstacle to peace in Ireland is the British presence and the partition of Ireland.' But the U.K. government's approach, during the years covered in this chapter, was one of trying simultaneously to reassure unionists and give concessions to nationalists. The 1985 Anglo-Irish Agreement and the 1993 Joint Declaration each, in their own way, reflected this policy. In November 1993 Secretary of State Mayhew set out the government's attitude in relation to Northern Ireland when he stated that

> The division which exists within the community – together with grievances which exist ... in the social, the economic, and constitutional fields – has led to inter-communal violence and terrorism, and it is the elimination of terrorism, from whatever quarter, that is the government's overriding objective. But the government believes that the underlying causes have to be addressed at the same time.

371

In recent years the government's way of addressing the underlying causes of conflict has revolved around the notion of affording equal respect, legitimacy and validity to the two main traditions in the region: protestant/unionist on the one hand, catholic/nationalist on the other. In his Coleraine speech of December 1992, Patrick Mayhew declared: 'We are committed ... to honouring our commitment to the wishes of a majority in Northern Ireland ... The reality is that the identity of unionists is safeguarded in fact, and also in national and international law; it is also recognised as wholly legitimate by constitutional nationalists. But there is also the aspiration to a united Ireland, an aspiration that is no less legitimate.' This symmetrical approach to respective unionist and nationalist aspirations underpins recent U.K. government policy in Northern Ireland. In his preface to the 1993 Joint Declaration, Mayhew asserted that the document set out 'constitutional principles and political realities which safeguard the vital interests of both sides of the community in Northern Ireland'. In the declaration itself, the U.K. government stressed the need for 'full respect for the rights and identities of both traditions in Ireland'.

When considering the various responses to the Northern Ireland conflict – governmental and non-governmental – it is important to reflect on two central realities, and it might be appropriate to end the first section of this chapter with a brief mention of each. First, scholars have firmly established the regionally varied nature of political experience in Northern Ireland. As Professor John Whyte pointed out, 'Areas only a few miles from each other can differ enormously – in religious mix, in economic circumstances, in the level of violence, in political attitudes. This means that the nature and intensity of the conflict can vary widely.' This in turn underlines the basic reality of Northern Ireland's politics, namely that any single political arrangement is likely to leave a significant section of the population disaffected. Second, any discussion of Northern Ireland which fails to acknowledge certain economic realities will be bound to hinder, rather than advance, progress in the region. Northern Ireland exists on the periphery of a state whose post-war economic performance has been far from impressive. High levels of unemployment form a persistent part of the area's life and have contributed significantly to the pattern of recent political conflict. Moreover, the feebleness of Northern Ireland's economy must be taken fully into account when discussing possible political rearrangements or solutions. The British subvention to Northern Ireland, for example, is so large that it could not possibly be sustained by the Republic of Ireland. Economic arguments in favour of the continued union of Great Britain and Northern Ireland may not be the most emotionally charged defences of the unionist position, but they are certainly among the most persuasive.

As noted, the New Ireland Forum of 1983-4 examined three options for the future of Northern Ireland: that it become part of a unitary Irish state, part of a federal/confederal state, or be governed under a system of joint (Dublin-London) authority. The Fianna Fáil delegation to the Forum preferred the first of these options, and indeed the party's leader (Charles Haughey) argued that, 'The only solution is as stated in the report: a unitary state with a new constitution.' This more nationalistic public stance was typical of Haughey's style of rhetoric and gesture. Leader of Fianna Fáil from 1979 to 1992, Haughey's career contained both rhetorical flourishes and pragmatic compromises in relation to the north. Indeed, the recent attitudes of the Republic's political parties toward the Northern Irish conflict have reflected considerable ambiguities. The central ambiguity is rooted in the double message of the state's 1937 constitution:

> Article 2: the national territory consists of the whole island of Ireland, its islands, and the territorial seas.
> Article 3: pending the re-integration of the national territory and without prejudice to the right of parliament and government established by this constitution to exercise jurisdiction over the whole of that territory, the laws enacted by that parliament shall have the like area and extent of application as the laws of Saorstát Éireann and the like extra-territorial effect.

373

Similarly, political parties in the period under scrutiny in this chapter have tended to endorse the principle that (ideally) a united Ireland would be desirable, while simultaneously recognising that it is not practical in the foreseeable future to try to achieve such an arrangement. In this, the parties have echoed popular opinion. Thus, for example, when asked what were the main issues with which the parties should be concerned during the 1987 Republic of Ireland general election, only three per cent of respondents suggested that Northern Ireland should represent one of these main issues. When asked in 1989 about the importance of a listed series of issues during the general election campaign of that year, twenty-nine per cent of respondents said that Northern Ireland was very important. But this should be set against the fact that, when asked (unprompted) to list the main issues about which the electioneering parties should be concerned, Northern Ireland did not even feature as one of these main issues. Thus, the desire for a united Ireland is very much a low level priority among the Republic's electorate.

The sequence of governments in the Republic during the 1980s saw Garret FitzGerald lead a Fine Gael-Labour coalition (1981-2), Charles Haughey head a Fianna Fáil administration (1982), FitzGerald return to power with a Fine Gael-Labour government (1982-7), and then Haughey lead first a Fianna Fáil team (1987-9) and then a coalition with the Progressive Democrats (1989-92). In 1981 Garret FitzGerald outlined his aim of rendering the Republic of Ireland more attractive to northern protestants. In what became known as his constitutional crusade, the Fine Gael leader set out to rid the state's constitution of features that might be unattractive to Ulster protestants. But the first of the major constitutional battles to be fought out via referendum during the 1980s did not fit into this pattern. FitzGerald himself has publicly referred not only to his own 'personal antipathy to abortion', but also to 'the opposition of the vast majority of people in Ireland, north and south, catholic and protestant, to abortion'. The 1981-3 campaign to insert a constitutional prohibition on abortion aimed to provide constitutional backing to the existing, restrictive abortion

374

legislation. The Pro-Life Amendment Campaign (P.L.A.C.) argued the case for such a constitutional amendment on the grounds that it was necessary in order to prevent the future legalisation of abortion. In contrast the Anti-Amendment Campaign (A.A.C.) contested the issue, although the A.A.C. was more loosely organised than P.L.A.C. In September 1983 the referendum saw sixty-seven per cent of those voting support the amendment (prohibiting the legalisation of abortion) and thirty-three per cent oppose it. The turn-out was low, at fifty-four per cent.

More relevant to FitzGerald's liberalising crusade was the 1986 campaign to remove the constitutional ban on divorce. FitzGerald himself intended both that the proposed change would help north-south relations by rendering the Republic more pluralistic, and also that the citizens of the Republic themselves would benefit from the alteration. In April 1986 FitzGerald announced that the government would, the following month, introduce the wording of the Divorce Amendment Bill, and that in June a referendum on the issue would be held. At the end of April 1986 the Anti-Divorce Campaign (A.D.C.) was launched. In contrast to the relative feebleness of the pro-divorce campaign, the A.D.C.'s approach was characterised by a well co-ordinated efficiency. Locally as well as nationally the anti-divorce case was shrewdly put across, while a mixture of catholic pulpit pressure and popular alarm about the (supposedly) possible effects which the introduction of divorce would have on property rights helped to push enough voters toward the anti-divorce stance. With a 60.5 per cent turn-out, the June 1986 referendum saw 36.5 per cent vote in favour of the amendment permitting the legalisation of divorce, and 63.5 per cent vote against.

The pattern which emerged from these two referendums is extremely complicated. Regional variation needs to be taken into account. For example, the five constituencies which produced a 'no' vote in the abortion referendum, and the six constituencies which produced a 'yes' vote in the divorce referendum, were all in Dublin. Again, the role of the catholic church raised intriguing political and historical questions.

Catholic church support for the anti-abortion amendment, and hostility to divorce, played a significant part in the two campaigns. Moreover, this raised the issue of the relationship between, on the one hand, the Republic's political and social ethos and, on the other, the expressed desire of the state's Irish nationalists for Irish unification. As noted, pro-abortion sentiment was hardly a central component of Ulster unionist politics but the divorce question was, perhaps, more relevant. After the rejection of the amendment permitting the legalisation of divorce, Garret FitzGerald observed that this result was 'something of a set-back to the long-term prospect of the two parts of Ireland coming closer together politically'. Indeed, while it is hardly surprising that the ethos of so overwhelmingly catholic a state should – to a significant degree – reflect catholic thinking, the implications of this for irredentist nationalism were hardly encouraging. Professor Whyte shrewdly observed that while northern protestants might agree with the catholic bishops' argument that it is only natural for a majority ethos to prevail, such protestants 'might conclude that, in that case, they would prefer to remain in their own state with its protestant majority than join a state which would have a catholic majority'. Attitudes on social issues in the Republic have, during the period under scrutiny in this chapter, been both complex and changing. The campaigns surrounding abortion and divorce have to be set against the increasing liberalisation, in recent years, of legislation relating to the availability of contraceptives. Moreover, in 1992 further referendums saw the electorate vote in favour of the right to travel outside the state for an abortion and of the right to information concerning the availability of abortion in other states. Again there was regional variation, with the vote against the right to travel and the right to information being highest in rural constituencies.

The general election of February 1987 resulted in Charles Haughey forming a minority Fianna Fáil government. The party increased its number of Dáil seats from seventy-five to eighty-one, while Fine Gael's share of seats fell from seventy to fifty-one. The Labour Party's share of first preference votes fell from 9.4 per cent to 6.4 per cent, while its share of seats dropped from sixteen to twelve. A significant development was the emergence as an electoral force of the Progressive Democrats (P.D.s). Founded in 1985 by ex-Fianna Fáil cabinet minister Desmond O'Malley – who had had a long-running feud with Charles Haughey – the P.D.s advocated the rationalisation and reform of the state apparatus, together with the limiting of the economic role of the state. In the 1987 election they secured 11.9 per cent of first preference votes and obtained fourteen seats in the Dáil. A much less impressive debut was made by Sinn Féin, whose 1986 decision to break with abstentionism meant that they contested the February 1987 election with the intention of taking any Dáil seats which they might win. The party's performance, however, was dismal. Having put up twenty-seven candidates and having fought vigorously during the campaign, Sinn Féin only managed to secure 1.9 per cent of first preference votes and failed to win a single seat.

It is important to note certain key points about the political party system in the Republic during these years. The first concerns the position of (and relations between) Fianna Fáil's political rivals. From 1973 onwards Fine Gael-Labour governments alternated with Fianna Fáil administrations: 1973-7, 1981-2, 1982-7 Fine Gael-Labour; 1977-81, 1982, 1987-9 Fianna Fáil. By 1987, however, divisions had deepened between Fine Gael and Labour. The former had shifted in the direction of fiscal rectitude, while the latter had seen its support suffer as a result of coalition. Moreover, the appearance of the P.D.s, together with the small but significant challenge posed on the left by the Workers' Party, meant that the non-Fianna Fáil parties represented a distinctly fragmented alternative. Second, the 1989 general election witnessed the end of what might be termed the Fianna Fáil-versus-the-rest model of Irish party politics. Traditionally, Fianna Fáil had stressed its distinctive capacity to form single-party government; since it had first taken office in 1932, Fianna Fáil had been the only party which had governed without coalition partners. This (supposedly) brought greater stability, strength, and efficiency and contrasted with the alliances which rival parties were forced to make in order to form governments. In 1989 the pattern changed. Fianna Fáil won seventy-seven seats, Fine Gael fifty-five, Labour fifteen, others nineteen, and Fianna Fáil went into coalition with the Progressive Democrats. Having followed the coalition path, Fianna Fáil took on a different role in the party system. In some ways, its position was strengthened. As the largest party, it represented the most powerful player in the coalition game: if a coalition had to be formed, then Fianna Fáil would find it easier to form the necessary deal than would any of its smaller rivals.

It has been argued that the 1989 election represented a turning point in the history of the Irish party system, and certainly Fianna Fáil's subsequent maintenance of governmental power by means of coalition (1989-92 with the P.D.s; 1993 onwards with Labour) would seem to support such a thesis. Grand claims were also made by some observers when Mary Robinson was elected President of the Republic in 1990. All previous Presidents had been men and, with the exception of Douglas Hyde, all had been of Fianna Fáil pedigree. Robinson – who had a distinguished record in law and also in campaigning on human rights and minority issues – was nominated and supported as Presidential candidate by the Labour Party, and also had the backing of (among others) the Workers' Party. During the summer of 1990 she followed an exacting schedule of countrywide campaigning, but the most dramatic feature of the Presidential race involved the Fianna Fáil candidate, Brian Lenihan. In a television debate Lenihan denied that he had made a telephone call in 1982 to the then President Patrick Hillery in an attempt to pre-empt a dissolution of the Dáil. But in a taped interview with a research student Lenihan had already admitted that he *had* in fact made such a call. The tape being made available, Lenihan's credibility was significantly damaged and this situation was only worsened by the fact that the Fianna Fáil candidate persisted in his denials.

Despite this setback, Lenihan attracted more first preference votes than his two rivals, winning 44.1 per cent, against Robinson's 38.9 per cent, and Fine Gael's Austin Currie's 17.0 per cent. But the Currie

163 Mary Robinson (RTE)

transfers went overwhelmingly to Robinson, who was duly elected President with a second count total of 52.8 per cent. Robinson's victory reflected a successful attempt to woo voters with what might be termed more progressive instincts. But while she has emerged as a highly visible President, too much significance should not be read into the election. The Presidency is primarily a ceremonial office. Moreover, the supposed liberal triumph of 1990 was, in fact, part of a broader series of developments. Thus, for example, Fianna Fáil's first Presidential defeat mirrored the new vulnerability which recent electoral experience had exposed. It is also important that the extent of the progressive victory should not be overstated. Robinson's election certainly solidified the position of Labour Party leader Dick Spring. But when Labour achieved the impressive total of thirty-three seats in the 1992 general election, it was with Fianna Fáil that the party came to share governmental authority. As has been noted, recent changes in the Irish party system have not necessarily weakened the position of the previously dominant political party.

Of vital significance to any appreciation of this period of Irish history is the increasingly influential role played in Irish political life by the European Community (E.C.), and it might be appropriate to finish our chapter on this note. Most issues of domestic public policy now have a European dimension. In May 1987 Irish voters voted, by referendum, to permit the state to ratify the Single European Act (S.E.A.), which reflected the desire for closer union between the E.C.'s member states. The treaty of Maastricht further developed the process of European union – union which was to involve economic, monetary, foreign, security, and justice policies. In June 1992 a referendum saw Irish voters permit the ratification of this treaty. Indeed, the process of European integration is the essential context for understanding contemporary Irish politics. European law plays a vital role in influencing Irish political life, and European union increasingly determines the nature of the framework within which the Irish state must operate.

The June 1994 European elections saw the Republic's fifteen seats distributed as follows: Fianna Fáil 7, Fine Gael 4, Green Party 2, Labour Party 1, Independent 1. In Northern Ireland the European elections saw the three sitting members returned. The D.U.P.'s Ian Paisley topped the poll (163,246), closely followed by the S.D.L.P.'s John Hume (161,992), with the U.U.P.'s Jim Nicholson (133,459) being elected on the strength of D.U.P. transfers. Tellingly, Northern Ireland politicians offered widely divergent interpretations of these results. Paisley argued that, having topped the poll, he had received endorsement in his vehement opposition to the Downing Street Declaration; Hume argued that his vote, which had risen since the 1989 election, indicated popular support for the peace process (of which the Downing Street statement was a significant part); Nicholson suggested that his own increased vote pointed to a popular preference for the U.U.P.'s calmer strategy over the more confrontational style of the D.U.P. The I.R.A.'s declaration (on 31 August 1994) of a 'complete cessation of military operations' raised enormous hopes in relation to Northern Ireland, but the sharp divergence between unionist and nationalist aspirations remained.[1]

NOTES

CHAPTER 3 (pp 43-60)

1 Prologue to *Félire Óengusso;* see Whitley Stokes, *On the calendar of Oengus* (1880), pp xviii ff.
2 *Crith Gablach,* ed. D.A. Binchy (1941), p. 23, § 46; cf. Eoin MacNeill, in *Proceedings of the Royal Irish Academy,* 36 C 16 (1923), pp 305 ff.
3 Ibid.
4 Ibid., pp 7 ff, § 14, 15.
5 Ibid., p. 16, § 27.
6 Ibid.

CHAPTER 4 (pp 61-75)

1 *The works of St Patrick,* translated by Ludwig Bieler (1953), p. 28.
2 Whitley Stokes and J. Strachan (ed.), *Thesaurus palaeohibernicus,* ii (1903), p. 247 (spelling modernised).
3 *Sancti Columbani opera,* ed. G. S. M. Walker (1957), pp 122 ff.
4 *Betha Colaim Chille,* ed. A. O'Kelleher and G. Schoepperle (1918), p. 294.
5 *Sancti Columbani opera,* pp 46-9.
6 Ibid., p. 190, 11 4-9; English rendering by Tomás Ó Fiaich.

CHAPTER 5 (pp 76-90)

1 *Ancient laws of Ireland,* iii, 88.
2 R. Thurneysen (ed.), *Scéla Mucce Meic Datho* (Mediaeval and Modern Irish series, vi), pp 15-16.
3 *Thesaurus palaeohibernicus* ii, 246.
4 G. Calder (ed.), *Auraicept na n-Éces* (1917), p. 6, translated by Robin Flower, in *The Irish tradition* (1947), p. 45.
5 W. Stokes (ed.), *Félire Óengusso* (1905), p. 26, translated by Frank O'Connor, in *Kings, lords, and commons* (London, 1962), p. 4.
6 *Félire Óengusso,* p. 25, translated by Frank O'Connor, in *Kings, lords, and commons,* p. 3.
7 *Thesaurus palaeohibernicus* ii, 327.

8 Migne, *Patrologia Latina*, lxxii, col. 789.
9 J. J. O'Meara (ed.), Giraldus Cambrensis Topographia Hibernie, in *Proceedings of the Royal Irish Academy*, 52 C 4, pp 151-2 (1940; translated by J. J. O'Meara, in *The history and topography of Ireland by Gerald of Wales* (Penguin Books, 1982), p. 84.

CHAPTER 6 (pp 91-106)

1 From Latin verses by Donatus, bishop of Fiesole, in *Monumenta Germaniae historica, Poet. Lat. aevi Carol.*, iii (1890), pp 691-2, translated by Liam de Paor.
2 Poem in margin of St Gall Priscian, in *Thesaurus palaeohibernicus*, ii, 290, translated by Liam de Paor.
3 Johs. Bøe, 'An ornamented bronze object found in a Norwegian grave' in *Bergens Museums Aarbok*, 1924-5, Hist.-Antikv. Raekke, no. 4, p. 34.
4 *Cogadh Gaedhel re Gallaibh*, translated by J.H. Todd (1867), p. 41.
5 P. F. Wallace, 'Anglo-Norman Dublin: continuity and change' in Donnchadh Ó Corráin (ed.), *Irish antiquity* (Cork, 1981), pp 247-67 ; 'The origins of Dublin' in B. G. Scott (ed.) *Studies in early Ireland: essays in honour of M. V. Duignan* (Belfast, 1982), pp 129-43.
6 *Cogadh Gaedhel re Gallaibh*, p. 79.
7 From Njal's Saga, translated by Holger Arbman, in *The vikings* (1961), p. 72.

CHAPTER 7 (pp 107-22)

1 *The bardic poems of Tadhg Dall Ó Huiginn* (Irish Texts Society, vol. xxi), ed. Eleanor Knott, poem 17.
2 Edmund Curtis and R. B. McDowell (ed.), *Irish historical documents 1172-1922*, p. 17.
3 For some account of this grammatical material see Osborn Bergin, 'The native Irish grammarian' in *Proceedings of the British Academy,*xxiv; Brian Ó Cuiv, 'Linguistic terminology in the mediaeval Irish bardic tracts' in *Transactions of the Philological Society*, 1965, and *The linguistic training of the mediaeval Irish poet* (1973).
4 The three manuscripts are (i) Lebor na hUidre, now in the Royal Irish Academy, Dublin, (ii) Rawlinson B. 502, now in the Bodleian Library, Oxford, (iii) Lebor na hUachongbála, commonly known as the 'Book of Leinster', now in part in Trinity College, Dublin, and in part in the Franciscan Library in Dún Mhuire, Killiney, County Dublin. It has been argued recently by Professor Pádraig Ó Riain (in *Éigse*, xvii, 161-76) that the main part of the Rawlinson MS is the codex which was known as Lebor Glinne Dá Loch, or Book of Glendalough.
5 *Early Irish lyrics*, ed. G. Murphy (1956), pp 70-71.
6 Book of Armagh, f. 16 r°. See fig. 41.
7 The hereditary nature of *comarbas Pátraic* between the tenth and twelfth centuries can be seen from the following genealogical table in which members of the Uí Shínaig family are shown. The names of those who held the office of *comarba Pátraic* and of two members who contested the abbacy in the time of St Malachy are printed in italics and the dates of tenure of office added in brackets:

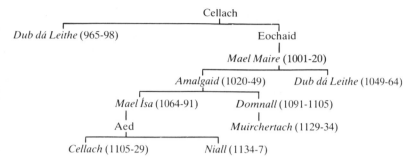

Cellach

Dub dá Leithe (965-98)   Eochaid

Mael Maire (1001-20)

Amalgaid (1020-49)   *Dub dá Leithe* (1049-64)

Mael Ísa (1064-91)   *Domnall* (1091-1105)

Aed   *Muirchertach* (1129-34)

Cellach (1105-29)   *Niall* (1134-7)

CHAPTER 8 (pp 123-43)

1 *Annals of the Four Masters*, ed. John O'Donovan, 1145, 1171.
2 Geoffrey Keating, *Foras Feasa ar Éirinn*, ed. David Comyn and P. S. Dineen, iii, 318 (319).
3 Giraldus Cambrensis, *Expugnatio Hibernica, The conquest of Ireland*, ed. A. B. Scott and F. X. Martin (1974), p. 41.
4 *The Song of Dermot and the earl*, ed. G. H. Orpen (1892), pp 22-5.
5 Ibid., p. 34-5.
6 Giraldus Cambrensis, as above, pp 87, 89
7 Ibid., p. 77.

Professor Martin wishes to express in a special way his gratitude to Dr Jocelyn Otway-Ruthven, of Trinity College, Dublin, who read this chapter in its final draft and made candid comments and corrections.

CHAPTER 9 (pp 144-57)

1 *Calendar of the justiciary rolls, Ireland 1308-14*, p. 103.
2 Séan Ó Tuama, 'The new love poetry' in Brian Ó Cuív (ed.), *Seven centuries of Irish learning* (1961), p. 111.
3 Kathleen Hoagland, *1000 years of Irish poetry* (1953), p. 313.
4 J.T. Gilbert, *Facsimiles of the national manuscripts of Ireland* (1884), pp 98-100.
5 Aubrey Gwynn, 'The black death in Ireland' in *Studies*, Mar. 1935, pp 27-8.

CHAPTER 10 (pp 158-73)

1 *The libelle of Englyshe polycye*, ed. G.F. Warner (1926), p. 36.
2 Cited by H. G. Richardson and G. O. Sayles, *The Irish parliament in the middle ages* (1952), p. 180, n. 40.

3 *Statute rolls of the parliament of Ireland, Henry VI*, p. 567.
4 *Register of John Swayne*, ed. D. A. Chart (1935), p. 108.
5 *Annals of the Four Masters*, ed. John O'Donovan, iv, 965.
6 *Statute rolls of the parliament of Ireland, Henry VI*, p.50.
7 Edmund Curtis, 'The viceroyalty of Richard, duke of York' in *Journal of the Royal Society of Antiquaries of Ireland*, lxii (1932), p. 166.
8 *Annals of the Four Masters*, iv, 1051-3.
9 *Statute rolls of the parliament of Ireland, 1st to 12th years Edward IV*, p. 139.
10 Margaret Griffith, 'The Talbot-Ormond struggle for control of the Anglo-Irish government, 1414-47' in *Irish Historical Studies*, ii, no. 8 (Sept. 1941), p. 396.
11 P.R.O., Council and Privy Seal Warrants, E 28/89, 30 Mar., 3 Edward IV.
12 *Annals of Ulster*, iii, 219-21.
13 G. O. Sayles, 'The vindication of the earl of Kildare from treason, 1496' in *Irish Historical Studies*, vii, no. 25 (Mar. 1950), p. 43.
14 Constantia Maxwell (ed.) *Irish history from contemporary sources* (1923), p. 113.
15 *Vetera monumenta Hibernorum et Scotorum historiam illustrantia, 1216-1547*, ed. Augustine Theiner (Rome, 1864), p. 521.
16 *State papers, Henry VIII, Ireland*, ii, 15.
17 See Art Cosgrove, *Late medieval Ireland, 1370-1541* (Dublin, 1981), pp 116-20.

CHAPTER 11 (pp 174-88)

1 Skeffington and the Irish councii to Henry VIII, 26 Mar. 1535 *(State papers, Henry VIII, Ireland*, ii, 236 ff).
2 'A certain information for our sovereign lord's commissioners in Ireland, 1537' (ibid., ii, 480).
3 Henry VIII to Surrey, 1520 (ibid., ii, 52 ff).
4 Henry VIII to lord deputy and Irish council, 1541 (ibid., iii, **332 ff**).
5 28 Henry VIII c. 5 (*Irish statutes* (1786), i, 90).
6 Statement of Thomas Lynch of Galway *(State papers, Henry VIII, Ireland*, iii, 141).
7 William Camden, *Annals* (1615), p. 78.
8 Ibid.
9 Lord justice and Irish council to privy council, 5 Nov. 1597 *(Calendar of state papers, Ireland, 1596-7*, p. 436).

CHAPTER 12 (pp 189-203)

1 Sir John Davies to earl of Salisbury, 12 Sept. 1607 *(Calendar of state papers, Ireland, 1606-8*, p. 273).

CHAPTER 13 (pp 204-16)

1 Thomas Carte, *Life of Ormonde* (1736), ii, 140.
2 Jonathan Swift, *Works,* ed. T. Scott (1910), iv. 94.
3 *Poems of David Ó Bruadair,* ed. J. C. MacErlean (1917), iii, 15.
4 *Clarendon correspondence,* ed. S. W. Singer (1828), ii, 475.
5 'Lilliburlero' in T. C. Croker, *Historical songs of Ireland* (1841), pp 6-7.

CHAPTER 14 (pp 217-31)

1 3 William and Mary, c. 2.
2 George Berkeley, *The querist,* in *The works of George Berkeley, bishop of Cloyne,* ed. A.
  A. Luce and T. E. Jessop, vi (1953), p. 128.
3 Arthur Young, *A tour of Ireland* (1780), ii, pt 2, pp 35,36.
4 *Dánta Diadha Uladh,* ed. Énri Ó Muirgheasa (1936), pp 281-3.
5 John Burke, *A general and heraldic dictionary of the peerage and baronetage of the British
  Empire* (1828), p. 89.
6 *Amhráin Phiarais Mhic Gearailt,* ed. Risteard Ó Foghludha (1905), p. 23.

CHAPTER 16 (248-62)

1 Quoted in J.A. Reynolds, *The catholic emancipation crisis in Ireland* (1954), p ??
2 *Dublin Evening Post,* 3 July 1828.
3 C. Gavan Duffy, *Young Ireland* (1880), pp 344-7.
4 *First series of reports of the Loyal National Repeal Association of Ireland* (1840), pp viii-
  ix.
5 Duffy, op. cit., p. 217.

CHAPTER 18 (pp 275-93)

1 Lord Eversley, *Gladstone and Ireland* (1912), p. 18.
2 *Freeman's Journal,* 9 June 1879, quoted in Michael Davitt, *The fall of feudalism in
  Ireland,* p. 154.
3 R. Barry O'Brien, *Life of Charles Stewart Parnell* (1898), i, 240.
4 John Morley, *Life of William Ewart Gladstone* (1903), iii, 240.
5 *Speech by Mr Charles Stewart Parnell in the house of commons, on the motion for the
  second reading of the bill for the future government of Ireland, 7 June 1886,* p. 13.

Notes to Chapters 19-22 (pp 294-361)

CHAPTER 19 (pp 294-312)

1 W.B. Yeats, *Nine one-act plays* (1937), p. 36.
2 T. M. Kettle, 'Would the Hungarian policy work?' in *New Ireland Review*, Feb. 1905.
3 W. B. Yeats, 'Under Ben Bulben' (1938), in *Collected poems* (1961), p. 398.
4 P. H. Pearse, *Political writings and speeches* (1922), pp 177-8.
5 *The Workers' Republic*, 8 Apr. 1916.
6 Erskine Childers, *The framework of home rule* (1911), p. 168.
7 Dorothy Macardle, *The Irish republic* (new. ed., 1951), pp 89-90; see also Ian Colvin, *Life of Lord Carson*, ii (1934), 206.
8 *The Workers' Republic*, 6 Nov. 1915.

CHAPTER 20 (pp 313-23)

1 Ian Colvin, *Life of Lord Carson*, ii (1934), p. 298.
2 *Commons' in. N.I.*, ii, 603.
3 *Belfast News Letter*, 7 Dec. 1925.
4 St John Ervine, *Craigavon* (1949), p. 416.
5 *Hansard N.I. (commons)*, viii, 2272.
6 *Annual Register, 1942*, p. 98.
7 *Hansard N.I. (commons)*, lix, 15.

CHAPTER 21 (pp 324-41)

1 Treaty debates, 19 Dec. 1921, p. 32.
2 Ibid., 7 Jan. 1922, p. 337.

CHAPTER 22 (pp 342-61)

1 For the vast literature on this subject see *A social science bibliography of Northern Ireland, 1945-83,* compiled by Bill Rolston, Mike Tomlinson, Liam O'Dowd, Bob Miller, and Jim Smyth. Belfast 1983.

CHAPTER 23 (pp 362-38⁸1)

1 For excellent surveys of the scholarship relevant to recent Irish politics and history, see J. Whyte, *Interpreting Northern Ireland* (Oxford, Clarendon, 1990) and J. Coakley and M. Gallagher (eds.), *Politics in the Republic of Ireland* (Dublin, Folens, 1993 edn.).

388

A BIBLIOGRAPHY OF IRISH HISTORY

The following is a bibliography of published works in English or Irish on the history of Ireland. Most of them were written in the present century and the latest date of publication is 1982 – for an update on the bibliography consult the 'Writings in Irish History' published annually in *Irish Historical Studies*. With some exceptions it does not include source material, printed or in manuscript, but the reader who seeks for guidance to this vast field is referred to section XV below.

The arrangement within most sections is broadly according to chronological order of subject.

Works in section I relate to more than one of the periods covered by sections IV-XII. Section II comprises works ranging widely over Irish history. Works in section XIII relate to all the periods covered by sections VI-X. Some works that cross period divisions appear in more than one section.

I   GENERAL HISTORY OF IRELAND

SOURCE COLLECTIONS

Edmund Curtis and R. B. McDowell (ed.). *Irish historical documents, 1172-1922.* London, 1943; reprint, 1968.

Constantia Maxwell (ed.). *Irish history from contemporary sources, 1509-1610.* London, 1923.

James Carty (ed.). *Ireland from the flight of the earls to Grattan's parliament, 1607-1782.* Dublin, 1949.

James Carty (ed.). *Ireland from Grattan's parliament to the great famine, 1783-1850.* Dublin, 1949.

James Carty (ed.). *Ireland from the great famine to the treaty, 1851-1921.* Dublin 1951.

Basil Chubb (ed.). *A source book of Irish government.* Dublin, 1964.

GENERAL WORKS

Edmund Curtis. *A history of Ireland.* London, 1936; 6th edition, 1950.

Sean O'Faolain. *The Irish.* Penguin Books, 1947; new edition, 1978.

J. C. Beckett. *A short history of Ireland.* London, 1952; 6th edition, 1979; reprint, 1981.

Brian Inglis, *The story of Ireland.* London, 1956; 2nd edition, 1965.

Robert Kee. *Ireland: a history.* London, 1980.

Eoin MacNeill. *Phases of Irish history.* Dublin, 1919.

Edmund Curtis. *A history of medieval Ireland, from 1086 to 1513.* London, 1923; 2nd edition, 1938; reprint, 1968.

A. J. Otway-Ruthven. *A history of medieval Ireland*. With an introduction [on Ireland before the coming of the Normans] by Kathleen Hughes. London, 1968; reprint 1980. Extended review by F. X. Martin, in *Studia Hibernica*, no. 14 (1974), pp 143-60.

J. C. Beckett. *The making of modern Ireland, 1603-1923*. London, 1966; paperback edition, 1969; new edition, 1981.

J. C. Beckett. *Confrontations: studies in Irish history*. London, 1972.

F. G. James. *Ireland in the empire, 1688-1770*. Cambridge (Mass), 1973.

W. O'Connor Morris. *Ireland, 1798-1898*. London, 1898.

P. S. O'Hegarty. *A history of Ireland under the union, 1801-1922*. London, 1952.

Oliver MacDonagh. *Ireland: the union and its aftermath*. London, 1977. (First published as *Ireland*, Englewood Cliffs (N.J.), 1968.)

F. S. L. Lyons, *Ireland since the famine*. London, 1971; revised edition, 1973.

F. S. L. Lyons. *Culture and anarchy in Ireland, 1890-1939*. Oxford, 1974.

Dorothy Macardle. *The Irish republic: a documented chronicle of the Anglo-Irish conflict. . .* Preface by Éamon de Valéra, London, 1937; 4th edition, Dublin, 1951; American edition, New York, 1965.

The Gill History of Ireland. Edited by J. F. Lydon and Margaret MacCurtain. 11 vols. Dublin, 1972-5.

The Helicon History of Ireland. Edited by Art Cosgrove and Elma Collins. To be completed in 10 vols. Dublin, 1981–.

A New History of Ireland. Edited by T. W. Moody, F. X. Martin, and F. J. Byrne. To be completed in 10 vols. Oxford, 1976–. (A cooperative history, under the auspices of the Royal Irish Academy)

II GENERAL WORKS IN SPECIAL FIELDS

THE CELTS

T. G. E. Powell. *The Celts*. London, 1958.

Joseph Raftery (ed.). *The Celts*. Cork, 1964.

Myles Dillon and Nora K. Chadwick. *The Celtic realms*. London, 1967; 2nd edition, 1972.

Proinsias Mac Cana. *Celtic mythology*. London, 1970.

ECONOMIC AND SOCIAL HISTORY

D. A. Chart. *The economic history of Ireland*. Dublin, 1920.

Charles Doherty. 'Exchange and trade in early medieval Ireland' in *Journal of the Royal Society of Antiquaries of Ireland*, cx (1980), pp 67-89.

M. D. O'Sullivan. *Italian merchant bankers in Ireland in the thirteenth century*. London, 1962.

Jacques Bernard. 'The maritime intercourse between Bordeaux and Ireland, c. 1450-c. 1520' in *Irish Economic and Social History*, vii (1980), pp 7-21.

A. K. Longfield. *Anglo-Irish trade in the sixteenth century*. London, 1929.

Bibliography: general works in special fields

George O'Brien. *The economic history of Ireland in the seventeenth century.* Dublin and London, 1919.
George O'Brien. *The economic history of Ireland in the eighteenth century.* Dublin, 1918.
George O'Brien. *The economic history of Ireland from the union to the famine.* London, 1921.
A. E. Murray. *A history of the commercial and financial relations between England and Ireland from the period of the restoration.* London, 1903.
L. M. Cullen. *The emergence of modern Ireland, 1600-1900.* London, 1981.
L. M. Cullen and T. C. Smout (ed.). *Comparative aspects of Scottish and Irish economic and social history, 1600-1900.* Edinburgh, [1977].
L. M. Cullen and François Furet (ed.). *Ireland and France, 17-20th centuries: towards a comparative study of social history.* Paris, 1980.
L. M. Cullen. *An economic history of Ireland since 1660.* London, 1972.
L. M. Cullen. *Anglo-Irish trade, 1660-1800.* Manchester, 1968.
L. M. Cullen and Paul Butel (ed.). *Négoce et industrie en France et en Irlande aux XVIIIe et XIXe siècles.* Paris, 1980.
L. M. Cullen (ed.). *The formation of the Irish economy.* Cork, 1969.
K. B. Nowlan (ed.). *Travel and transport in Ireland.* Dublin and New York, 1973.
R. N. Salaman. *The history and social influence of the potato.* Cambridge, 1949; reprint, 1970.
K. H. Connell. 'The potato in Ireland' in *Past & Present,* no. 23 (Nov. 1962), pp 57-71.
Conrad Gill. *The rise of the Irish linen industry.* Oxford, 1925; reprint, 1964.
Patrick Lynch and John Vaizey. *Guinness's brewery in the Irish economy, 1759-1876.* Cambridge, 1966.
E. B. McGuire. *Irish whiskey: a history of distilling, the spirit trade, and excise controls in Ireland.* Dublin, 1973.
K. H. Connell. *The population of Ireland, 1750-1845.* Oxford, 1950.
Michael Drake. 'Marriage and population growth in Ireland, 1750-1845' in *Economic History Review,* xvi, no. 2 (Dec. 1963), pp 301-13.
R. D. C. Black. *Economic thought and the Irish question, 1817-1870.* Cambridge, 1960.
Elizabeth R. Hooker. *Readjustments of agricultural tenure in Ireland.* Chapel Hill, (N.C.), 1938.
R. D. Crotty. *Irish agricultural production: its volume and structure.* Cork, 1966.
E. J. Riordan. *Modern Irish trade and industry.* London, 1920.
David O'Mahony. *The Irish economy.* Cork, 1962; 2nd edition, 1967.
James Meenan. *The Irish economy since 1922.* Liverpool, 1970.
Commission of inquiry into banking, currency and credit [1934-]1938, reports. Dublin, Stationery Office, [1938]. (P.2628)
Maurice Moynihan. *Currency and central banking in Ireland, 1922-1960.* Dublin, 1975.
Economic development. Dublin, Stationery Office, 1958. (Pr. 4803)
Science and Irish economic development: report of the research and technology survey team appointed by the minister for industry and commerce in November 1963 (in association with OECD). 2 vols. Dublin, Stationery Office, 1966. (Pr. 8975, Pr. 9093)
N. J. Gibson and J. E. Spencer (ed.). *Economic activity in Ireland: a study of two open economies.* Dublin, 1977.

Barry Moore, John Rhodes, and Roger Tarling. 'Industrial policy and economic development: the experience of Northern Ireland and the Republic of Ireland' in *Cambridge Journal of Economics,* ii (1978).

K. A. Kennedy and B. R. Dowling. *Economic growth in Ireland: the experience since 1947.* Dublin, 1975.

B. R. Dowling and J. Durkan (ed.). *Irish economic policy: a review of major issues.* Dublin, 1978.

J. W. O'Hagan (ed.). *The economy of Ireland: policy and performance.* 3rd edition. Dublin, 1981.

L. M. Cullen. *Life in Ireland.* London and New York, 1968.

Constantia Maxwell. *The stranger in Ireland.* London, 1954.

Constantia Maxwell. *Country and town in Ireland under the Georges.* London, 1940; new edition, Dundalk, 1949.

S. J. Connolly. *Priests and people in pre-famine Ireland, 1780-1845.* Dublin, 1982.

L. M. Cullen. *Six generations: life and work in Ireland from 1790.* Cork, 1970.

R. B. McDowell (ed.). *Social life in Ireland, 1800-45.* Dublin, 1957.

K. H. Connell. *Irish peasant society: four historical essays.* Oxford, 1968.

Terence Brown. *Ireland: a social and cultural history, 1922-1979.* Fontana Paperbacks, 1981.

TOWNS

R. A. Butlin (ed.). *The development of the Irish town.* London and Totowa (N.J.), 1977.

David Harkness and Mary O'Dowd (ed.). *The town in Ireland.* Belfast, 1981.

H. B. Clarke. *Dublin, c. 840-c.1560: the medieval town in the modern city.* Dublin, 1978.

A. P. Smyth. *Scandinavian York and Dublin,* Vol. i, Dublin, 1975; vol. ii, 1981.

National Museum of Ireland. *Viking and medieval Dublin.* Dublin, 1973.

P. F. Wallace. 'Dublin's waterfront at Wood Quay: 900-1317' in G. Milne and B. Hobley (ed.). *Waterfront archaeology in Britain and Northern Europe* (Council for British Archaeology, Research report no. 41, London, 1981), pp 109-18.

P. F. Wallace. 'Anglo-Norman Dublin: continuity and change' in D. Ó Corráin, (ed.). *Irish antiquity* (Cork, 1981), pp 247-67.

P. F. Wallace. 'The origins of Dublin' in B. G. Scott (ed.). *Studies on early Ireland: essays in honour of M. V. Duignan* (Belfast, 1982), pp 129-43.

P. F. Wallace. 'Carpentry in Ireland, A.D. 900-1300: the Wood Quay evidence' in S. McGrain (ed.). *Woodworking techniques before A.D. 1500* (British Archaeological Reports, International series no. 129, Oxford, 1982), pp 263-99.

John Ryan. 'Pre-Norman Dublin' in *Journal of the Royal Society of Antiquaries of Ireland,* lxxix (1949), pp 64-83.

M. D. O'Sullivan. *Old Galway: the history of a Norman colony in Ireland.* Cambridge, 1942.

William O'Sullivan. *The economic history of Cork city from the earliest times to the act of union.* Dublin and Cork, 1937.

J. F. Lydon. 'The city of Waterford in the later middle ages' in *Decies,* xii (1979), pp 9-15.

Gearóid Mac Niocaill. *Na buirgéisi, XII-XV aois.* I vol. in 2, Dublin, 1964.

Gearóid Mac Niocaill. 'Socio-economic problems of the late medieval town' in David Harkness and Mary O'Dowd (ed.). *The town in Ireland* (Belfast, 1981), pp 7-21.

M. J. Craig. *Dublin, 1660-1860.* London, 1952.

Bibliography: general works in special fields

J. G. Simms. 'Dublin in 1685' in *Irish Historical Studies,* xiv, no. 55 (Mar. 1965), pp 212-26.

Constantia Maxwell. *Dublin under the Georges, 1714-1830.* London, 1936; 2nd edition, London and Dublin, 1946; revised edition, London, 1956.

LAW, GOVERNMENT, AND PARLIAMENT

Eoin MacNeill. *Early Irish laws and institutions.* Dublin, [1935].

Eoin MacNeill. 'Ancient Irish law: the law of status and franchise' in *Proceedings of the Royal Irish Academy,* 36 C 16 (1923).

D. A. Binchy. *Crith Gablach.* Dublin, 1941.

D. A. Binchy. *The linguistic and historical value of the Irish law tracts* (Sir John Rhys memorial lecture). London, British Academy, 1943.

Liam Ó Buachalla. 'Some researches in ancient Irish law' in *Journal of the Cork Historical and Archaeological Society,* lii (1947), pp 41-54, 135-48; liii (1948), pp 1-18.

Bryan Murphy. 'The status of the native Irish after 1331' in *Irish Jurist,* ii (1967), pp 116-38.

G. J. Hand. *English law in Ireland, 1200-1324.* Cambridge, 1967.

A. G. Donaldson. *Some comparative aspects of Irish law.* Durham (N.C.), 1957.

H. G. Richardson and G. O. Sayles. *The Irish parliament in the middle ages.* Philadelphia, 1952; new impression, 1966.

H. G. Richardson and G. O. Sayles. *Parliament in medieval Ireland.* Dublin Historical Association, 1964.

Brian Farrell (ed.). *The Irish parliamentary tradition.* Dublin, 1973.

D. B. Quinn. 'The early interpretation of Poynings' Law' in *Irish Historical Studies,* ii, no. 7 (Mar. 1941), pp 141-54.

R. Dudley Edwards and T. W. Moody, 'The history of Poynings' Law, 1494-1615' in *Irish Historical Studies,* ii, no. 8 (Sept. 1941), pp 415-24.

T. W. Moody. 'The Irish parliament under Elizabeth and James I: a general survey' in *Proceedings of the Royal Irish Academy,* 45 C 6 (1939), pp 41-81.

V. W. Treadwell. 'The Irish parliament of 1569-71' in *Proceedings of the Royal Irish Academy,* 65 C 4 (1966), pp. 55-89.

Aidan Clarke. 'The history of Poynings' Law, 1615-41' in *Irish Historical Studies,* xviii, no. 70 (Sept. 1972), pp. 207-22.

J. L. McCracken. *The Irish parliament in the eighteenth century.* Dublin Historical Association, 1971.

V. W. Treadwell. 'The Irish customs administration in the sixteenth century' in *Irish Historical Studies,* xx, no. 80 (Sept. 1977), pp 384-417.

T. J. Kiernan. *History of the financial administration of Ireland to 1817.* London, 1930.

R. B. McDowell. *The Irish administration, 1801-1914.* London, 1964.

J. H. Whyte. 'The influence of the catholic clergy on elections in nineteenth-century Ireland' in *English Historical Review,* lxxv, no. 295 (Apr. 1960).

Peter Jupp. 'Irish parliamentary elections and the influence of the catholic vote, 1801-20' in *Historical Journal,* x (1967), pp 183-96.

Brian Walker. 'The Irish electorate, 1806-1915' in *Irish Historical Studies,* xviii, no. 71 (Mar. 1973), pp 359-406.

Nicholas Mansergh. *The Irish Free State: its government and politics.* London, 1934.

D. N. Haire. 'In aid of the civil power, 1868-90' in F. S. L. Lyons and R. A. J. Hawkins (ed.),

Ireland under the union (Oxford, 1980), pp 115-48.

Brian Farrell. *The founding of Dáil Éireann: parliament and nation building.* Dublin, 1971.

J. L. McCracken. *Representative government in Ireland: a study of Dáil Éireann, 1919-1948.* London, 1958.

Donal O'Sullivan. *The Irish Free State and its senate.* London, 1940.

F. B. Chubb. *The government and politics of Ireland.* With a historical introduction by David Thornley. Stanford and London, 1970; paperback edition, 1974; 2nd edition, 1982.

R. K. Carty. *Party and parish pump: electoral politics in Ireland.* Waterloo, Ontario, 1981.

Ronan Fanning. *The Irish Department of Finance, 1922-58.* Dublin, 1978.

Seán Reámonn. *History of the revenue commissioners.* Dublin, 1981.

THE CHURCHES

Kathleen Hughes. *The church in early Irish society.* Cambridge, 1966.

P. J. Corish (ed.). *A history of Irish catholicism.* Dublin, 1967-72. (An incomplete series of brief studies by various authors issued in 16 separate fascicles)

N. K. Chadwick. *The age of the saints in the early Celtic church.* London, 1961.

D. D. C. Pochin Mould. *The Irish saints.* Dublin, 1964.

John Ryan. *Irish monasticism: origins and early development.* Dublin, 1934; reprint, Shannon 1972, with new introduction.

J. A. Watt. *The church in medieval Ireland.* Dublin, 1972.

J. A. Watt. *The church and the two nations in medieval Ireland.* Cambridge, 1970.

Kathleen Hughes and Anne Hamlin. *The modern traveller to the medieval Irish church.* London, 1977.

Aubrey Gwynn and R. N. Hadcock. *Medieval religious houses: Ireland.* London, 1970.

Aubrey Gwynn. 'The twelfth and thirteenth centuries' in Aubrey Gwynn and D. F. Gleeson, *A history of the diocese of Killaloe* (Dublin, [1962]) pp 135-291. (An account of the general reform movement in the church)

F. X. Martin. 'The Irish friars and the Observant movement in the fifteenth century' in *Proceedings of the Irish Catholic Historical Committee,* 1960, pp 10-16.

F. X. Martin. 'The Irish Augustinian reform movement in the fifteenth century' in J. A. Watt, J. B. Morrall, and F. X. Martin (ed.), *Medieval studies presented to Aubrey Gwynn* (Dublin, 1961), pp 230-64.

Aubrey Gwynn. *The medieval province of Armagh, 1470-1545.* Dundalk, 1946.

Aubrey Gwynn. 'Ireland and the English nation at the council of Constance' in *Proceedings of the Royal Irish Academy,* 45 C 8 (1940), pp 183-233.

Canice Mooney. 'The Irish church in the sixteenth century' in *Irish Ecclesiastical Record,* xcix (1963) pp 102-113.

Brendan Bradshaw. *The dissolution of the religious orders in Ireland under Henry VIII.* Cambridge, 1974.

F. X. Martin. 'Confusion abounding: Bernard O'Higgins, O.S.A., bishop of Elphin, 1542-1561' in Art Cosgrove and Donal McCartney (ed.), *Studies in Irish history presented to R. Dudley Edwards* (Dublin, 1979), pp 38-84.

F. X. Martin. *Friar Nugent: a study of Francis Lavalin Nugent (1569-1635), agent of the counter-reformation.* Rome and London, 1962.

D. F. Cregan. 'The social and cultural background of a counter-reformation episcopate,

Bibliography: general works in special fields

1618-60' in Art Cosgrove and Donal McCartney (ed.), *Studies in Irish history presented to R. Dudley Edwards* (Dublin, 1979), pp 85-117.

James McCaffrey. *History of the catholic church in the nineteenth century.* 2 vols. Dublin, 1909.

P. J. Corish. 'Gallicanism at Maynooth: Archbishop Cullen and the royal visitation of 1853' in Art Cosgrove and Donal McCartney (ed.), *Studies in Irish history presented to R. Dudley Edwards* (Dublin, 1979) pp 176-89.

Emmet Larkin. *The making of the Roman Catholic church in Ireland, 1850-1860.* Chapel Hill, (N.C.), 1980.

Emmet Larkin. *The Roman Catholic church and the creation of the modern Irish state, 1878-86.* Philadelphia and Dublin, 1975.

Emmet Larkin. *The Roman Catholic church and the Plan of Campaign in Ireland, 1886-8.* Cork, 1978.

Emmet Larkin. *The Roman Catholic church in Ireland and the fall of Parnell, 1886-1891.* Liverpool, 1979.

W. A. Phillips (ed.). *The history of the Church of Ireland.* 3 vols. Oxford, 1933-4.

D. H. Akenson. *The Church of Ireland: ecclesiastical reform and revolution, 1800-1885.* New Haven and London, 1971.

T. J. Johnston, J. L. Robinson, and R. W. Jackson. *A history of the Church of Ireland.* Dublin, 1953.

Kenneth Milne. *The Church of Ireland: a history.* Dublin, 1966.

R. B. McDowell. *The Church of Ireland, 1869-1969.* London, 1978.

Michael Hurley. *Irish anglicanism, 1869-1969: essays on the role of anglicanism in Irish life presented to the Church of Ireland, on the occasion of the centenary of its disestablishment, by a group of methodist, presbyterian, quaker, and Roman catholic scholars.* Dublin, 1970.

J. S. Reid. *History of the presbyterian church in Ireland.* Edited by W. D. Killen. 3 vols. Belfast, 1867.

J. M. Barkley. *A short history of the Presbyterian Church in Ireland.* Belfast, 1959.

J. L. M. Haire (ed.). *Challenge and conflict: essays in Irish presbyterian history and doctrine.* Belfast, 1981.

C. H. Crookshank. *History of methodism in Ireland.* 3 vols. Belfast, 1885-8.

R. L. Cole. *History of methodism in Ireland. . . 1860-1960.* London, 1960.

Isabel Grubb. *Quakers in Ireland, 1654-1900.* London, 1927.

Louis Hyman. *The Jews of Ireland. . .* Shannon, 1972.

EDUCATION

N. D. Atkinson. *Irish education: a history of educational institutions.* Dublin, 1969.

D. H. Akenson. *The Irish education experiment: the national system of education in the nineteenth century.* London and Toronto, 1970.

Mary Daly. 'The development of the national school system, 1831-40' in Art Cosgrove and Donal McCartney (ed.), *Studies in Irish history presented to R. Dudley Edwards* (Dublin, 1979), pp 150-63.

D. H. Akenson. *A mirror to Kathleen's face: education in independent Ireland, 1922-1960.*

Montreal and London, 1975.

John Coolahan. *Irish education: its history and structure.* Dublin, 1981.

Constantia Maxwell. *A history of Trinity College, Dublin, 1591-1892.* Dublin, 1946.

K. C. Bailey. *A history of Trinity College, Dublin, 1892-1945.* Dublin, 1947.

R. B. McDowell and D. A. Webb. *Trinity College, Dublin, 1592-1952: an academic history.* Cambridge, 1982.

John Healy, *Maynooth College, 1798-1895.* Dublin, 1895.

T. W. Moody. 'The Irish university question of the nineteenth century' in *History,* xliii, no. 148 (1958), pp 90-109.

T. W. Moody and J. C. Beckett. *Queen's, Belfast, 1845-1949: the history of a university.* 2 vols. London, 1959.

Robert Allen. *The Presbyterian College, Belfast, 1853-1953.* Belfast, 1954.

Fergal McGrath. *Newman's university: idea and reality.* Dublin, 1951.

Michael Tierney (ed.). *Struggle with fortune: a miscellany for the centenary of the Catholic University of Ireland, 1854-1954.* Dublin, [1954].

Fathers of the Society of Jesus. *A page of Irish history: story of University College, Dublin, 1883-1909.* Dublin, 1930.

Report of the Council of Education: (1) the function of the primary school; (2) the curriculum to be pursued in the primary school. Dublin, Stationery Office, [1954]. (Pr. 2583)

Report of the Council of Education: the curriculum of the secondary school. Dublin, Stationery Office, [1962]. (Pr. 5996)

The restoration of the Irish language. Dublin, Stationery Office, 1965. (Pr. 8061)

Investment in education: report of the survey team appointed by the minister for education in October 1962. 2 vols. Dublin, Stationery Office, 1965. (Pr. 8311), 1966 (Pr. 8527)

Commission on Higher Education (1960-67), presentation and summary of report. Dublin, Stationery Office, 1967. (Pr. 9326)

Commission on Higher Education (1960-67), report. 2 vols. Dublin, Stationery Office, 1967. (Pr. 9389, Pr. 9588)

Higher Education Authority, first report, 1968-9. Dublin, Stationery Office, [1969]. (The first of a continuing series)

LANGUAGE, LITERATURE, AND LEARNING

Brian Ó Cuív (ed.). *A view of the Irish language.* Dublin, 1969.

David Green. *The Irish language.* Dublin, 1966.

Douglas Hyde. *A literary history of Ireland from the earliest times to the present day.* London, 1899; new edition, with an introduction by Brian Ó Cuív, London and New York, 1967.

A. de Blacám. *Gaelic literature surveyed.* Dublin and Cork, 1933.

K. H. Jackson. *The oldest Irish tradition.* Cambridge, 1964.

Myles Dillon (ed.). *Irish sagas.* Dublin, 1959; reprint with new introduction, 1968.

Myles Dillon. *Early Irish literature.* Chicago, 1948.

Myles Dillon. *The cycles of the kings.* Oxford, 1946.

Eleanor Knott and Gerard Murphy. *Early Irish literature.* Introduction by James Carney. London, 1966.

[Liam de Paor.] *Great books of Ireland.* Dublin, 1967.

James Carney. *Early Irish poetry.* Cork, 1965.

Bibliography: general works in special fields

Frank O'Connor. *Kings, lords, and commons: an anthology from the Irish.* Translated by Frank O'Connor. London, 1961; reprint, 1962.
Frank O'Connor. *The backward look: a survey of Irish literature.* London, 1967.
Proinsias Mac Cana. *Literature in Irish.* Dublin, 1980.
Proinsias Mac Cana. *The learned tales of medieval Ireland.* Dublin, 1981.
Brian Ó Cuív (ed.). *Seven centuries of Irish learning, 1000-1700.* Dublin, 1961.
Robin Flower. *The Irish tradition.* Oxford, 1947.
Roger McHugh and Maurice Harmon. *Short history of Anglo-Irish literature from its origins to the present day.* Dublin, 1982.
St John D. Seymour. *Anglo-Irish literature, 1200-1582.* Cambridge, 1929.
Thomas MacDonagh. *Literature in Ireland: studies in Irish and Anglo-Irish literature.* Dublin, 1916.
Seán Ó Tuama (ed.). *The Gaelic League idea.* Cork and Dublin, 1971.
Malcolm Brown. *The politics of Irish literature from Thomas Davis to W. B. Yeats.* London, 1972.
Peter Costello. *The heart grown brutal: the Irish revolution in literature from Parnell to the death of Yeats.* Dublin, 1977.
Benedict Kiely. *Modern Irish fiction: a critique.* Dublin, 1950.
T. J. B. Flanagan. *Irish novelists, 1800-1850.* New York, 1959.
Robert Farren. *The course of Irish verse.* London, 1948.
W. B. Stanford. *Ireland and the classical tradition.* Dublin and Totowa (N.J.), 1976.
J. J. O'Meara. *Eriugena.* Cork, 1963.
Katherine Walsh. *A fourteenth-century scholar and primate: Richard FitzRalph in Oxford, Avignon, and Armagh.* Oxford, 1981.
K. T. Hoppen. *The common scientist in the seventeenth century: a study of the Dublin Philosophical Society, 1683-1708.* London, 1970.
J. G. Simms. *William Molyneux of Dublin.* Edited by P. H. Kelly. Blackrock (Co. Dublin), 1982.

THE THEATRE

W. S. Clark. *The early Irish stage: the beginnings to 1720.* Oxford, 1955.
W. S. Clark. *The Irish stage in the county towns, 1720-1800.* Oxford, 1965.
Mícheál Mac Liammóir. *Theatre in Ireland.* Dublin, 1950.
Robert O'Driscoll. *Theatre and nationalism in twentieth century Ireland.* London, 1971.
Lennox Robinson (ed.). *The Irish theatre: lectures delivered during the Abbey Theatre festival held in Dublin in August 1938.* London, 1939.
Hugh Hunt. *The Abbey: Ireland's national theatre, 1904-79.* Dublin, 1979.

THE VISUAL ARTS AND MUSIC

Peter Harbison, Homan Potterton, and Jeanne Sheehy. *Irish art and architecture from prehistory to the present.* London, 1978.
Françoise Henry. *Early Christian Irish art.* Dublin, 1954.
Françoise Henry. *Irish art in the early Christian period (to 800 A.D.)* London, 1940; revised edition, 1965.
Françoise Henry. *Irish art during the Viking invasions (800-1020 A.D.)* London, 1967.
Françoise Henry. *Irish art in the romanesque period (1020-1170 A.D.).* London, 1970.

Bibliography: general works in special fields

Françoise Henry and G. L. Marsh-Micheli. 'A century of Irish illumination (1070-1170)' in *Proceedings of the Royal Irish Academy*, 62 C 5 (1962).

[G. F. Mitchell and others.] *Treasures of early Irish art, 1500 B.C. to 1500 A.D., from the collections of the National Museum of Ireland, Royal Irish Academy, [and] Trinity College, Dublin.* New York: Metropolitan Museum of Art, 1977.

R. A. Stalley. *Architecture in Ireland, 1150-1350.* Dublin, 1971.

H. G. Leask. *Irish churches and monastic buildings.* 3 vols. Dundalk, 1955, 1958, 1960.

John Hunt. *Irish medieval figure sculpture, 1200-1600.* 2 vols. Dublin, 1974.

M. J. Craig. *Dublin, 1660-1860.* London, 1952; reprint, 1980.

M. J. Craig. *The architecture of Ireland from the earliest times to 1880.* Dublin, 1982.

Anne Crookshank and the Knight of Glin. *The painters of Ireland, c. 1660-1920.* London, 1978.

Anne Crookshank. *Irish art from 1600 to the present day.* Dublin, 1979.

Jeanne Sheehy. *The rediscovery of Ireland's past: the Celtic revival, 1830-1930.* London, 1980.

Records of eighteenth-century domestic architecture and decoration in Ireland. 5 vols. Dublin, Georgian Society, 1909-13.

Brian Boydell (ed.). *Four centuries of music in Ireland.* London, 1979.

Donal O'Sullivan. *Irish folk music, song, and dance.* Dublin, 1952; revised reprint, 1961, 1969.

Donal O'Sullivan. *Songs of the Irish.* Dublin, 1967; reprint, Cork, 1981.

Donal O'Sullivan. *Carolan: the life, times, and music of an Irish harper.* 2 vols. London, 1958.

NATIONALISM

T. W. Moody (ed.). *Nationality and the pursuit of national independence.* Belfast, 1978.

J. G. Simms. *Colonial nationalism, 1698-1776.* Dublin, 1976.

Emil Strauss. *Irish nationalism and British democracy.* London, 1951.

Robert Kee. *The green flag: a history of Irish nationalism.* London, 1972.

A. C. Hepburn (ed.). *The conflict of nationality in modern Ireland.* London, 1980.

T. W. Moody (ed.). *The Fenian movement.* Cork, 1968; reprint, Dublin and Cork, 1978.

Erhard Rumpf and A. C. Hepburn. *Nationalism and socialism in twentieth-century Ireland.* Liverpool, 1977.

Tom Garvin. *The evolution of Irish nationalist politics.* Dublin, 1981.

L. M. Cullen. 'The cultural basis of modern Irish nationalism' in Rosalind Mitchison (ed.), *The roots of nationalism: studies in northern Europe* (Edinburgh, 1980).

UNIONISM

Hugh Shearman. *Not an inch: a study of Northern Ireland and Lord Craigavon.* London, 1942.

Patrick Buckland. *Irish unionism 1: the Anglo-Irish and the new Ireland, 1885-1922.* Dublin and New York, 1972.

Patrick Buckland. *Irish unionism 2: Ulster unionism and the origins of Northern Ireland, 1886-1922.* Dublin and New York, 1973.

Patrick Buckland (ed.). *Irish unionism, 1885-1923: a documentary history.* Belfast, 1973.

Bibliography: general works in special fields

Patrick Buckland. *Irish unionism, 1885-1922.* London, Historical Association, 1973.

Peter Gibbon. *The origins of Ulster unionism: the formation of popular protestant politics and ideology in nineteenth-century Ireland.* Manchester, 1975.

Sybil Gribbon. 'The social origins of Ulster unionism' in *Irish Economic and Social History,* iv (1977), pp 66-72. (A review article on the preceding)

D. C. Savage. 'The origins of the Ulster unionist party, 1885-6' in *Irish Historical Studies,* xii, no. 47 (Mar. 1961), pp 185-208.

J. F. Harbinson. *The Ulster unionist party, 1882-1973: its development and organisation.* Belfast, 1973.

THE LAND QUESTION

W. F. T. Butler. *Confiscation in Irish history.* Dublin, 1917; 2nd edition, 1918.

J. P. Prendergast. *The Cromwellian settlement of Ireland.* London, 1865; revised edition, 1870; 3rd edition, 1922.

Margaret MacCurtain. 'Rural society in post-Cromwellian Ireland' in Art Cosgrove and Donal McCartney (ed.), *Studies in Irish history presented to R. Dudley Edwards* (Dublin, 1979), pp 118-36.

J. G. Simms. *The Williamite confiscation in Ireland, 1690-1703.* London, 1956.

David Large. 'The wealth of the greater Irish landowners, 1750-1815' in *Irish Historical Studies,* xv, no. 57 (Mar. 1966), pp 21-47.

J. E. Pomfret. *The struggle for land in Ireland, 1800-1923.* Princeton, 1930.

Brian O'Neill. *The war for the land in Ireland.* With an introduction by Peadar O'Donnell. New York, 1933.

J. S. Donnelly jr. *The land and the people of nineteenth-century Cork; the rural economy and the land question.* London and Boston, 1975.

W. E. Vaughan. 'Landlord and tenant relations between the famine and the land war, 1850-75' in L. M. Cullen and T. C. Smout (ed.), *Comparative aspects of Scottish and Irish economic and social history, 1600-1900* (Edinburgh, [1971]), pp 216-26.

W. E. Vaughan. 'An assessment of the economic performance of the Irish landlords, 1851-81' in F. S. L. Lyons and R. A. J. Hawkins (ed.), *Ireland under the union* (Oxford, 1980), pp 173-99.

E. D. Steele. *Irish land and British politics: tenant right and nationality, 1865-1870.* Cambridge, 1974.

Barbara L. Solow. *The land question in the Irish economy, 1870-1903.* Cambridge (Mass.), 1971.

N. D. Palmer. *The Irish Land League crisis.* New Haven, 1940.

Paul Bew. *Land and the national question.* Dublin, 1978.

S. D. Clark. *Social origins of the Irish land war.* Princeton, 1979.

H. E. Socolofsky. *Landlord William Scully.* Lawrence (Kansas), 1979.

T. W. Moody. *Davitt and Irish revolution, 1846-82.* Oxford, 1981.

THE LABOUR MOVEMENT

James Connolly. *Labour in Ireland.* Introduction by Robert Lynd. Dublin, 1917. New edition, introduction by Cathal O'Shannon, Dublin, [1960]. (Comprises 'Labour in Irish history' and 'The reconquest of Ireland')

W. P. Ryan. *The Irish labour movement, from the twenties to our own day.* Dublin and London, 1919.

T. W. Moody. 'Michael Davitt and the British labour movement, 1882-1906' in *Transactions of the Royal Historical Society,* 5th series, iii (1953), pp 53-76.

J. D. Clarkson. *Labour and nationalism in Ireland.* New York, 1925; reprint, 1970.

J. W. Boyle (ed.). *Leaders and workers.* Cork, [1965].

Arthur Mitchell. *Labour in Irish politics, 1890-1930: the Irish labour movement in an age of revolution.*

Charles McCarthy. *Trade unions in Ireland, 1894-1960.* Dublin, 1977.

Charles McCarthy. *The decade of upheaval: the Irish trade unions in the nineteen sixties.* Dublin, 1973.

C. D. Greaves. *The life and times of James Connolly.* London, 1961.

Emmet Larkin. *James Connolly, Irish labour leader, 1876-1947.* London, 1965.

J. A. Gaughan. *Thomas Johnson, 1872-1963.* Dublin, 1980.

Dermot Keogh. *The making of the Irish working class: the Dublin trade union movement and labour leadership, 1880-1914.* Belfast, 1981.

IRISH EMIGRATION AND THE IRISH ABROAD

Sylvia L. Thrupp. 'A survey of the alien population of England in 1440' in *Speculum,* xxxii (1957), pp 262-72.

John Denvir. *The Irish in Britain from the earliest times to the fall and death of Parnell.* London, 1894.

J. A. Jackson. *The Irish in Britain.* London, 1963.

M. A. G. Ó Tuathaigh. 'The Irish in nineteenth-century Britain' in *Transactions of the Royal Historical Society,* 5th series, xxxi (1981), pp 149-73.

Fergus D'Arcy. 'The Irish in 19th century Britain: reflections on their role and experience' in *Irish History Workshop,* i (1981), pp 3-12.

Barbara Kerr. 'Irish seasonal migration to Great Britain, 1800-38' in *Irish Historical Studies,* iii, no. 12 (Sept. 1943), pp 365-80.

James E. Handley. *The Irish in Scotland, 1798-1845.* Cork, 1943.

James E. Handley. *The Irish in modern Scotland.* Cork, 1947.

D. N. Doyle and Owen Dudley Edwards. *America and Ireland, 1776-1976.* Westport (Conn.), 1979.

D. N. Doyle. *Ireland, Irishmen, and revolutionary America, 1760-1820.* Dublin and Cork, 1981.

W. F. Adams. *Ireland and Irish emigration to the new world from 1815 to the famine.* New Haven, 1932.

S. H. Cousens. 'Emigration and demographic change in Ireland, 1851-61' in *Economic History Review,* xiv, no. 2 (Dec. 1961), pp 275-88.

Arnold Schrier. *Ireland and the American emigration, 1870-1900.* Minneapolis, 1958.

T. N. Brown. *Irish-American nationalism, 1870-1890.* Philadelphia and New York, 1966.

T. W. Moody. 'Irish-American nationalism' in *Irish Historical Studies,* xv, no. 60 (Sept. 1967), pp 438-45. (A review article on the preceding)

K. A. Miller, with Bruce Boling and D. N. Doyle. 'Emigrants and exiles: Irish cultures and Irish emigration to North America, 1790-1922' in *Irish Historical Studies,* xxii,

Bibliography: general works in special fields

no. 86 (Sept. 1980), pp 97-125.

Cormac Ó Gráda. 'Some aspects of nineteeth-century Irish emigration' in L. M. Cullen and T. C. Smout (ed.), *Comparative aspects of Scottish and Irish economic and social history, 1600-1900* (Edinburgh, [1972]), pp 65-71.

David Fitzpatrick. 'Irish emigration in the late nineteenth century' in *Irish Historical Studies*, xxii, no. 86 (Sept. 1980), pp 126-43.

Carl Wittke. *The Irish in America*. Baton Rouge (Louisiana), 1950.

George Potter. *To the golden door: the story of the Irish in Ireland and America*. Boston, 1960.

W. V. Shannon. *The American Irish*. New York, 1963.

Commission on emigration and other population problems, 1948-1954, reports. Dublin, Stationery Office, 1954. (Pr. 2541)

OTHER SUBJECTS

K. W. Nichols. 'The Irish genealogies; their value and defects' in *Irish Genealogist*, v (1975), pp 256-61.

Gearóid Mac Niocaill. *The medieval Irish annals*. Dublin Historical Association, 1975.

Michael Dolley. *Medieval Anglo-Irish coins*. London, 1972.

G. A. Hayes-McCoy. *The Irish at war*. Cork, 1964.

G. A. Hayes-McCoy. *Irish battles*. London, 1969.

Katharine Simms. 'Warfare in the medieval Gaelic lordships' in *Irish Sword*, xii (1976), pp 98-108.

R. E. Glasscock and T. E. McNeill. 'Mottes in Ireland: a draft list' in *Bulletin of the Group for the Study of Irish Historical Settlement*, iii (1972), pp 27-51.

Terence Barry. *Medieval moated sites of S. E. Ireland: Counties Carlow, Kilkenny, Tipperary, and Wexford*. Oxford, 1977.

Kevin Danaher. 'Irish tower houses and their regional distribution' in *Béaloideas*, xlv-xlvii (1977-9), pp. 158-63.

H. G. Leask. *Irish castles and castellated houses*. Dundalk, 1941.

Hugh Shearman. *Anglo-Irish relations*. London, 1948.

J. C. Beckett. *The Anglo-Irish tradition*. London, 1976.

P. J. O'Farrell. *Ireland's English question: Anglo-Irish relations, 1534-1970*. London, 1971.

P. J. O'Farrell. *England and Ireland since 1800*. London, 1975.

C. Cruise O'Brien. *States of Ireland*. London, 1972.

Elizabeth Malcolm. 'Temperance and Irish nationalism' in F. S. L. Lyons and R. A. J. Hawkins (ed.), *Ireland under the union* (Oxford, 1980), pp 69-114.

H. F. Kearney. 'Fr Mathew: apostle of modernisation' in Art Cosgrove and Donal McCartney (ed.), *Studies in Irish history presented to R. Dudley Edwards* (Dublin, 1979), pp 164-75.

Margaret MacCurtain and Donncha Ó Corráin (ed.). *Women in Irish society: the historical dimension*. Dublin, 1978.

L. P. Curtis. *Anglo-Saxons and Celts: a study of anti-Irish prejudice in Victorian Britain*. Bridgeport (Conn.), 1968.

L. P. Curtis. *Apes and angels: the Irishman in Victorian caricature*. Washington (D.C.), 1971.

Katharine Simms. 'The legal position of Irishwomen in the late middle ages' in *Irish Jurist,*
v (1975), pp 96-111.

Marcus de Búrca (Bourke). *The G.A.A.: a history.* Dublin, 1980.

N. P. Canny. 'The formation of the Irish mind: religion, politics, and Gaelic Irish literature,
1580-1750' in *Past & Present,* no. 95 (May 1982), pp 91-116.

Maurice Gorham. *Forty years of Irish broadcasting.* Dublin, 1967.

Gay Byrne. *To whom it may concern: ten years of the Late Late Show.* Dublin, 1972.

Broadcasting review committee, report 1974. Dublin, Stationery Office, 1974. (Pr. 3827)

III HISTORICAL GEOGRAPHY OF IRELAND

T. W. Freeman. *Ireland: a general and regional geography.* London, 1950; 4th edition, 1972.

A. R. Orme. *Ireland.* London, 1970. (The World's Landscapes, 4)

G. F. Mitchell. *The Irish landscape.* London, 1976.

F. H. A. Aalen. *Man and the landscape in Ireland.* London, 1978.

E. E. Evans. *The personality of Ireland: habitat, heritage and history.* Cambridge, 1973.

Nicholas Stephens and R. E. Glasscock (ed.). *Irish geographical studies in honour of E.
Estyn Evans.* Belfast, 1970.

E. E. Evans. *Irish folkways.* London, 1957.

M. W. Heslinga. *The Irish border as a cultural divide.* Assen, 1962; reprint, 1971.

Eileen McCracken. *The Irish woods since Tudor times: their distribution and exploitation.*
Newton Abbot, 1971.

W. J. Smyth. 'The western isle of Ireland and the eastern seaboard of America – England's
first frontiers' in *Irish Geography,* xi (1978), pp 1-22.

T. W. Freeman. *Pre-famine Ireland: a study in historical geography.* Manchester, 1957.

T. Jones Hughes. 'Society and settlement in nineteenth-century Ireland' in *Irish Geography,*
v (1965), pp 79-96.

Ruth Dudley Edwards. *An atlas of Irish history.* London, 1973; 2nd edition, London, 1981.

J. H. Andrews. *Irish maps.* Dublin, 1978.

J. H. Andrews. *A paper landscape: the ordnance survey in Ireland.* Oxford, 1975.

R. N. Hadcock. *Map of monastic Ireland, scale 1:625,000.* Dublin, Ordnance Survey, 1960;
2nd edition, 1964.

Atlas of Ireland, prepared under the direction of the Irish National Committee for Geography.
Dublin, Royal Irish Academy, 1979.

403

IV PREHISTORIC IRELAND

S. P. Ó Ríordáin. *Antiquities of the Irish countryside*. Cork, 1942; 5th edition, revised by Ruaidhri de Valera, London, 1979.
Joseph Raftery. *Prehistoric Ireland*. London, 1951.
P. C. Woodman. *The mesolithic in Ireland*. Oxford, 1978.
Michael Herity and George Eogan. *Ireland in prehistory*. London, 1977.
Peter Harbison. *Guide to the national monuments of Ireland*. Dublin, 1970; 2nd revised edition, 1979.

V IRELAND FROM THE FIRST TO THE TWELFTH CENTURY

J. F. Kenney, *Sources for the early history of Ireland: ecclesiastical*. New York, 1929; reprint, New York, 1966, with preface by Ludwig Bieler.
E. R. Norman and J. K. S. St Joseph. *The early development of Irish society: the evidence of aerial photography*. Cambridge, 1969.
Myles Dillon (ed.). *Early Irish society*. Dublin, 1954.
Eoin MacNeill. *Celtic Ireland*. Dublin and London, 1921; 2nd edition, with introduction and notes by Donncha Ó Corráin, Dublin, 1981.
Cecile O'Rahilly (ed.). *Táin bó Cúailnge, from the Book of Leinster*. Dublin, 1967.
Cecile O'Rahilly (ed.). *Táin bó Cúailnge, recension I*. Dublin, 1976.
T. F. O'Rahilly. *Early Irish history and mythology*. Dublin, 1946.
Kathleen Hughes. *Early Christian Ireland: introduction to the sources*. London, 1972.
Máire and Liam de Paor. *Early Christian Ireland*. London, 1958.
Libri Sancti Patricii: the Latin writings of St Patrick. Edited and translated by Newport J. D. White. Dublin, 1905.
Libri epistolarum Sancti Patricii episcopi. Edited by Ludwig Bieler. 2 vols. Dublin, 1952.
The works of St Patrick; St Secundinus, Hymn on St Patrick. Edited and translated by Ludwig Bieler. Westminster (Maryland) and London, 1953.
J. B. Bury. *The life of St Patrick and his place in history*. London, 1905.
Eoin MacNeill. *Saint Patrick*. London, 1934; new edition, edited by John Ryan, with other Patrician writings by MacNeill, and a bibliography of Patrician literature by F. X. Martin. Dublin and London, 1964.
T. F. O'Rahilly. *The two Patricks*. Dublin, 1942; reprint, 1957.
Ludwig Bieler. *The life and legend of Saint Patrick: problems of modern scholarship*. Dublin, 1949.
John Ryan (ed.). *Saint Patrick*. Dublin, 1958.
James Carney. *The problem of Saint Patrick*. Dublin, 1961.
D. A. Binchy. 'Patrick and his biographers, ancient and modern' in *Studia Hibernica*, 2 (1962).

R. P. C. Hanson. *Saint Patrick, his origins and career.* Oxford, 1968.

Muirchú's Life of Patrick. Translated by N. J. D. White, in *St Patrick, his writings and life* (London, 1920).

Adomnan's Life of Columba. Edited and translated by A. O. and M. O. Anderson. London, 1961.

Frank MacManus. *Saint Columban.* Dublin, 1963.

Liam de Paor. 'A survey of Sceilg Mhichíl' in *Journal of the Royal Society of Antiquaries of Ireland,* lxxxv (1955).

Ludwig Bieler. *Ireland, harbinger of the middle ages.* London, 1963.

D. Whitelock, R. McKitterick, and D. Dumville. *Ireland in early medieval Europe.* Cambridge, 1982.

Donncha Ó Corráin. *Ireland before the Normans.* Dublin, 1972.

F. J. Byrne. *Irish kings and high-kings.* London, 1973.

Martin MacNamara. *The apocrypha in the Irish church.* Dublin, 1975.

Brian Ó Cuív. *The impact of the Scandinavian invasions on the Celtic-speaking peoples, c.800-1100 A.D.* Dublin, 1975.

A. P. Smyth. *Scandinavian kings in the British Isles, 850-880.* Oxford, 1977.

Johannes Brondsted. *The vikings.* Penguin Books, 1960.

Gwyn Jones. *A history of the vikings.* Oxford, 1968.

James Graham-Campbell. *The vikings.* London, 1980.

P. H. Sawyer. *The age of the vikings.* 2nd edition. London, 1971.

P. G. Foote and D. M. Wilson. *The viking achievement.* London, 1970.

Michael Dolley. *Viking coins of the Danelaw and of Dublin.* London, 1965.

A. B. Scott. *Malachy.* Dublin, 1976.

VI   MEDIEVAL IRELAND

J. F. O'Doherty. 'St Laurence O'Toole and the Anglo-Norman invasion' in *Irish Ecclesiastical Record* l (1937), pp 449-77; li (1938), pp 131-46.

J. F. O'Doherty. 'The Anglo-Norman invasion, 1167-71' in *Irish Historical Studies,* i, no. 2 (Sept. 1938), pp 154-7.

G. H. Orpen. *Ireland under the Normans, 1169-1333.* 4 vols. Oxford, 1911-20; reprint, 1968.

G. H. Orpen. 'Ireland to 1315' in *Cambridge Medieval History,* vii (1932), pp. 527-47.

G. H. Orpen. 'The effects of Norman rule in Ireland, 1169-1333' in *American Historical Review,* xix (1913-14), pp 245-56.

R. Dudley Edwards. 'Anglo-Norman relations with Connacht, 1169-1224' in *Irish Historical Studies,* i, no. 2 (Sept. 1938), pp 135-53.

W. L. Warren. *Henry II.* London, 1973. (Section on Ireland, pp 187-206)

W. L. Warren. 'John in Ireland, 1185' in John Bossy and Peter Jupp (ed.), *Essays presented to Michael Roberts* (Belfast, 1976), pp 11-23.

W. L. Warren. 'King John and Ireland' in J. F. Lydon (ed.), *England and Ireland in the later middle ages'* (Dublin, 1981), pp 26-42.

Bibliography: medieval Ireland

Michael Richter. 'The first century of Anglo-Irish relations' in *History*, lix (1974), pp 194-210.

M. P. Sheehy. 'The bull Laudabiliter: a problem in medieval diplomatique and history' in *Journal of the Galway Archaeological and Historical Society*, xxix (1960-61), pp 45-70.

Giraldus Cambrensis. *Expugnatio Hibernica, The conquest of Ireland*. Edited, with translation, by A. B. Scott and F. X. Martin. Dublin, 1978.

Gerald of Wales. *The history and topography of Ireland*. Edited, with translation, by John J. O'Meara. Penguin Books, 1982.

F. X. Martin. *No hero in the house: Diarmait Mac Murchada and the coming of the Normans to Ireland*. Dublin, 1977. (O'Donnell Lecture, 1975)

Michael Dolley. *Anglo-Norman Ireland, c.1100-1318*. Dublin, 1972.

K. W. Nicholls. *Gaelic and gaelicised Ireland in the middle ages*. Dublin, 1972.

J. F. Lydon. *The lordship of Ireland in the middle ages*. Dublin, 1972.

J. F. Lydon. *Ireland in the later middle ages*. Dublin, 1973.

Robin Frame. *Colonial Ireland, 1169-1369*. Dublin, 1981.

Brian Graham. 'The towns of medieval Ireland' in R. A. Butlin (ed.), *The development of the Irish town*. (London and Totowa (N.J.), 1977), pp 28-60.

Robin Frame. *English lordship in Ireland, 1318-1361*. Oxford, 1982.

Barry W. O'Dwyer. *The conspiracy of Mellifont, 1216-1231*. Dublin Historical Association, 1970.

Robin Frame. 'The Bruces in Ireland, 1315-18' in *Irish Historical Studies*, xix, no. 73 (Mar. 1974), pp 3-37.

J. F. Lydon. 'The Bruce invasion of Ireland' in *Historical Studies*, iv, edited by G. A. Hayes-McCoy (London, 1963), pp 111-25.

Robin Frame. 'Power and society in the lordship of Ireland, 1272-1377' in *Past & Present*, no. 76 (1977), pp 3-33.

J. F. Lydon. 'The problem of the frontier in medieval Ireland' in *Topic: a journal of the liberal arts* (Washington, Pa), no. 13 (spring 1967), pp 5-22.

C. A. Empey. 'The Butler lordship' in *Butler Society Journal*, i (1971), pp 174-87.

Bryan Murphy. 'The status of the native Irish after 1331' in *Irish Jurist*, ii (1967), pp 116-38.

Aubrey Gwynn. 'The Black Death in Ireland' in *Studies*, xxiv (1935), pp 558-72.

Art Cosgrove. *Late medieval Ireland, 1370-1541*. Dublin, 1981.

Art Cosgrove. 'The execution of the earl of Desmond, 1468' in *Journal of the Kerry Archaeological and Historical Society*, viii (1975), pp 11-27.

Art Cosgrove. 'Hiberniores ipsis Hibernicis' in Art Cosgrove and Donal McCartney (ed.), *Studies in Irish history presented to R. Dudley Edwards* (Dublin, 1979), pp 1-14.

C. A. Empey and Katharine Simms. 'The ordinances of the White Earl and the problem of coign in the later middle ages' in *Proceedings of the Royal Irish Academy*, 75 C 8 (1975), pp 161-87.

A. J. Otway-Ruthven. 'The character of Norman settlement in Ireland' in J. L. McCracken (ed.), *Historical Studies*, v (London, 1965), pp 75-84.

A. J. Otway-Ruthven. 'Knight service in Ireland' in *Journal of the Royal Society of Antiquaries of Ireland*, lxxxix (1959), pp 1-15.

A. J. Otway-Ruthven. 'The organisation of Anglo-Irish agriculture in the middle ages' in *Journal of the Royal Society of Antiquaries of Ireland*, lxxxi (1951), pp 1-13.

J. F. Lydon. 'Richard II's expeditions to Ireland' in *Journal of the Royal Society of Antiquaries of Ireland,* xciii (1963), pp 135-49.

R. J. Mitchell. *John Tiptoft.* London, 1938.

Donough Bryan. *The Great Earl of Kildare.* Dublin, 1933.

G. O. Sayles. 'The vindication of the earl of Kildare from treason, 1496' in *Irish Historical Studies,* vii, no. 25 (Mar. 1950), pp 39-47.

Agnes Conway. *Henry VII's relations with Scotland and Ireland.* Cambridge, 1932.

Steven Ellis. 'Henry VII and Ireland, 1491-6' in J. F. Lydon (ed.), *Ireland in the later middle ages* (Dublin, 1981), pp 237-54.

VII   IRELAND IN THE SIXTEENTH CENTURY

T. W. Moody, F. X. Martin, and F. J. Byrne (ed.). *Early modern Ireland, 1534-1691.* Oxford, 1976. (*A New History of Ireland,* vol. iii)

Margaret MacCurtain. *Tudor and Stuart Ireland.* Dublin, 1972.

Richard Bagwell. *Ireland under the Tudors.* 3 vols. London, 1885-90; reprint, 1963.

Philip Wilson. *The beginnings of modern Ireland.* Dublin and London, 1912.

James Hogan. *Ireland in the European system.* London, 1920.

R. Dudley Edwards. *Church and state in Tudor Ireland.* Dublin, 1935.

Brendan Bradshaw. *The Irish constitutional revolution of the sixteenth century.* Cambridge, 1979.

D. B. Quinn. 'Henry VIII and Ireland, 1509-34' in *Irish Historical Studies,* vii, no 48 (Sept. 1961), pp 318-44.

W. F. T. Butler. *Gleanings from Irish history.* London, 1925.

David Mathew. *The Celtic peoples and renaissance Europe.* London, 1933.

G. A. Hayes-McCoy. 'Gaelic society in Ireland in the late sixteenth century' in *Historical Studies,* iv, edited by G. A. Hayes-McCoy (London, 1963), pp 45-61.

Steven Ellis. 'Tudor policy and the Kildare ascendancy in the lordship of Ireland' in *Irish Historical Studies,* xx, no. 79 (Mar. 1977), pp 235-71.

Steven Ellis. 'The Kildare rebellion and the early Henrician reformation' in *Historical Journal,* xix (1976), pp 807-30.

Brendan Bradshaw. 'Cromwellian reforms and the origins of the Kildare rebellion' in *Transactions of the Royal Historical Society,* xxvii (1977), pp 69-93.

Steven Ellis. 'Thomas Cromwell and Ireland, 1532-40' in *Historical Journal,* xxiii (1980), pp 497-519.

James Hogan. 'Shane O'Neill comes to the court of Elizabeth' in Séamas Pender (ed.), *Féilscríbhinn Torna: essays and studies presented to Professor Tadhg Ua Donnchadha* (Cork, 1947), pp 154-70.

N. P. Canny. *The Elizabethan conquest of Ireland: a pattern established, 1565-1576.* Hassocks, 1976.

N. P. Canny. *The upstart earl: a study of the social and mental life of Richard Boyle, first earl of Cork, 1566-1643.* Cambridge, 1982.

Bibliography: Ireland in the seventeenth century

Captain Cuellar's adventures in Connaught and Ulster, 1588. Edited by Hugh Allingham. London, 1897.

R. E. Hardy. *Survivors of the armada.* London, 1966.

Cyril Falls. *Elizabeth's Irish wars.* London, 1950.

G. A. Hayes-McCoy. 'Strategy and tactics in Irish warfare, 1593-1601' in *Irish Historical Studies,* ii, no. 7 (Mar. 1941),pp 255-79.

G. A. Hayes-McCoy. 'The Army of Ulster, 1593-1601' in *The Irish Sword,* i (1949-53), pp 105-17.

G. A. Hayes-McCoy.'The tide of victory and defeat: I The battle of Clontibret, 1595 ; II The battle of Kinsale, 1601' in *Studies,* xxxviii (1949), pp 158-68, 307-17.

J. J. Silke. 'Spain and the invasion of Ireland, 1601-2' in *Irish Historical Studies,* xiv, no. 56 (Sept. 1965), pp 295-312.

D. B. Quinn. *The Elizabethans and the Irish.* Ithaca (New York), 1966.

Edmund Spenser. *A view of the present state of Ireland [1596].* Edited by W. L. Renwick. Oxford, 1934; reissue, 1970.

VIII IRELAND IN THE SEVENTEENTH CENTURY

T. W. Moody, F. X. Martin, and F. J. Byrne (ed.). *A new history of Ireland,* vol. iii *Early modern Ireland, 1534-1691.* Oxford, 1976.

Margaret MacCurtain. *Tudor and Stuart Ireland.* Dublin, 1972.

Richard Bagwell. *Ireland under the Stuarts.* 3 vols. London, 1909-16; reprint, 1963.

George O'Brien. *The economic history of Ireland in the seventeenth century.* Dublin and London, 1919.

P. J. Corish. *The catholic community in the seventeenth and eighteenth centuries.* Dublin, 1981.

N. P. Canny. *The upstart earl: a study of the social and mental life of Richard Boyle, first earl of Cork, 1566-1643.* Cambridge, 1982.

N. P. Canny. 'The flight of the earls, 1607' in *Irish Historical Studies,* xvii, no. 67 (Mar. 1971), pp 380-99.

Sir John Davies. *A discovery of the true causes why Ireland was never entirely subdued. . until his majesty's happy reign.* London, 1612; facsimile reprint, Shannon, 1969.

George Hill. *An historical account of the plantation in Ulster,. . ., 1608-20.* Belfast, 1877; reprint, Shannon, 1970.

T. W. Moody. *The Londonderry plantation, 1609-1641: the City of London and the plantation in Ulster.* Belfast, 1939.

Aidan Clarke. *The Old English in Ireland, 1625-42.* London, 1966.

Aidan Clarke. *The Graces, 1625-41.* Dublin Historical Association, 1968.

H. F. Kearney. *Strafford in Ireland, 1633-41.* Manchester, 1959.

Aidan Clarke. 'The genesis of the Ulster rising of 1641' in Peter Roebuck (ed.), *Plantation to partition* (Belfast, 1981), pp 29-45.

St J. D. Seymour. *The puritans in Ireland, 1647-61.* Oxford, 1921; reprint, 1969.

Aidan Clarke. 'Ireland and the general crisis' in *Past & Present*, no. 48 (1970), pp 79-99.

C. P. Meehan. *The confederation of Kilkenny*. Dublin, 1905.

J. C. Beckett, 'The confederation of Kilkenny reviewed' in M. Roberts (ed.), *Historical Studies,* ii (London, 1959), pp 29-41.

David Stevenson. *Scottish covenanters and Irish confederates: Scottish-Irish relations in the mid-seventeenth century*. Belfast, 1981.

T. C. Barnard. *Cromwellian Ireland: English government and reform in Ireland, 1649-1660.* Oxford, 1975.

J. P. Prendergast. *The Cromwellian settlement of Ireland*. London, 1865; revised edition, 1870; 3rd edition, 1922.

Edward MacLysaght. *Irish life in the seventeenth century: after Cromwell*. Dublin and Cork, 1939; 2nd edition, Cork, 1950; reprint, Shannon, 1969.

W. E. H. Lecky. *History of Ireland in the eighteenth century*. Vol. i. London, 1892.

J. G. Simms. *Jacobite Ireland, 1685-91*. London and Toronto, 1969.

J. C. Beckett. *Protestant dissent in Ireland, 1687-1780*. London, 1948.

Thomas Davis. *The patriot parliament of 1689*. Edited by C. Gavan Duffy. London, 1893.

J. G. Simms. *The Williamite confiscation in Ireland, 1690-1703*. London, 1958.

J. G. Simms. *The treaty of Limerick*. Dublin Historical Association, 1961; reprinted, 1965.

J. G. Simms. *The Jacobite parliament of 1689*. Dublin Historical Association, 1966.

IX   IRELAND IN THE EIGHTEENTH CENTURY

J. A. Froude. *The English in Ireland in the eighteenth century*. 3 vols. London, 1872-4; 2nd edition, 1881.

W. E. H. Lecky. *History of Ireland in the eighteenth century*. 5 vols. London, 1892.

W. E. H. Lecky. *The leaders of public opinion in Ireland*. 2nd edition, London, 1871. (Studies of Swift, Flood, Grattan, and O'Connell)

E. M. Johnston. *Ireland in the eighteenth century*. Dublin, 1974.

Thomas Bartlett and D. W. Hayton (ed.). *Penal era and golden age: essays in Irish history. 1690-1800*. Belfast, 1979.

R. B. McDowell. *Ireland in the age of imperialism and revolution, 1760-1800*. Oxford, 1979.

George O'Brien. *The economic history of Ireland in the eighteenth century*. Dublin, 1918.

L. M. Cullen. 'Problems in the interpretation and revision of eighteenth-century Irish economic history' in *Transactions of the Royal Historical Society*, 5th series, xvii (1967), pp 1-22.

H. F. Kearney. 'The political background to English mercantilism, 1695-1700' in *Economic History Review*, xi (1959), pp 484-96.

Patrick Kelly. 'The Irish woollen export prohibition act of 1699: Kearney revisited' in *Irish Economic and Social History*, vii (1980), pp 22-43.

L. M. Cullen. 'The smuggling trade in Ireland in the eighteenth century' in *Proceedings of the Royal Irish Academy*, 67 C 5 (1969), pp 149-75.

Daniel Corkery. *The hidden Ireland: a study of Gaelic Munster in the eighteenth century*. Dublin, 1925; 4th impression, 1956.

Bibliography: Ireland in the eighteenth century

L. M. Cullen. 'The hidden Ireland; reassessment of a concept' in *Studia Hibernica,* no. 9 (1969), pp 7-47.

Oliver W. Ferguson. *Jonathan Swift and Ireland.* Urbana (Illinois), 1962.

Jonathan Swift. *The Drapier's letters to the people of Ireland against receiving Wood's halfpence [1724].* Edited by Herbert Davis. Oxford, 1935; reprint, 1965.

George Berkeley. *The querist.* Dublin, 1735. (Best edition in *The works of George Berkeley, bishop of Cloyne,* ed. A. A. Luce and T. E. Jessop, vi (London, 1953)).

Michael Drake. 'The Irish demographic crisis of 1740-41' in *Historical Studies,* vi, edited by T. W. Moody (London, 1968), pp 101-24.

J. G. Simms. 'Connacht in the eighteenth century' in *Irish Historical Studies,* xi, no. 42 (Sept. 1958), pp 116-33.

J. C. Beckett. *Protestant dissent in Ireland, 1687-1780.* London, 1948.

Maureen Wall. *The penal laws, 1691-1760.* Dublin Historical Association, 1961.

Maureen Wall. 'The catholics of the towns and the quarterage dispute in eighteenth-century Ireland' in *Irish Historical Studies,* viii, no. 30 (Sept. 1952), pp 91-114.

Maureen Wall. 'The rise of a catholic middle class in eighteenth-century Ireland' in *Irish Historical Studies,* xi, no. 42 (Sept. 1958), pp 91-115.

Maureen Wall. 'Catholic loyalty to king and pope in eighteenth-century Ireland' in *Proceedings of the Irish Catholic Historical Committee,* (1960), pp 17-24.

Thomas Wall. *The sign of Dr Hay's Head.* Dublin, 1958.

R. B. McDowell. *Irish public opinion, 1750-1800.* London, 1944.

J. S. Donnelly jr. 'The Whiteboy movement, 1761-6' in *Irish Historical Studies,* xxi, no. 80 (Mar. 1978), pp 20-54.

J. S. Donnelly jr. 'The Rightboy movement, 1785-8' in *Studia Hibernica,* nos 17-18 (1977-8), pp 120-202.

Arthur Young. *A tour in Ireland. . . made in the years 1776, 1777, and 1778, and brought down to the end of 1779.* London, 1780; edited by A. W. Hutton. 2 vols, 1892; reprint, Shannon, 1970.

Maurice R. O'Connell. *Irish politics and social conflict in the age of the American revolution.* Philadelphia, 1965.

S. J. Connolly. *Priests and people in pre-famine Ireland, 1780-1845.* Dublin, 1982.

J. C. Beckett. 'Anglo-Irish constitutional relations in the later eighteenth century' in *Irish Historical Studies,* xiv, no. 53 (Mar. 1964), pp 20-38.

Edith M. Johnston. *Great Britain and Ireland, 1760-1800: a study in political administration.* Edinburgh, 1963.

A. P. W. Malcolmson. *John Foster: the politics of the Anglo-Irish ascendancy.* Oxford, 1978.

Patrick Rogers. *The Volunteers and catholic emancipation, 1778-93.* London, 1934.

R. R. Madden. *The United Irishmen, their lives and times.* 7 vols. London, 1842-6; revised edition, 4 vols, 1857-60.

Rosamund Jacob. *The rise of the United Irishmen, 1791-4.* London, 1937.

Robert Dunlop. *Henry Grattan.* London, 1889.

W. E. H. Lecky. *Leaders of public opinion in Ireland.* 3rd edition. Vol. i: FLood and Grattan, London, 1903.

Stephen Gwynn. *Henry Grattan and his times.* London, 1939.

Theobald Wolfe Tone. *Life of Theobald Wolfe Tone. . . written by himself and continued by his son.* Edited by W. T. W. Tone. 2 vols. Washington, 1826. (A new edition of Tone's writings, including much new material, is in preparation by T. W. Moody and R. B. McDowell.)

Frank MacDermot. *Theobald Wolfe Tone: a biographical study.* London, 1939; new edition, Tralee, 1968.

The Drennan letters. . *1776-1819.* Edited by D. A. Chart. Belfast, 1931.

Hereward Senior. *Orangeism in Ireland and Britain, 1795-1836.* London and Toronto, 1966.

E. H. Stuart Jones. *An invasion that failed: the French expedition to Ireland, 1796.* Oxford, 1950.

Charles Dickson. *The Wexford rising in 1798: its causes and course.* Tralee, 1955.

Charles Dickson. *Revolt in the north: Antrim and Down in 1798.* Dublin and London, 1960.

Thomas Pakenham. *The year of liberty: the story of the great Irish rebellion of 1798.* London, 1969.

Richard Hayes. *The last invasion of Ireland: when Connacht rose.* Dublin, 1937; 2nd edition, 1939.

G. C. Bolton. *The passing of the Irish act of union.* London, 1966.

X IRELAND, 1800-50

M. A. G. Ó Tuathaigh. *Ireland before the famine, 1798-1848.* Dublin, 1972.

S. J. Connolly. *Priests and people in pre-famine Ireland, 1780-1845.* Dublin, 1982.

D. A. Chart. *Ireland from the union to catholic emancipation.* London, 1910.

R. B. McDowell. *Public opinion and government policy in Ireland, 1801-1846.* London, 1952.

R. B. McDowell (ed.). *Social life in Ireland, 1800-45.* Dublin, 1957.

Desmond Bowen. *The protestant crusade in Ireland, 1800-70: a study of protestant-catholic relations between the act of union and disestablishment.* Dublin and Montreal, 1978.

R. W. Postgate. *Robert Emmet.* London, 1931.

Leon Ó Broin. *The unfortunate Mr Robert Emmet.* Dublin and London, 1958.

Galen Broeker. *Rural disorder and police reform in Ireland, 1812-36.* London and Toronto, 1970.

Ian Dalton. *Protestant society and politics in Cork, 1812-1844.* Cork, 1981.

James A. Reynolds. *The catholic emancipation crisis in Ireland, 1823-29.* New Haven, 1954.

M. A. G. Ó Tuathaigh. *Thomas Drummond and the government of Ireland, 1835-41.* The O'Donnell lecture delivered at University College, Galway, on 15 December 1977. Dublin: National University of Ireland.

K. B. Nowlan. *The politics of repeal: a study in the relations between Great Britain and Ireland, 1841-50.* London, 1965.

D. A. Kerr. *Peel, priests, and politics: Sir Robert Peel's administration and the Roman Catholic church in Ireland, 1841-1846.* Oxford, 1982.

W. E. H. Lecky. *Leaders of public opinion in Ireland.* 3rd edition. Vol. ii: Daniel O'Connell. London, 1903.

Bibliography: Ireland, 1800-1850

Robert Dunlop. *Daniel O'Connell and the revival of national life in Ireland.* New York and London, 1908.

Sean O'Faolain. *King of the beggars.* London, 1938.

Michael Tierney (ed.). *Daniel O'Connell: nine centenary essays.* Dublin, 1949.

Angus Macintyre. *The liberator: Daniel O'Connell and the Irish party, 1830-47.* London, 1965.

L. J. McCaffrey. *Daniel O'Connell and the repeal year.* Lexington (Kentucky), 1966.

Rachel O'Higgins. 'Irish trade unions and politics, 1830-50' in *Historical Journal*, iv (1961), pp 208-17.

F. A. D'Arcy. 'The artisans of Dublin and Daniel O'Connell, 1830-47: an unquiet liaison' in *Irish Historical Studies*, xvii, no. 66 (Sept. 1970), pp 221-43.

Jacqueline Hill. 'The protestant response to repeal: the case of the Dublin working class' in F. S. L. Lyons and R. A. J. Hawkins (ed.), *Ireland under the union* (Oxford, 1980), pp 35-68.

J. H. Whyte. 'Daniel O'Connell and the repeal party' in *Irish Historical Studies*, xi, no. 44 (Sept. 1959), pp 297-316.

David Large. 'The house of lords and Ireland in the age of Peel, 1832-50' in *Irish Historical Studies*, ix, no. 36 (Sept. 1955), pp 367-9.

Randall Clarke. 'The relations between O'Connell and the Young Irelanders' in *Irish Historical Studies*, iii, no. 44 (Sept. 1959), pp 297-315.

J. F. Broderick. *The holy see and the Irish movement for the repeal of the union with England, 1829-47.* Rome, 1951.

Charles Gavan Duffy. *Young Ireland: a fragment of Irish history, 1840-50.* (Ends in 1845 with the death of Davis. A revised edition (London, 2 vols, 1896) has the same title except that the terminal dates are given (correctly) as 1840-1845.)

Charles Gavan Duffy. *Four years of Irish history, 1845-1849: a sequel to 'Young Ireland'.* London, 1883.

Charles Gavan Duffy. *Thomas Davis: the memoirs of an Irish patriot, 1840-1846.* London, 1890.

T. W. Moody. *Thomas Davis, 1814-1845.* Dublin, 1945.

T. W. Moody. 'Thomas Davis and the Irish nation' in *Hermathena*, ciii (1966), pp 5-31. (Includes a bibliography of Davis's writings and of writings on Davis.)

K. B. Nowlan. *Charles Gavan Duffy.* Dublin, [1964].

Denis Gwynn. *Young Ireland and 1848.* Cork, 1949.

C. E. Trevelyan. *The Irish crisis.* London, 1848.

Transactions of the central relief committee of the Society of Friends during the famine in Ireland in 1846 and 1847. Dublin, 1852.

John O'Rourke. *The history of the great Irish famine of 1847, with notices of earlier famines.* Dublin, 1875.

W. P. O'Brien. *The great famine in Ireland and a retrospect of the fifty years 1845-95.* London, 1896.

R. Dudley Edwards and T. D. Williams (ed.). *The great famine: studies in Irish history, 1845-1852.* Dublin, 1956; reprint, with introduction by E. R. R. Green, New York, 1976.

Cecil Woodham-Smith. *The great hunger: Ireland 1845-9.* London, 1962.

S. H. Cousens. 'The regional variation in mortality during the great Irish famine' in *Proceedings of the Royal Irish Academy*, 63 C 3 (1963), pp 127-49.

XI IRELAND, 1850-1921

F. S. L. Lyons. *Ireland since the famine.* London, 1971; revised edition, 1973. (Full, classified bibliography)

Joseph Lee. *The modernisation of Irish society, 1848-1918.* Dublin, 1973.

Nicholas Mansergh. *The Irish question, 1840-1921.* London, 1948; new edition, 1965.

J. H. Whyte. *The independent Irish party, 1850-59.* Oxford, 1958.

Charles Gavan Duffy. *The league of north and south.* London, 1886.

T. K. Hoppen. 'National politics and local realities in mid-nineteenth century Ireland' in Art Cosgrove and Donal McCartney (ed.), *Studies in Irish history presented to R. Dudley Edwards* (Dublin, 1979), pp 190-227.

S. H. Cousens. 'The regional variations in population changes in Ireland, 1861-1881' in *Economic History Review,* xvii, no. 2 (Dec. 1964), pp 301-21.

T. N. Brown. *Irish-American nationalism, 1870-1890.* Philadelphia and New York, 1966.

Desmond Ryan. *The phoenix flame: a study of Fenianism and John Devoy.* London, 1937.

T. W. Moody (ed.). *The Fenian movement.* Cork, 1968; reprint, Dublin and Cork, 1978.

John O'Leary. *Recollections of Fenians and Fenianism.* 2 vols. London, 1896; reprint, Shannon, 1969.

John Devoy. *Recollections of an Irish rebel.* . . New York, 1929; reprint, Shannon, 1969.

William O'Brien and Desmond Ryan (ed.). *Devoy's post bag, 1871-1928.* 2 vols. Dublin, 1948, 1953.

Mark Ryan. *Fenian memories.* Dublin, 1945.

Leon Ó Broin. *Fenian fever: an Anglo-Irish dilemma.* London, 1971.

Leon Ó Broin. *Revolutionary underground: the story of the Irish Republican Brotherhood, 1858-1924.* Dublin, 1976.

Marcus Bourke. *John O'Leary: a study in Irish separatism.* Tralee, 1967.

Desmond Ryan. *The Fenian chief: a biography of James Stephens.* [Edited by Patrick Lynch and Owen Dudley Edwards.] Dublin and Sydney, 1967.

R. V. Comerford. *Charles J. Kickham: a study in Irish nationalism and literature.* Portmarnock, 1979.

R. V. Comerford. 'Anglo-French tension and the origins of Fenianism' in F. S. L. Lyons and R. A. J. Hawkins (ed.), *Ireland under the union* (Oxford, 1980), pp. 149-72.

R. V. Comerford. 'Patriotism as pastime: the appeal of Fenianism in the mid-1860s' in *Irish Historical Studies,* xxii, no. 87 (Mar. 1981), pp. 239-50.

Mark Tierney. *Croke of Cashel: the life of Archbishop Thomas William Croke, 1823-1902.* Dublin, 1976.

E. R. Norman. *The catholic church and Ireland in the age of rebellion, 1859-73.* London, 1965.

Lord Eversley. *Gladstone and Ireland: the Irish policy of parliament, 1850-94.* London, 1912.

J. L. Hammond. *Gladstone and the Irish nation.* London, 1938; new impression, with introduction by M. R. D. Foot, 1964.

E. D. Steele. 'Gladstone and Ireland' in *Irish Historical Studies,* xvii, no. 65 (Mar. 1970), pp 58-88.

Bibliography: Ireland, 1850-1921

J. R. Vincent. 'Gladstone and Ireland' in *Proceedings of the British Academy*, lxii (1977), pp 193-238.

Michael MacDonagh, *The home rule movement*. Dublin, 1920.

T. P. O'Connor. *The Parnell movement*. London, 1886; new edition, 1887.

T. de V. White. *The road of excess*. (A biography of Isaac Butt) Dublin, [1946].

D. A. Thornley. *Isaac Butt and home rule*. London, 1964.

R. B. O'Brien. *The life of Charles Stewart Parnell, 1846-1891*. 2 vols. London, 1898.

Henry Harrison. *Parnell vindicated: the lifting of the veil*. London, 1931.

M. M. O'Hara. *Chief and tribune: Parnell and Davitt*. Dublin and London, 1919.

Leon Ó Broin. *Parnell: beathaisnéis*. Dublin, 1937.

C. Cruise O'Brien. *Parnell and his party, 1880-90*. Oxford, 1957; corrected impression, 1964.

F. S. L. Lyons. *Charles Stewart Parnell*. London, 1977; paperback edition, 1978.

F. S. L. Lyons. *The fall of Parnell, 1890-91*. London, 1960.

F. Sheehy Skeffington. *Michael Davitt: revolutionary, agitator and labour leader*. London, 1908; reprint, with introduction by F. S. L. Lyons, 1967.

T. W. Moody. *Davitt and Irish revolution, 1846-82*. Oxford, 1981.

Michael Davitt. *The fall of feudalism in Ireland, or the story of the Land League revolution*. London and New York, 1904.

N. D. Palmer. *The Irish Land League crisis*. New Haven, 1940.

T. W. Moody. 'Michael Davitt and the British labour movement, 1882-1906' in *Transactions of the Royal Historical Society*, 5th series, iii (1953), pp 53-76.

F. S. L. Lyons. *John Dillon: a biography*. London, 1968.

J. V. O'Brien. *William O'Brien and the course of Irish politics, 1881-1918*. Berkeley (Cal.), 1976.

L. P. Curtis. *Coercion and conciliation in Ireland, 1880-92*. Princeton and London, 1963.

K. R. M. Short. *The dynamite war: Irish-American bombers in Victorian Britain*. Dublin, 1971.

C. J. Woods. 'Ireland and Anglo-papal relations, 1880-85' in *Irish Historical Studies*, xviii, no. 69 (Mar. 1972), pp 29-60.

Richard Hawkins. 'Gladstone, Forster, and the release of Parnell, 1882-8' in *Irish Historical Studies*, xvi, no. 64 (Sept. 1969), pp 417-45.

Tom Corfe. *The Phoenix Park murders: conflict, compromise, and tragedy in Ireland, 1879-1882*. London, 1968.

W. F. Mandle. 'The I.R.B. and the beginnings of the Gaelic Athletic Association' in *Irish Historical Studies*, xx, no. 80 (Sept. 1977), pp 418-38.

A. B. Cooke and J. R. Vincent. *The governing passion: cabinet government and party politics in Britain, 1885-86*. Brighton, 1974.

Alan O'Day. *The English face of Irish nationalism: Parnellite involvement in British politics, 1880-86*. Dublin, 1977.

F. S. L. Lyons. *The Irish parliamentary party, 1890-1901*. London, 1951.

C. Cruise O'Brien (ed.). *The shaping of modern Ireland [1891-1916]*. London, 1960.

Catherine B. Shannon. 'The Ulster liberal unionists and local government reform, 1885-98' in *Irish Historical Studies*, xviii, no. 71 (Mar. 1973), pp 407-23.

C. J. Woods. 'The general election of 1892: the catholic clergy and the defeat of the

Parnellites' in F. S. L. Lyons and R. A. J. Hawkins (ed.), *Ireland under the union* (Oxford, 1980), pp 149-72.

D. W. Miller. *Church, state, and nation in Ireland, 1898-1921.* Dublin, 1973.

A. J. Ward. *Ireland and Anglo-American relations, 1899-1921.* London, 1969.

R. M. Henry. *The evolution of Sinn Féin.* Dublin, 1920.

J. J. Horgan. *Parnell to Pearse.* Dublin, 1948.

Denis Gwynn. *The Life of John Redmond.* London, 1932.

Padraic Colum. *Arthur Griffith.* Dublin, 1959.

Seán Ó Lúing. *Art Ó Gríofa.* Dublin, 1953.

R. P. Davis. *Arthur Griffith and non-violent Sinn Féin.* Dublin, 1974.

R. P. Davis. *Arthur Griffith.* Dublin Historical Association, 1976.

W. Alison Phillips. *The revolution in Ireland, 1906-1923.* 2nd edition, 1926.

Leon Ó Broin. *The chief secretary: Augustine Birrell in Ireland.* London, 1969.

W. B. Stanford and R. B. McDowell. *Mahaffy: a biography of an Anglo-Irishman.* London, 1971.

Brian Inglis. *Roger Casement.* London, 1973.

Pádraic H. Pearse. *Political writings and speeches.* Dublin, 1922; reprint, 1958.

Pádraic H. Pearse. *Plays, stories, poems.* Dublin, 1917; reprint, 1952.

Ruth Dudley Edwards. *Patrick Pearse: the triumph of failure.* London, 1977.

James Connolly. *Socialism and nationalism.* Introduction and notes by Desmond Ryan. Dublin, 1948.

James Connolly. *The workers' republic.* Introduction by William McMullen. Dublin, 1951.

James Connolly. *Labour and Easter week.* Introduction by William O'Brien. Dublin, 1949.

C. D. Greaves. *The life and times of James Connolly.* London, 1961.

Proinsias Mac an Bheatha. *Tart na Córa – Séamus Ó Congaile, a shaol agus a shaothar.* Dublin, [1963].

Emmet Larkin. *James Larkin, Irish labour leader, 1876-1947.* London, 1965.

A. P. Ryan. *Mutiny at the Curragh.* London, 1956.

James Fergusson. *The Curragh incident.* London, 1963.

F. X. Martin (ed.). *The Irish Volunteers, 1913-15: recollections and documents.* Dublin, 1963.

F. X. Martin (ed.). *The Howth gun-running and the Kilcoole gun-running, 1914: recollections and documents.* Dublin, 1964.

Diarmuid Lynch. *The I.R.B. and the 1916 rising.* Edited by F. O'Donoghue, Cork, 1957.

Desmond Ryan. *The rising: the complete story of Easter week.* Dublin, 1949; 3rd edition, 1957.

Owen Dudley Edwards and Fergus Pyle (ed.). *1916: the Easter rising.* London, 1968.

K. B. Nowlan (ed.). *The making of 1916: studies in the history of the rising.* Dublin, 1969.

J. Bowyer Bell. *The secret army: a history of the I.R.A., 1916-1979.* London, 1970; 3rd edition, Dublin, 1979.

T. P. Coogan. *The I.R.A.* London, 1970; 2nd edition, Glasgow, 1980.

Leon Ó Broin. *Dublin Castle and the 1916 rising: the story of Sir Matthew Nathan.* Dublin, 1966.

F. X. Martin (ed.). *Leaders and men of the Easter rising: Dublin 1916.* London and Ithaca, 1967.

Bibliography: Ireland, 1921-82

F. X. Martin. '1916 – Myth, fact and mystery' in *Studia Hibernica,* 1967 [1968], pp 7-126. Review article of published literature, 1916-1966, on the Easter rising.
T. D. Williams (ed.). *The Irish struggle, 1916-1926.* London, 1966.
Edgar Holt. *Protest in arms: the Irish troubles. 1916-23.* London, 1960.
F. X. Martin (ed.). 'Eoin MacNeill on the 1916 rising' in *Irish Historical Studies,* xii, no. 47 (Mar. 1961), pp 226-71.
F. X. Martin and F. J. Byrne (ed.). *The scholar revolutionary: Eoin MacNeill, 1867-1945, and the making of the new Ireland.* Shannon, 1973.
Michael Tierney. *Eoin Mac Neill: scholar and man of action, 1867-1945.* Edited by F. X. Martin. Oxford, 1980.
Margery Forester. *Michael Collins – the lost leader.* London, 1971.
F. X. Martin (ed.). *1916 and University College, Dublin.* Dublin, 1966.
Florence O'Donoghue. *No other law: the story of Liam Lynch and the Irish Republican Army, 1916-1923.* Dublin, 1954.
Tomás Ó Néill and Pádraig Ó Fiannachta. *De Valera.* 2 vols. Dublin, 1968.
Frank Pakenham and T. P. O'Neill. *Eamonn de Valera.* London, 1970.
C. D. Greaves. *Liam Mellows and the Irish revolution.* London, 1971.
Andrew Boyle. *The riddle of Erskine Childers.* London, 1977.
Thomas Jones. *Whitehall diary: iii, Ireland, 1918-25.* Edited by Keith Middlemas. London, 1971.
Charles Townshend. *The British campaign in Ireland, 1919-1921.* London, 1969.
D. G. Boyce. *Englishmen and Irish troubles: British public opinion and the making of Irish policy, 1918-22.* London, 1972.
Frank Pakenham. *Peace by ordeal.* London, 1955; new edition, 1962.
David Fitzpatrick. *Politics and Irish life, 1913-21: provincial experience of war and revolution.* Dublin, 1977.

XII   IRELAND, 1921-82

John A. Murphy. *Ireland in the twentieth century.* Dublin, 1975.
T. P. Coogan. *Ireland since the rising.* London, 1966.
Denis Gwynn. *The Irish Free State, 1922-7.* London, 1928.
J. M. Curran. *The birth of the Irish Free State, 1921-1923.* Alabama, 1980.
Terence Brown. *Ireland: a social and cultural history, 1922-79.* Fontana Paperbacks, 1981.
George O'Brien. *The four green fields.* Dublin, 1936.
Peadar O'Donnell. *There will be another day.* Dublin, 1963.
T. D. Williams (ed.). *The Irish struggle, 1916-26.* London, 1966.
Francis MacManus (ed.). *The years of the great test, 1926-39.* Cork, 1967.
K. B. Nowlan and T. D. Williams (ed.). *Ireland in the war years and after, 1939-51.* Dublin, 1969.
J. T. Carroll. *Ireland in the war years.* Newton Abbot, 1975.
J. J. Lee (ed.). *Ireland, 1945-70.* Dublin, 1979.

Sáorstát Éireann, Irish Free State, Official handbook. Dublin, 1932.
T. de V. White. *Kevin O'Higgins.* London, 1948.
Mary C. Bromage. *De Valéra and the march of a nation.* London, 1956.
Tomás Ó Néill and Pádraig Ó Fiannachta. *De Valera.* 2 vols. Dublin, 1968.
Lord Longford and T. P. O'Neill. *Eamon de Valera.* Dublin and London, 1970.
John Bowman. *De Valera and the Ulster question, 1917-1973.* Oxford, 1982.
D. W. Harkness. *The restless dominion: the Irish Free State and the British Commonwealth of Nations, 1921-31.* London and Dublin, 1969.
G. J. Hand (ed.). *Report of the Irish boundary commission, 1925.* Shannon, 1969.
Nicholas Mansergh. *Survey of British Commonwealth affairs: problems of external policy, 1931-39.* London, 1952.
Nicholas Mansergh. *Survey of British Commonwealth affairs: problems of wartime cooperation and post-war change, 1939-52.* London, 1958.
J. Bowyer Bell. *The secret army: a history of the I.R.A., 1916-79.* London, 1970; 3rd edition, Dublin, 1979.
T. P. Coogan. *The I.R.A.* London, 1970; 2nd edition, Glasgow, 1980.
Calton Younger. *Ireland's civil war.* London, 1968.
Maurice Manning. *The Blueshirts.* Dublin, 1971.
J. H. Whyte. *Church and state in modern Ireland, 1923-1970.* Dublin, 1971; 2nd edition, 1980.
Patrick Keatinge. *A place among the nations: issues of Irish foreign policy.* Dublin, 1978.
D. R. O'Connor Lysaght. *The republic of Ireland.* Cork, 1970.
Jack White. *Minority report: the anatomy of the southern Irish protestant.* Dublin, 1975.
Frank Litton (ed.). *Unequal achievement: the Irish experience, 1957-1982.* Dublin, 1982.
T. Ryle Dwyer. *Michael Collins and the Treaty.* Dublin and Cork, 1981.
T. Ryle Dwyer. *De Valera's darkest hour: in search of national independence, 1919-1932.* Dublin and Cork, 1982.
T. Ryle Dwyer. *De Valera's finest hour: in search of national independence, 1932-1959.* Dublin and Cork, 1982.
Kevin Boland. *The rise and decline of Fianna Fáil.* Dublin and Cork, 1982.

XIII   ULSTER HISTORY

T. E. McNeill. *Anglo-Norman Ulster: the history and archaeology of an Irish barony, 1177-1400.* Edinburgh, 1980.
Katharine Simms. 'The archbishops of Armagh and the O'Neills, 1347-1471' in *Irish Historical Studies,* xix, no. 73 (Mar. 1974), pp 38-55.
Katharine Simms. '"The king's friend"; O'Neill, the crown, and the earldom of Ulster' in J. F. Lydon (ed.), *England and Ireland in the later middle ages* (Dublin, 1981), pp 214-36.
George Hill. *An historical account of the MacDonnells of Antrim.* Belfast, 1873; reprint, 1976.
George Hill. *An historical account of the plantation in Ulster. . ., 1608-20.* Belfast, 1877; reprint, Shannon, 1970.

Bibliography: Ulster history

Cyril Falls. *The birth of Ulster.* London, 1936.
T. W. Moody. *The Londonderry plantation, 1609-41: the City of London and the plantation in Ulster.* Belfast, 1939.
T. W. Moody (ed.). 'The revised articles of the Ulster plantation, 1610' in *Bulletin of the Institute of Historical Research,* xii, no. 36 (Feb. 1935), pp 178-83.
T. W. Moody. 'The treatment of the native population under the scheme for the plantation in Ulster' in *Irish Historical Studies,* i, no. 1 (Mar. 1938), pp 59-63.
J. B. Woodburn. *The Ulster Scot: his history and religion.* London, 1915.
M. Perceval Maxwell. *The Scottish migration to Ulster in the reign of James I.* London, 1973.
C. D. Milligan. *History of the siege of Londonderry.* Belfast, 1951.
J. G. Simms. *The siege of Derry.* Dublin, 1966.
Peter Roebuck (ed.). *Plantation to partition: essays in Ulster history in honour of J. L. McCracken.* Belfast, 1981.
R. J. Dickson. *Ulster emigration to colonial America, 1718-1775.* London, 1966.
E. R. R. Green (ed.). *Essays in Scotch-Irish history.* London, 1969.
Mary McNeill. *The life and times of Mary Ann McCracken, 1770-1866: a Belfast panorama.* Dublin, 1960.
Finlay Holmes, *Henry Cooke,* Belfast, 1982.
Peter Jupp. 'County Down elections, 1783-1831' in *Irish Historical Studies,* xviii, no. 70 (Sept. 1972), pp 177-206.
Desmond Murphy. *Derry, Donegal, and modern Ulster, 1790-1921.* Londonderry, 1981.
D. H. Akenson. *Between two revolutions: Islandmagee, County Antrim, 1798-1920.* Ontario, 1979.
T. W. Moody and J. C. Beckett (ed.). *Ulster since 1800: a political and economic survey.* London, 1955; reprint, with corrections, 1957.
T. W. Moody and J. C. Beckett (ed.). *Ulster since 1800: a social survey.* London, 1957; reprint, with corrections, 1958.
E. R. R. Green. *The Lagan valley, 1800-1850: a local history of the industrial revolution.* London, 1949.
W. E. Coe. *The engineering industry of the north of Ireland.* Newton Abbot, 1969.
J. A. McCutcheon. *The industrial archaeology of Northern Ireland.* Belfast, 1980.
R. W. Kirkpatrick. 'Origins and development of the land war in mid-Ulster, 1879-85' in F. S. L. Lyons and R. A. J. Hawkins (ed.), *Ireland under the union* (Oxford, 1980), pp 201-36.
R. F. Foster. 'To the Northern Counties station: Lord Randolph Churchill and the prelude to the Orange card' in F. S. L. Lyons and R. A. J. Hawkins (ed.), *Ireland under the union* (Oxford, 1980), pp 237-88.
Patrick Buckland. *Irish unionism 2: Ulster unionism and the origins of Northern Ireland, 1886-1922.* Dublin and New York, 1973.
A. T. Q. Stewart. *The Ulster crisis.* London, 1967; reprint, 1979.
Liam de Paor. *Divided Ulster.* Penguin Books, 1970.
Hugh Shearman. *Not an inch: a study of Northern Ireland and Lord Craigavon.* London, 1942.
T. W. Moody. *The Ulster question, 1603-1973.* Dublin and Cork, 1974. (Extensive bibliography)

A. T. Q. Stewart. *The narrow ground: aspects of Ulster, 1609-1969.* London, 1977.

D. W. Miller. *Queen's rebels: Ulster loyalism in historical perspective.* Dublin and New York, 1978.

St John Ervine. *Craigavon, Ulsterman.* London, 1949.

Edward Marjoribanks and Ian Colvin. *Life of Lord Carson.* 3 vols. London, 1932, 1934, 1936.

A. T. Q. Stewart. *Edward Carson.* Dublin, 1981.

John Bowman. *De Valera and the Ulster question, 1917-1973.* Oxford, 1982.

Hugh Shearman. *Northern Ireland, 1921-1971.* Belfast, 1971. (Many valuable illustrations)

Patrick Buckland. *A history of Northern Ireland.* Dublin, 1981.

R. J. McNeill. *Ulster's stand for union.* London, 1922.

W. S. Armour. *Armour of Ballymoney.* London, 1934.

Denis Gwynn. *The history of partition, 1912-1925.* Dublin, [1950].

J. W. Blake. *Northern Ireland in the second world war.* Belfast, 1956.

Nicholas Mansergh. *The government of Northern Ireland.* London, 1936.

Thomas Wilson (ed.). *Ulster under home rule: a study of the political and economic problems of Northern Ireland.* London, 1955.

R. J. Lawrence. *The government of Northern Ireland: public finance and public services, 1921-1964.* Oxford, 1965.

K. S. Isles and N. Cuthbert. *An economic survey of Northern Ireland.* Belfast, 1957.

D. P. Barritt and C. F. Carter. *The Northern Ireland problem: a study in group relations.* London, 1962; 2nd edition, 1972.

Sydney Elliott *Northern Ireland parliamentary election results, 1921-71.* Chichester, 1973.

Paul Bew, Peter Gibbon, and Henry Patterson. *The state in Northern Ireland, 1921-72.* Manchester, 1979.

D. H. Akenson. *Education and enmity: the control of schooling in Northern Ireland, 1920-1950.* Newton Abbot and New York, 1973.

Michael Farrell. *Northern Ireland: the Orange state.* London, 1976.

Liam O'Dowd, Bill Rolston, and Mike Tomlinson. *Northern Ireland between civil rights and civil war.* London, 1980.

Derek Birrell and Alan Murie. *Policy and government in Northern Ireland: lessons of devolution.* Dublin, 1980.

Richard Rose. *Governing without consensus: an Irish perspective.* London, 1971.

Paul Arthur. *Government and politics in Northern Ireland.* London, 1980.

Patrick Buckland. *The factory of grievances: devolved government in Northern Ireland, 1921-39.* Dublin, 1979.

Martin Wallace. *British government in Northern Ireland from devolution to direct rule.* Newton Abbot, 1982.

David Watt (ed.). *The constitution of Northern Ireland: problems and prospects.* London, 1981.

Rosemary Harris. *Prejudice and tolerance in Ulster.* Manchester, 1972.

David Boulton. *The U.V.F., 1966-73: an anatomy of loyalist rebellion.* Dublin, 1973.

John Darby. *Conflict in Northern Ireland: the development of a polarised community.* Dublin, 1976.

Terence O'Neill. *Ulster at the crossroads.* London, 1969.

Terence O'Neill. *Autobiography.* London, 1972.

419

Bibliography: biographical and other works of reference

Brian Faulkner. *Memoirs of a statesman*. Edited by John Houston. London, 1978.
Sunday Times Insight Team. *Ulster*. 2nd edition. Penguin Books, 1972.
Ian MacAllister. *The Northern Ireland Social Democratic and Labour Party*. London, 1977.
Robert Fisk. *The point of no return: the strike which broke the British in Ulster*. London, 1975.
Dervla Murphy. *A place apart*. Penguin Books, 1978.
Bob Rowthorn. 'Northern Ireland: an economy in crisis' in *Cambridge Journal of Economics*, v, (1981).
J. M. Mogey. *Rural life in Northern Ireland: five regional studies*. London, 1937.
Hugh Shearman. *Ulster*. London, 1949. (County Books)
Lord Longford and Anne Hardy. *Ulster*. London, 1981.
J. C. Beckett and R. E. Glasscock (ed.). *Belfast: origin and growth of an industrial city*. London, 1967.
Jonathan Bardon. *Belfast: an illustrated history*. With picture research by Henry V. Bell. Belfast, 1982; reprint, with corrections, 1983.
Ian Budge and Cornelius O'Leary. *Belfast: approach to crisis: a study of Belfast politics, 1613-1970*. London, 1973.
Henry Patterson. *Class conflict and sectarianism: the protestant working class and the Belfast labour movement, 1868-1920*. Belfast, 1980.
Gilbert Camblin. *The town in Ulster*. London, 1951.
C. E. B. Brett. *Buildings of Belfast, 1700-1914*. London, 1967.
Alistair Rowan. *The buildings of Ireland: north-west Ulster: the counties of Londonderry, Donegal, Fermanagh, and Tyrone*. Harmondsworth, 1979.
Emrys Jones. *A social geography of Belfast*. London, 1960.
Richard Deutsch and Vivien Magowan. *Northern Ireland, 1968-73: a chronology of events*. Vol. i: 1968-71; vol. ii: 1972-73. Belfast, 1973, 1974. (Includes valuable bibliography and appendices.)
Richard Deutsch. *Northern Ireland, 1921-1974: a select bibliography*. New York and London, 1975.

XIV   BIOGRAPHICAL AND OTHER WORKS OF REFERENCE

T. W. Moody, F. X. Martin, and F. J. Byrne (ed.). *A new history of Ireland*. Vol. viii: *A chronology of Irish history to 1976*. Oxford, 1982.
Alfred Webb. *Compendium of Irish biography*. . . Dublin, 1878.
J. S. Crone. *A concise dictionary of Irish biography*. Dublin, 1928; 2nd edition, [1937].
Henry Boylan. *A dictionary of Irish biography*. Dublin, 1878
Edward MacLysaght. *Irish families: their names, arms, and origins*. Dublin, 1957.
Edward MacLysaght. *More Irish families*. Galway and Dublin, 1960.
Edward MacLysaght. *Supplement to Irish families*. Dublin, 1964.
Edward MacLysaght. *Guide to Irish families*. Dublin, 1964.
Dictionary of national biography. Edited by Leslie Stephen and Sidney Lee. 66 vols. London, 1885-1901. Reprinted with corrections, 22 vols, 1908-9. (The main dictionary to

1900; continued from 1901 in decadal volumes, of which the latest is for 1961-1970. Contains innumerable Irish biographies.)

Concise dictionary of national biography. 2 vols: (1) to 1900 (corrected impression, London, 1959); (2) 1901-1970 (1982).

Dictionary of American biography. Edited by Allen Johnson and Dumas Malone. 20 vols. New York and London, 1928-37. (Contains many Irish-American biographies.)

John Lodge. *Peerage of Ireland.* Revised edition, by Mervyn Archdall. 7 vols. Dublin, 1789.

G.E.C. *Complete peerage of England, Scotland, Ireland, Great Britain and the United Kingdom. . .* Edited by Vicary Gibbs and others. 13 vols. London, 1910-59.

Aubrey Gwynn and R. N. Hadcock. *Medieval religious houses.* London, 1970.

F. E. Ball. *The judges in Ireland, 1121-1921.* 2 vols. London, 1926.

Thom's Irish almanac and official directory for the year 1844 [etc.]. Dublin, 1844 [etc.].

Ulster year book, 1926 [etc.]. Belfast: H.M. Stationery Office, 1926 [etc.].

Samuel Lewis. *A topographical dictionary of Ireland.* 2 vols. and atlas. London, 1837.

Census of Ireland, 1901: general topographical index. Dublin: H.M. Stationery Office, 1904 (Cd 2071).

Brian Cleeve (ed.). *Dictionary of Irish Writers.* 3 vols. Cork, 1967, 1969, 1971.

D. J. Hickey and J. E. Doherty. *A dictionary of Irish history since 1800.* Dublin, 1980.

W. E. Vaughan and A. J. Fitzpatrick. *Irish historical statistics: population, 1821-1971.* Dublin, 1978. (New History of Ireland Ancillary Publications II)

B. M. Walker. *Parliamentary election results in Ireland, 1801-1922.* Dublin, 1978. (New History of Ireland Ancillary Publications IV)

Lord Killanin and M. V. Duignan. *Shell guide to Ireland.* London, 1962.

Department of Foreign Affairs. *Facts about Ireland.* 5th edition. Dublin, 1981.

XV BIBLIOGRAPHIES, SERIAL PUBLICATIONS, AND FESTSCHRIFTS

BIBLIOGRAPHIES

Edith M. Johnston. *Irish history: a select bibliography.* London, Historical Association, 1969; revised reprint, 1972.

J. F. Kenney. *The sources for the early history of Ireland: ecclesiastical.* New York, 1929; reprint New York 1966, with preface by Ludwig Bieler.

P. W. A. Asplin. *Medieval Ireland, c.1170-1498: a bibliography of secondary works.* Dublin, 1971.

For the period 1485-1914 a bibliography of Irish history is provided by the Irish sections of the Royal Historical Society's *Bibliography of British history, 1485-1603* (2nd edition, London, 1959); —, *1603-1714* (1928); —, *1714-89* (1951); —, *1789-1851* (1977); —, *1851-1914* (1976).

James Carty. *Bibliography of Irish history, 1870-1911.* Dublin, 1940.

James Carty. *Bibliography of Irish history, 1911-21.* Dublin, 1936.

Writings on Irish history, 1936-78. A bibliography of current publications, published annually in *Irish Historical Studies* from 1938 to 1979.

Select bibliography of publications in Irish economic and social history published in 1973 [etc.]. Published annually in *Irish Economic and Social History* since 1974.

Royal Historical Society. *Annual bibliography of British and Irish history: publications of*

Bibliography: bibliographies, serial publications, and festschrifts

1975 [etc.]. Edited by G. R. Elton. Hassocks, 1976–.

T. W. Moody (ed.). *Irish historiography, 1936-70.* Dublin, 1971.

J. J. Lee (ed.). *Irish historiography, 1970-79.* Cork, 1980.

Irish Manuscripts Commission, catalogue of publications issued and in preparation, 1928-1966. Dublin, Stationery Office, 1966.

A guide to the reports on collections of manuscripts. . . issued by the royal commissioners for historical manuscripts. Part I – Topographical [index]. London, Stationery Office, 1914.

Guide to the reports of the royal commission on historical manuscripts, 1870-1911. Part II *– Index of persons.* 2 vols. London, Stationery Office, 1935, 1938.

R. J. Hayes (ed.). *Sources for the history of Irish civilisation: articles in Irish periodicals.* 9 vols. Boston (Mass.), 1970.

R. J. Hayes (ed.). *Manuscript sources for the history of Irish civilisation.* 11 vols. Boston (Mass.), 1966; *Supplement.* 3 vols. 1979.

A. R. Eager. *A guide to Irish bibliographical material: a bibliography of Irish bibliographies and sources of information.* London, 1964; 2nd edition, 1980.

PERIODICALS

Irish Historical Studies (Dublin, 1938–; biannual).

Historical Studies: papers read before the Irish Conference of Historians (London, 1958–).

Irish Economic and Social History (1974; annual).

Proceedings of the Royal Irish Academy, section C (Dublin, 1836–).

Journal of the Royal Society of Antiquaries of Ireland (Dublin, 1892–).

Studia Hibernica (Dublin, 1961–; annual).

Proceedings of the Irish Catholic Historical Committee (Dublin, 1955–; annual).

The Irish Sword (Dublin, 1949–; biannual).

Ulster Journal of Archaeology (Belfast, 1853-62; 1895-1911; 1938–; annual).

Dublin Historical Record (Dublin, 1938–).

Journal of the Cork Historical and Archaeological Society (Cork, 1892–).

Journal of the Galway Historical and Archaeological Society (Galway, 1900–).

Journal of the County Louth Archaeological Society (Dundalk, 1904–).

Studies (Dublin, 1912–; quarterly).

Irish Ecclesiastical Record (Dublin, 1864-1968; monthly).

Ulster Genealogical & Historical Guild Newsletter (Belfast, 1978–).

SERIES

Studies in Irish History. Edited by T. W. Moody and others. First series, vols i-vii, London, 1944-56; second series, vols i-x, 1960–75.

New History of Ireland Ancilliary Publications. Edited by T. W. Moody, F. X. Martin, and F. J. Byrne. Dublin, 1971–.

Dublin Historical Association. Irish history series. Dundalk, 1961–.

Dublin Historical Association. Medieval Irish history series. Dundalk, 1964–.

Irish Life and Culture: a series of pamphlets issued by the Cultural Relations Committee of Ireland. Dublin, 1950–.

Bibliography: bibliographies, serial publications, and festschrifts

The Thomas Davis Lectures. A continuing programme of half-hour talks, mainly on Irish history, culture, and social life, broadcast annually by Radio Telefís Éireann from 1953. Many Thomas Davis series have been published in book form, especially as paperbacks; a complete list for 1953-67 by F. X. Martin, is in *Irish Historical Studies,* xv, no. 59 (Mar. 1967). Most of the published Thomas Davis series are included in sections II-XII above.

Insights into Irish History. Edited by L. M. Cullen. Dublin, 1971–

The O'Donnell Lectures. An annual series of lectures on Irish history, given in rotation at the colleges of the National University of Ireland. Dublin: National University of Ireland, 1957–.

Public Record Office of Northern Ireland. Education Facsimiles. Belfast: H.M. Stationery Office, 1969–. (Packs of 20 loose documents with general introduction, notes, and illustrations; 14 packs published to date)

National Library of Ireland. Facsimile Documents. Dublin: Coordinating Committee for Educational Services based on the institutions of science and art, 1976–. (Packs of loose documents, on similar plan to preceding; 9 packs published to date)

FESTSCHRIFTS

John Ryan (ed.). *Féil-sgríbhinn Eóin Mhic Néill; Essays and studies presented to Eoin Mac Neill.* Dublin, 1940.

H. A. Cronne, T. W. Moody, and D. B. Quinn (ed.). *Essays in British and Irish history in honour of James Eadie Todd.* London, 1949.

J. A. Watt, J. B. Morrall, and F. X. Martin (ed.). *Medieval studies presented to Aubrey Gwynn, S.J.* Dublin, 1961.

John Bossy and Peter Jupp (ed.) *Essays presented to Michael Roberts, sometime professor of modern history in the Queen's University of Belfast.* Belfast, 1976.

K. R. Andrews, N. P. Canny, and P. E. H. Haire (ed.). *The westward enterprise: English activities in Ireland, the Atlantic, and America, 1480-1650.* Liverpool, 1978. (Essays in honour of D. B. Quinn)

Art Cosgrove and Donal McCartney (ed.). *Studies in Irish history presented to R. Dudley Edwards.* Dublin, 1979.

Thomas Bartlett and D. W. Hayton (ed.). *Penal era and golden age, 1690-1800.* Belfast, 1979. ('A tribute to J. C. Beckett')

F. S. L. Lyons and R. A. J. Hawkins (ed.). *Ireland under the union: varieties of tension: essays in honour of T. W. Moody.* Oxford, 1980.

J. F. Lydon (ed.). *England and Ireland in the later middle ages: essays in honour of Jocelyn Otway-Ruthven.* Dublin, 1981.

Peter Roebuck (ed.). *Plantation to partition: essays in Ulster history in honour of J. L. McCracken.* Belfast, 1981.

J. M. Goldstrom and L. A. Clarkson (ed.). *Irish population, economy, and society: essays in honour of the late K. H. Connell.* Oxford, 1981.

A CHRONOLOGY OF IRISH HISTORY

We are grateful to the Oxford University Press for generous permission to draw upon *A new history of Ireland*, vol. viii: *A chronology of Irish history to 1976* (Oxford, 1982). A hyphen between dates (e.g. 742-8) signifies a period or process; a solidus (e.g. 1161/2) signifies alternative dates for a specific event or events; a saltire (e.g. 1145 x 1151) signifies the period within which a specific event, which cannot be more precisely dated, occurred. Dates between 1582 and 1752 are given according to Old Style for the day and the month but according to New Style for the year. The following abbreviations are used:

a.	*ante* (before)
c.	*circa* (about)
con.	Conservative party
d.	died
D.U.P.	Democratic Unionist Party
F.F.	Fianna Fáil party
F.G.	Fine Gael party
G.B.	Great Britain
I.F.S.	Irish Free State
I.R.A.	Irish Republican Army
lab.	Labour party
lib.	Liberal party
N.I.	Northern Ireland
N.I.L.P.	Northern Ireland Labour Party
N.U.I.	National University of Ireland
P.M	prime minister
R.I.	Republic of Ireland
R.U.C.	Royal Ulster Constabulary
R.T.E.	Radio Telefís Éireann
S.D.L.P.	Social Democratic and Labour Party
T.C.D.	Trinity College, Dublin
U.C.C.	University College, Cork
U.C.D.	University College, Dublin
U.C.G.	University College, Galway
U.D.A.	Ulster Defence Association
U.D.R.	Ulster Defence Regiment
U.K.	United Kingdom

2,000,000-30,000 B.C.	Pleistocene period: intense cold of great ice age. Topography of Ireland much as today; sea-level fluctuating.
3000 B.C.	Sea-level stabilised: building of megalithic tombs begins.
2500 B.C.	Radiocarbon dating for building of passage grave at Newgrange (Co. Meath): wheat cultivated at Newgrange.
1800 B.C.	Tin (probably from Cornwall) alloyed with copper to make bronze; gold worked.

Chronology of Irish history

1200 B.C.	Later phase of bronze age: gold ornaments very numerous; many new types of object, including weapons and ornaments, made under influences from northern Europe.
680 B.C.	Radiocarbon dating for first circular inhabitation enclosure at Emain Machae (Navan fort, near Armagh).
500 B.C.	Iron metallurgy in Ireland, though bronze-age economy still in evidence.
200 B.C.	Bronze and iron objects: sculpture in stone and wood; Turoe stone.
1-500 A.D.	Building of crannogs, hill forts, and ring forts continues; earliest examples of La Tène-influenced art-styles in Ireland.
c.130-80	Ptolemy's 'Geography'; includes detailed map of Ireland with identifiable names of rivers, towns and tribes.
297-c.450	Irish raids on Roman Britain.
431	Palladius sent as first bishop to Irish Christians by Pope Celestine; 'Annals of Ulster' begin.
432	Traditional date of St Patrick's mission.
c.445-53	Probable floruit of Niall Noígiallach, founder of Uí Néill dynasty.
a.c.490	St Éndae founds earliest Irish monastery at Aran.
493	Traditional date for death of St Patrick (Wed., 17 Mar.).
c.500-700	Archaic Old Irish linguistic period.
520-c.620	Efflorescence of early Irish monasticism.
524/6	Death of St Brigit of Kildare (1 Feb.).
546	Derry founded by St Colum Cille (Columba).
547/8	Clonmacnoise founded by St Ciarán.
c.550	Beginnings of monastic Hiberno-Latin writing: hymns and penitentials.
c.550-c.600	Earliest Irish law texts committed to writing.
563	Iona founded by St Colum Cille (Pentecost Sunday, 13 May).
575	Convention of Druim Cett (Co. Londonderry).
c.580-c.680	Latin literature flourishes in Ireland: works of Latin grammar and biblical exegesis.
c.590	St Columbanus begins Irish mission on Continent: founds Annegray, Luxeuil, and Fontaines.
a.597	The Cathach psalter: earliest Irish MS, allegedly written by St Colm Cille, now in Royal Irish Academy, Dublin.
615	Death of St Columbanus at Bobbio (Sun., 23 Nov.).
622	Death of St Cóemgen (Kevin) of Glendalough (3 June).
635-51	St Aidan's mission from Iona to Northumbria: founds Lindisfarne.
649-50	Death of St Fursu in France (16 Jan.); buried at Péronne (Peronna Scottorum, Picardy) by founder, Erchinoald, mayor of the palace in Neustria.
c.650-750	High achievement in Irish metal-working; stone sculpture: Ossory group of high crosses; classical period of Old Irish laws.
664	Synod of Whitby: Roman Easter accepted in Northumbria; Colmán, bishop of Lindisfarne, and his adherents retire to Ireland; found Inishbofin (668).
c.668-730	Gradual transition from tribalism to dynastic polity in Ireland.

426

670-*c*.690	Armagh seeks to establish its primacy; Muirchú and Tírechán write hagiographical works on St Patrick.
680 x 691	Antiphonary of Bangor written.
689	Martyrdom of St Kilian at Würzburg (8 July).
c.692 x 697	Adomnán's 'Vita Columbae'.
698-700	Three years of famine and pestilence; cannibalism rumoured.
c.700-750	Moylough belt shrine; Tara brooch; Ardagh chalice.
c.700-*c*.900	Classical Old Irish linguistic period.
710 x 725	Compilation of Irish canon law ('Collectio Hibernensis') by Cú Chuimne of Iona and Rubin mac Connad of Dairinis (Molana Island, near Youghal).
716	Iona accepts Roman Easter.
720	Othmar founds monastery of St Gallen, Switzerland.
c.740	Compilation of 'Senchas Már', Irish legal corpus.
	Ending of Iona chronicle; compilation of annals continued in Ireland; earliest genealogical corpus for whole of Ireland compiled.
742-8	St Boniface clashes with St Vergilius and other Irish missionaries in Germany.
c.750-800	St Gall Gospels and Book of Kells illuminated.
c.750-75	Composition of Irish World Chronicle at Bangor.
c.770-*c*.840	Céle Dé (Culdee) reform movement within Irish church.
795	First viking raids on Ireland.
c.800	'Félire Óengusso', martyrology in Old Irish verse, by Óengus mac Óengobann 'the Culdee'; Stowe Missal written.
802	Iona raided by vikings.
806	Iona raided by vikings; chief relics removed to Kells.
807-13	Vikings raid western seaboard.
823	Bangor raided by vikings: bishops and scholars killed.
824	Bangor again raided by vikings; Skellig raided by vikings.
825	Dícuil's geography, 'De mensura orbis terrarum', written at Frankish court; Dúngal teaches at Pavia.
837-76	Intense viking activity in Ireland: semi-permanent bases established.
841	Permanent Norse encampment (*longphort*) at Annagassen, Co. Louth, and at Dublin (nucleus of later kingdom of Dublin).
845	Viking leader Turgéis drowned by Máel Sechnaill mac Máele Ruanaid, king of Mide.
	Johannes Scottus Eriugena joins royal school at Laon.
848-58	Sedulius Scottus at Liège.
853	Olaf (Amlaíb) 'son of king of Laithlind' assumes sovereignty over Norse kingdom of Dublin.
861-2	Áed Findliath, king of Ailech, allies with Dublin Norse against high-king.
876-916	'Forty years peace': relative respite from viking attacks on Ireland.
900-*c*.911	Hiberno-Norse infiltration of Cumberland, Lancashire, and Cheshire.
900-*c*.1050	Early Middle Irish linguistic period
	Decline of Latin learning; elaboration of Irish native traditions; *dindshenchas* poetry

900 *(cont.)*	Secularisation of monastic schools.
908	Flann Sinna, king of Tara, defeats Cormac mac Cuilennáin, king-bishop of Cashel, at Belach Mughna, Co. Carlow.
*c.*909 x 916	Flann's cross (Cross of Scriptures) erected at Clonmacnoise.
914	Large viking fleet establishes a base at Waterford.
916-19	Reign of High-king Niall Glúndub.
916-37	Renewed viking activity in Ireland.
920-52	Dublin kings strike coins at York.
921-6/7	Sitric, grandson of Ivar, king of Dublin, reigns in York Godfrid, grandson of Ivar, rules in Dublin.
922	Foundation of Norse town of Limerick.
*a.*924	Muiredach's cross at Monasterboice.
964	Rise of Dál Cais: Mathgamain mac Cennétig seizes kingship of Cashel.
*c.*970-80	St Catroe of Armagh founds monastery at Metz.
975	Death of Cináed ua hArtacáin, 'chief poet of Ireland'. Monastery of St Martin's at Cologne assigned to Irish monks.
978	Brian Bóruma mac Cennétig defeats Máel Muad mac Brain and becomes king of Munster.
980	Máel Sechnaill II mac Domnaill, king of Mide, defeats Olaf Cuarán, king of Dublin, and Hebridean Norse, at battle of Tara, and succeeds to high-kingship on death of Domnall Ua Néill at Armagh.
981,989	Máel Sechnaill II captures Dublin.
995	Máel Sechnaill II captures Dublin for third time; seizes ring of Thor and sword of Carlus.
999	Brian Bóruma defeats Máel Mórda, king of Leinster, and Sitric Silkbeard at Glen Máma (near Saggart, Co. Dublin).
1000	Brian Bóruma captures Dublin (Jan.) and burns Wood of Thor: Sitric Silkbeard submits.
1002	Máel Sechnaill II acknowledges Brian Bóruma as high-king of Ireland.
1005	Brian Bóruma visits Armagh: leaves 20 ounces of gold on altar and confirms primacy of Armagh (entry by his secretary Máel Suthain in Book of Armagh).
1006	Brian Bóruma claims hostages from north: undisputed high-king of Ireland.
1014	Battle of Clontarf (23 Apr., Good Friday): Munster forces under Brian Bóruma defeat and kill Máel Mórda, king of Leinster, and Jarl Sigurd of Orkney, with much slaughter on both sides; Brian killed (buried at Armagh).
1014	Máel Sechnaill II resumes high-kingship; continues till his death in 1022.
1022-72	High-kingship in abeyance. Age of scholarly activity; synthetic historians; compilation of 'Lebor Gabála'; translations of Latin epics into Irish; devotional literature.
1028	Sitric Silkbeard, king of Dublin, and Flannacán, king of Brega, go on pilgrimage to Rome.
*c.*1028 x 1036	Christ Church cathedral founded by Sitric and Dúnán, first bishop of Dublin.

1049	Irish monk, Aaron of Cologne, consecrated archbishop of Cracow (d. 1060).
c.1050-c.1200	Late Middle Irish linguistic period: reworking of traditional sagas; elaboration of pseudo-historical tracts; new recensions of genealogical tracts.
1066	Irish missionary bishop, Johannes, martyred in Mecklenburg.
1068	Sons of Harold Godwinson attack Bristol with Irish fleet.
1074	Death of Dúnán, first bishop of Dublin (6 May); Patricius (Gilla Pátraic) consecrated by Lanfranc; Lanfranc's letters to Toirrdelbach Ua Briain and Gofraid, king of Dublin, urging ecclesiastical reforms.
1075	Church of St Peter at Regensburg granted to Marianus Scottus II and Irish pilgrims.
c.1090-1130	Flowering of Irish romanesque metalwork.
1092	Manuscript of 'Annals of Inisfallen' written; continued by various hands until 14th century.
c.1100	Gerald of Windsor, castellan of Pembroke, marries Nest, daughter of Rhys ap Tewdwr.
1101	First synod of Cashel: Muirchertach Ua Briain grants Cashel to church; Máel Ísu Ua hAinmere bishop of Cashel (and papal legate?).
1102	Muirchertach Ua Briain marries one daughter to Sigurd, king of Man, son of Magnus Bareleg, king of Norway, and another to Arnulf of Montgomery, who sends Gerald of Windsor as his envoy to Ireland. St Anselm, archbishop of Canterbury, writes to Muirchertach Ua Briain urging ecclesiastical reforms
c.1107	Gilla Espuic of Limerick corresponds with St Anselm; composes 'De statu ecclesiae'.
1111	Synod of Ráith Bressail: diocesan organisation of Irish church planned. Domnall Ua Briain assumes kingship of the Hebrides.
1120	Óenach Tailten revived by Toirrdelbach Ua Conchobair.
1124	Round tower at Clonmacnoise finished by Gilla Críst Ua Máel Eóin and Toirrdelbach Ua Conchobair.
1124-7	St Malachy bishop of Down and Connor and abbot of Bangor.
1127-34	Building of Cormac's chapel at Cashel.
1127-1226	Irish romanesque architecture and sculpture flourish.
1130	Compilation of Leinster codex, Rawlinson B 502: earliest Irish genealogical manuscript extant.
1132	St Malachy consecrated archbishop of Armagh.
1134	Cormac's chapel at Cashel consecrated.
1137	Conchobar Ua Briain and Diarmait Mac Murchada with 200 ships from Dublin and Wexford lay siege to Waterford; Ua Briain submits to Mac Murchada in return for overlordship of Desmond.
1139	St Malachy visits Rome to ask Innocent II for two pallia; visits St Bernard at Clairvaux.
1142	First Irish Cistercian house founded at Mellifont.
1145 x 1151	St Bernard of Clairvaux writes to Diarmait Mac Murchada 'king of Ireland' admitting him to membership of Cistercian confraternity.

1151	Battle of Móin Mór (in north Co. Cork): Toirrdelbach Ua Briain, king of Munster, defeated by Toirrdelbach Ua Conchobair and Diarmait Mac Murchada: 7,000 Munstermen killed.
1152	Synod of Kells convened (6 Mar.); later transferred to Mellifont: Cardinal Paparo brings four pallia and completes diocesan organisation of Irish church; departs (24 Mar.).
	Diarmait Mac Murchada abducts Dervorgilla, wife of Tigernán Ua Ruairc.
1155	Proposal for invasion of Ireland by Henry II discussed at council of Winchester but rejected (29 Sept.).
1155-6	John of Salisbury visits Pope Adrian IV at Rome (Nov.– July); obtains papal privilege (bull *Laudabiliter?*) approving projected conquest of Ireland by Henry II.
1162	Synod of Clane, in presence of Diarmait Mac Murchada and Gilla Meic Liac: primacy of Armagh reaffirmed; ordinance that only alumni of Armagh should be recognised as *fir léigind* (lectors) in Irish churches.
	Lorcán Ua Tuathail consecrated archbishop of Dublin by Gilla Meic Liac, archbishop of Armagh.
	Diarmait Mac Murchada gains complete control over Dublin.
1166	Tigernán Ua Ruairc marches to Ferns: destroys castle of Diarmait Mac Murchada; Ruaidrí Ua Conchobair banishes Mac Murchada from Ireland (1 Aug.); Mac Murchada flees to Bristol.
1167	Mac Murchada returns from Wales with small force of Flemings under Richard fitz Godebert of Rhos; recovers kingdom of Uí Chennselaig (Aug.).
1169	Robert fitz Stephen, Hervey de Montmorency, and Maurice de Prendergast land at Bannow Bay, Co. Wexford (May).
	Wexford captured by Diarmait Mac Murchada, assisted by Normans.
1170	Richard de Clare (Strongbow), earl of Strigoil, lands near Waterford (23 Aug.); captures the city, and marries Aífe, daughter of Mac Murchada (25 Aug.).
	Dublin captured by Mac Murchada and Norman allies (21 Sept.); custody given to Miles de Cogan (1 Oct.).
1171	Mac Murchada dies at Ferns (*c.* 1 May); succeeded by his son-in-law, Strongbow.
	Henry II lands at Crook, near Waterford (17 Oct.).
	Henry II at Dublin; submission of kings of north Leinster, Bréifne, Airgialla, and Ulster (11 Nov.).
1171-2	Second synod of Cashel in session (winter).
1171/1172	Henry II grants charter to Dublin.
1172	Meath (Ua Máel Sechlainn kingdom of Mide) granted to Hugh de Lacy by Henry II (*c.* 1 Apr.).
	Pope Alexander III writes to the Irish kings enjoining fealty to Henry II (20 Sept.).
1174	Death of Flann Ua Gormáin, 'arch-lector of Armagh and of all Ireland' (since 1154; had studied in France and England for 21 years).

*c.*1174	Henry II grants charter to Dublin, conceding free-trading rights throughout his dominions.
1175	Treaty of Windsor between Henry II and Ruaidrí Ua Conchobair (6 Oct.).
1177	John de Courcy invades Ulster and captures Downpatrick; builds castle (*c.*1 Feb.).
	Council of Oxford: John, 10-year-old son of Henry II, designated 'Lord of Ireland' (May).
*p.*1179	Irish monks of Schottenkloster at Vienna take control of German monastery at Kiev (Russia).
*c.*1180	John de Courcy marries Affreca, daughter of Godred, king of Man; Hugh de Lacy marries daughter of Ruaidrí Ua Conchobair.
1180 x 1190	Carrickfergus castle built by de Courcy.
1183	First visit to Ireland of Gerald of Wales (Feb.).
1185	Pope Lucius III orders annual convocation of abbots of Irish Benedictine monasteries in Germany to be held at Regensburg.
	John, lord of Ireland, lands at Waterford (25 Apr.); leaves Ireland (17 Dec).
*c.*1188	Gerald of Wales completes 'Expugnatio Hibernica'.
*c.*1200	Standardisation of classical Modern Irish grammar and of poetic diction and metre by bardic schools.
*c.*1200-*c.*1650	Classical Modern Irish linguistic period.
1204	Dublin castle established as centre of royal administration.
1207	First national coinage, carrying symbol of the harp.
1210	King John lands at Waterford (20 June).
	Carrickfergus captured by John; the de Lacys flee; Maud de Braose and her son William captured (28 July).
1213	Philip II Augustus prepares to invade England; William Marshal leads '500' Anglo-Irish barons to England in support of John.
1215	Schottenklöster formally organised as 'national' order under abbot of St Jakob at Regensburg.
1216-27	The 'conspiracy of Mellifont' by Irish Cistercians.
1216	Magna Carta issued for Ireland (12 Nov.; transmitted, Feb. 1217).
1217	Royal mandate against promotion of Irishmen to cathedral benefices (14 Jan; repudiation of mandate by Honorius II, 1220).
1224	First Irish Dominican foundations, at Dublin and Drogheda.
*c.*1224-30	First Irish Franciscan foundations, at Youghal and Cork.
1226	Abbot of Clairvaux appointed by general chapter to reform Irish Cistercian houses.
1227	All Connacht granted as fief to Richard de Burgh (21 May).
1237-8	Encastellation of Connacht by Anglo-Irish.
*c.*1239	Thomas Aquinas, pupil of Peter of Ireland, (professor of philosophy at University of Naples).
*a.*1247	Connacht shired.
1250	Pope revokes ordinance of certain Irish prelates excluding Irishmen from Irish canonries (24 Sept.).
1251	Mint opened at Dublin (Oct.; over £43,000 coined before closure, 1254).

1252	'Irish riot' at Oxford University; written agreement of peace (similarly in 1267 and 1274).
1257	Battle of Credran (Co. Sligo): Fitz Gerald advance northwards halted by O'Donnells.
1258	At Caeluisce, on the river Erne, the sons of the kings of Thomond and of Connacht acknowledge Brian O'Neill as king of Ireland.
1259	Áed Ó Conchobair marries daughter of Dubgall Mac Sumarlaide, who brings dowry of 160 *gallóclaig*.
1260	Battle of Downpatrick (16 May): Brian O'Neill defeated and killed by justiciar.
1261	Battle of Callan (near Kenmare): Fíngen Mac Carthaig defeats justiciar (William of Dene); numerous castles destroyed.
1262-3	Irish kings offer high-kingship to Haakon IV, king of Norway, for support in expelling English from Ireland.
1264	Parliament at Castledermot (18 June).
1265	Norman-French poem composed on building of defences at New Ross.
1270	Battle of Áth in Chip (near Carrick-on-Shannon): Walter de Burgh defeated by Áed Ó Conchobair; his brother William Óc killed.
1280	Anglo-Irish magnates directed to assemble for purposes of examining Irish petition for English law.
1297	Parliament at Dublin: liberties and counties represented; beginning of widespread representation.
1299	Parliament at Dublin (20-27 Jan; 3 May): towns represented.
1300	Parliament at Dublin (24 Apr.): counties and towns represented.
1301	Large Irish army serves with Edward I in Scotland, under command of justiciar (Wogan).
1310	Parliament at Kilkenny: statute against reception of Irishmen as members of Anglo-Irish religious houses (9 Feb.).
1311	Papal permit for establishment of university *(studium generale)* at Dublin (see 1320).
1315	Edward Bruce lands at Larne (26 May); captures Dundalk and is inaugurated as 'high king' (29 June).
1315-17	Famine in western Europe, including Ireland.
1316	Edward Bruce crowned king of Ireland near Dundalk (*c.* 1 May).
1316-31	Friar James, O.F.M., of Ireland, accompanies Odoric de Pordenone as far as China.
1318	Battle of Faughart: Edward Bruce defeated and killed by John de Bermingham (14 Oct.).
1320	Parliament at Dublin: approval for foundation of university at Dublin (27 Apr. see 1311, 1465).
1323	Dame Alice Kyteler convicted of heresy by Richard Ledred (Leatherhead), bishop of Ossory (2 July).
c. 1325	'Book of Kildare' compiled: collection of literary and religious pieces, in Latin, English, and Norman-French
c. 1327/8	Petition from 'divers men of Ireland' to Edward III that English law be available to Irishmen without special charter.

*c.*1330	Manuscript collection of poems and other literary composition in Hiberno-English, Norman-French, and Latin, compiled (B.L., Harl.MS913).
1331	Ordinances for conduct of Irish government: include decree that there should be one law *(una et eadem lex)* for Irish and Anglo-Irish, except for betaghs.
1337-44	Richard FitzRalph at papal court, Avignon.
1348	Black Death appears at Howth and Drogheda (early Aug.).
1351	'Nodlaig na Garma': convention of poets and men of learning held by Uilliam Buidhe Ó Ceallaigh; Gofraidh Fionn Ó Dálaigh's poem 'Filidh Éireann go haointeach' (Christmas).
1366	Parliament at Kilkenny: 'statute of Kilkenny' promulgated (19 Feb.).
1378 x 1392/4	'Book of Uí Mhaine' written for Muircheartach Ó Ceallaigh, bishop of Clonfert.
1394	Richard II arrives at Waterford (2 Oct.).
1395	Irish kings submit to Richard II (Jan.–Apr.); Richard returns to England (15 May).
1399	Richard II again in Ireland (1 June–27 July).
1409-10	League of mendicant friars in Ireland against attacks of John Whitehead at Oxford.
1416-18	Great Book of Lecan compiled by Giolla Íosa Mór Mac Fir Bhisigh with assistance of Murchadh Riabhach Ó Cuíndlis and Ádhamh Ó Cuirnín.
1422	Further proclamation for expulsion of Irishmen and Irish students from England.
1423	Observant priory (O.S.A.) established at Banada, Co. Sligo; first house of friars observant movement in Ireland.
1431	Polyphonic choir established at St Patrick's cathedral, Dublin.
1435	Ordinance prohibiting Irish poets and musicians from being in Anglo-Irish areas (1 Apr.).
1445	Uilliam Ó Raghallaigh becomes first Irish-born provincial of Franciscans in Ireland.
1446	Royal charter to guild of barbers and surgeons at Dublin (18 Oct.). First known use of term 'Pale' to denote area under Dublin control.
1449	Richard, duke of York, arrives in Ireland as lieutenant; returns to England (22 Aug.).
1459	Yorkists defeated at Ludford Bridge (12 Oct.); duke of York takes refuge in Ireland.
1460	Parliament at Drogheda: duke of York confirmed as lieutenant by Anglo-Irish in opposition to Ormond; declaration that only acts of Irish parliament should bind Ireland (8 Feb.). Yorkists defeated at battle of Wakefield; duke of York killed (30 Dec.).
1461	Henry VI deposed (4 Mar.); replaced by Edward IV, son of Richard, duke of York; Lancastrians defeated at Towton (29 Mar.).
1462	Battle of Pilltown, Co. Kilkenny: Ormond's supporters defeated by Thomas Fitzgerald, earl of 7th earl of Desmond.
1463	Thomas Fitzgerald succeeds his father as 8th earl of Desmond; appointed lord deputy by Edward IV (1 Apr.).
1465	Desmond's project to set up a university at Drogheda.

1468	Tiptoft holds parliament at Drogheda: earls of Desmond and Kildare and Edward Plunkett attainted; Desmond executed (4 Feb.).
1478-1513	Supremacy of Gerald or Garret Fitzgerald, 8th earl of Kildare (Gearóid Mór, 'the great earl').
1485	Battle of Bosworth: Richard III defeated and killed; succeeded by Lancastrian Henry VII.
1487	Lambert Simnel crowned king of England as Edward VI at Christ Church, Dublin (24 May).
	First recorded use of firearms in Ireland, by troops of Aodh Ruadh Ó Domhnaill.
1491	Perkin Warbeck (claiming to be Richard, son of Edward IV) lands at Cork (Nov.).
1494-5	Sir Edward Poynings lord deputy.
1494	Parliament at Drogheda: 'Poynings' law' enacted (1 Dec; see 1782).
1495	Waterford besieged by supporters of Perkin Warbeck (July).
1499-1506	Maurice O'Fihely, O.F.M., Conv., of Tuam edits works of Duns Scotus (printed at Venice).
c. 1500	Book of Lismore written for Finghín Mac Carthaigh Riabhach.
1504	Battle of Knockdoe, near Galway: earl of Kildare with Ó Domhnaill and English of Pale defeat Clanricard and Ó Briain (19 Aug.).
1513	Garret More, 8th earl of Kildare, dies of gunshot wounds; succeded as 9th earl and lord deputy by his son Garret Oge.
1519	Kildare summoned to London (12 Jan.).
1520	Thomas Howard, earl of Surrey, appointed lord lieutenant (10 Mar.) and sent to Ireland with 500 troops (23 May).
	Henry VIII directs Surrey to subdue Irish lords 'rather. . . by sober ways. . . and amiable persuasions, founded in law and reason, than by. . . strength or violence' (Sept.[?]).
1521	Surrey submits plan for reconquest to Henry VIII (30 June).
	Henry VIII sends livery of knighthood to Conn Bacach Ó Néill.
1529	Gonzalo Fernandez, chaplain of Charles V, arrives in Ireland to treat with earl of Desmond (24 Feb.).
1532	Garret, 9th earl of Kildare (Gearóid Óg) appointed deputy; James Butler, son of earl of Ossory, treasurer; George Cromer, archbishop of Armagh, chancellor (5 July).
1533	Henry VIII marries Anne, daughter of Sir Thomas Boleyn, earl of Wiltshire and Ormond (25 Jan.).
1534	Kildare leaves for England; his son, Thomas, Lord Offaly ('Silken Thomas'), appointed as his deputy (Feb.).
	Revolt of Silken Thomas (June).
1535	Surrender of Silken Thomas (Aug.).
1536	'Reformation parliament' in Dublin (1-31 May): Silken Thomas and others attainted; royal supremacy enacted.
1537	Execution of Silken Thomas and his five uncles in London (3 Feb.).
	Acts of parliament (Oct.–Dec.): against authority of pope; for suppression of monasteries.

434

1538	Brian O'Connor of Offaly submits to Lord Deputy Grey: gives undertakings containing germ of 'surrender and regrant' policy (6 Mar.).
1539	Dissolution of monasteries within Pale begins.
	O'Neill and O'Donnell routed by Lord Deputy Grey at Bellahoe, on Meath-Monaghan border (Aug.).
1540-43	Lord Deputy St Leger's pacification: introduction of 'surrender and regrant'.
1541	Henry VIII declared 'king of Ireland' by act of Irish parliament (18 June).
1542	First Jesuit mission to Ireland (Feb.–Mar.).
	Conn O'Neill created earl of Tyrone, with succession to his illegitimate son, Matthew, created baron of Dungannon (1 Oct.).
1547-53	Edwardian reformation in Ireland.
1549	First English act of uniformity prescribes use of Book of Common Prayer (14 Mar.).
	English Book of Common Prayer ordered to be used in Ireland (9 June).
1550-57	Plantation in Leix and Offaly.
1552	Second English act of uniformity prescribing use of second Book of Common Prayer (14 Apr.).
1553-8	Marian reaction in Ireland: restoration of papal authority.
1555	Bull of Pope Paul IV making Ireland a kingdom.
1558	Matthew, baron of Dungannon, killed by order of Shane O'Neill.
1559	Shane O'Neill succeeds Conn as The O'Neill (*a.* 17 July).
1560	Elizabeth's first Irish parliament (11/12 Jan.–1 Feb.) restores royal supremacy and prescribes use of second English Book of Common Prayer (with amendments).
1561 7	Rebellion of Shane O'Neill.
1561	Shane O'Neill proclaimed a traitor (8 June).
1562	Shane O'Neill submits to Elizabeth at Whitehall (6 Jan.); returns to Ireland (26 May); again in rebellion (Nov.).
	Brian O'Neill, 2nd baron of Dungannon, killed by Turlough Luineach O'Neill, tanist to Shane O'Neill (12 Apr.); Brian's brother taken to England.
1564	Shane O'Neill campaigns against MacDonnells of Antrim (Sept.).
1565	Shane defeats MacDonnells at Glenshesk (2 May).
1566	Shane O'Neill burns cathedral of Armagh (Aug.).
1567	Shane O'Neill defeated by O'Donnell at Farsetmore, near Letterkenny (8 May); takes refuge with MacDonnells, and killed by them at Cushendun, Co. Antrim (2 June).
1568	Hugh O'Neill recognised as baron of Dungannon (1 Mar.).
1568-73	First Desmond rebellion.
1569	Act for the attainder of Shane O'Neill (11 Mar.).
	Sir Edward Fitton appointed president of Connacht (1 June).
1570	Pope Pius V excommunicates Queen Elizabeth by bull *Regnans in excelsis* (25 Feb.).
	Sir John Perrot appointed president of Munster (13 Dec.).
1571	First printing in the Irish language in Dublin (June).
1573-6	Earl of Essex's attempt to set up colony in Antrim.

1575	Massacre on Rathlin Island by Essex's soldiers (26 July).
1579	Sir Nicholas Malby appointed president of Connacht (31 Mar.).
1579-83	Second Desmond rebellion.
1580	Revolt in Leinster headed by Viscount Baltinglass and Fiach MacHugh O'Byrne (July); government force defeated by O'Byrne in Glenmalure (25 Aug.).
	Papal force at Smerwick massacred by government force under Lord Deputy Grey (10 Nov.).
1582	Bull of Pope Gregory XIII for reform of calendar: 4 Oct. 1582 to be followed by 15 Oct.; year to begin on 1 Jan. (24 Feb.; see 1751).
1584	Hugh O'Neill, baron of Dungannon, made tanist to Turlough Luineach O'Neill (Mar.).
	Dermot O'Hurley, archbishop of Cashel, hanged in Dublin (20 June).
1585	Parliament in Dublin (26 Apr.–25 May): Baltinglass attainted; Hugh O'Neill takes seat in house of lords as earl of Tyrone.
	Commissioners make agreements with Connacht landowners – 'composition of Connacht' (July–Oct.).
1585	Scheme for plantation in Munster (Dec.).
1586	Parliament in Dublin (26 Apr.–14 May): Desmond and his supporters attainted.
	Agreement made by Lord Deputy Perrot with Sorley Boy MacDonnell and his nephew Angus: greater part of the Route (region in north Antrim extending south-east of Coleraine to Ballymoney and east to Dunluce) granted to Sorley Boy; the Glens (east Antrim from Ballycastle to Larne) granted to Angus (18 June).
1587	Hugh O'Neill granted patent conferring title of earl of Tyrone.
1588	About 25 ships of Spanish armada wrecked off Irish coasts (Sept.).
1590	Foundation of first Irish college, Alcalá, on the Continent.
1591	Earl of Tyrone marries Mabel Bagenal, sister of Sir Henry Bagenal, marshal of the army (3 Aug.).
	Hugh Roe O'Donnell (kidnapped by government at Rathmullen, Sept. 1587), escapes from Dublin castle (26 Dec.).
1592	Charter incorporating Trinity College, Dublin (3 Mar.).
1595-1603	Rebellion of Hugh O'Neill, earl of Tyrone.
1595	Earl of Tyrone defeats Bagenal's force at Clontibret, Co Monaghan (13 June).
	Turlough Luineach dies (Sept.); succeeded as The O'Neill by earl of Tyrone.
1596	Fiach MacHugh O'Byrne revolts (Sept.; killed May 1597).
1598	Bagenal defeated by Tyrone at the Yellow Ford, between Armagh and Blackwater (14 Aug.).
	Munster plantation attacked by *súgán* earl of Desmond (Oct.).
1599	Phelim MacFeagh O'Byrne routs English force at Deputy's Pass, near Wicklow (29 May).
	Sir Conyers Clifford, president of Connacht, killed in engagement with Hugh Roe O'Donnell in Curlew mountains, Co. Roscommon (5 Aug.).

436

1600	Tyrone campaigns in Munster (Feb.-Mar.). Expedition to Lough Foyle under Sir Henry Docwra lands at Culmore (15 May) and establishes strong position at Derry.
1601	Spanish army under Don Juan del Águila to support Tyrone lands at Kinsale (Sept.); invested by government forces under Lord Deputy Mountjoy (26 Oct.); Tyrone and O'Donnell, attempting to cooperate with the besieged, are heavily defeated by Mountjoy (24 Dec.). O'Donnell leaves Ireland for Spain (27 Dec.); Tyrone withdraws to Ulster.
1602	Águila surrenders Kinsale to Mountjoy. Tyrone's principal vassal, Donal O'Cahan, submits to Docwra (27 July). Hugh Roe O'Donnell dies at Simancas (Aug.). O'Neill inaugural chair at Tullahogue, Co. Tyrone, destroyed by Mountjoy (Sept.). Rory O'Donnell, brother and successor of Hugh Roe, submits to Mountjoy (Dec.).
1603	Death of Elizabeth and accession of James I (24 Mar.). Surrender of Tyrone at Mellifont (30 Mar.). First assizes held in Donegal; first sheriffs appointed for Donegal and Tyrone. Rory O'Donnell, brother of Hugh Roe, created earl of Tyrconnell (29 Sept.).
1605	Proclamation declaring all persons in the realm to be the free, natural and immediate subjects of king and not subjects of any lord or chief (11 Mar.).
1606	Irish custom of gavelkind declared illegal by royal judges (Jan./Feb.). Foundation of St Anthony's Franciscan College, Louvain.
1607	Earls of Tyrone and Tyrconnell and others secretly sail from Lough Swilly – 'flight of the earls' (4 Sept.). Fugitive earls and their associates charged with high treason, and their lands declared forfeited (Dec.).
1608	Tanistry declared illegal by court of king's bench (Jan./Feb.). Revolt of Sir Cahir O'Doherty, of Inishowen (Apr.–July).
1608-10	Preparations for plantation in six escheated counties in Ulster – Donegal, Coleraine, Tyrone, Armagh, Fermanagh, and Cavan.
1610	Agreement between crown and city of London for plantation of city of Derry, town of Coleraine, county of Coleraine, and barony of Lough-insholin, Co. Tyrone (28 Jan.). Settlers from England and Scotland begin to arrive in Ulster.
1612	Cornelius O'Devany, O.F.M., bishop of Down and Connor, convicted of treason (Jan.) and hanged in Dublin (Feb.). Dungannon incorporated (27 Nov.) – first of 40 new boroughs, many in Ulster, incorporated between Nov. 1612 and May 1613.
1613	Charter incorporating Derry as city of Londonderry, creating new county of Londonderry, incorporating Irish Society of London, and granting to it most of temporal land in Co. Londonderry (29 Mar.; see 1635).
1613-5	James I's Irish parliament.
1621	Authorisation for plantations in parts of Leitrim, King's County, Queen's County, and Westmeath (20 Jan.).

1625	England at war with Spain.
1626	Charles I offers concessions ('graces') to his Irish subjects in return for grants to maintain an expanded army (22 Sept.).
1627	England at war with France.
1628	Charles issues 'graces' in return for promise of £40,000 a year for 3 years.
1632	Compilation of the Annals of the Four Masters by Michael O'Clery and others, begins at Donegal (completed 10 Aug. 1636).
1633	Viscount Wentworth (created earl of Strafford, 12 Jan. 1640) lord deputy (July).
1634-5	Charles I's first Irish parliament.
1635	City of London and Irish Society found guilty of mismanagement and neglect of Londonderry plantation; sentenced to fine of £70,000 and forfeiture of Londonderry property etc. (28 Jan.; see 1657).
1635-6	Wentworth prepares for a plantation in Connacht.
1640	Charles I's second Irish parliament meets (16 Mar.).
1641	Bill for the attainder of earl of Strafford passed by English house of commons (21 Apr.; Strafford executed, 12 May).
	Rising begins in Ulster (22 Oct.).
	Government forces defeated at Julianstown Bridge, near Drogheda, by Ulster rebels (29 Nov.).
	Meeting at Knockcrofty, near Drogheda, between Ulster Irish and Old English (Dec.), leads to alliance between them.
1642	Scottish army under Robert Munro lands at Carrickfergus (15 Apr.).
	First regularly constituted presbytery in Ireland meets at Carrickfergus (10 June).
	Owen Roe O'Neill arrives in Ulster (8/9 July).
	Civil war begins in England (22 Aug.).
	Catholic confederacy ('confederation of Kilkenny') instituted (Oct.).
1643	Cessation of hostilities between royalists and confederates (15 Sept.).
1645	End of civil war in England; last pitched battle at Langport, Som. (10 July).
	Secret 'Glamorgan treaty' between king and confederates (25 Aug.).
	Archbishop Giovanni Rinuccini, papal envoy to confederates, arrives at Kenmare, Co. Kerry (12 Oct.).
	Second secret 'Glamorgan treaty' (20 Dec.).
1646	'Ormond peace' with confederates (28 Mar.).
	Monro defeated at Benburb, Co. Tyrone, by Owen Roe O'Neill (5 June).
	Rinuccini and O'Neill repudiate 'Ormond peace' (Aug.–Sept.).
1647	Ormond surrenders Dublin to parliamentary forces under Col. Michael Jones (July).
	Jones defeats confederates at Dungan's Hill, near Trim (8 Aug.).
1648	Second civil war in England (May-Aug.); Scots defeated by Cromwell at Preston, Lancs. (17 Aug.).
	Open breach between O'Neill and confederate council (Sept.).
1649	Second 'Ormond peace' with confederates (17 Jan.).
	Execution of Charles I (30 Jan.).
	Departure of Rinuccini from Ireland (23 Feb .).

438

1649 *(cont.)*   Jones defeats Ormond at Rathmines (2 Aug.).
Cromwell arrives at Dublin as commander-in-chief (15 Aug.).
Cromwell takes Drogheda by storm: massacre of garrison (about 2,600) and
townspeople (11 Sept.).
Cromwell takes Wexford: second massacre (about 2,000) (11 Oct.).
New Ross surrenders to Cromwell (19 Oct.).
Owen Roe O'Neill dies at Cloughoughter, Co. Cavan (6 Nov.).
1650   Cromwellian conquest completed (Jan.-May).
1652   Act for the settlement of Ireland (12 Aug.).
1652-3   Cromwellian land-confiscation.
1653   'Barebones' parliament (4 July–12 Dec.), in which Ireland and Scotland are
represented by 6 and 5 members respectively.
1654   First Protectorate parliament meets (3 Sept.); Ireland represented by 30
members.
1657   Charter of Cromwell restoring Londonderry property etc. to city of London
(see 1635, 1662).
1658   Death of Cromwell (3 Sept.).
1660   Restoration of monarchy in England (Feb.–May); Charles II proclaimed
king in Dublin (14 May).
Navigation act, for controlling England's external trade (13 Sept.); treats
England and Ireland as an economic unit.
1660-65   Restoration land settlement (act of settlement, 1662; court of claims,
1662-3; act of explanation, 1665).
1661-6   Charles II's Irish parliament.
1662   Charter of Charles II replacing Cromwell's charter of Londonderry (10 Apr.;
see 1657).
1662-9   Ormond lord lieutenant.
1663   England act restricts Irish trade with colonies and importation of Irish cattle
into England (27 July).
1666   English act prohibits importation of Irish cattle into England (18 Jan.).
1671   Second English navigation act prohibits direct importation from colonies to
Ireland (22 Apr.); act expires in 1681 (18 Jan.) but is renewed in 1685
(2 July).
1672   First grant of *regium donum* to presbyterian ministers (*c.* Oct.).
1677-85   Ormond again lord lieutenant.
1678-81   'Popish plot'.
1681   Execution of Archbishop Oliver Plunkett in London (1 July).
1685   Death of Charles II and accession of James II (6 Feb.).
1687   Richard Talbot, earl of Tyrconnell, lord deputy (Feb.).
1688   Derry and Enniskillen defy James II (Dec.).
1689   James II arrives at Kinsale (12 Mar.).
Siege of Derry (18 Apr. – to 28 July).
James II's Irish parliament (7 May – 18 July).
Defenders of Enniskillen defeat Jacobite force at Newtownbutler, Co.
Fermanagh (31 July).

Chronology of Irish history

1690	William III lands at Carrickfergus (14 June), defeats James II at Oldbridge on River Boyne (1 July); departure of James II to France.
	First siege of Limerick (9-30 Aug.).
	Jacobite force under Patrick Sarsfield destroys Williamite baggage train at Ballyneety (11 Aug.).
1691	Williamite victory at Aughrim (12 July).
	Second siege of Limerick (Sept.–Oct.).
	Treaty of Limerick (3 Oct.) marks end of war: Irish army allowed to go to France and continue in James II's service; catholics promised the religious privileges they enjoyed in Charles II's reign.
	First recorded meeting of presbyterian general synod of Ulster (at Antrim, 30 Sept.).
	Catholics effectively excluded from parliament and public office in Ireland by act of English parliament (24 Dec.).
1691-1703	Williamite land confiscation.
1693	Death of Patrick Sarsfield, after battle of Landen (23 July).
1695-1709	Penal legislation against catholics.
1698	William Molyneux's tract, *The case of Ireland's being bound by acts of parliament in England stated,* published in Dublin (Apr.).
1699	English act restricting export of Irish woollens (26 Jan.).
1700	Subsidy authorised to Louis Crommelin for establishing a linen industry (14 Feb.).
1701	James II dies at St Germains (6 Sept.); his son recognised by Louis XIV as James III.
1702	William III dies (8 Mar.); succeeded by Anne.
1704	Sacramental test for public office, applicable both to catholics and protestant dissenters (4 Mar.).
1705	English act permits direct export of Irish linen to American colonies (14 Mar.).
1707	Union of English and Scottish parliaments takes effect (1 May).
1709	Irish house of lords expresses hope that Irish union with England will follow union of England and Scotland (9 May).
1710	Board of trustees for linen manufacture established (28 Aug.).
1713	Jonathan Swift installed as dean of St Patrick's cathedral, Dublin (13 June).
1714	Anne dies (1 Aug.); succeeded by George I, first of Hanoverian line.
1715	Jacobite rising in Scotland under earl of Mar (Sept.–Nov.).
1718	Beginning of extensive migration of Ulster Scots to American colonies (June-July).
1719	Toleration act for protestant dissenters (2 Nov.).
1720	British act (6 George I, c.5) declaring right of British parliament to legislate for Ireland and denying appellate jurisdiction of Irish house of lords (7 Apr.).
1722	Patent to William Wood to coin copper halfpence for circulation in Ireland (12 July).
1724	First of Swift's 'Drapier's letters' (Feb./Mar.; 2nd letter, 6 Aug.; 3rd letter, 5 Sept.; 4th letter, *To the whole people of Ireland,* 22 Oct.; 5th letter, 31 Dec.).

1726	Abraham Shackleton, quaker, opens school at Ballitore, Co. Kildare (1 Mar.; continues as headmaster till 1756; Edmund Burke a pupil, 1741-3). Non-subscribing presbyterians separate from main presbyterian body to form presbytery of Antrim (June).
1727	George I dies (11 June): succeeded by George II.
1729	Foundation stone laid of Edward Lovet Pearce's new parliament building in College Green (3 Feb.; parliament meets there for first time, 5 Oct. 1731). New wave of emigration of Ulster Scots to American colonies.
1731	Dublin Society for Improving Husbandry, etc. formed (25 June; 'Royal Dublin Society', 19 June 1820).
1736	House of commons condemns tithe of agistment on pasturage for dry and barren cattle (18 Mar.).
1737	First number of *Belfast News Letter* (1 Sept.).
1739	British act removing duties on import of Irish woollen yarn into G.B. (14 June).
1739-41	Severe weather, bad harvest, fever, and famine.
1742	Handel's 'Messiah' performed for first time in Music Hall, Fishamble St., Dublin (13 Apr.; first performance in Cork, 6 Dec. 1744).
1745	Jacobite rising under 'Young Pretender' begins in Scotland (July; Jacobite victory at Prestonpans, 21 Sept.; defeat at Culloden, 16 Apr. 1746). Earl of Chesterfield lord lieutenant (31 Aug.; till Mar. 1746).
1751	British act for reform of calendar (22 May; see above, 1582; takes effect on 2 Sept. 1752, next following day becoming 14 Sept.). Irish parliament authorises application of revenue surplus to reduction of national debt (19 Dec.); dispute between house of commons and government.
1752	Building of west front of Trinity College begins (completed, 1759).
1753	Renewed dispute between house of commons and government over revenue surplus.
1757	Lying-in hospital (known as Rotunda from 1767) opened in Dublin (8 Dec.).
1758	'Wide street commissioners' for Dublin appointed by Irish parliament (29 Apr.). British act permitting the importation of salted beef, pork, and butter from Ireland (20 June).
1759	British act removing restrictions on import of Irish cattle into G.B. (5 Apr.). Henry Flood enters parliament (21 Nov.); becomes leader of opposition. Rioting in Dublin on rumour of legislative union with G.B. (3 Dec.).
1760	François Thurot enters Belfast Lough with three French ships and takes Carrickfergus (21 Feb.; withdraws 26 Feb.). Origin in Dublin of Catholic Committee on initiative of Dr John Curry, Charles O'Conor, and Thomas Wyse (c.31 Mar.). George II dies (25 Oct.); succeeded by George III.
1761	Beginning of Whiteboy movement in Munster (c.Oct.–Dec.).
1763	Oakboy or Hearts of Oak disturbances begin in Ulster. First number of *Freeman's Journal* (10 Sept.; last number, 19 Dec. 1924).
1764	Rotunda concert hall built (see 1757).

1766	Fr Nicholas Sheehy, convicted of inciting Whiteboys to murder, executed at Clonmel (15 Mar.)
	Tumultuous risings act, against Whiteboys (7 June).
1767-72	Lord Townsend lord lieutenant.
1768	Octennial act, limiting life of parliament to 8 years (16 Feb.).
1769	Steelboy or Hearts of Steel disturbances in Ulster (July).
1768-9	Money bill dispute between house of commons and government.
1771	Benjamin Franklin in Ireland (5 Sept.–*c.*23 Oct.); attends meeting of house of commons (10 Oct.).
1772	Act to repress Steelboy disturbances in five Ulster counties (28 Mar.; repealed in 1774).
	'Bogland act' enables catholics to take bog reclamation leases of 61 years (2 June).
1773	First performance, at Covent Garden Theatre, London, of Oliver Goldsmith's 'She stoops to conquer' (15 Mar.).
1774	Act enabling catholics to testify their allegiance to king (2 June).
1775	First performance, at Covent Garden Theatre, London, of R. B. Sheridan's 'The rivals' (17 Jan.).
1775-83	War of American independence.
1775	Henry Flood appointed vice-treasurer (27 Oct.), abandoning parliamentary opposition.
	Henry Grattan's maiden speech in house of commons (15 Dec.); takes Flood's place as leader of opposition.
1776	New anti-Whiteboy act (Apr.; made perpetual in 1800).
	Arthur Young begins tour of Ireland (20 June; continued in 1777 and 1778; his *Tour of Ireland* published in 1780).
	American declaration of independence (4 July).
1778	Volunteer movement begins with enrolling of company in Belfast (17 Mar.).
	John Paul Jones, American privateer, twice raids Belfast Lough (Apr.).
	Gardiner's first catholic relief act, enabling catholics to take leases for 999 years and to inherit in same way as protestants (14 Aug.).
1779	Belfast Charitable Society decides to set up cotton manufacturing in Poorhouse (19 May).
	Volunteers, parading in College Green, demand removal of restrictions on Irish trade (4 Nov.).
1780	British act allows Ireland to trade with British colonies on equal terms with G.B. (24 Feb.).
	Grattan in house of commons moves resolutions in favour of legislative independence (19 Apr.).
	Relief act repeals sacramental test for protestant dissenters (2 May; see 1704).
	Mutiny act (Aug.) (perpetual; see 1782).
	John Beresford appointed chief commissioner of revenue (16 Dec.).
1781	British force under Cornwallis surrenders to Washington at Yorktown (Va): virtual end of war of American independence.
	First stone of James Gandon's Custom House, Dublin, laid (8 Aug.; opened, 7 Nov. 1791).

1782   Habeas corpus act (12 Feb.).

Ulster Volunteer convention at Dungannon adopts resolutions in favour of legislative and judicial independence and relaxation of penal laws (15 Feb.).

Grattan again moves for an address to king declaring Ireland's right to legislative independence (22 Feb.).

Grattan for third time moves declaration of rights, which is carried unanimously by both houses of parliament (16 Apr.).

Gardiner's second catholic relief act allowing catholics to acquire land, except in parliamentary boroughs, and removing other disabilities, including various restrictions on catholic clergy and catholic worship (4 May).

Act validating marriages by presbyterian ministers (4 May).

Act establishing Bank of Ireland (4 May; bank opens, 25 June 1783).

House of commons votes £50,000 to purchase lands to be settled on Grattan (31 May).

British act repealing declaratory act of 1720, and thereby conceding parliamentary independence (21 June).

Poynings' law (see 1494) amended: all bills approved by both houses of parliament to be transmitted unaltered to London—Yelverton's act (27 July).

Act for securing the independence of the judiciary—Forbes's act (27 July).

Gardiner's third catholic relief act, allowing catholics to be teachers and to act as guardians (27 July).

Mutiny act (annual; see 1700) (July).

1783   British renunciation act acknowledging exclusive right of Irish parliament to legislate for Ireland and exclusive jurisdiction of Irish courts (17 Apr.).

Second Volunteer convention at Dungannon to prepare for parliamentary reform (8 Sept.).

National Volunteer convention on parliamentary reform, at Rotunda, Dublin (10 Nov.–2 Dec.).

Volunteers' parliamentary reform bill rejected by house of commons by 157 to 77 (19 Nov.).

William Pitt P.M. of G.B. (19 Dec.).

1784   Act regulating corn trade—Foster's corn law (14 May).

Opening of St Mary's catholic chapel, Belfast, attended by First Belfast Volunteer Company (30 May).

Formation of Peep o'Day Boys (protestant) and Defenders (catholic) arising out of dispute (4 July) at Markethill, Co. Armagh.

Radical reform congress in William Street, Dublin (25-7 Oct.; second session, 20 Jan.–4 Feb. 1785; third session, 20-30 Apr.).

1785   Pitt's proposals for regulating trade between G.B. and Ireland introduced in Irish house of commons by Thomas Orde, chief secretary (7 Feb.; scheme abandoned, Aug.).

First meeting of Irish Academy (3 May; title changed to Royal Irish Academy by charter, 28 Jan. 1786).

1785 *(cont.)*   Renewed disturbances of Whiteboys, now called Rightboys, in Munster (Sept.).
1786   First stone of James Gandon's Four Courts laid (3 Mar.; first sitting of judges there, 3 Nov. 1796).
               Belfast Academy opened (1 May; becomes Belfast Royal Academy, 1887).
1788   George III becomes insane (5 Nov.; regency crisis; king declared to have recovered, 10 Mar. 1789).
1789   John Fitzgibbon (earl of Clare, 12 June 1795) appointed lord chancellor.
               Meeting of States General at Versailles (5 May) opens the way to revolution in France.
               Whig Club formed in Dublin (26 June).
               Fall of Bastille, in Paris (14 July).
1790   Northern Whig Club formed in Belfast (28 Feb.).
               Edmund Burke's *Reflections on the revolution in France* published (1 Nov.).
1791   Thomas Paine's *Rights of man,* pt 1, published (13 Mar.; pt 2, 1792).
               Demonstrations in Dublin, Belfast, and elsewhere commemorating fall of Bastille (14 July).
               Wolfe Tone's *Argument on behalf of the catholics of Ireland (c.* 22 Aug.).
               Tone's first visit to Belfast (Oct.): Society of United Irishmen founded (14 Oct.).
               First meeting of Dublin Society of United Irishmen (9 Nov.).
               Viscount Kenmare and 67 others secede from Catholic Committee, in which John Keogh is now dominant (27 Dec.).
1792   First number of *Northern Star,* organ of Belfast United Irishmen (4 Jan.); editor, Samuel Neilson.
               Langrishe's catholic relief act, allowing catholics to practise as solicitors and barristers (18 Apr.) and repealing laws against intermarriage of protestants and catholics.
               Gathering of Irish harpers in Belfast (11-14 July).
               Wolfe Tone appointed agent and assistant secretary of Catholic Committee (25 July).
               Catholic convention in Tailors' Hall, Dublin (3-8 Dec.).
               Catholic delegates, accompanied by Tone, travel from Dublin to London via Belfast to present petition to king (Dec.).
1793   Execution of Louis XVI in Paris (21 Jan.).
               France declares war on G.B. (1 Feb.).
               Convention of Ulster Volunteers at Dungannon (15-16 Feb.); proclamation suppressing them (11 Mar.).
               Hobart's catholic relief act, giving catholics the parliamentary franchise and removing most of their remaining disabilities, but leaving them excluded from parliament, judgeships, and the higher public offices (9 Apr.).
               Act establishing militia, at strength of 14,948 (9 Apr.; strength increased to 21,660 in 1795).
               Convention act, prohibiting any assembly, other than parliament, chosen to represent the people (16 Aug.).

1793 *(cont.)*   Opening of St Patrick's College, Carlow, the first catholic college for
                 higher studies in Ireland (1 Oct.).
1794   United Irishmen's plan of parliamentary reform published (15 Feb.).
                 Rev. William Jackson, agent of French revolutionary government,
                 arrested in Dublin (28 Apr.).
                 Dublin Society of United Irishmen suppressed (23 May).
1795   Fitzwilliam's viceroyalty (Jan.–Mar.); disaster for catholic expectations.
                 Suicide of William Jackson (30 Apr.).
                 Act providing for establishing catholic seminary at Maynooth (5 June;
                 Royal College of St Patrick opened, *c.* 1 Oct.).
                 Tone embarks at Belfast for America (13 June).
                 'Battle of the Diamond', near Loughgall, Co. Armagh, between Peep
                 o' Day Boys and Defenders (21 Sept.), leads to foundation of Orange
                 Society.
1796   Tone arrives in France from U.S.A. (1 Feb.).
                 Insurrection act (24 Mar.).
                 Habeas corpus suspension act (26 Oct.; continued to 1 June 1799).
                 Act regulating new yeomanry corps (9 Nov.).
                 French invasion fleet, with Tone on board, in Bantry Bay (22-7 Dec.).
1797   Bank of Ireland suspends gold payments (26 Feb.).
                 General Gerard Lake begins disarming of Ulster (13 Mar.).
                 William Orr, United Irishman, hanged at Carrickfergus (14 Oct.).
1798   Leaders of Leinster directory of United Irishmen arrested (12 Mar.).
                 Arrest of Lord Edward Fitzgerald (19 May; dies from wound 4 June).
                 United Irish rising in Leinster (May-June): insurgents initially successful in
                 Co. Wexford, but defeated at Tara (26 May), Curragh (29 May), New Ross
                 (5 June), Arklow (9 June), and Vinegar Hill, near Enniscorthy (21 June);
                 massacre of protestants at Scullabogue, Co. Wexford (5 June).
                 United Irish rising in Ulster (June): insurgents defeated at Antrim (7 June),
                 and Ballynahinch (13 June).
                 French force under General Humbert in Connacht (Aug.–Sept.): defeats
                 government forces at Castlebar (27 Aug.); surrenders to Cornwallis, lord
                 lieutenant, at Ballinamuck (8 Sept.).
                 French squadron under Admiral Bompart, with Tone on board, defeated
                 outside Lough Swilly (12-20 Oct.); Tone captured at Buncrana (3 Nov.).
                 Tone convicted of high treason by court martial in Dublin and sentenced to
                 be hanged (10 Nov.); cuts his throat (12 Nov.) and dies in provost marshal's
                 prison, Dublin barracks (19 Nov.).
1799   Last session of Irish parliament (15 Jan.–2 Aug.): Pitt in British house of
                 commons advocates parliamentary union of G.B. and Ireland (31 Jan.);
                 Irish house of commons passes union proposals (5-6 Feb.); union bills
                 introduced in Irish house of commons (21 May); and in British (17 June);
                 British act of union (2 July), Irish act (1 Aug.).
                 Orange lodges pass resolutions against union (Feb.–Mar.).
1801   Union of Great Britain and Ireland begins (1 Jan.).
1802   Peace of Amiens between Britain and France (27 Mar.).

1803	Renewed war between G.B. and France (18 May). Rising of Robert Emmet in Dublin (23 July); Emmet convicted of high treason (19 Sept.) and executed (20 Sept.). Thomas Russell convicted at Downpatrick of high treason (20 Oct.); executed (21 Oct.). Michael Dwyer, in revolt in Wicklow since 1798, surrenders to government (14 Dec.).
1808	Work on site in Sackville Street for monument to Viscount Nelson begins (30 Jan.). Controversy over proposed royal veto on appointments to catholic bishoprics (May–Sept.); veto proposals rejected by bishops (14-15 Sept.); rise of Daniel O'Connell. Christian Brothers, lay teaching order, founded by Edmund Rice at Waterford (Aug.).
1811	Kildare Place Society founded to conduct non-denominational schools (2 Dec.).
1813	Catholic relief bill introduced by Grattan in U.K. house of commons (30 Apr.; defeated by 251 to 247, 24 May).
1814	Belfast Academical Institution opened (1 Feb.; 'Royal' prefixed to title, 1831).
1815	Napoleon defeated at Waterloo (18 June); end of war with France.
1816	Failure of potato crop causes famine, aggravated by typhus epidemic (Aug.–Oct.).
1817	Typhus epidemic widespread (continues till Dec. 1819, causes some 50,000 deaths). Exchequers of G.B. and Ireland amalgamated as from 5 Jan., under consolidated fund act (1 July 1816). Foundation stone of Wellington obelisk in Phoenix Park laid (17 June; completed 1820).
1820	Grattan dies in London.
1821	George IV visits Ireland (12 Aug.–3 Sept.): Dunleary harbour renamed Kingstown. Failure of potato crop (Sept.–Nov.).
1822	Fever follows famine in west of Ireland (June; continues till Dec.).
1823	Catholic Association founded in Dublin (12 May).
1826	Irish currency assimilated with British as from 5 Jan., under currency act of 27 June 1825. Act providing for uniform valuation of lands and tenements for purpose of local taxation (26 May; Richard Griffith later appointed commissioner of valuation). Fever epidemic and collapse of textile industry in Dublin, Belfast, Cork, and other towns (*c.*July). General election (June-July): O'Connell successfully mobilises catholic electors for Villiers Stuart against Lord George Beresford in Co. Waterford; sitting M.P.s similarly defeated in counties Westmeath, Louth, and Monaghan by supporters of catholic emancipation.

446

1828	O'Connell returned M.P. in by-election in Clare (24 June), defeating Vesey Fitzgerald by 2,057 votes to 982.
1829	Relief act enabling catholics to enter parliament, belong to any corporation, and hold higher offices in state—'catholic emancipation' (13 Apr.).

Act raising county franchise from 40s. to £10 freehold (13 Apr.).

O'Connell returned unopposed for Clare (30 July; enters parliament (4 Feb. 1830) after taking new oath of allegiance).

Non-subscribing presbyterians withdraw from synod of Ulster (Aug.–Sept.; they form the remonstrant synod of Ulster, 25 May 1830).

1830 George IV dies (26 June); succeeded by William IV.

1831 'Tithe war' beings: 120 police move into Graiguenamanagh, Co. Kilkenny, to seize cattle in payment of the tithe (3 Mar.); 'tithe massacre' at Newtownbarry, Co. Wexford (18 June); 12 police killed serving processes at Carrickshock, Co. Kilkenny (14 Dec.).

Scheme of primary education instituted (Nov.).

1832 Asiatic cholera appears in Belfast and Dublin (Jan.; spreads throughout Ireland and continues till 1833).

Parliamentary reform act (7 Aug.): Irish seats increased from 100 to 105, and £10 franchise introduced in boroughs; electorate increased to 1.2% of population.

1833 Church temporalities act (14 Aug.) abolishes 10 bishoprics and provides for appointment of ecclesiastical commissioners.

Tithe arrears act (29 Aug.).

1834 Repeal of union debated in house of commons on motion of O'Connell (22-30 Apr.).

National bank founded under O'Connell's auspices in London (21 June).

Opening of Dublin-Kingstown railway, the first in Ireland (17 Dec.).

1835 'Lichfield House compact' between whigs, radicals, and O'Connellites (Feb.–Mar.).

First and second reports of select committee of house of commons on Orangeism presented to house (20 July); followed by two other reports (presented on 6 Aug. and 7 Sept.).

Thomas Drummond under-secretary (25 July 1835); dies in office (15 Apr. 1840).

Association of Non-subscribing Presbyterians formed by combination of remonstrant synod, presbytery of Antrim, and synod of Munster.

1836 Grand Orange Lodge of Ireland decides to dissolve (14 Apr.).

Act amalgamating county constabulary and peace preservation force into centralised police force under inspector general (20 May; 'Royal Irish Constabulary' from 1867).

1837 William IV dies (20 June); succeeded by Victoria.

1838 Fr Theobald Mathew, O.F.M. Cap., with support of William Martin, a quaker, founds total abstinence movement, at Cork (10 Apr.).

Poor relief act (31 July) extends English poor law system to Ireland: elected boards of guardians, responsible to a poor law commission, set up to administer a workhouse system.

Act converting tithe into a rent charge (15 Aug.).

1839	The 'big wind' (6-7 Jan.).
1840	O'Connell forms National Association (15 Apr.; renamed Loyal National Repeal Association, 16 July).
	General synod of Ulster and secession synod combine to form General Assembly of the Presbyterian Church in Ireland (10 July).
	Municipal reform act (10 Aug.).
1841	Thomas Davis joins Repeal Association (17 Apr.).
	Defeat of whig ministry; Sir Robert Peel P.M. (30 Aug.).
	O'Connell elected lord mayor of Dublin (1 Nov.; till 1 Nov. 1842).
1842	Fr Mathew's total abstinence crusade at its peak (Jan.); 3 million pledged adherents.
	First number of *Nation* – the weekly founded by Young Ireland group – Thomas Davis, Charles Gavan Duffy, and John Blake Dillon.
1843	Repeal debate in Dublin corporation, Butt leading the case against O'Connell (28 Feb.–2 Mar.).
	Monster repeal meetings at Trim (9 Mar.) and Hill of Tara (15 Aug.).
	Meeting announced by O'Connell for 8 Oct. at Clontarf proclaimed by government (1 Oct.); O'Connell cancels meeting.
	O'Connell charged with conspiracy (14 Oct.).
	Devon commission into state of law and practice relating to occupation of land appointed (20 Nov.; reports, 14 Feb. 1845, recommending compensation for improvements and minor reforms).
1844	O'Connell and others found guilty (Jan.–Feb.); O'Connell sentenced to one year's imprisonment etc. (30 May); judgment reversed by house of lords (4 Sept.).
	Act to establish board of charitable donations and bequests (9 Aug.).
1845	Earl of Rosse's telescope at Birr castle comes into operation (15 Feb.) – the largest in the world; dismantled, 1908.
	Dispute between O'Connell and Young Ireland over Queen's Colleges scheme (May).
	Act providing for capital grant to Maynooth College of £30,000 and increasing annual grant from £8,928 to £26,360 (30 June).
	Queen's Colleges act (31 July; see 1849).
	Arrival of potato blight in Ireland reported in press (9 Sept.).
	Thomas Davis dies in Dublin (16 Sept.).
	Peel orders purchase in U.S.A. of £100,000 of Indian corn for Ireland (*c.*9-10 Nov.).
	Relief committee appointed by government (18 Nov.).
1846	Act authorising public works to relieve distress (5 Mar.).
	Act authorising county relief works (5 Mar.).
	Peel's act in effect repealing corn laws (26 June).
	Peel replaced as P.M. by Lord John Russell (30 June).
	Breach between O'Connell and Young Ireland over principle of physical force (28 July).
	Complete destruction of potato crop (Aug.–Sept.).
	Central Relief Committee of Society of Friends set up (13 Nov.).

448

1847   Irish Confederation formed (13 Jan.).
        Soup-kitchens system established; famine at its height (Feb.).
        O'Connell dies at Genoa (15 May; funeral in Dublin, 5 Aug.).
        Poor relief act (8 June) empowering boards of guardians to grant outdoor
            relief, but persons holding above one-quarter acre of land are excluded
            from benefit.
        First collection of agricultural statistics, undertaken by constabulary (*c*.June).
        Potato harvest good but small; corn harvest good (July).
        John Mitchel breaks away from *Nation* (Dec.; starts militant *United
            Irishman*, 12 Feb. 1848).
1848   Revolution in Paris (22-4 Feb.); Louis-Philippe abdicates.
        Treason-felony act (22 Apr.).
        Mitchel convicted under treason-felony act and sentenced to 15 years trans-
            portation (26-7 May).
        Last number of *United Irishman* (27 May); first number of John Martin's
            Irish Felon (24 June) includes first three articles by James Fintan Lalor
            on linking repeal to land question.
        General failure of potato crop (July–Sept.).
        Fifth and last number of *Irish Felon* (22 July).
        Young Ireland rising in Munster under William Smith O'Brien and others
            (July–Aug.); engagement between Confederates and police near Ballingarry,
            Co. Tipperary (29 July).
        O'Brien, Thomas Francis Meagher, Terence Bellew McManus, and Patrick
            O'Donohoe convicted of high treason and sentenced to death (7-9 Oct.;
            sentences commuted to transportation for life, 5 June 1049).
        Cholera reappears (Nov.; continues into 1849).
1849   William Crolly, catholic archbishop of Armagh, dies of cholera at Drogheda
            (6 Apr.).
        Potato blight reappears (May).
        Sectarian affray at Dolly's Brae, near Castlewellan, Co. Down (12 July).
        Encumbered estates act providing for creation of encumbered estates
            court (28 July).
        Queen Victoria and Prince Albert in Ireland (3-12 Aug.).
        Queen's Colleges at Belfast, Cork, and Galway opened to students (Oct.).
1850   Paul Cullen, catholic archbishop of Armagh (24 Feb.; translated to Dublin,
            3 May 1852; archbishop of Dublin, 1852-78).
        Tenant right conference in Dublin (6-9 Aug.), concluding in formation of
            Irish Tenant League.
        National synod of catholic bishops at Thurles: one of its statutes declares
            Queen's Colleges to be fraught with 'grave and intrinsic dangers' to catholics
            (22 Aug.–10 Sept.).
        Charter founding the Queen's University in Ireland (3 Sept.).
1851   Ecclesiastical titles act (1 Aug.), prohibiting assumption in U.K. of territorial
            titles by catholic bishops.
        Catholic Defence Association of Great Britain and Ireland formed (19 Aug.)
            — the 'Irish Brigade'.

1852	General election (July): about 40 M.P.s returned in Tenant League interest (July).
	Conference of Tenant League in Dublin: policy of independent opposition in parliament adopted (8-9 Sept.).
	William Keogh and John Sadleir, members of independent Irish party, accept office in Aberdeen's ministry (19 Dec.).
1853	Act extending income tax to Ireland (28 June).
	Queen Victoria and Prince Albert visit Dublin (29 Aug.–4 Sept.).
	Assembly's College, Belfast, opened for theological training of presbyterian clergy (5 Dec.).
	Robert Hickson opens yard at Queen's Island, Belfast, for building iron ships (Edward J. Harland becomes manager, Dec. 1854).
1854	Act making provision for establishment of National Gallery in Dublin (10 Aug.).
	Catholic University of Ireland opened (3 Nov.); J. H. Newman first rector.
1855	Emmet Monument Association formed in New York by Michael Doheny and John O'Mahony to work for Irish independence (*c.* Feb.).
	Cecilia Street School of Medicine opened as part of Catholic University (2 Nov.).
	Gavan Duffy emigrates to Australia (6 Nov.).
1856	James Stephens, former Young Irelander, returns to Ireland from exile in France (Jan.).
	Suicide of John Sadleir (17 Feb.).
	Phoenix Society formed at Skibbereen by Jeremiah O'Donovan (later called O'Donovan Rossa).
1857	Sectarian rioting in Belfast (13-19 July, Sept.).
1858	Secret organisation, later known as I.R.B. (Irish Republican Brotherhood), founded in Dublin by James Stephens (17 Mar.; parallel body, Fenian Brotherhood, founded in New York by John O'Mahony, Apr. 1859).
	Act providing for creation of General Medical Council to maintain standards in medical education and for registration of medical practitioners in U.K. (2 Aug.).
	Edward Harland buys Robert Hickson's shipyard at Belfast (see 1853), and takes into partnership Gustav Wilhelm Wolff (firm assumes name Harland & Wolff, 1 Jan. 1862).
1859	First number of *Irish Times* (29 Mar.).
	Independent Irish party splits (31 Mar); break up of Tenant League.
	Evangelical revival in Ulster; reaches its height with mass prayer-meeting in Botanic Gardens, Belfast (29 June).
1860	Series of excessively cold and wet seasons begins (Jan.; lasts till 1862, followed by droughts in 1863 and 1864); severe agricultural depression.
	Napier's land act (28 Aug.).
	Deasy's land act (28 Aug.).
	Partry (Co. Mayo) evictions.
1861	John George Adair evicts 47 tenants on his estate at Derryveagh, Co. Donegal (8-10 Apr.).

450

1861 *(cont.)*	American civil war begins (12 Apr.; ends, 26 Apr. 1865).
	Funeral of Terence Bellew McManus in Dublin (10 Nov.).
1862	Poor relief act (7 Aug.), extending provisions for outdoor relief and abolishing 'quarter acre' restriction of 1847 act.
1863	First number of *Irish People,* Fenian weekly (28 Nov.): Thomas Clarke Luby, proprietor, O'Donovan Rossa manager, John O'Leary editor.
1864	Laying of foundation-stone of O'Connell monument in Dublin (8 Aug.) leads to two weeks of sectarian rioting in Belfast.
	Stephens declares 1865 to be the date for the Fenian insurrection (*c.* Aug.).
1865	Dublin International Exhibition opened in Earlsfort Terrace (9 May).
	Police raid offices of *Irish People* (15 Sept.); Rossa, Luby, and O'Leary arrested; last number of paper, 16 Sept.
	Magee College, Londonderry, opened as combined arts and presbyterian theological college (10 Oct.).
	Stephens arrested (11 Nov.); rescued from Richmond prison, Dublin (24 Nov.).
1866	Habeas corpus suspended (17 Feb.; suspension continued till 1869).
	Fenian council of war rejects Devoy's plan for an immediate rising (20-21 Feb.).
	Devoy arrested (23 Feb.).
	Fenian raids on Canada (Apr.–June).
	Archbishop Cullen created cardinal (22 June), first Irishman to achieve this rank.
	Stephens deposed as head centre of Fenian Brotherhood (17 Dec.).
1867	Abortive Fenian attempt to seize Chester castle (11 Feb.).
	Fenian rising in counties of Kerry, Dublin, Cork, Limerick, Tipperary, and Clare (Feb.–Mar.).
	United Brotherhood or Clan na Gael founded at New York by Jerome J. Collins (20 June).
	Act providing for establishment of Public Record Office at Four Courts, Dublin (12 Aug.).
	I.R.B. convention at Manchester appoints Col. Thomas J. Kelly to succeed Stephens (17 Aug.).
	Rescue of Kelly and Capt. Timothy Deasy in Manchester (18 Sept.).
	Execution of Allen, Larkin, and O'Brien at Manchester (23 Nov.).
	Clerkenwell explosion (13 Dec.).
1868	Irish parliamentary reform act (13 July): borough franchise reduced from £8 to £4 rated occuperiship; lodger franchise introduced.
	General election (Nov.): liberal victory, Gladstone P.M. (3 Dec.).
	Thomas O'Hagan (Lord O'Hagan, 14 June 1870) lord chancellor of Ireland (18 Dec.); first catholic to hold this office since reign of James II.
1869	Release of 40 Fenian prisoners, including Charles Joseph Kickham (Mar.).
	Amnesty Association formed in Dublin (June).
	Act disestablishing and disendowing Church of Ireland (26 July; act takes effect, 1 Jan. 1871).

451

Chronology of Irish history

1870	First chapter of Kickham's *Knocknagow* published in New York *Emerald* and Dublin *Shamrock* (Mar.; whole work published in book form; Dublin, June 1873).
	Home rule movement launched by Isaac Butt in Dublin (19 May).
	Michael Davitt sentenced to 15 years penal servitude (18 July).
	Gladstone's first land act (1 Aug.).
1871	Release of 33 Fenian prisoners, including Devoy, Rossa, O'Leary, and Luby (Jan.).
	'Westmeath act' allowing detention without trial for agrarian offences (16 June).
	Fenian invasion of Canada (5 Oct.).
1872	Ballot act introduces secret voting (18 July).
	Sectarian rioting in Belfast (15-20 Aug.).
1873	Home Rule Confederation of Great Britian founded at Manchester (Feb.).
	Gladstone's university bill defeated (12 Mar.).
	Home rule conference at Rotunda, Dublin (18-21 Nov.): Home Rule League founded.
1874	General election: 59 professing home rulers returned (Feb.); Gladstone resigns; conservative ministry under Disraeli (20 Feb.).
	Butt's motion on home rule defeated in house of commons by 458 to 61 (30 June–2 July).
1875	John Mitchel elected M.P. for Tipperary (16 Feb.); barred from taking his seat; reelected (12 Mar); dies (20 Mar.).
	Parnell returned to parliament as member for Meath (19 Apr.).
	O'Connell centenary celebrations (5-7 Aug.).
	National synod of bishops at Maynooth (30 Aug.–20 Sept.): renews condemnation of Queen's Colleges (see 1850) and applies it to Trinity College (see 1970).
1876	'Skirmishing fund' instituted at New York by O'Donovan Rossa (Mar.).
	Catalpa rescue of six Fenian convicts from Western Australia (17-18 Apr.).
	Seventh annual convention of Clan na Gael in Philadelphia decides to form joint revolutionary directory with I.R.B. (8-15 Aug.).
	Supreme council of I.R.B. resolves to withdraw all support from home rule movement (20 Aug.).
1877	Parnell, Joseph Gillis Biggar, Frank Hugh O'Donnell, and other Irish 'obstructives' prolong sitting of house of commons for over 24 hours (31 July–1 Aug.).
	Parnell elected president of Home Rule Confederation of Great Britain in place of Butt (28 Aug.).
	First of three years of bad harvests and agricultural depression (culminating in major economic crisis in 1879).
	Davitt released from Dartmoor (19 Dec.).
1878	Earl of Leitrim murdered near Milford, Co. Donegal (2 Apr.).
	Intermediate education act (16 Aug.).
	Davitt on lecturing tour in America (Sept.–Dec.): he and Devoy propose 'new departure' for Fenian movement.
	'New departure' announced by Fenian leaders in New York (27 Oct.).

452

1879	Supreme council of I.R.B., at Paris, rejects 'new departure' proposals presented by Davitt and Devoy (Jan.).
	Land agitation launched with meeting at Irishtown, Co. Mayo (20 Apr.).
	Isaac Butt dies (5 May).
	Parnell at Westport land meeting (8 June): 'hold a firm grip of your homesteads and lands'.
	Repeal of convention act of 1793 (21 July).
	Land League of Mayo founded at Castlebar (16 Aug.).
	Irish National Land League founded in Dublin (21 Oct.).
	Duchess of Marlborough's fund for relief of distress opened (Dec.).
1879-82	The 'land war'.
1880	Mansion House fund for relief of distress opened (Jan.).
	Parnell addresses U.S. house of representatives on situation in Ireland (2 Feb.).
	Parnell launches Irish National Land League of the United States (11 Mar.).
	General election (Mar.–Apr.): triumph for Parnell and Land League; Gladstone again P.M. (23 Apr.); William Edward Forster chief secretary for Ireland (Apr.).
	Charter founding Royal University of Ireland (27 Apr.).
	Parnell elected chairman of Irish parliamentary party (17 May).
	'Boycotting' of Capt. Charles C. Boycott, of Lough Mask House, Co. Mayo (25 Sept.–26 Nov.).
	Viscount Mountmorres murdered near Clonbur, Co. Galway (25 Sept.)
	Parnell's speech at Galway (24 Oct.).
	Ladies' Land League of New York founded by Fanny Parnell (15 Oct.).
	Trial of Parnell and others for conspiracy begins in court of queen's bench (28 Dec.; ends, 25 Jan., in disagreement of jury).
1881	Ladies' committee under Anna Parnell set up by Land League (26 Jan.) – origin of Ladies' Irish National Land League.
	Davitt rearrested, in Dublin (3 Feb.).
	Protection of person and property act (2 Mar.).
	Peace preservation act (21 Mar.).
	Land League of Great Britain founded in London (25 Mar.).
	First number of *United Ireland,* weekly organ of Parnellites (13 Aug.), edited by William O'Brien.
	Second Gladstone land act (22 Aug.): '3 Fs' legalised.
	Arrest of Parnell (13 Oct.) and other Land League leaders.
	No-rent manifesto (18 Oct.).
	New land court opened at 24 Upper Merrion Street, Dublin (20 Oct.).
	Land League proclaimed as an unlawful association (20 Oct.).
1882	Queen's University in Ireland dissolved (3 Feb.).
	'Kilmainham treaty' (Apr.) accepted by cabinet (2 May); Forster resigns.
	Parnell, John Dillon, and James J. O'Kelly released from Kilmainham (2 May); Davitt from Portland (6 May).
	Lord Frederick Cavendish, new chief secretary, and Thomas Henry Burke, under-secretary, murdered in Phoenix Park (6 May; trial and

1882 *(cont.)* execution of Invincibles, Apr.–June 1883).
Davitt at Liverpool advocates land nationalisation in preference to peasant proprietorship as principle of land settlement (6 June).
New coercion act (12 July).
Arrears of rent act (18 Aug.).
Labourers' cottages and allotments act (18 Aug.).
Irish National League founded in Dublin, in succession to Land League (17 Oct.).

1883 Irish National League of America founded in Philadelphia in succession to American Land League (25-7 Apr.).
Letter of Roman Congregation of Propaganda 'De Parnellio' to Irish bishops and clergy forbidding them to take part in collection for Parnell tribute (11 May; Parnell receives cheque for over £37,000 at public meeting in Rotunda, 11 Dec.).

1884 Dynamite campaign in G.B.: Thomas James Clarke and three others sentenced to life imprisonment (June).
Gaelic Athletic Association founded at Thurles (1 Nov.).
Bill to redistribute parliamentary seats introduced by Gladstone (1 Dec.).
Franchise act (6 Dec.) gives vote to householders: immense increase in Irish rural electorate.

1885 Chamberlain's first draft of central board scheme (5 Jan.).
Parnell's 'ne plus ultra' speech at Cork (21 Jan.).
Irish Loyal and Patriotic Union founded to defend union of Great Britain and Ireland (1 May).
Chamberlain's central board scheme rejected by cabinet (9 May).
Defeat of Gladstone's second ministry (23 June); Salisbury P.M.
Act redistributing parliamentary seats (25 June).
Ashbourne act, providing for land purchase with advance by state of entire purchase money (14 Aug.).
Labourers act (14 Aug.).
Parnell's manifesto to Irish voters in G.B. calling on them to vote against liberals in forthcoming general election (21 Nov.).
General election (23 Nov.–19 Dec.): Parnell wins 85 seats and holds balance between liberals and conservatives.
Gladstone's conversion to home rule announced prematurely by his son (17 Dec.).

1886 Salisbury's government defeated (27 Jan.); Gladstone forms his third administration (1 Feb.).
Gladstone introduces home rule bill in house of commons (8 Apr.).
Rioting in Belfast (4-10 June, 7 July–19 Sept.).
Home rule bill defeated in house of commons by 341 to 311, some 93 liberals voting with the majority (8 June).
General election (July): Gladstone defeated; Salisbury ministry formed (25 July).
'Plan of Campaign' announced in *United Ireland* (23 Oct.).

1887   Arthur James Balfour chief secretary (Mar.; till Aug. 1892).
        'Parnellism and crime' articles published in *The Times* (Mar.-Dec.).
        Mgr Persico, papal envoy to Ireland (7 July – 24 Oct.).
        New coercion act (19 July).
        'Mitchelstown massacre' (9 Sept.).
        Radicals and nationalists demonstrating in Trafalgar Square, London, against imprisonment of William O'Brien, clash with police and troops: over 100 casualties — 'Bloody Sunday' (13 Nov.).

1888   Roman circular condemning Plan of Campaign (20 Apr.) and boycotting (20 Apr.).
        Parnell addresses the Eighty Club in London on Plan of Campaign and Roman circular (8 May).
        Special commission appointed to investigate charges against Parnell and others (13 Aug.).

1889   Pigott forgeries exposed before special commission (20-22 Feb.).
        Parnell and Gladstone at Hawarden (8-19 Dec., discussion on home rule).
        O'Shea files petition for divorce, citing Parnell as co-respondent (24 Dec.).

1890   Report of special commission (13 Feb.): Parnell and associates exonerated from most serious charges, including complicity in Phoenix Park murders (13 Feb.).
        Opening of Science and Art Museum and of National Library of Ireland (29 Aug.).
        First number in London of Davitt's weekly *Labour World* (26 Sept.; continues till 30 May 1891).
        Hearing of O'Shea divorce suit (15, 17 Nov.); verdict against Mrs O'Shea and Parnell (17 Nov.).
        Parnell reelected chairman of Irish parliamentary party (25 Nov.).
        Publication of Gladstone's letter to Morley urging Parnell's resignation (25 Nov.).
        Parnell's manifesto to the Irish people published (29 Nov.).
        Debates in Committee Room 15 on Parnell's leadership: majority decide against him (1-6 Dec.).

1891   Irish National Federation, organisation of anti-Parnellites, inaugurated in Dublin (10 Mar.).
        Conference in Dublin decides to form Irish Labour League (24 Mar.).
        O'Shea's divorce decree made absolute (June); Parnell marries Katharine O'Shea at Steyning, Sussex (25 June).
        Balfour act extends facilities for land purchases and establishes congested districts board (5 Aug.).
        Death of Parnell in Brighton (6 Oct.); funeral in Dublin, 11 Oct.
        John Redmond leader of Parnellites (Dec.).

1892   Ulster convention in Belfast (17 June): 12,000 delegates resolve to have nothing to do with any home rule parliament.
        General election (July); fourth Gladstone ministry formed (Aug.).
        Belfast Labour Party formed (29 Sept.), first labour party in Ireland.

1893	Gladstone introduces second home rule bill (13 Feb.).
	Report of evicted tenants commission (25 Feb.).
	Disturbances in Belfast (21-2 Apr.) as a result of second reading of home rule bill.
	Foundation of Gaelic League (31 July),
	Home rule bill passes house of commons (2 Sept.); defeated in house of lords (9 Sept.).
	Trade Union Congress meets in Belfast (5-9 Sept.).
1894	Resignation of Gladstone (3 Mar.); Rosebery P.M.
	Irish Agricultural Organisation Society formed by Horace Plunkett (28 Apr.).
	First Irish Trade Union Congress (27-8 Apr.).
	Childers commission appointed to inquire into financial relations between G.B. and Ireland (26 May; final report, 5 Sept. 1896).
	Alfred Webb, home rule M.P. for West Waterford, elected president Indian National Congress (26 Dec.).
1895	Rosebery ministry (lib.) defeated (11 June); Salisbury (con.) P.M. (25 June).
	General Election (July); defeat of liberals.
1896	Dillon elected chairman of anti-Parnellites (18 Feb.).
	Irish Socialist Republican Party formed in Dublin (29 May); secretary James Connolly.
	Irish race convention in Dublin (1-3 Sept.).
1898	William O'Brien launches United Irish League at Westport to agitate for dividing up grazing lands among small farmers (23 Jan.).
	Ancient Order of Hibernians (Board of Erin) unites with A.O.H. of America at Trenton, N.J. (27 June–1 July).
	Local government act provides for creation of elected county and district councils (12 Aug.).
	First number of Connolly's *Workers' Republic* (13 Aug.).
	T. J. Clarke released from Portland (29 Sept.).
	Davitt (M.P. since 1892) withdraws from parliament to protest against Boer war (25 Oct.).
	Queen Victoria in Ireland (3-26 Sept.).
1899	Irish Literary Theatre founded (May).
	First number of Arthur Griffith's *United Irishman* (4 Mar.).
	First number of *An Claidheamh Soluis,* official organ of Gaelic League (18 Mar.).
1900	Redmond elected leader of reunited Irish parliamentary party (6 Feb.).
	First number of D. P. Moran's *The Leader* (1 Sept.).
	Cumann na nGaedheal founded by Griffith (30 Sept.).
1901	Queen Victoria dies (22 Jan.); succeeded by Edward VII.
	Robertson commission on university education appointed (1 July; final report, 28 Feb. 1903).
	United Irish League of America formed at New York (4 Dec.).
1902	Ancient Order of Hibernians achieves unity in Ireland under Board of Erin (4 Mar.).
	Arthur James Balfour (con.) succeeds Salisbury as P.M. (12 July).

1902 *(cont.)*   Emergence of Ulster branch of Irish Literary Theatre (Nov.; renamed
                Ulster Literary Theatre, 1904).
                Dunraven land conference (20 Dec.; report, 3 June 1903).
1903   Irish Literary Theatre becomes Irish National Theatre Society (1 Feb.).
                Independent Orange Order formed in Belfast (11 June).
                Edward VII in Ireland (21 July–1 Aug.).
                Wyndam land act (14 Aug.).
1904   First instalment of Griffith's 'The resurrection of Hungary' in *United
                Irishman* (2 Jan.).
                Annie Fredericks Horniman adapts disused Mechanics' Institute, Abbey
                Street, Dublin, as a theatre and offers it rent-free to the National Theatre
                Society (Apr.); first performance in Abbey theatre, 27 Dec.
1905   Ulster Unionist Council formed (Mar.).
                First Dungannon Club formed by Bulmer Hobson in Belfast (8 Mar.).
                Magheramorne manifesto of Independent Orange Order (13 July); author
                Robert Lindsay Crawford.
                Scheme of devolution proposed in manifesto of Dunraven's Irish Reform
                Association (26 Aug.).
                Sinn Féin policy proposed by Griffith (28 Nov.).
                Resignation of Balfour; liberal administration formed by Sir Henry
                Campbell-Bannerman (5 Dec.).
1906   General election: victory for liberals (Jan.).
                First number of *Sinn Féin* edited by Griffith (5 May).
                Fry commission to inquire into Trinity College, Dublin (2 June; reports,
                31 Aug., 12 Jan. 1907).
                Dudley commission on congestion in Ireland (20 July; reports, 14 Nov.,
                5 May 1908).
                Peace preservation act of 1881 expires (31 Dec.): controls on possession and
                importation of arms relaxed.
1907   Sinn Féin League inaugurated through amalgamation of Dungannon
                Club with Cumann na nGaedheal (21 Apr.).
                Irish International Exhibition opens at Ballsbridge, Dublin (4 May; ends,
                9 Nov.).
                Irish council bill (May-June).
                Theft of state jewels from Dublin castle discovered (6 July).
                Mutiny of police in Belfast (24 July).
                Pius X issues *Ne temere* decree on mixed marriages (2 Aug.).
                Evicted tenants act (28 Aug.).
                Sinn Féin League amalgamates with National Council (5 Sept.; name Sinn
                Féin adopted Sept. 1908).
1908   C. J. Dolan defeated as Sinn Féin candidate for North Leitrim (21 Feb.).
                Herbert Henry Asquith P.M. (8 Apr.).
                Irish universities act, providing for institution of National University of
                Ireland and the Queen's University of Belfast (1 Aug.).
                Old age pensions act (1 Aug.).

1908 *(cont.)* Patrick Pearse opens St Enda's school for boys (8 Sept.).
Irish Transport and General Workers' Union formed; James Larkin general
secretary (29 Dec.).
1909 David Lloyd George introduces 'people's budget' (29 Apr.).
Fianna Éireann, headed by Countess Markievicz, formed by Bulmer Hobson
(16 Aug.).
Birrell's land act (3 Dec.) gives powers of compulsory purchase to congested
districts board.
1910 General election (Jan.–Feb.): Irish party hold balance.
Sir Edward Carson elected chairman of Irish unionist party (21 Feb.).
Edward VII dies (6 May); succeeded by George V.
James Connolly's *Labour in Irish history,* first published in book form, in
Dublin (Nov.).
First number of I.R.B. monthly, *Irish Freedom,* edited by Patrick McCartan
(Nov.; suppressed Dec. 1914).
General election (Dec.): Irish party again hold balance.
1911 George V in Dublin and neighbourhood (7-12 July).
Parliament act (18 Aug.).
1912 Winston Churchill visits Belfast (8 Feb.), and with Redmond addresses
large crowd on home rule in Celtic Park.
Andrew Bonar Law at demonstration at Balmoral, Belfast, pledges support
of Belfast unionists for Ulster resistance to home rule (9 Apr.).
Titanic, White Star line, built in Belfast by Harland and Wolff, sinks on
maiden voyage to New York (14-15 Apr.).
Solemn League and Covenant subscribed in Ulster (28 Sept.).
1913 Third home rule bill passes house of commons by 367 to 257 (16 Jan.); bill
defeated in house of lords by 326 to 69 (30 Jan.).
Ulster Volunteer Force formally established (31 Jan.).
Home rule bill again passes house of commons (7 July) and is again defeated
in house of lords (15 July).
Conflict in Dublin between workers, led by James Larkin, and employers,
led by William Martin Murphy (30 Aug.–1 Sept.).
Lock-out of workers by Employers' Federation begins (2 Sept.; some
25,000 workers locked-out by 22 Sept.; lock-out continues till Feb. 1914).
Provisional government of Ulster, backed by Ulster Volunteer Force,
provided for (24 Sept.).
Æ's open letter 'To the masters of Dublin' published in *Irish Times* (7 Oct.).
Irish Citizen Army founded (19 Nov.).
Irish Volunteers founded (25 Nov.).
1914 'The Curragh incident' (20 Mar.).
Cumann na mBan founded as women's counterpart to Irish Volunteers
(2 Apr.).
Ulster Volunteers' gun-running at Larne, Bangor, and Donaghadee
(24-5 Apr.).
Home rule bill passes house of commons for third time (25 May).
James Joyce's *Dubliners* (15 June).

1914 *(cont.)* Murder of Archduke Franz Ferdinand at Sarajevo (28 June).
Buckingham Palace conference (21-24 July).
Austrian ultimatum to Serbia (23 July).
Howth gun-running (26 July).
Kilcoole gun-running (1-2 Aug.).
Britain declares war on Germany (4 Aug.).
Supreme council of I.R. B. decides on insurrection before end of war (Sept.).
Third home rule bill receives royal assent, but its operation is suspended
(18 Sept.).
Redmond at Woodenbridge, Co. Wicklow, appeals to Irish Volunteers to
serve 'not only in Ireland itself but wherever the firing line extends, in
defence of right, of freedom, and religion in this war' (20 Sept.); MacNeill
and other members of original committee of Volunteers repudiate
Redmond's leadership (24 Sept.).

1915 *Lusitania* sunk off Old Head of Kinsale (7 May).
Coalition ministry formed under Lloyd George; includes Bonar Law and
Carson (25 May).
Pearse's oration at funeral of O'Donovan Rossa (1 Aug.).

1916 The *Aud* arrives in Tralee bay (20 Apr.).
Casement lands at Banna strand (21 Apr.).
Easter rising begins in Dublin (24 Apr.).
Francis Sheehy-Skeffington and two others murdered by Capt. J. C.
Bowen-Colthurst (26 Apr.).
Pearse orders surrender (29 Apr.).
Execution of 15 leaders of rising (3-12 May).
Casement hanged (3 Aug.).
Lloyd George P.M. of coalition government (7 Dec.; continues till Oct.
1922).

1917 Count Plunkett elected as Sinn Féin candidate for North Roscommon
(5 Feb.).
Revolution in Russia (8-15 Mar.); abdication of Tzar Nicholas II (15 Mar.)
(O.S. 23 Feb. – 2 Mar.).
Eamon de Valera elected as Sinn Féin candidate for East Clare (10 July).
Irish convention meets in Trinity College, Dublin (25 July; last meeting,
5 Apr. 1918).

1918 Report of Irish convention published (12 Apr.).
One-day general strike (except in Ulster) against conscription (23 Apr.).
Mail boat *Leinster* sunk by German submarine between Kingstown and
Holyhead; some 500 drowned (10 Oct.).
End of first world war (11 Nov.).
Act entitling women to sit and vote in house of commons (21 Nov.).
General election (14-28 Dec.): Sinn Féin 73, home-rulers 6, unionists 25,
independent unionists 6. Countess Markievicz, Sinn Féin M.P., first woman
elected to house of commons.

1919 War of independence begins with ambush at Soloheadbeg, Co. Tipperary
(21 Jan.; ends July 1921).

1919 *(cont.)*	Sinn Féin representatives meet in Dublin as Dáil Éireann (21 Jan.). Dáil Éireann adopts provisional constitution and declaration of independence (21 Jan.).
	De Valera elected president of Dáil Éireann (1 Apr.).
	Dáil resolves that Irish Volunteers must swear allegiance to Irish Republic and to dáil (20 Aug.; Volunteers become known as I.R.A.).
1920	First enrolments of 'Black and Tans' (2 Jan.).
	Disturbances in Derry (Apr., May, June).
	Disturbances in Belfast, expulsions of catholics from shipyards and engineering works (21-4 July).
	More disturbances in Belfast (22-3 Aug.): some 30 deaths; curfew imposed.
	Black and Tan raid on Balbriggan, Co. Dublin (20 Sept.).
	Terence MacSwiney, lord mayor of Cork, dies in Brixton prison on 74th day of hunger strike (25 Oct.).
	'Bloody Sunday' (21 Nov.): 14 suspected secret service agents shot dead in Dublin by I.R.A. groups; Black and Tans fire on crowd at Gaelic football match in Croke Park, killing 12.
	Cork sacked by Black and Tans (11-12 Dec.).
	Government of Ireland act (23 Dec.), providing for subordinate parliaments and administrations at Dublin and Belfast.
1921	Carson resigns as leader of Ulster unionists (4 Feb.). Sir James Craig elected by Ulster Unionist Council in his place.
	General election to parliaments of Southern Ireland and Northern Ireland (May); all candidates nominated for Southern Ireland parliament (Sinn Féin 124, independents 4) returned unopposed; in Northern Ireland elections 40 unionists, 6 nationalists, 6 Sinn Féin returned.
	Custom House, Dublin, destroyed by I.R.A. (25 May).
	House of commons of Northern Ireland meets (7 June): cabinet appointed under Sir James Craig (Viscount Craigavon, 1927) as P.M. (continues till 24 Nov. 1940).
	Northern Ireland parliament opened by George V (22 June).
	Truce between I.R.A. and British army in Ireland (9 July).
	Sinn Féin M.P.s elected to Southern Ireland parliament meet in Mansion House, Dublin, as second Dáil Éireann (16 Aug.; see 21 Jan. 1919).
	Anglo-Irish treaty signed in London (6 Dec.); involves split in Sinn Féin.
	Election of Eamon de Valera as chancellor of the National University of Ireland (Dec.).
1922	Treaty approved by Dáil Éireann by 64 to 57 (7 Jan.).
	Violence in Belfast; many killed (12-15 Feb., 20-22 May).
	Special Powers Act, Northern Ireland (7 Apr.; made permanent in 1933).
	I.R.A. declared illegal organisation by N.I. government (23 May).
	N.I. act, establishing Royal Ulster Constabulary (31 May).
	General election for Dáil Éireann (16 June): pro-treaty majority.

1922 *(cont.)* Field Marshal Sir Henry Wilson assassinated in London by I.R.A. (22 June).
Civil war begins (28 June; Four Courts destroyed, 30 June).
Death of Arthur Griffith (12 Aug.).
Michael Collins killed at Bealnablath, Co. Cork (22 Aug.).
William Thomas Cosgrave elected head of provisional government by dáil (9 Sept.): president of executive council and minister for finance (6 Dec.; continues till Mar. 1932).
Constitution of Irish Free State Bill approved by dáil (25 Oct.).
Erskine Childers convicted by military court of unlawful possession of revolver (17 Nov.; shot, 24 Nov.).
First of 77 executions of Irregulars by shooting (17 Nov.; last 2 May 1923).
Irish Free State Constitution Act (U.K.) (5 Dec.), ratifies constitution as approved by dáil, and Anglo-Irish treaty.

1923   First meeting of United Council of Christian Churches and Religious Communions, combining representatives of Church of Ireland, presbyterian church, and methodist church (23 Jan.; see 1966).
Cumann na nGaedheal founded by Cosgrave as party of supporters of treaty (Mar.); in government till Mar. 1932.
End of civil war (May).
Boyne obelisk (memorial of battle of 1690) blown up by persons unknown (31 May).
Education act (N.I.) providing for non-denominational schools under local authority (22 June.)
I.F.S. act to establish Gárda Siochána (Civic Guard) (8 Aug.).
Hogan act, to provide for completion of land purchase in I.F.S. (9 Aug.).
I.F.S. admitted to League of Nations (10 Sept.).

1924   Opening of Belfast station (2BE) of B.B.C. (15 Sept.).
First meeting, in London, of boundary commission (6 Nov.).

1925   Northern Ireland land act to complete land purchase in N.I. (28 May).
I.F.S. act authorising Shannon hydro-electric scheme (4 July).
Morning Post publishes forecast of boundary commission's report (7 Nov.; report, not published till 1969, confirms prediction).
Agreement between governments of U.K., I.F.S., and N.I. revoking powers of boundary commission and maintaining existing boundary of N.I. (3 Dec.).

1926   I.F.S. broadcasting station (2RN) opened in Dublin (1 Jan.).
Fianna Fáil party launched by de Valera in Dublin (16 May).

1927   I.F.S. act providing for establishment of Agricultural Credit Corporation (28 May).
Kevin O'Higgins, I.F.S. minister for justice, assassinated (10 July).
I.F.S. General election (9 June): Fianna Fáil largest opposition party; de Valera and Fianna Fáil enter dáil (11 Aug.).

1928	Irish Manuscripts Commission appointed (10 Oct.); Eoin MacNeill chairman (till 1945).
1929	Proportional representation in parliamentary elections abolished in N.I. (16 Apr.).
1930	First censorship board in I.F.S. appointed (12 Feb.).
	I.F.S. elected to council of League of Nations (17 Sept.).
1931	An Óige (Irish Youth Hostels Association) inaugurated (7 May).
	First number of *Irish Press,* founded by de Valera (5 Sept.).
	Statute of Westminster (11 Dec.).
1932	Army Comrades Association formed (9 Feb.; renamed National Guard, 20 July 1933).
	General election in I.F.S. (16 Feb.): Cosgrave (see 1922) succeeded by de Valera (F.F.) as president of executive council (9 Mar.; continues till 1948).
	Payment of land annuities to British government withheld by de Valera (30 June); 'economic war' with Britain begins (July; continues till 1938).
	De Valera makes inaugural speech as chairman of League of Nations assembly at Geneva (26 Sept.).
	Strikes, marches, and riots in Belfast in protest against unemployment (4-13 Oct.).
	Northern Ireland parliament buildings at Stormont, Belfast, formally opened by Prince of Wales (16 Nov.).
1933	O'Duffy dismissed as chief commissioner of Gárda Síochána (22 Feb.).
	Army Comrades Association adopts blue shirt and black beret as distinctive dress (24 Mar.); association, under leadership of General Eoin O'Duffy adopts name National Guard (20 July).
	National Guard proclaimed unlawful association (22 Aug.).
	United Irish party (later known as Fine Gael) launched under presidency of O'Duffy (2 Sept.).
1934	O'Duffy resigns from Fine Gael party (21 Sept.).
	Anglo-Irish 'cattle and coal' agreement (21 Dec.).
1935	Disturbances in Belfast (6-9 May, 12 July).
1936	George V dies (20 Jan.); succeeded by Edward VIII.
	I.F.S. act abolishing senate (29 May; restored 29 Dec. 1937).
	I.R.A. declared illegal in I.F.S. (18 June).
	I.F.S. act providing for formation of Aer Lingus as national airline (14 Aug.).
	O'Duffy and followers leave Ireland for Spain to fight for Franco rebels as 'Irish brigade' (20 Nov.; return on 22 June 1937).
	Edward VIII abdicates (11 Dec.) and is succeeded by George VI; I.F.S. constitutional amendment act removing from constitution all reference to crown and governor general (11 Dec.); external relations act giving effect to abdication and recognising crown for purposes of external relations (12 Dec.).

1936 *(cont.)* Left-wing Irish unit led by Frank Ryan joins government forces in Spain (16 Dec.).

1937 New constitution approved by dáil (14 June); referendum gives favourable majority of 685,105 to 526,945 (1 July).
George VI in N. I. (28-9 July).
New constitution of Éire comes into effect (29 Dec.).

1938 Anglo-Irish agreement on 'treaty ports', finance, and trade (25 Apr.); act of dáil gives effect to agreement (16 May).
Douglas Hyde, first president of Éire inaugurated (25 June; continues till June 1945).
New movement for better understanding between north and south announced (23 Dec.; becomes Irish Association for Cultural, Economic, and Social Relations).

1939 First of series of I.R.A. bomb attacks in England (16 Jan.; ends, Mar. 1940).
Offences against the State Act, Éire (14 June).
I.R.A. bomb explosion in Coventry (25 Aug.) kills 5, wounds 70.
Second world war begins with German invasion of Poland (1 Sept.); de Valera announces government's intention to remain neutral (2 Sept.); N.I. belligerent as part of U.K.
Britain and France declare war on Germany (3 Sept.).
I.R.A. raid on Magazine Fort, Phoenix Park (23 Dec.).

1940 Two emergency bills against I.R.A. passed by oireachtas (3 Jan.).
Act providing for Dublin Institute for Advanced Studies (19 June)
German aircraft bomb creamery at Campile, Co. Wexford (26 Aug.).
Viscount Craigavon, P.M. of N.I. dies (24 Nov.); succeeded by J.M. Andrews (continues till 20 Apr. 1943).

1941 German bombs dropped in Counties Carlow, Dublin, Kildare, Louth, Meath, Wexford, and Wicklow (1-3 Jan.).
German air raids on Belfast (15-16 Apr.): over 700 killed and over 400 seriously wounded; Dublin and Dun Laoghaire fire brigades sent to assistance of Belfast.
German bombs on North Strand, Dublin: 34 killed, 90 injured, 300 houses destroyed or damaged (31 May).

1942 American troops arrive in N.I. (Jan.); protest by de Valera.
Federated Union of Employers formed in Dublin (25 Mar.).
I.R.A. attacks on R.U.C. in Dungannon (3 Apr.) and in Belfast (5 Apr.).
Act establishing Central Bank in Dublin as currency authority, replacing Currency Commission (4 Nov.).

1943 Arts Council established in N.I. (1 Feb.).
J.M. Andrews resigns as P.M. of N.I. (28 Apr.); succeeded by Sir Basil Brooke (Viscount Brookeborough, 4 July; continues till 25 Mar. 1963).
Comhdháil Náisiúnta na Gaeilge, coordinating body for Irish language organisations, formed (26 Oct.).

1944 Córas Iompair Éireann, Irish transport company, set up (8 Dec.).

463

1945	Act providing for N.I. Housing Trust (6 Feb.).
	Congress of Irish Trade Unions formed (25 Apr.).
	'V.E. day' (8 May): end of war in Europe.
	Churchill's victory speech (13 May); de Valera's reply (16 May).
	Seán T. O'Kelly elected president of Éire (16 June) in succession to Douglas Hyde (see 1939, 1952).
1946	Turf development act, Éire, establishing Bord na Mona (1 June).
	Clann na Poblachta founded under Seán MacBride (6 July).
	Ireland's application for admission to United Nations (July-Aug.; see 1955).
	Act establishing Institute for Industrial Research and Standards in Dublin (27 Aug.).
	Act provides for setting up of labour court in Dublin.
1947	Education act, N.I. (27 Nov.).
	Health Act, Éire (13 Aug.); R.C. bishops express disapproval of some clauses, especially those concerning mother-and-child services.
1948	General election in Éire (4 Feb.): de Valera (see 1932) succeeded by John A. Costello (F.G.) as taoiseach, heading inter-party government (18 Feb.; continues till May 1951) (See 1951).
	Health services act, N.I. (4 Feb.).
	Organisation for European Economic Development instituted (16 Apr.); Éire and U.K. members.
	An Taisce, national trust for planning and conservation in R.I., established (15 July; recognised as statutory body by ministerial regulation, 7 Sept. 1964).
	Ulster Transport Authority established (10 Aug.).
	Costello announces government's intention to repeal external relations act (7 Sept.).
	Judgment in high court, Dublin, against Foyle and Bann Fisheries Ltd concerning fishing in Clonleigh, Co. Donegal (13 Oct.; Belfast and Dublin governments agree on joint control of Foyle fisheries, 9 July 1950; and see 1952).
	Republic of Ireland act (21 Dec.) repeals external relations act, 1936, and provides for declaration of republic.
1949	North Atlantic treaty against armed aggression signed in Washington by U.S.A., Canada, G.B., France, and other states (4 Apr.).
	Éire formally declared a republic (18 Apr.).
	Convention signed in London by ten European states, including R.I. and U.K., establishing Council of Europe, with seat at Strasbourg (5 May).
	Ireland act, U.K. (2 June), declares that R.I. is not part of British dominions, but that it is not to be regarded as a foreign country, and that N.I. shall not cease to be part of U.K. without consent of N.I. parliament.
1950	Holy Year begins (1 Jan.).

1950 *(cont.)* Act of oireachtas implementing agreement between Dublin and Belfast governments for Erne drainage and electricity scheme (13 June; corresponding act by N.I. parliament, 27 June).
Judgment of supreme court, Dublin, in Tilson case (5 Aug.).
Industrial Development Authority Act, R.I. (20 Dec.).
Bank strike in R.I. (23 Dec.; continues till 16 Feb. 1951).

1951 Agreement between governments of R.I. and N.I. on running of Great Northern Railway (9 Jan.).
Dr Noel Browne, minister for health, resigns over 'mother-and-child' scheme (11 Apr.).
Arts Council founded in R.I. (8 May)
General election in R.I. (30 May): Costello (see 1948) succeeded by de Valera (F.F.) as taoiseach (continues till June 1954) (See 1948, 1954).
Abbey Theatre, Dublin, destroyed by fire (18 July; see 1966).

1952 Social welfare act for coordinated system of social insurance in R.I. (14 June).
Seán T. O'Kelly (see 1945) president for second term (25 June; till June 1959)
Act providing for legal adoption in R.I. (13 Dec.).
Joint commission on Foyle fisheries set up by governments of R.I. and N.I.

1953 Comhairle Radio Éireann, appointed by Erskine Childers, minister for posts and telegraphs, with non-statutory control over broadcasting, takes office with Maurice Gorham as director of broadcasting (1 Jan.; see 1960).
Car ferry *Princess Victoria* sinks off Co. Down coast (31 Jan.).
Gael-linn, financed by football pools, for promotion of Irish language, established (3 May).
Library of Alfred Chester Beatty (mining engineer, art collector, and philanthropist), containing his unique collection of oriental manuscripts, pictures, etc., officially opened at Shrewsbury Road, Dublin (8 Aug.; see 1968).
First of Thomas Davis Lectures, a continuing series, broadcast by Radio Éireann (27 Sept.).

1954 General election in R.I.(18 May): de Valera (see 1951) succeeded by Costello (F.G.) as taoiseach, heading second inter-party government (2 June; continues till Mar. 1957) (See 1951,1957).
I.R.A. raid on Gough military barracks, Armagh (12 June).
Bank officials in R.I. begin working short hours (4 Dec.), leading to closure of banks till 23 Mar. 1955. (see 1950, 1966).

1955 First regular television service in N.I. begins transmission from Divis (21 July).
Saor Uladh, a breakaway from I.R.A., attack police barracks at Rosslea, Co. Fermanagh (26 Nov.).
R.I. admitted to United Nations Organisation (14 Dec.).

465

1956	Balance of payments crisis in R.I.
	T.K. Whitaker appointed secretary to R.I.'s department of finance (30 May).

Maura Lyons, 15 year old catholic, disappears from her home in Belfast, after becoming converted to protestantism through preaching of Rev. Ian Paisley (23 Oct.; reappears at Paisley's home, 10 May 1957, and is placed in remand centre; petition to make her a ward of court granted by Lord MacDermott, lord chief justice, 20 May 1957).

I.R.A. campaign in N.I. begins with attacks on border customs posts by Saor Uladh (11 Nov.; continues till Feb. 1962).

Ronnie Delaney wins gold medal during the world Olympic Games at Melbourne, Australia (1 Dec.).

1957	General election in R.I. (5 Mar.): Costello (see 1954) succeeded by de Valera (F.F.) as taoiseach (20 Mar.; continues till June 1959) (See 1961).

Treaty of Rome instituting European Economic Community signed by France, West Germany, Italy, Belgium, Holland, and Luxembourg (25 Mar.).

Boycott of protestants at Fethard-on-Sea, Co. Wexford, begins (13 May).

Gough monument in Phoenix Park wrecked by explosion (23 July).

1958	Act providing for establishment of An Foras Talúntais (Agricultural Research Institute) (19 Feb.).

General election in N.I. (20 Mar.): unionists 37, nationalists 7, independent nationalists 1, N.I.L.P. 4, independent labour 1, republican labour 1, independent 1 (See 1962).

Aer Lingus service to North America inaugurated (28 Apr.).

Economic Development, by T. K. Whitaker and others, completed (May); published Dec.

Act for establishing Ulster Folk Museum (10 June; see 1964).

50 Irish officers appointed as observers with United Nations peace-keeping forces in Lebanon (July; see 1978).

First *Programme for economic expansion* laid by the government before each house of the oireachtas (Nov.; see 1963).

First programme of economic expansion published (11 Nov.).

1959	Congress of Irish Trade Unions and Irish Trade Union Congress decide to combine in Irish Congress of Trade Unions, with separate committee for N.I. (10 Feb.).

De Valera elected president of R.I. (17 June) in succession to Seán T. O'Kelly (see 1952; continues till 1966).

Seán Lemass (F.F.), minister for industry and commerce, elected taoiseach in succession to de Valera (23 June; continues till Nov. 1966).

Rev. Donald Soper prevented from delivering address at open-air meeting at Ballymena by heckling of Paisley and others (1 Aug.; Paisley fined £5 for causing breach of the peace).

1959 *(cont.)* General election in U.K. (8 Oct.): in G.B. – con. 333, lab. 258, nat. lib
        and con. 20, lib. 6, others 1; in N.I. – unionists 12 (see 1964)
        Agreement between U.K. and R.I. on Sir Hugh Lane pictures announced
        by Lemass (12 Nov.).

1960   Act of oireachtas establishing broadcasting authority (Radio Éireann) of
        nine members to conduct national radio and television services (12
        Apr.; see 1953; name altered to Radio Telefís Éireann by act of 8
        Mar. 1966).
        Ireland sends troops to serve with U.N. forces in Congo (27 July).
        Appointment of commission on higher education (Sept.; report, Feb.
        1967).

1961   Ireland applies for membership of European Economic Community (1
        Aug.).
        Ireland enters U.N.E.S.C.O. (3 Oct.).
        General election in R.I. (4 Oct.): F.F. 70, F.G. 47, lab. 16, Clann na
        Talmhan 2, National Progressive Democratic Party 2, Clann na
        Poblachta 1, independents and others 6 (see 1957, 1965)
        Television service of Radio Éireann inaugurated (31 Dec.).

1962   General election in N.I. (31 May): unionists 34, nationalists 9, N.I.L.P.
        4, independent labour 1, republican labour 1, Irish labour 1,
        independent 1 (see 1957, 1965).
        First transmission of R.T.E. television series 'The late, late show';
        compere Gay Byrne (6 July).
        Motorway (M1) from Belfast to Lisburn opened (10 July); first in
        Ireland.

1963   Capt. Terence O'Neill succeeds Viscount Brookeborough as P.M. of
        N.I. (25 Mar.; continues till 28 Apr. 1969).
        Pope John XXIII dies (3 June; Paisley leads protest against action of
        Belfast City Council in paying tribute to him, 4 June).
        John F. Kennedy, President of U.S.A., in Ireland (26-9 June).
        Second programme for economic expansion laid by the government
        before each house of the oireachtas (Aug.); part II follows in July 1964;
        see 1969.
        Second programme of economic expansion in R.I. published (22 Aug.).
        Committee under Sir John Lockwood appointed to review facilities for
        higher education in N.I. (20 Nov.; report, 10 Feb. 1965).
        Survey team under Patrick Lynch appointed, in association with
        O.E.C.D., to estimate technological needs of R.I. (Nov.; see 23 Dec.
        1965).
        President John F. Kennedy assassinated in Dallas, Texas (22 Nov.).

1964   R.I. decides to send troops to serve with U.N. forces in Cyprus (24
        Mar.).
        An Foras Forbartha (National Institute for Physical Planning and
        Construction Research) incorporated (26 Mar.).
        Ulster Folk Museum opened, at Cultra, Co. Down (2 July).

1964 *(cont.)* N.I. Committee of Irish Congress of Trade Unions recognised by N.I.
government (24 Aug.).
Rioting in Belfast (28 Sept.-3 Oct.).
General election in U.K.(15 Oct.): in G.B. – lab. 317, con. 292, lib. 9; in
N.I. – unionists 12; Harold Wilson (lab.) succeeds Alec Douglas-Home
(con.) as P.M. (16 Oct.; continues till June 1970) (See 1959,1966).

1965 Lemass, taoiseach, visits O'Neill, P.M. of Northern Ireland, in Belfast
(14 Jan.).
Nationalist party decides to accept role of official opposition in N.I.
parliament, Edward McAteer leader in house of commons (2 Feb.).
O'Neill visits Lemass in Dublin (9 Feb.).
Report of Lockwood committee (10 Feb.) recommends second university
for N.I., at Coleraine (see 1 Oct. 1968) and an Ulster polytechnic (see 1
Apr. 1971).
General election in R.I. (7 Apr.): F.F. 72, F.G. 47, lab. 22, Clann na
Poblachta 1, others 2 (see 1961, 1969).
New towns act, N.I. (24 June; leads to establishment of new town,
Craigavon, near Portadown).
W. T. Cosgrave dies (16 Nov.).
General election in N.I. (25 Nov.): unionists 36, nationalists 9, N.I.L.P. 2
republican labour 2, national democratic party 1, liberal 1, independent
1.
Anglo-Irish free trade agreement (14 Dec.).
Act altering law relating to succession in Republic (22 Dec.).
*Investment in education: report of the survey team appointed. . . in
October 1962*, vol. i, published (23 Dec.; vol. ii, 8 August 1966).

1966 R.T.E. television series , 'The course of Irish history', edited by T. W.
Moody and F. X. Martin (24 Jan.-13 June; published in book form,
26 Jan. 1967).
Nelson Pillar, Dublin, wrecked by explosion (8 Mar.).
General election in U.K. (31 Mar.): in G.B. – lab. 364, con. 239, national
lib. and con. 3, lib. 12; in N.I. – unionists 11, republican labour 1. (See
1964,1970).
Commemoration of 50th anniversary of Easter rising begins (10 Apr.).
Ulster Volunteer Force, first of protestant paramilitary organisations,
founded (Apr./May).
Banks throughout Ireland closed by strike of junior officials (6 May;
reopened to public, in N.I. on 21 June, in R.I. on 5 Aug.; see 1954,
1970).
De Valera reelected president of R.I. (1 June; continues till May 1973).
Paisley demonstrates outside Church House, Belfast, against 'Romeward
trend in presbyterian church' (6 June).
Catholic bishops, as trustees of Maynooth College, announce proposal to
develop it as 'an open centre of higher studies, admitting students of
both sexes, clerical and lay'.

1966 *(cont.)* Peter Ward, catholic barman (aged 18) shot dead in Malvern Street, Belfast (26 June; Gusty Spence and other U.V.F. men convicted of the murder, 14 Oct.).

U.V.F. declared illegal organisation by N.I. government (28 June).

First public performance in new Abbey Theatre, Dublin (18 July).

Paisley and others each fined £30 for unlawful assembly on 6 June (19 July; refusing to pay fine and enter into recognisances to keep the peace they are imprisoned, 26 July-19 Oct.).

First section of Belfast–Ballymena motorway (M2) opened (24 Oct.).

Ulster Council of Christian Churches and Religious Communions in Ireland (see 1923) renamed Irish Council of Churches (4 Nov.).

Lemass (see 1959) announces intention to resign as taoiseach (8 Nov.); Jack Lynch elected leader of Fianna Fáil party by 52 votes to 19 for George Colley, Charles J . Haughey having withdrawn his candidature (9 Nov.).

Lemass resigns; Jack Lynch elected to succeed him (10 Nov.; continues till Mar. 1973).

Seán T. O'Kelly, president of R.I., 1945-59, dies (25 Nov.).

Meeting in London between Lynch, taoiseach, and Wilson, P.M., for discussion of common interests of Ireland and Great Britain in relation to European Economic Community (19 Dec.).

1967 Northern Ireland Civil Rights Association (N.I.C.R.A.) formed (29 Jan.).

Act to establish An Chomhairle Oiliúna (AnCo), industrial training authority (7 Mar.)

Commission on higher education, 1960-67, presentation and summary of report published (22 Mar.).; recommendations include: National University to be defederated and its constituent colleges to become independent universities; Trinity College, Dublin, to remain a separate university; university governing bodies to be reformed; Council of Irish Universities and Commission for Higher Education to be set up.

Donogh O'Malley, R.I. minister for education, announces government's intention to combine Trinity College, Dublin, and University College, Dublin, in one university of Dublin (18 Apr.; strong opposition to plan in both colleges eventually results in its abandonment).

R.I. and U.K. reapply for membership of E.E.C. (11 May; see 1972).

Agreement between R.I and N.I. for linking electricity system by line from Maynooth to Tandragee (5 Oct.) .

Lynch visits O'Neill at Stormont Belfast (11 Dec.).

O'Neill visits Lynch in Dublin (8 Jan.).

Sir Alfred Chester Beatty, first honorary citizen of Ireland (1956), dies aged 92 (20 Jan.); in his will his library (see 1953) becomes the property of the Irish nation (9 Sept.).

Donogh O'Malley dies (10 Mar.), aged 47.

1968 *(cont.)* Austin Currie, nationalist M.P., 'squats' in house at Caledon, Co. Tyrone (20 June), after protesting against its allocation by Dungannon Rural District Council to a single girl, aged 19.

'Lenihan plan' for higher education announced by R.I. minister for education (6 July): N.U.I. to be dissolved; U.C.C. and U.C.G. to become separate universities; T.C.D. and U.C.D. to be combined but each to retain its identity; Higher Education Authority and Conference of Irish Universities to be established.

Paul VI encyclical, *Humanae vitae,* condemning artificial forms of contraception (29 July).

Civil rights march (first of a series) from Coalisland to Dungannon, Co. Tyrone (24 Aug.).

First meeting of Higher Education Authority (12 Sept.); Dr Tarlach Ó Raifeartaigh chairman.

Maynooth College admits first lay students for degree courses (14 Sept.).

New University of Ulster opened at Coleraine (1 Oct.).

William Craig, minister of home affairs, N.I. bans intended civil rights march and Apprentice Boys' parade in Derry announced for 5 Oct. (3 Oct.).

Clash between civil rights marchers and police in Derry (5 Oct.), followed by rioting (5-6 Oct.).

Derry Citizens' Action Committee formed (9 Oct.).

Student demonstration in Belfast; People's Democracy formed (9 Oct.).

Referendum to amend R.I. constitution so as to abolish proportional representation heavily defeated (16 Oct.).

O'Neill announces 5-point reform programme for N.I. (22 Nov.) conceding N.I.C.R.A. demands except 'one man one vote' in local government elections.

William Craig dismissed as N.I. minister of home affairs (11 Dec.).

1969 People's Democracy march from Belfast to Derry (1-4 Jan.); marchers ambushed by militant protestants at Burntollet bridge, Co. Londonderry (4 Jan.).

Brian Faulkner, minister of commerce, resigns (23 Jan.), succeeded by Roy Bradford (24 Jan.).

New Ulster Movement launched (6 Feb.).

General election in N.I. (24 Feb.): unionists 36 (24 pro- O'Neill, 12 anti-O'Neill), independent unionists 3, nationalists 6, N.I.L.P. 2, republican labour 2, independents 3 (see 1965, 1973).

Cameron commission appointed to investigate violence in N.I. since 5 Oct. 1968 (3 Mar.); its report (12 Sept.) very critical of conduct of R.U.C.

Third programme: economic and social development 1969-72, laid by the government before each house of the oireachtas (Mar.).

1969 *(cont.)* Explosions at electricity substation at Castlereagh, near Belfast (30 Mar.), and at Belfast city reservoir (20 Apr.), caused by protestant extremists.

Rioting in Derry (19 Apr., 12-16 July, 12-14 Aug.); at request of N.I government British troops move in.

O'Neill wins small majority of unionist party for 'one man one vote' principle in local government elections (23 Apr.).

O'Neill resigns as P.M. of N.I. (28 Apr.); succeeded by James Chichester-Clark (1 May; continues till Mar. 1971).

General election in R.I. (18 June): F.F. 75, F.G. 50, lab. 18, independent 1 (see 1965, 1973).

U.V.F. bomb explodes at R.T.E. headquarters, Dublin, first of a series (5 Aug.).

Rioting in Belfast (2-5, 15 Aug.); British troops move in (15 Aug.).

'Downing Street declaration' (19 Aug.), joint communiqué by U.K. and N.I. ministers on responsibilities of U.K. government for N.I. and on cooperation between the two governments to restore normality there.

Joint communiqué by P.M.s of U.K. and N.I.: G.O.C will have overall responsibility for security in N.I. (19 Aug.).

British government issues seven-point statement, 'The Downing Street declaration' (19 Aug.), stating its ultimate responsibility for the protection of the people of N.I., welcoming reforms already made by the N.I. government, and reaffirming that every citizen of N.I. is 'entitled to the same equality of treatment and freedom from discrimination as obtains in the rest of the United Kingdom.'

Joint communiqué issued by governments of U.K. and N.I. on measures being taken by N.I. government to implement reforms indicated in Downing Street declaration, and marking out areas in which it is agreed that effective reforms are fundamental to the creation of confidence (29 Aug.).

Report of Hunt committee (10 Oct.) on reform of police.

N.I. electoral law act (25 Nov.): qualifying age lowered to 18; 'one man one vote' in local government elections.

Act to establish Ulster Defence Regiment, part-time security force under army control (18 Dec.).

Press report (28 Dec.) of split in I.R.A. between 'Officials' and 'Provisionals'.

1970 Split between 'Officials' and 'Provisionals' at Sinn Féin convention in Dublin (11 Jan.).

Banks in R.I. restrict service owing to labour dispute (2 Mar.); banks closed (30 Apr.); reopened (17 Nov.; see 1966, 1976).

Act establishing police authority etc. in N.I. (26 Mar.).

Easter rising commemorations lead to rioting in Derry, Armagh, and Belfast (28 Mar.-2 Apr.); beginning of fighting between republicans and British army .

471

1970 *(cont.)* Agreement between T.C.D. and N.U.I. on distribution of certain faculties
between them (7 Apr.).
Alliance Party combining liberal protestants and catholics in N.I.
founded 21 Apr.).
'B Specials' disbanded and their duties transferred to Ulster Defence
Regiment (30 Apr.).
Macrory report on new structure of local government in N.I. (29 May);
general acceptance by N.I government announced (17 Dec.).
Bernadette Devlin, M.P. arrested (26 June), leading to renewed
demonstrations in Derry and Belfast (26-9 June); Provos in action for
first time, in Belfast.
Charles J . Haughey, R.I. minister for finance, and Neil Blaney, minister
for agriculture, dismissed by Lynch (6 May); arrested on charges of
illegal importation of arms for I.R.A. (28 May); Blaney discharged (2
July); Haughey acquitted (23 Oct.).
General election in U.K. (18 June): in G.B. – con. 322, lab. 288, lib. 6,
others 2; in N.I. – unionists 8, protestant unionist 1, republican labour
1, unity 2 (see Feb. 1974); Wilson (see 1964) succeeded as P.M. by
Edward Heath (con.) (19 June; continues till Mar. 1974).
Catholic bishops announce removal of restrictions on catholics attending
Trinity College, Dublin (25 June).
Social Democratic and Labour Party, N.I., formed by combination of
opposition M.P.s (21 Aug.); leader Gerry Fitt.
Irish School of Ecumenics (director Rev. Michael Hurley, S.J.)
inaugurated at Milltown Park by Rev. Eugene Carson Blake, general
secretary of World Council of Churches (9 Nov.).

1971 First British soldier killed in Belfast (6 Feb.).
Fighting between Provos and Officials in Belfast (10 Mar.).
Chichester-Clark (see 1969) resigns as P.M. (20 Mar.); succeeded by
Brian Faulkner (23 Mar.; continues till 24 Mar. 1972).
Seán Lemass, taoiseach 1959-1966 dies (11 May).
Reintroduction of internment without trial (9 Aug.): 342 arrested.
Ulster Defence Association (U.D.A.), paramilitary organisation of
working class protestants, emerges in Belfast (Aug.).
Tripartite talks at Chequers between Heath, Lynch, and Faulkner (27-8
Sept.).
Discovery-well in gas field off Old Head of Kinsale completed (7 Nov.).
Senator John Barnhill shot dead at his home near Strabane by Officials
(12 Dec.).

1972 Treaty of accession to E.E.C. signed in Brussels by R.I., U.K., and
Denmark (22 Jan.)
'Bloody Sunday': 13 civilians shot dead by paratroopers in Derry,
following banned civil rights march (30 Jan.); Lynch declares 2 Feb.
day of national mourning (31 Jan.); British embassy in Dublin burned
(2 Feb.).

1972 *(cont.)* Bomb explosion, work of Officials, at officers' mess in Aldershot, killing six civilians (22 Feb.).

Attempt to assassinate John Taylor, N.I. minister of state at Armagh (25 Feb.).

Explosion at Abercorn Restaurant, Belfast (4 Mar.).

Marcus McCausland shot dead near Derry by Officials (6 Mar.).

Faulkner's government resigns, having refused to accept transfer of responsibility for security from Stormont to Westminster; N.I. parliament and government suspended; direct rule introduced under William Whitelaw as secretary of state for N.I.(24 Mar.; N.I. parliament abolished, 18 July 1973).

R.I. sets up special criminal court, to consist of three judges without a jury under Offences against the State Act, 1939 (26 May).

Officials suspend operations in N.I. (29 May).

Truce between Provos and British army (26 June; continues till 9 July).

'Bloody Friday' in Belfast (21 July): 22 explosions by Provos, killing 19 and injuring 130.

Whitelaw's green paper, *The future of Northern Ireland,* published (30 Oct.).

Seán MacStíofáin, Provos chief of staff, arrested by R.I. police (19 Nov.), after giving an interview to R.T.E. reporter, Kevin O'Kelly; interview broadcast later that day.

R.T.E. Authority dismissed by government (24 Nov.) over broadcast of MacStíofáin interview.

Referendum in R.I. reduces minimum age for voting to 18 and approves omission from constitution of special position of R.C. church (7 Dec.).

1972 peak year for violence in N.I.: 467 killed, out of total killings of 678 since 1969.

1973　　R.I. becomes member of E.E.C. along with U.K. and Denmark (1 Jan.).

Car bomb explosion in Dublin, killing one and injuring 17 (20 Jan.).

General election in R.I. (28 Feb.): F.F. 69, F.G. 54, lab. 19, independents 2; majority for Fine Gael-Labour coalition; Lynch (see 1966) succeeded as taoiseach by Liam Cosgrave (F.G.) heading inter-party government (14 Mar.; continues till June 1977).

Two car bomb explosions in London, killing one and injuring 180 (8 Mar.).

Act providing for assembly of 78 in N.I., to be elected by proportional representation (3 May).

Erskine Hamilton Childers elected president of R.I. (30 May; continues till 17 Nov. 1974).

Elections in N.I. to new district councils, first to be held since 1967 (30 May); final results: official unionists 210, loyalist coalition 81, S.D.L.P. 82, Alliance 63, others 83 (total 519).

1973 *(cont.)* General election for N.I. assembly (28 June); final results: official
unionists 23, Alliance 8, N.I.L.P. 1, (total pro-assembly unionists 32);
unpledged unionists 10, loyalist coalition 15, other loyalists 2 (total
dissident unionists 27); S.D.L.P.19 (total membership 78) (See 1969,
1975).

N.I. Constitution Act (U.K.) (18 July).

First meeting of N.I. Assembly ends in disorder (31 July).

Heath and Cosgrave meet at Baldonnell Aerodrome, Co. Dublin (17
Sept.).

First inter-church meeting at Ballymascanlon, Co. Louth, attended by
representatives of all main churches in Ireland (26 Sept.); the first of an
annual series of ecumenical conferences.

Six oil-producing countries on Persian Gulf increase price of crude oil
from $3 to $8 per barrel (16 Oct.); to $11.50 on 23 Dec.; world
economic recession follows .

Official unionists, Alliance, and S.D.L.P. agree to form 'power-sharing'
executive under Faulkner (22 Nov.).

United Ulster Unionist Council, combination of loyalist parties, formed
to oppose power-sharing (6 Dec.).

Whitelaw (see 1972) succeeded by Francis Pym as secretary of state for
N.I. (2 Dec.; continues till Mar. 1974).

Conference at Sunningdale, Berks, between representatives of Irish and
British governments and of N.I. executive designate (6-9 Dec.),
resulting in agreement on status of N.I., setting up of a Council of
Ireland, and co-operation between the two Irish governments, including
measures to bring to justice persons committing crimes of violence,
however motivated, in any part of Ireland (9 Dec.).

1974   N.I. executive takes office under Faulkner (1 Jan.).

Bomb kills 11 in bus carrying army personnel to Catterick, Yorks (4
Feb.). General election in U.K. (28 Feb.): in G.B. – lab. 301, con. 297,
lib. 14, others 11; in N.I. – unionists 7, D.U.P. 1, Vanguard Unionist
Progressive Party 3, S.D.L.P. 1 (United Ulster Unionist Council (see 6
Dec. 1973) gain 11 out of 12 seats) (see 1970, Oct. 1974); Wilson
succeeds Heath (see 1970) as P.M. (4 Mar.; continues till Apr. 1976);
Merlyn Rees (lab.) succeeds Pym (see 1973) as secretary of state for
N.I. (continues till Sept. 1976).

Ulster Workers' Council declares general strike (14 May).

Three car bomb explosions in Dublin kill 25, and one in Monaghan kills
6 (17 May).

Faulkner and unionist members of executive resign (28 May).

N. I. assembly prorogued and direct rule from Westminster reimposed
(29 May); strike called off.

U.K. act providing for constitutional convention on N.I. (17 July).

General election in U.K.(10 Oct.): in G.B. – lab. 319, con. 277, lib. 13,
others 14; in N.I. – unionists 6, D.U.P. 1, Vanguard Unionist
Progressive Party 3, S.D.L.P. 1, independent 1 (see Feb. 1974,1979).

1974 *(cont.)* Erskine Childers, president of R.I., dies (17 Nov.); Cearbhall Ó Dálaigh, elected unopposed to succeed him (3 Dec.; continues till Oct. 1976).
Richard Burke, R. I. minister for education, announces new plan for higher education (16 Dec.): U.C.D. to become independent university, T.C.D. to retain independence with loss of certain faculties.

1975 General election for N.I. convention (1 May): Unionist Party of Northern Ireland 5; Official Unionist Party 19; D.U.P. 12; Vanguard Unionist Party 14; N.I.L.P. 1; S.D.L.P. 17; Alliance 8; independents 2 (total membership 78); convention meets 8 May (see 1973, 1982).
Eamon de Valera dies, aged 92 (29 Aug.).
Dr Tiede Herrema kidnapped in Limerick (3 Oct.); released after 18 days siege of house in Monasterevan (7 Nov.).
Convention votes by 42 to 31 to present report of United Ulster Unionist Council (rejecting power-sharing) as report of convention, while appending minority report (7 Nov.).
Detention without trial in N.I. ends (5 Dec.).

1976 John A. Costello, taoiseach 1948-51 and 1954-7, dies, aged 84 (5 Jan.).
N.I. convention dissolved and report rejected by United Kingdom government (5 Mar.; see 23 Oct. 1982).
James Callaghan (lab.), succeeds Wilson (see 1974) as P.M. of U.K. (5 Apr.; continues till May 1979).
National Trust Archive, for historical records of Irish architecture, established (12 April; title changed to Irish Architectural Archive, 9 June 1981).
Strike of bank officials closes banks in R.I. (28 June); banks reopen, 6 Sept. (See 1966,1970).
Bomb explosions in special criminal court, Dublin: 4 prisoners escape (15 July).
Christopher Ewart-Biggs, U.K. ambassador to R.I., and Judith Cooke, civil servant, killed by land-mine at Sandyford, Co. Dublin (21 July).
Galway, and Maynooth College are to become independent universities (30 July).
Deaths of three children struck by car driven by Provo pursued by soldiers in Belfast (10 Aug.) leads to movement called 'Peace People' headed by Mairead Corrigan and Betty Williams.
Faulkner announces intention to retire from politics (18 Aug.; succeeded as leader of Unionist Party of Northern Ireland by Mrs Anne Letitia Dickson, 15 Sept.).
Roy Mason succeeds Rees (see 1974) as secretary of state for N.I. (10 Sept.; continues till May 1979).
President Ó Dálaigh, after being described by Patrick Donegan, minister for defence, as 'a thundering disgrace' (18 Oct.), resigns to protect the dignity of his office (22 Oct.); Patrick Hillery returned unopposed to succeed him (9 Nov.).

1976 *(cont.)* Heritage Trust, to reconcile economic development and conservation of the physical heritage of Ireland, established (27 Oct.).
Rally of Peace People from north and south at new bridge over Boyne at Drogheda (5 Dec.).

1977 Treasures of Ireland, covering from 1500 B.C. to 1500 A.D., loaned by National Museum, Trinity College Dublin, and Royal Irish Academy, go on public exhibition to different centres in U.S.A., 1979-1982, to Paris, Cologne, Berlin, Amsterdam, and Copenhagen, 1982-4.
Brian Faulkner (created Lord Faulkner, Jan.) dies in riding accident, aged 56 (3 Mar.).
General election in R.I. (June): F.F. 84, F.G. 43, lab. 17, others 4; Cosgrave (see 1973) succeeded as taoiseach by Lynch (F.F.) (5 July; continues till Dec. 1979); Cosgrave succeeded in leadership of Fine Gael by Garret FitzGerald (see 1973, 1981).

1978 Cearbhall Ó Dálaigh, president 1974-6, dies aged 67 (21 Mar.).
Lynch, taoiseach, addresses special session on disarmament of United Nations General Assembly (25 May).
Irish battalion sent to Lebanon to serve with United Nations peace-keeping forces there (June).
High court declares portion of Wood Quay site, Dublin, to be a national monument, the first such declaration by an Irish court (30 June; see 1979, 1 June).

1979 Whiddy Island disaster (8 Jan.): the 150,000 ton French oil-tanker *Betelgeuse* explodes at Gulf Oil terminal on Whiddy Island, Bantry Bay, killing 50 people; inquiry (May-Dec.) conducted by Judge Declan Costello in Dublin, finds owners of tanker and Gulf Oil responsible (report of inquiry published, July 1980).
European Monetary System instituted (13 Mar.); R.I. a member, U.K. not; R.I. announces ending of one-for-one parity with sterling (30 Mar.).
General election in U.K. (3 May): in G.B. – con. 339, lab. 269, lib. 11, others 4; in N.I. – official unionists 5, D.U.P. 3, S.D.L.P. 1, others 3; Callaghan (lab.; see 1976) succeeded as P.M. by Mrs Margaret Thatcher (con.; 4 May); Mason (see 1976) succeeded by Humphrey Atkins as secretary of state for N.I. (continues till Sept. 1981) (See Oct. 1974).
To halt destruction of national monument at Wood Quay, Dublin, for building of civic offices, site occupied peacefully by group of distinguished citizens (1-20 June; see 1978, 30 June).
Citizens of the nine member-states of E.E.C. vote for 410 representatives (M.E.P.s) in first direct elections to European parliament (7 June): R.I. returns 15 members (5 F.F., 4 F.G., 4 lab., 2 independents); N.I. returns 3 members (1 Official Unionist Party, 1 D.U.P., 1 S.D.L.P.).
Earl Mountbatten assassinated on his boat off Mullaghmore, Co. Sligo (27 Aug.).
Pope John Paul II in Ireland (29 Sept.-1 Oct.).

476

1979 *(cont.)* Lynch (see 1977) announces his intention to resign as taoiseach (5 Dec.);
Charles J. Haughey, minister for health and social welfare, elected to
succeed him (11 Dec.; continues till June 1981).

1980 Chalice and accompanying objects unearthed at Derrynavlan, barony of
Slieveardagh, Co. Tipperary (17 Feb.). Derrynavlan chalice is superb
example of 9th century Irish art.
Meeting in London of Haughey with Mrs Thatcher (21 May): friendly
exchange of views on N.I. situation .
Connemara National Park, Letterfrack, opened (Oct.).
Seven republican prisoners in Maze prison, Co. Antrim, begin hunger
strike as protest against prison regulations (27 Oct.); 3 women in
Armagh prison join hunger strike (1 Dec.); 23 additional prisoners in
Maze join (15 Dec.): strike ends at Maze (18 Dec.), at Armagh (19
Dec.; see Mar. 1981).
Meeting in Dublin of Haughey and Mrs Thatcher (8 Dec.): they agree to
begin consideration of the 'totality of relationships within these
islands'.

1981 Stardust Ballroom, Artane, Co. Dublin, destroyed by fire (14 Feb.); 48
killed, over 160 injured.
'Bobby' Sands, O.C. Provisional I.R.A. in Maze prison, begins hunger
strike (1 Mar.; see 27 Oct. 1980); later joined by other republican
prisoners; elected Sinn Féin M.P. in by-election for Fermanagh-South
Tyrone (20 Apr.); dies (5 May); 9 other hunger-strikers die (12 May-10
Aug.); strike called off (3 Oct.); 64 killed in disturbances in N.I. (1
Mar.-3 Oct.).
Atkins (see May 1979) succeeded by James Prior as secretary of state
for N.I. (Sept.) .
General election in R.I (11 June): F.F. 78, F.G. 65, lab. 15, others 8;
Haughey (see 1979) succeeded as taoiseach by Garret FitzGerald
(F.G.), heading F.G.–lab. coalition government (30 June; continues till
Mar. 1982). (See 1977, Feb. 1982).
Official opening of new National Concert Hall in Earlsfort Terrace,
Dublin, by President Hillery (9 Sept.).
Meeting between taoiseach and Mrs Thatcher (6 Nov.): Anglo-Irish
Inter-governmental Council to be set up (first meeting of council, 19
Jan. 1982).

1982 General election in R.I. (18 Feb.): F.F. 81, F.G. 63, lab. 15, others 7;
FitzGerald (see 1981) succeeded as taoiseach by Haughey (F. F.) (9
Mar.). (See Nov. 1982) .
Argentine forces occupy Falkland Islands (2 Apr.); first ships of British
task force sent to reoccupy them leave Portsmouth (5 Apr.); R.I.
government affirms Irish neutrality (2 May); announces that, in view of
open hostilities in Falklands, it regards use of economic sanctions
against Argentina by E.E.C. as inappropriate (4 May); sanctions
renewed by E.E.C. (17 May), R.I. and Italy refusing to concur;
Argentine forces in Falklands surrender to British (15 June).

477

1982 *(cont.)* Prior's white paper, *Northern Ireland: a framework for devolution,*
published (6 Apr.) – 'rolling devolution' (see 20 Oct.).

Haughey, taoiseach, addresses second special session on disarmament of
United Nations General Assembly (11 June).

Provisional I.R.A. explode bombs in Hyde Park and in Regent's Park,
London, killing 10 British servicemen, members of mounted
detachments of Household Cavalry and of band of Royal Green Jackets
(20 July).

F.F. parliamentary party reject by 58 to 22 a vote of no confidence in
Haughey as taoiseach moved by Charles McCreevy (6 Oct.); minority
includes Desmond O'Malley and Martin O'Donoghue, who resign as
ministers of trade, commerce, and tourism, and of education in order to
vote against Haughey.

General election for N.I. Assembly (20 Oct.); final results: Official
Unionist Party 26, D.U.P. 21, other unionists 2, Alliance 10, S.D.L.P.
14, Sinn Féin 5 (total membership 78) (see 1975).

Bomb at Droppin Well Inn, Ballykelly, Co. Londonderry, kills 16 (11
British soldiers of Cheshire Regiment and 5 civilians) and injures many
others (6 Dec.); Irish National Liberation Army claims responsibility.

General election in R.I. (24 Nov.): F.F. 75 F.G. 70, lab. 16, others 5;
Haughey (see above, 9 Mar.) succeeded as taoiseach by FitzGerald,
heading F.G.-lab. coalition government (14 Dec.). (See Feb. 1982).

1983   Peter Barry, R.I., minister for foreign affairs, pays a fact-finding visit to
Belfast and Derry to acquaint himself with the N.I. situation on the
ground (18-20 Jan).

Garret FitzGerald, taoiseach, Charles Haughey, leader F.F. party, Dick
Spring, tánaiste and John Hume, leader S.D.L.P. meet for the first
session of New Ireland Forum, which invited the views of all people
who wish for lasting peace and stability in a new Ireland (30 May).
Chairman Colm Ó hEocha, president U.C.G. The Forum consisted of
F.G. 8, F.F. 9, lab. 5, S.D.L.P. 5.

Referendum to amend the constitution to prevent possibility of laws
permitting abortion. In a poll of 54.59%, 66.45% voted for the
amendment, and 32.87% against.

Death of George Colley, T.D., who served as minister in several F.F.
governments, and twice contended for the leadership. He was tánaiste
from 1977 to 1981 (17 Sept.).

Garret FitzGerald, taoiseach, and Margaret Thatcher, P.M., meet at
Chequers for the first session of the Anglo-Irish Intergovernmental
Council (A.I.I.C.), which will discuss issues in Anglo-Irish relations (7
Nov.).

Michael Mills, political correspondent of the *Irish Press,* appointed to
the new post of ombudsman, to examine complaints concerning the
actions of public officials (8 Nov.).

1983 *(cont.)* Niels J. Haagerup, a Danish representative, presents a draft resolution on N.I. to the European Parliament's Political Affairs Committee (12 Dec.).
(This report is adopted in March 1984, and welcomed by the government of the R.I. as a recognition of the problem as one of the gravest in the European community.)
Dr Patrick Hillery inaugurated as the 7th president for his second consecutive term (31 Dec.). He is an agreed candidate and no election is held.

1984 Death of Seán MacEntee (9 Jan.).
Death of Professor T.W. Moody (11 Feb.). Co-editor of the first two editions of *The Course of Irish History,* 1967, 1984; he also planned the ambitious multi-volume, *A New History of Ireland* published jointly by the Royal Irish Academy and Oxford University Press, 1976 –. To date (1994) 7 volumes have appeared; the final volumes are due for completion in 1994.
Publication of the Report of the New Ireland Forum, which put forward three possibilities for discussion: a unitary state, a federal/confederal state, and joint sovereignty (2 May).
John Stalker, deputy chief constable of Manchester, appointed to lead inquiry into the killing of 6 unarmed men (May).
US President Regan visits Balyporeen, Ireland (1-4 June).
European election in R.I.: F.F. 8, F.G. 6, ind. 1; in N.I.: Ian Paisley, John Taylor and John Hume elected (18 June).
John Treacy wins a silver medal for the marathon at the Olympic games (12 Aug.).
Death of writer Liam O'Flaherty (7 Sept.).
Douglas Hurd succeeds James Prior as secretary of state in N.I. (10 Sept.).
Grand Hotel Brighton bombed during Conservative Party Conference, 4 people killed and one died later (12 Oct.).

1985 First commercial flight from Knock Airport (25 Oct).
Anglo-Irish Agreement signed by Garret FitzGerald and Margaret Thatcher at Hillsborough (15 Nov.)
Dáil passes Anglo-Irish Agreement (21 Nov.)
House of Commons passed Anglo-Irish Agreement (27 Nov.)
Progressive Democrats Party formed by Desmond O'Malley and Mary Harney (21 Dec.).

1986 John Stalker removed from Inquiry (June see 1984).
Divorce referendum in R.I. – ban on divorce confirmed (June).
Republican Sinn Féin founded by R. Ó Brádaigh and D. Ó Conaill (Nov.).

1987 General election in R.I. (19 Feb.): F.F. 81, F.G 51, lab 12, P.D. 14, others 5. C.J. Haughey taoiseach.
Alan Dukes succeeds Garret FitzGerald as leader of F.G. (Mar.).

1987 *(cont.)* S.A.S. kill 8 P.I.R.A. at Loughgall, Co. Armagh (8 May).
Referendum on Single European Act (24 May).
Stephen Roche wins Tour de France cycle race (26 July).
P.I.R.A. bomb kills 11 and injures 63 at Remembrance Day Service in Enniskillen (8 Nov.).

1988 Death of Séan MacBride, winner of Nobel and Lenin peace prizes (15 Jan.).
S.A.S. kill 3 unarmed members of P.I.R.A. in Gibraltar: Máiréad Farrell, Seán Savage and Daniel McCann (6 Mar.).
European Court rules against 7 day detention without charge (Nov.).
British government sought 'temporary' derogation (Dec.).
1988-1989 Bi-centenary of foundation of Australia as a British convict settlement. Amongst the convicts the Irish were prominent. Altogether some 23,000 Irish were transported between 1788 and 1876.

1989 European elections in R.I.: F.F. 6, F.G. 4, lab. 1, ind. 2, W.P. 1, P.D. 1.
General election in R.I.: F.F. 77, F.G. 55, lab. 15, P.D. 6, W.P. 7, D.S.P. 1. C.J. Haughey taoiseach of F.F./P.D. coalition.
Peter Brooke succeeds Tom King as secretary of state for N.I. (24 July).
University of Limerick opened (14 Sept).
Guildford Four released (19 Oct.).
Author Samuel Beckett, winner of Nobel Prize for Literature, dies (27 December).

1990 N.I. Fair Employment Act becomes law (1 Jan.).
Cardinal T. Ó Fiaich dies on visit to Lourdes (8 May).
Death of Terence O'Neill, prime-minister of N.I. 1963-9 (14 June).
Brian Keenan released (24 Aug.).
Painting by Michelanglo Merisi da Caravaggio (1571-1610) 'The Taking of Christ' discovered in Dublin. Originally given to Jesuits by Dr Marie Lee-Wilson. Experts first called to examine it in August 1990. Information revealed to public in April 1993 by Noel Barber, S.J., and given on indefinite loan to the National Gallery. First exhibited in November 1993.
Mary Robinson elected president of R.I. (7 Nov.). Installed 3 December.
John Bruton succeeds Alan Dukes as leader of F.G. (Nov.)
John Major succeeds Margaret Thatcher as leader of Conservative party (Nov.)

1991 Mortar bombs fired by P.I.R.A. at 10 Downing Street (7 Feb.).
Release of Birmingham Six (14 Mar.).
Maguire 7 convictions quashed (26 June).

1992 C.J. Haughey resigns as taoiseach and succeeded by Albert Reynolds (Feb.).
Democratic Left Party formed after split in Worker's Party (Feb.).
In N.I. election Gerry Adams of Sinn Féin loses his West Belfast seat to Dr Joe Hendron of the S.D.L.P. Conservatives elected in U.K. with 21 seat majority (April).

1992 *(cont.)* Patrick Mayhew succeeds Peter Brooke as secretary of state in N.I. (April).
Referendum on Maastrict Treaty (18 June).
Nelson Mandela of A.N.C. visits Ireland and addresses dáil (July).
Michael Carruth, boxer, wins a gold medal as a welter-weight, at the Olympic Games (Aug.).
U.D.A. banned (Aug.)
General election in R.I.: F.F. 88, F.G. 45, lab. 33, P.D. 10, D.L. 4, others 5 (Nov.).
Referendum on Right to Life (25 Nov.).
Referendum on Right to Travel (25 Nov.).
Referendum on Right to Information (25 Nov.).

1993 Albert Reynolds elected taoiseach of F.F./lab. coalition (12 Jan.).
European Commission accepts case brought by relatives of the people killed in Gibraltar (Sept. see 1988).
Mary Harney succeeds Desmond O'Malley as leader of the P.D.s (Oct.).
Downing Street Declaration signed by Albert Reynolds and John Major (15 Dec.).

1994 Amnesty Report on political killings in N.I. published (Feb.).
European elections in R.I.: F.F. 7, F.G. 4, lab. 1, G.P. 2, ind. 1.
Sonia O'Sullivan's athletic victory at the Helsinki European contest on 10 August won her a gold medal (10Aug.).
The I.R.A. begins a ceasefire (30 August) 1994.

INDEX

Act of Settlement (1662), 204
Adams, Gerry, 362, 368-9, Fig. 160
Adomnán, St, 57, 68, 70, 72 78, 85
Adrian IV, Pope, 108, 120, 125-6
Aer Lingus, 336
Aés dána (learned class), 51, 59
Affreca, wife of de Courcy, 139
Aghaboe, 67
Agrarian disturbances: 18th c., 228-9;
19th c., 285-9
Agricultural Credit Corporation, 334
Agriculture: neolithic, 33-4, Fig. 12;
systematic (Norman), 139; 18th c.,
221, 234, 265-6 ;19th c., 266-8, 274
Aherlow, Glen of, Fig. 7
Aidan, St, 88
Aiken, Frank, 340, Figs 124, 139
Ailech· kingdom of, 115, kings of, 121,
124
Ailill, King, 82
Aimser chue (coshering), 54
Aire túise (nobleman), 54
Airgialla: kingdom of, 45, 115; king of,
116, 120
Alexander II, Pope, 123
Allegiance, *see* Oath of,
Allen, fortress of, 46
Amber, 40
Ambrosian Library (Milan), 72
America: and Ireland, 26; and
emigration, 26, 272; and Fenianism,
279, 284-5
American war of independence, 231,
232-3
Anchorites, 73
Andrews, John Miller, 319, 321, Fig.
136

Anglo-Irish literature, 14th c., 147;
literary revival, 295, 303-4
Anglo-Irish trade agreements, *1938*,
329-30; *1965*, 337-8, Fig. 146
Anglo-Irish Treaty (1921), 311-12,
315, 320, 324-7, 331-2
Anglo-Irish War (1919-21), 311-12
Annagassan, 95
Annals of the Four Masters, 46, 163
Anselm, St, 118
Antrim: Dál Riata of, 44; earl of, 220,
battle of, 245, *see also* Lyle's Hill,
Rathlin Island
Aran Islands, 67
Ardagh chalice, 91, Fig. 30
Ardagh, 172
Ards, Co. Down, 56, 141
Arklow, 135, 245
Arles, Co. Leix, Fig. 85
Armada, Spanish, 183
Armagh, founded, 45; adopts monastic
system, 65-6; monastery at, 82; Brian
Boru visits, 113; primacy confirmed,
113; joins reform movement, 118,
receives pallium, 120; diocese of,
171; plantation of county, 191; in
ruins, Fig. 68; Book of, Fig. 22
'Arms crisis', 357
Army Comrades Association, 329
Army of Ireland, 333, 340-1
Art, Irish (7th-8th c.), 86-90
Ashbourne land act (1885), 288
Askulv, Norse king of Dublin, 132-3
Asquith, Herbert, H., 305-6
Astronomical treatise, earliest, 154
Áth in Chip, battle of, 141, 142
Athenry, 127, 140
Athlone, alternative capital, 23;

483

Johannes Eriugena, 102
John I, king of England, 138, 145
John of Ireland, 117
John Paul II, pope, 354
Joyce, James, 339
Julianstown Bridge, 200
Jury system, 138

Kavanaghs of Leinster, 177
Keating, Seatrún, 124
Kells, Book of, 20, 87, 91-2, Fig. 33
Kells, Co. Kilkenny, 140
Kells, Co. Meath, 92,101; Synod of,
  120
Kenmare, Lord, 227
Keogh, John, 240
Keogh, William, 277
Kerry, 138,141
Kettle, Andrew, J., 288
Kettle, T. M., 299-300
Kevin, St, 67
Keynes, J. M., 336
Kickham, Charles, 278, Fig. 111
Kilclief, 64
Kilcommodon hill, 213
Kildare, diocese of, 56; monastery, 67,
  82; tomb of St Brigid, 86; and Gerald
  of Wales, 87-8; liberty of, 138; Friar
  Michael of, 147
Kildare, earls of, *see* FitzGeralds
Kildare, fall of house of, 176
Kildreelig monastery, 83
Kilfenora, 57, 111
Kilkenny, 23, 139; St Canice's
  cathedral, 141; Black Death in, 150-1
Kilkenny, Confederation of, 199-202
Kilkenny, Statutes of, 155, 168-9
Killagh, Co. Kerry, 140
Killala, 245
Killaloe, 56, 111
Killeady, Co. Limerick, 67
Killeavy, 67
Kilmacduagh, 57
Kilmainham Treaty, 288
Kilmalkedar, 111

Kilmore, diocese of, 57
Kiltullagh, 64
Kings with opposition (*rí co fresabra*),
  115-6, 121
Kingsland, Lord, 220
Kinsale, battle of, 188, Fig. 69; James
  II at, 210, Fig. 80
Kite, John, archbishop of Armagh, 171
Knockdoe, battle of, 170

La Tène, 43
Labour Party (English), 344
Labour Party(Irish), 331, 356, 357,
  358-9, 363, 374, 376, 377, 378, 379,
  380
Lacys, and conquest of Connacht, 136
Ladies' Land League, 288
Lagore, Co. Meath, 46
Laigin (Leinstermen), 45, 56, 57, 97,
  98
Laigin Desgabair, 56
Laigin Tuathgabair, 56
Lake, General, 243-4, 245
Lalor, James Fintan, 262, 276
Lambay Island, 92
Lancastrians, 157,158, 162-3, 166, 167
Land annuities dispute, 328-9
Land League, 285-8
Land nationalisation, 287-8
Land purchase system, 288
Land question, 248-9, 274, 276; land
  act (1870), 281; land war (1879-82),
  286-88; land act (1881), 287, 288;
  state-aided purchase, 288, 312;
  nationalisation, 287-8; land act
  (1923), 334
Land system, 265-6, 274, 275-6
Land, percentage owned by catholics,
  201, 203, 205, 216, 219-20, Fig. 76;
  see also Plantations
Landen, battle of, 216
Lane, Ralph, 175
Langrishe, Sir Hercules, 231
Language, Irish, *see* Irish language
Larcom, Captain Thomas, 26